Voting as a Rite

HARVARD EAST ASIAN MONOGRAPHS 417

Voting as a Rite

A History of Elections in Modern China

Joshua Hill

Published by the Harvard University Asia Center
Distributed by Harvard University Press
Cambridge (Massachusetts) and London 2019

© 2019 by The President and Fellows of Harvard College
Printed in the United States of America

The Harvard University Asia Center publishes a monograph series and, in coordination with the Fairbank Center for Chinese Studies, the Korea Institute, the Reischauer Institute of Japanese Studies, and other facilities and institutes, administers research projects designed to further scholarly understanding of China, Japan, Vietnam, Korea, and other Asian countries. The Center also sponsors projects addressing multidisciplinary and regional issues in Asia.

Library of Congress Cataloging-in-Publication Data

Names: Hill, Joshua, 1977– author.
Title: Voting as a rite : a history of elections in modern China / Joshua Hill.
Other titles: Harvard East Asian monographs ; 417.
Description: Cambridge, Massachusetts : Harvard University Asia Center, 2019. | Series: Harvard East Asian monographs ; 417 | Includes bibliographical references and index.
Identifiers: LCCN 2018034039| ISBN 9780674237216 (hardcover : alk. paper) | ISBN 9780674237223 (pbk. : alk. paper)
Subjects: LCSH: Elections—China—History. | Voting—China—History.
Classification: LCC JQ1518 .H55 2019 | DDC 324.951—dc23
LC record available at https://lccn.loc.gov/2018034039

Index by Matthew White

♾ Printed on acid-free paper

Last figure below indicates year of this printing
28 27 26 25 24 23 22 21 20 19

Contents

List of Tables and Figures — vii

Acknowledgments — ix

Introduction — 1

1. Rectifying Names: Inventing Terms for Elections, 1840–1898 — 11

2. Transmission and Re-Creation: Writing Laws for Voting, 1898–1908 — 40

3. The First Elections and the Last Emperor: Voting and Campaigning, 1909–1911 — 74

4. Free Elections and the First Republic: Parties and the Press, 1911–1913 — 106

5. Warlord Democracy: Coercion and Coordination, 1913–1921 — 137

6. Elections as Education: Political Tutelage, 1921–1987 — 163

7. Voting without a Choice: Elections in the People's Republic, 1949–2018 — 192

Conclusion: Democratization and the Discourse
of Elections in China   219

Character List   231

Notes   235

Bibliography   273

Index   291

Tables and Figures

Tables

1. Primary-Stage Voting and Revoting in Wu County, 1909 — 91

Figures

1. Frequency of terms *gongju* and *xuanju* to mean "election/voting" in *Shenbao* headlines, 1872–1901 — 46
2. Frequency of terms *gongju* and *xuanju* to mean "election/voting" in *Shenbao* headlines, 1905–1911 — 47
3. Frequency of terms *gongju* and *xuanju* to mean "election/voting" in headlines of forty-one Chinese periodicals, 1872–1911 — 47
4. Relative frequency of the use of the term *yundong* to mean "election campaigning" during the 1909 provincial assembly elections — 94
5. "Yuzhong xuanju yundong [Election Campaigning in the Rain]" — 97
6. "Xuanju yundong [Election Campaigning]" — 98
7. "Xuanju yundong er [Election Campaigning 2]" — 99
8. A model ballot for the 1912 parliamentary election — 124
9. "Miss Mei Votes in China's First General Election" — 183

10	"Women you xuanjuquan he bei xuanjuquan" [We Have the Right to Vote and to Be Elected] (1953)	201
11	"Use your democratic rights in accordance with the law/ Cast a sacred ballot." Propaganda slogan for the 2016 local People's Congress election in Changsha, Hunan	215
12	The former provincial legislature building in Changsha, Hunan	220

Acknowledgments

Twenty years ago, a fortuitous part-time job in the Yale-China Association's New Haven office changed the trajectory of my life. I will always be extremely grateful to Edie MacMullen for finding that position for me—and for everything else she taught me about being a teacher and a historian. Nancy Chapman, then executive director of the association, inspired my initial interest in China and the Chinese language; without her mentorship, I would not be where I am now. After graduation I spent three years as an English language instructor for the Yale-China Association at Huizhen Academy in Ningbo and at Yali Middle School in Changsha. I am grateful to all of my former colleagues at those institutions.

As a graduate student at Harvard University, I had the good fortune to be taught by several inspiring scholars. My adviser, Bill Kirby, guided this project at every step, from its origins in a conversation we had while walking to Lamont Library in 2007 to its final publication as a book. Henrietta Harrison's careful commentary on my drafts challenged me to express myself with clarity and interrogate my source materials with acuity. Liz Perry pushed me to think through the contemporary implications of my work. Mark Kishlansky provided characteristically sharp commentary on my arguments and my writing style. Mark passed away before I finished this book, but his influence is evident. Hue-Tam Ho Tai and Mark Elliott read and commented on several chapters of my dissertation, and David Armitage provided additional inspiration and advice. Feng

Xiaocai gave extensive guidance and feedback while a visiting scholar at the Harvard-Yenching Institute.

During my final years at Harvard, the Fairbank Center for Chinese Studies gave me office space, access to a coffee machine, and an amazing environment for friendship and conversation. For this, I am thankful to Lydia Chen and Linda Kluz, as well as my officemates, Allison Miller, Cole Roskam, and Guo Rui. Other graduate school classmates and friends, including Alexander and Tracy Akin, Craig Colbeck, Wayne and Sukja de Fremery, Nick Kapur, Konrad Lawson, Ben Levey, Li Ren-yuan, Lo Shih-chieh, Tristan Stein, Wei Yang, Yen Hsiao-pei, and Zhao Hui offered advice, feedback, and support at various stages of this project. As a postdoctoral fellow at the Center for Chinese Studies at the University of California, Berkeley, I began revisions on this project under the exacting gaze of Wen-hsin Yeh. Her suggestions pushed my work in several new directions. While at Berkeley, I benefited from conversations with Charlotte Cowden, He Jianye, Elinor Levine, Kevin O'Brien, Angel Ryono, and Jonathan Tang. I was fortunate to overlap at Berkeley with Zhang Jishun; her thinking about Chinese elections in the 1950s shaped my own. My thanks go to the many people at several institutions who have invited me to give talks based on this project, including Hideo Fukamachi, Jan Kiely, Lin Hsiao-ting, Tom Mullaney, Pan Kuang-che, and Christopher Reed. I am especially thankful for the detailed commentary that Chang Peng-yuan offered after my talk at Academia Sinica's Institute of Modern History.

Research for this project in China occurred in several stages between 2008 and 2016. My initial trip was supported by a Fulbright IIE grant. Many individuals in mainland China offered help and encouragement, particularly Chen Qianping of Nanjing University and Ye Lijun of the Hunan University of Chinese Medicine. I am grateful to the staff at various libraries and archives, including the Nanjing Library's Rare Books Room and Republican Documents Room, the Hunan Provincial Library's Rare Books Room, the Jiangsu Provincial Archives, the Shanghai Library, the Shanghai Municipal Archives, and the Chinese University of Hong Kong's Universities Service Centre for China Studies. In 2016, I completed a version of this manuscript in a Mawangdui, Changsha, rooftop writing studio generously lent to me by Yan Shuiliang and Mo Dongyun.

Acknowledgments

During the twilight period between submitting my dissertation and receiving my degree, I taught on an adjunct basis for the Tufts University Department of History and the Fletcher School of Law and Diplomacy. I appreciate the support offered by several colleagues at those institutions, especially Elizabeth Foster, Gary Leupp, Elizabeth Remick, and Peter Uvin. At Fletcher, I was a temporary replacement for Alan Wachman, who was on medical leave for what proved to be a terminal illness. Over the course of numerous phone calls in his final months, Alan generously shared his ideas on teaching, on China, and on pursuing a career in academia. Getting to know him, even if only for a short while, had an immense impact on me, and I think back to our conversations often.

I am particularly grateful for the advice and support offered by my colleagues in the History Department at Ohio University, especially Patrick Barr-Melej, Robert Ingram, and Katherine Jellison. Victoria Lee's careful commentary on my final draft resulted in a greatly improved book. At Alden Library, He Yan provided crucial help in obtaining needed materials, as has the Inter-Library Loan staff. I am grateful to Bob Graham at the Harvard University Asia Center Publications Program and the two anonymous reviewers who read my manuscript.

More than anything else, I am thankful to my family, both in the United States and in China: my parents, Charles and Sara Hill; my brothers, Nathanael and Zack; and my mother-in-law, Mo Chunhua. I am grateful to my children, Liya and Ian, for providing ample motivation for me to complete this project.

In the past ten years, Peng Xiaojia has moved from Hunan to Jiangsu to Massachusetts to California to Ohio to be with me as I tried to build an academic career. Without her, this book would not have been possible.

INTRODUCTION

Ensconced in a remote cave, a slender man with flowing hair told his story to a rapt foreign correspondent. This was an unusual discussion. Even among his inner circle, few knew much about the background of this leader of a nearly defeated, yet stubbornly persistent rebellion. Although he claimed to be "skeptical . . . about the necessity for supplying an autobiography," he crafted a tale that evinced remarkable thematic continuity. He recounted that from a young age he had delighted in defying established authority: he ran away from home and argued incessantly with his father, once even refusing to kowtow in apology. He highlighted the later acts of defiance that became deeply embedded in the lore of China's communist revolution, including his investigations of countryside life, experiences as a labor organizer, and opposition to arranged marriages. Yet in nearly the same breath, Mao Zedong (1893–1976) also spoke to Edgar Snow (1905–72) of a nearly forgotten event from his formative years: the storming of the Hunan provincial legislature building in Changsha on October 10, 1920.

"Our group," Mao explained, speaking of a period predating the founding of the Chinese Communist Party, "had demanded equal rights for men and women, and representative government, and in general approval of a platform for a bourgeois democracy. . . . We led an attack on the provincial parliament, the majority of whose members were landlords and gentry appointed by the militarists." This led to a brief occupation of the legislative chambers, constructed less than a decade earlier to house

Hunan's postimperial elected government. Once in possession of the elegant Western-style building, Mao claimed he and his allies "pull[ed] down the scrolls and banners, which were full of nonsensical and extravagant phrases." Even though he had come to disdain "bourgeois democracy" by the time of Snow's interview, he still judged this event to be an important milestone, "a big incident in Hunan" that "frightened the rulers."[1]

Mao's recollections mostly accorded with contemporary accounts from Changsha. Nearly 10,000 people gathered to march in protest around the city on the morning of October 10, 1920, the ninth anniversary of China's Republican Revolution. A persistent rain discouraged many, and only a few hundred completed the full route. At noon some hardy souls forced entry into the legislature, damaging a gate in the process. Once inside, they pulled down the national flag and the legislature's flag. Neither was seen again. Over the following days, this act of desecration sparked outrage from government officials and evoked criticism even from those sympathetic to the protests. Despite calls to punish the perpetrators, none were ever publicly identified.[2]

The only evidence for Mao's participation in this incident comes from his own words, but his critical role as a leader of Changsha's radical movement is incontrovertible.[3] In the fall of 1920, that community of activists had devoted itself to the cause of "Hunanese independence," which Mao defined for Snow as autonomy from the national authorities in Beijing. Yet the movement's platform called for a reorganization of political life that went well beyond just rebalancing center/province relations. In particular, Mao and his allies demanded a dramatic expansion of the role of elections in provincial political life. Of the thirteen slogans the October 1920 protest organizers suggested that marchers write on banners, five—among them "Universal Voting Rights [*putong xuanju*]," "Direct Elections [*zhijie xuanju*]," and "Male or Female, Rich or Poor, All Should Have Voting Rights [*wulun nan nü pin fu dou you xuanjuquan*]"—called for revising existing voting laws.[4] Mao himself endorsed these concepts and, in the weeks leading up to the protest, editorialized on their behalf in series of published essays.[5] For a brief moment in 1920, it appeared he believed that power might flow from the ballot box, rather than (as he later famously claimed) the barrel of a gun.

The twenty-seven-year-old Mao and his partners in that protest were not alone in their hope that elections could transform China's fate. Although living in a city removed from the center of national political life, the debate over voting they had joined was far from marginal. Speaking at the Beijing Institute of Law and Politics, near the heart of the nation's power structure, prominent intellectual Liang Qichao (1873–1929) argued in May 1922 that finding the right mechanism for popular participation was a critical task facing the Republic of China. Placing this challenge within the context of classical Chinese political thought, he claimed that "our ancestors knew that the will of the people ought to be respected; [but] they did not make a serious study of the method by which the ideal might be realized." As a result, they had no tools for resisting rulers who transgressed public opinion. This, Liang concluded, was "the greatest defect of Chinese political thought."[6]

Neither the students in Liang's audience nor the readers of his published talks could fail to note the contrast drawn between earlier centuries and the recent past, even though Liang studiously refrained from making concrete proposals for the present. The previous quarter of a century had been marked not only by "study of methods" for channeling the popular will but also by intensive experimentation with a variety of techniques for doing so. Voting and elections, as the demands of the Changsha protesters suggested, formed the core of these experiments. Before the 1911 revolution ended imperial rule, the last leaders of the Qing dynasty instituted elections for provincial and, later, local assemblies. The Republic of China held nationwide parliamentary elections in the winter of 1912–13, in 1918, and (abortively) in 1921. Provincial-level elections occurred in 1912–13, 1918, 1921, and at various other times in the 1920s, depending on the province. Liang had been involved in many of these elections either as an essayist or as a politician. Long after Liang's speech, the single-party governments that dominated mainland China after 1927 built on these early experiences to create their own systems of voting—and continue to do so today.

It is unsurprising that voting had become a common activity during this period. By the early twentieth century, nearly all aspects of Chinese governance and political structure were open to debate. Advocates of almost every conceivable political system found a platform for their views. Yet one area of consensus amid this diversity was the belief that voting was a necessity. This fact should make the history of Chinese elections an important area of study. At the very least, the immense resources that governments from the Qing to the People's Republic have dedicated to elections—the intellectual energy expended on researching and writing election laws, the labor devoted to promoting and administering elections, and the fiscal expenditures required to make all of that happen—should demand an accounting. Yet this has not occurred. For over a century there has been nearly continuous experimentation with elections in China, but there is still no comprehensive history of the ideas that shaped them, the values that animated them, and the impulses that have led governments to implement them.

The reason is obvious: mainland China has never had a national leader elevated to office on the basis of a popular election. Absent that, studying Chinese elections as a historical phenomenon seems little more than the exploration of dead-ends or the pondering of what-ifs. As a result, the scholarly literature on this topic is fragmented and constrained. Most major works are limited by time period, such as Chang Peng-yuan's monumental survey of elections before the 1949 fall of the Nationalist regime on the mainland, Ye Lijun's careful analysis of election laws in the pre-1927 Republic, Roger Thompson's archivally grounded exploration of late Qing local elections, and John Fincher's detailed reconstruction of elections between 1905 and 1914.[7] Narrow chronologies also characterize most studies of village elections in contemporary mainland China, which are typically written by political scientists focusing on the post-Mao era.[8] Other scholars focus on unique regions, such as Shelley Rigger's insightful work on elections in Taiwan, or on specific strands within the broader topic of elections, such as Louise Edwards's pathbreaking book on women's suffrage before 1949.[9] Collectively, the existing literature on Chinese elections takes specific sets of elections as discrete events and analyzes them as such, without placing them in a broader context.

The basic claim made in this book is that an intellectual history of Chinese elections across a wide-ranging time frame is both possible and useful. Possible because source materials—in the form of newspapers, rare books, and government archives—are plentiful and accessible to a greater extent today than in previous decades. For earlier periods, digitized historical newspapers (the Shanghai-based *Shenbao* in particular) allow extraordinary connections to be found through keyword searching. Biographies of otherwise obscure Republican individuals can now be written, the work of minor journalists can be traced through the years, and linguistic changes can be measured through word counts; previously, conducting such research would have required skimming thousands of pages of small text. Nondigitized local newspapers held in small and medium-sized cities throughout China are a rarely used resource for tracking the spread of ideas outside of major cities like Shanghai; viewing these requires travel to a particular library, but little else—most are open to researchers without any formalities required. Rare book rooms provide another avenue for locating previously unused materials. A surprising amount of "archival" early Republican material, including voter rolls and the proceedings of the Jiangsu provincial legislature, are preserved in these rooms, although locating such treasures can be tricky. Archives, once essentially off-limits for study of the post-1949 period, may still restrict access to exclude sensitive time periods or topics, but available materials reveal new insights into the nature of voting under the People's Republic. Through a combination of new sources and old ones revitalized with new technologies, it is now possible to write a history of Chinese elections that spans over 150 years.

Such a project is useful because when examined as a whole, rather than divided by the conventional chronological breaks (the 1911 Revolution, the 1926–28 Northern Expedition, the 1949 Revolution, the 1978 beginning of the Reform era, or the 1987 lifting of martial law on Taiwan), important continuities emerge. Viewed over the long term, Chinese political and intellectual elites have held a stable set of attitudes toward and expectations for elections. Disagreements and debates over the structure of elections (such as those highlighted by Mao's 1920 Changsha protest), as well as frequent regime change, can obscure this important fact. This book investigates a set of particularly dominant justifications for holding elections and influential explanations for what elections were supposed to accomplish. Despite their many differences, the late Qing constitutionalists who advocated for China's first official election law in 1908 and the communist cadres who pushed for village committee elections in the 1980s held unexpectedly compatible visions for elections.

There are good reasons for the conceptual and ideological continuity between these otherwise different groups. Although elections were universally understood as a foreign import, China's most important political and intellectual leaders placed voting within the framework of values and ideas derived from earlier Chinese political practice. Neither China's elections nor the debates about the nature of voting can be understood without an appreciation for the longer context of the Chinese past. Liang Qichao complained in 1922 that earlier generations had neglected to consider methods for channeling the "will of the people," but during his own lifetime a rich and influential series of discourses on voting had taken root in China. Some of these drew from nineteenth-century Chinese observations of Western politics, whereas others derived from the late imperial civil service examination system or from alternative systems of local appointment. The meaning of Chinese elections must be measured against the historical and cultural contexts of those who organized, participated in, or commented on them.

The values that have informed twentieth-century and twenty-first-century Chinese elections differ significantly from those that hold sway in contemporary democratic nations, but both sets of attitudes are primarily ideological structures conditioned by historical experience and memory. U.S. political scientists Christopher Achen and Larry Bartels suggest we understand mainstream views in established democracies as constituting a folk theory of democracy. Essentially, this folk theory is the idea that "what the majority wants becomes government policy," because thoughtful and engaged citizens cast ballots for representatives who will act in the voters' interests.[10] As the name "folk theory" implies, these views rest on a hazy set of inherited beliefs, observations, and anecdotes. Achen and Bartels, on the basis of empirical observations of contemporary U.S. politics, challenge the notion that U.S. elections (in particular) actually operate in anything like the manner that the folk theory suggests.[11] The folk theory, which romanticizes the sovereign role of the individual citizen as a decision maker, never found many adherents in China, but the designers of Chinese electoral systems from the Qing dynasty to the People's Republic have all operated under their own, profoundly different set of foundational expectations.

This Chinese conceptual framework, founded on long-standing concerns in the Chinese political tradition, described what elections can and should do. Chinese election advocates primarily saw elections as a way to enhance the government's power and efficacy. Chinese elections thus emphasized state-building, not the elevation of the will (or whim) of the voters. Liang Qichao's paean to the "will of the people" notwithstanding, he and other leading intellectuals already thought they knew what the people should want: national wealth and power, which could only be found through decisive state action. Such action could only be successful if strong, dense links between the populace and the authorities existed. The ballot box, a symbol of modernity imported from overseas, would simply be a method for fashioning such ties. Voting was intended to produce a strong and prosperous China by opening a newer, more intimate path for the people to work with the state. This goal remained consistent throughout the twentieth century and was embraced by ministers of the Qing throne, the elites of Republican society, and the cadres of the communist state alike.

These leaders believed that elections could strengthen the state in two specific ways that drew directly from the Chinese historical experience. The first was as a method to select the talented and the morally worthy for public office. In this sense, elections were seen as a successor to the pre-1905 civil service examination system and a variety of informal local selection practices from the late imperial era. As a consequence, voting laws that prioritized this goal restricted suffrage to the portion of the population—educated, wealthy, and male—assumed to be able to recognize talent and virtue objectively. Crucially, according to this notion, the point of voting was not for voters to exercise independent judgment based on personal preference but to select candidates who were universally acknowledged to have the right intellectual and moral qualities. Reformist officials feared that such paragons, presumed to exist and to be recognized by their neighbors as such, had been overlooked under the system of selection by written examination. Once that obstacle had been removed, this new pool of talent could be tapped.

China's earliest national election law, created in 1908 with the selection of talent as a primary goal, had an unintended consequence. The state did not determine winners in advance, thus creating an opportunity for candidates to compete for office. Direct observation of election campaigning—an activity that advantaged the most organized, most popular, and most unscrupulous candidates—led to the widespread abandonment of the belief that elections could select talent and virtue by the early 1920s. The authors of China's first election laws had hoped to create a system of selection but, as Mark Kishlansky suggests in his discussion of the English Parliament, selection and election are two very different things.[12] Campaigning may be unpleasant and even resented in every polity that holds elections, but in most places it does not present such a deep challenge to reigning notions of the purpose of elections. The tension between the reality of campaigning and this foundational expectation for elections in China, however, had serious consequences in the early twentieth century and beyond.

The second function of elections was to serve as a means of communication between the rulers and the ruled. Preparation for holding elections gave the state a chance to engage in a variety of educational, organizational, and propaganda activities. These were designed to inculcate the people with the attitudes and ideas deemed necessary for the re-creation of China as a modern nation-state. Elections that emphasized this particular foundational expectation, mainly conducted under the auspices of one-party governments after 1927, made use of universal suffrage and direct voting to reach the broadest possible segment of society. As the importance of elections lay in their impact on the subjectivity of voters, the authorities often selected winners (who would be incidental to the policy-making process in any event) in advance. Paired with new tools of social control, such as population censuses and ethnic classification schemes, elections provided an opportunity for states to create and impose new categories and subjectivities on the population.[13] Pedagogical elections of this kind became a method for governments to change the nature of their voters, rather than for voters to change the nature of their government. Yet this, too, proved to operate better in theory than in practice. Even the most extensive effort to use voting as a tool of education, the 1953–54 People's Congress election, revealed sharp limits to the state's ability to transform the popular mindset.

Both of the foundational expectations for elections in China rested on the notion that voting could act as a rite in the Confucian sense of the term. Political and social rituals had been constitutive elements of Chinese states long before the twentieth century.[14] The political and intellectual elite who designed China's earliest elections surely saw their work in the tradition of Confucian classics that repeatedly emphasized that the proper performance of ritual could transform the world. Primarily, such injunctions focused directly on social rituals. As a consequence, late imperial Chinese invested significant effort in the elaboration of appropriate social rituals and defined membership in their cultural community by participation in such rituals. Although fewer in number than social rituals, explicitly political rituals developed in the late imperial era as well. The most important of these spanned the empire, included the establishment of community compacts, and, under the Qing, monthly readings of the Kangxi emperor's Sacred Edict.[15] Like these earlier political rites, elections were supposed to confirm relationships that already existed; few advocates of elections thus understood them to be contests between opposing points of view in which the outcome might be in doubt. To conceptualize voting as a "rite" rather than a "right" is not, therefore, to dismiss Chinese elections as either mere spectacle or empty farce. Instead, this term highlights the notion that many in nineteenth- or twentieth-century China would have regarded ritual as a valuable tool for national renewal.

Rituals do not always perform as expected. Much like Achen and Bartels's folk theory, the Chinese foundational expectations existed in tension with the lived experience of watching and participating in Chinese elections. These challenges have been visible to observers from the late Qing to the present. At various times, particularly amid the chaos of the mid-1920s, disillusionment with the gap between the promises of the foundational expectations and the actual results of elections led many to lose interest in the process. Warfare in the 1930s and 1940s similarly made elections appear to be a luxury that an embattled nation could ill afford. By the late 1950s, an increasingly confident Mao abandoned the last shreds of his youthful interest in elections; during the Cultural Revolution, he jettisoned formal voting systems entirely. The gap from the last elections in 1965 until the resumption of voting under Mao's successors in 1980 was the longest period in mainland China's twentieth century without government-mandated voting. Although voting continued under the rump Nationalist regime on Taiwan, it appeared for decades to be more a facade than anything else.

Chinese elections and the foundational expectations that undergirded them did not come to an end in the mid-twentieth century. Since 1987, the nearly simultaneous introduction of village-level elections in mainland China and dramatic success of the Taiwanese democratization movement have combined to make an understanding of Chinese elections more important than ever. These developments on both sides of the Taiwan Straits over the past few decades need to be placed in the legacy of this long-standing framework to be fully understood. The continuities and (in the case of Taiwan) discontinuities between these more recent elections and those of the early twentieth century demonstrate the abiding appeal—and the democratic limitations—of a belief system that conceptualizes elections as a ritual of state-building, a rite of citizen education, and a ceremony of meritocratic selection.

CHAPTER I

Rectifying Names

Inventing Terms for Elections, 1840–1898

Early in the fifty-fourth year of the Qianlong reign era, village elders, scholars, and other local elites gathered in conclaves to select a new chieftain. Some traveled great distances across a barely settled countryside; others journeyed from the prosperous shipping towns dotting the coast. Members of these assemblies unanimously anointed the aristocratic warrior Hua-sheng-dun as their confederation's leader. No note of this event—better remembered in the United States as the electoral college's election of George Washington (1732–99) as president in 1789—was taken in Beijing, although the emergence of the new nation had been spotted as early as 1784, when the first American-flagged merchant ship docked in Guangzhou.

This oversight is not particularly remarkable. The Qianlong emperor (1711–99; r. 1736–95) had far more pressing issues to consume his attention in the 1780s. Had Washington's election been noticed, eighteenth-century Qing chroniclers would have lacked a vocabulary to articulate what had taken place. Not only did no Chinese term exist for the position Washington filled, there was no precise name for the process by which he had been selected. Despite the fitful publication of a handful of descriptive Chinese-language texts on the United States, Great Britain, and the West in the first decades of the nineteenth century, there was still no standard term for voting and elections in 1837, when a British general election brought to power a Parliament that narrowly voted to declare war on China three years later. Lacking even a name for the practice, no one in early nineteenth-century China evinced much interest in voting. It was neither a model to be embraced nor a horror to be avoided; it was not even a curiosity.

The emergence of a formidable overseas threat to Qing security, dramatically symbolized by the steam-powered *HMS Nemesis* sinking a Chinese fleet in January 1841, fueled an interest in European political ideas and institutions, including elections.[1] This interest came to be interpreted through and contextualized by long-standing domestic "constitutional" debates about "the legitimate ordering of public life" in late imperial China.[2] Thus, mid- and late nineteenth-century accounts of Western elections were not innocent descriptions devoid of ideological meaning, historical allusion, or moral connotation. Instead, they belonged, as Lydia Liu proposed in her notion of "translingual practice," to a process of re-creation. "Meanings," Liu argued, "are not so much 'transformed' when concepts pass from the guest language to the host language as invented within the local environment of the latter."[3] The invention of a Chinese discourse on elections in the nineteenth century that merged Chinese and Western concerns generated a complex of foundational expectations for the nature of voting and the consequences of holding elections.

Between the 1840s and the 1890s, two different conceptualizations of elections emerged from this new literature. The dominant vision depicted elections idealistically. A relatively cohesive group of officials and intellectuals, who believed the state would be strengthened by allowing several million holders of lower-level civil service examination degrees to legitimately participate in politics, articulated this view in print. Traditionally, the throne had seen holders of these degrees—generally ineligible for bureaucratic office yet unlikely to earn the higher degrees that might lead to such employment—as potential troublemakers requiring discipline. Amid the crises of the mid-nineteenth century, some in the Qing intellectual and political elite came to see this group as a potential buttress for the dynasty's revival. Reformers of this stripe imagined that Western-style elections, purportedly similar to procedures and institutions that existed deep in Chinese antiquity, could bring the population into harmony with the imperial will and thus "link the ruler and the ruled [*shang xia tong*, or any one of several variations of this phrasing]." Advocates never saw elections as the fundamental building block of democracy or popular sovereignty; instead, they reimagined voting as a solution to dynastic weakness.

Many of these late imperial Chinese political thinkers and statesmen ultimately coalesced around one particular character compound, *gongju*, translated here as "public appointment," to represent their notion of elections and voting. This phrase, unlike so many other "new terms for new ideas" in the late nineteenth century, was not an import from Japanese. Instead, it was reappropriated from Qing China's administrative lexicon. This long-circulating term designated loosely defined practices of choosing local leaders through a consensual, noncompetitive selection system over which the state retained ultimate veto power. Descriptions of foreign voting practices became grafted onto this term for deregulated, non-official management in the countryside; by implication, elections might not be completely foreign after all. By the 1890s, proposals for the adoption of some sort of voting system in China invariably employed the phrase "public appointment," and it became enshrined in late nineteenth-century dictionaries, newspapers, and political tracts. Although this term was soon abandoned in favor of the compound *xuanju* (which has remained the standard Chinese term for "elections" ever since), this change reflected the transformation of Chinese political institutions after 1900, rather than a shift in ideological concerns; the assumptions of harmony, consensus, and state oversight embedded in "public appointment" remained vibrant throughout China's experiments with elections in the early twentieth century.

A more pessimistic view of elections appeared in other nineteenth-century texts. Such writers emphasized the petty, divisive nature of elections and the propensity of elections to elevate private interests over the public good. Few drew any connection between Chinese practices, current or ancient, and voting; those who did rejected them outright. None claimed that elected institutions could bind ruler and ruled together in such a way as to strengthen the country. In contrast to more optimistic views, these writers had all directly observed elections overseas, seemingly lending their accounts an authenticity the others lacked. Yet their reactions to these elections were filtered through their imaginations just as much as those of the optimists. Rather than idealizing voting as a path to comity and harmony, they saw it as a road to partisanship and corruption.

Their view remained a quiet countertradition in the nineteenth century; few of these critical works were published before the late 1890s. Some descriptions did circulate to a limited extent, and echoes of such complaints emerged in the writings of other high officials.

The invention of competing Chinese cultural and intellectual concepts of elections in the nineteenth century proved to be profoundly durable. Voting in China would be shaped by this conversation and the foundational expectations that resulted from it. This legacy links the Chinese elections held in the twentieth century—no matter to what extent they might seem to resemble foreign models—to the ideas, institutions, and inclinations of the late imperial era.

Selection and "Public Appointment" in Late Imperial China

Chinese thinkers have preoccupied themselves with envisioning, debating, and critiquing different systems for selecting officials since the ancient past. Many of the systems that Chinese states have experimented with—most famously, the selection of officials via competitive civil service examinations—have been well studied. Others, however, are far more obscure. The earliest known Chinese description of a U.S. presidential election, an offhand remark in an 1817 confidential palace memorial from the governor-general of Guangdong and Guangxi to the throne, compared the process to one of these less well-known systems: Americans, the emperor was told, were ruled by a chief selected "by the public appointment [*gongju*] of several men, who serve in succession according to the drawing of lots [*nianjiu lunchong*]."[4]

The origins of much of this description, such as the claim that the U.S. presidency was determined by a game of chance, are unknown; the phrase "public appointment," however, is best understood as a direct reference to an established selection practice in China. Foreign observers of Qing politics in the late nineteenth century understood the term as such—it merited a brief entry in British diplomat Herbert Giles's comprehensive 1892 Chinese–English dictionary.[5] A few historians have conceptualized the compound as referring to a specific procedure, characterizing it as "some form of public approval of a choice arrived at by other means" or an "old way of reaching informal consensus."[6] Regardless of whether the 1817 memorial writer deliberately sought to draw a parallel between this practice and U.S. elections, later writers certainly did. It proved a slippery analogy, as "public appointment" functioned as a customary practice of local governance, rather than an institution of the dynastic state.

Although no single authoritative description of public appointment exists, the contours of the practice can be reconstructed through philosophical texts and administrative records dating back to at least the twelfth century. Zhu Xi (1130–1200), the influential reinterpreter of the Confucian tradition, helped popularize one of the earliest variants. As part of his program for political reconstruction at the local level, he envisioned a system of "community compacts [*xiangyue*]" that would promote Confucian values and behaviors. The activities mandated by these compacts, he envisioned, would be supervised by a "person of age and morality put forward by the people [*zhong tui*]," though he did not specify a particular mechanism for this.[7] Within two centuries of his death, Zhu's community compacts received imperial sanction and had become common across China.[8]

By the time of the Manchu conquest in 1644, this process of selecting community compact leaders was commonly referred to as public appointment. During the first years of the Qing dynasty, regents for the Shunzhi emperor (1638–61; r. 1643–61) ordered the reestablishment of community compacts in villages across the newly conquered majority Han areas. Their edict required the selection of men over sixty years of age who had led morally exemplary lives as compact overseers through "public appointment [*gongju*]."[9] Subsequent eighteenth- and nineteenth-century Qing emperors expanded this practice to the management of community granaries, the policing of salt production sites, the administration of lineages, the oversight of water conservancy projects, and the organization of self-defense groups.[10] Public appointment in this traditional sense continued to be practiced even in the dynasty's final years. A 1909 government-sponsored survey of rural social customs in Anhui Province, for instance, asked respondents if managers of public property were selected "by the people through public appointment [*you zhong gongju*]" or "by taking turns [*lunliu*]."¹¹ Founders of new social and economic institutions in the decade after 1895, including police departments and railway companies, tended to recommend that local leadership be selected through public appointment.¹²

"Public appointment" was thus a common phrase in Qing political discourse, yet it was never described in much detail. The evidence that survives of the process in action suggests that it differed significantly from voting or elections. Though the public appointment process began with an ill-defined "public," completion of the process required official confirmation. One description, issued in 1736 and enshrined in the Qing dynasty's collected statues, explained the public appointment process for a special honorary examination degree awarded when a new emperor ascended the throne:

> [Officials should order] local gentry, elders, and members of the community to jointly file a petition to select [the proposed recipient of the honorary degree] through public appointment [*gongju*]. Local officials from the formal bureaucracy should conduct interviews in order to learn the public's appraisal [of the candidate] [*caifang gongping*] and should carefully check the facts of the situation.¹³

Though the particular occasion described in this edict happened infrequently, this sort of supervised public appointment was also used on a regular basis for more common occurrences, such as selection of leaders for the village mutual responsibility (*baojia*) system.¹⁴

Qing emperors expressed great hope that the selection of village leaders through public appointment could result in improved government at the local level. The Jiaqing emperor (1760–1820; r. 1796–1820), for example, held that "in order to compile [accurate] population registers, localities must select honest local headmen through public appointment [*gongju*] who will be given this project to complete without interference from government clerks or scribes."¹⁵ The Jiaqing emperor was not alone in this belief. By the time he ascended the throne, a group within the scholar-official elite had come to think that the Qing state needed to create mechanisms that would allow greater formal participation for local elites in governance. This was a small political and intellectual movement inside the Qing bureaucracy—its ideas were controversial and not universally accepted.

Lin Zexu (1785–1850), long before taking up his fateful post as the anti-opium commissioner in Guangzhou, made a name for himself as an advocate of this policy. During his career as a provincial administrator, he worried over the dearth of talented officials provided by the civil service examination system and sought more paths to bring skilled individuals into government.[16] As a result, he established decentralized agencies to be led by individuals selected at the local level. He directed the use of "public appointment" to select local gentry leaders for water conservancy projects on at least three occasions: once in the early 1830s as governor of Jiangsu and twice near the end of the decade as governor-general of Hubei and Hunan.[17] He maintained his belief in the efficacy of such organizations even after assuming office in Guangzhou: on April 4, 1839, he authorized the creation of an anti–opium smuggling "local gentry office [*ju*]" to be managed by "upright and honest gentry elders 'selected and appointed' [*xuanju*] by the gentry."[18] Lin's vision attracted a following among a particular subset of like-minded officials, including Wei Yuan (1794–1856), a scholar from the Hunanese interior who had earned a measure of fame for his writings on administrative reform. Wei's interests led him to a deep concern for the foundations of the Qing state and the belief that political participation should be expanded to a broader segment of the population.[19] Lin, Wei, and other like-minded literati formed a powerful constituency of scholar-officials that supported public appointment as a concept and as the foundation for delegation of authority at the local level.

Despite the vagueness of this term, public appointment was a recognizable system of selection in eighteenth- and nineteenth-century China. It was outside of and separate from the much better-known path to bureaucratic appointment via examination. Selection via public appointment was theoretically made by local elites through a consensual, noncompetitive deliberative process, but the state reserved a decisive oversight role in the process. The actual mechanisms of the system were vague and probably differed from place to place. Yet when early translators and thinkers needed a Chinese term to represent imported notions of "elections," many would seize on it.

Imagining Elections from Afar

Ties of commerce and curiosity had linked Qing China with Europe and (later) North America for centuries. But until the catastrophic wars of the mid-nineteenth century, Chinese leaders and scholars had little reason to think deeply about the political systems of those places. The writers, thinkers, and strategists who first struggled to explain the nature of Qing China's new foes primarily focused on practical issues. What was the relationship between the various European countries? How did those countries interact with the rest of the world? What was the nature of the technology that European powers had used to such devastating effect during the Opium War and later conflicts? These writers aimed to provide more general overviews of government, politics, and society in the West.

They had little precedent to guide them in creating a vocabulary to describe such institutions and ideas. Few standardized reference works existed, and those that did provided little insight into the translation of unfamiliar political concepts. The only pre–Opium War English–Chinese bilingual dictionary, completed in 1823 by Robert Morrison, a Scottish missionary living in Guangzhou, did not include the words *election*, *vote*, or *Parliament*.[20] A handful of missionary-authored Chinese-language texts from that era did allude to voting in Western countries, but their circulation was small and their impact limited.

Pressure mounted to make something out of these materials as opium imports increased. The Daoguang emperor (1782–1850; r. 1820–50), after some debate, demanded the end of foreign opium imports and an end to opium smoking inside China. He appointed Lin Zexu, the advocate of local political activism, to implement his will. Lin brought an inquisitive bent to this new position. Soon after his March 1839 arrival in Guangzhou, the center of the opium trade, Lin tasked a small group of translators with compiling intelligence on the belligerent strangers who had come to peddle the drug. These translators, who all had deep personal ties to the English-speaking world, did not fit the Qing ideal of either a scholar or an official. None appear to have had a classical Chinese education, nor did any participate in the civil service examination system. Just one had held a position (albeit an irregular one) in government before working for Lin. This motley group worked feverishly to translate scraps of foreign newspapers, snippets of manuals of international law, and excerpts from Scotsman Hugh Murray's massive *Encyclopædia of Geography*.[21]

As crisis and ultimately war engulfed south China in 1839 and 1840, this team synthesized their sources of foreign information into a resource guide designed to introduce Qing officials to the global politics of the nineteenth century. Lin's involvement in this project was to serve as the work's nominal editor, although the text is typically, if misleadingly, ascribed to his hand. As the manuscript, which Lin named the *Sizhou zhi* [Gazetteer of the Four Continents], reached completion in 1840, the emperor dismissed him from office. Lin never had a chance to use the text to craft policy, but he retained a copy after his forced retirement.

The work of Lin's translators assumed a foundational place in creating a new Chinese terminology to represent foreign political practices. These men had no clear model for their translation choices, had limited resources for checking their translations, and worked against the backdrop of crisis, blockade, and, by the end of 1839, war. Thus they opted for brief descriptions of the election process and made little attempt to standardize their descriptions. They characterized the British House of Commons as being composed of "successful and accomplished people who were appointed through deliberation [*yiju*] by the various tribes," the French legislature as being filled by individuals selected through "mutual guarantees of fitness for office [*huxiang baochong*] from the various tribes," and U.S. elections as conducted by means of "public appointment [*gongju*]." These vague descriptions significantly parallel Murray's extremely truncated introductions to these representative institutions. The translators incorporated information from other unidentified sources, as well. They described majority voting in their discussion of the electoral college's elevation of "the person with the most recommendations [*yi tuijian zui duo zhe wei ru xuan*]" to the presidency, despite Murray's silence on this topic.[22] Similarly, they (but not Murray) note the existence of written ballots and the importance of counting votes.[23]

Translation is always fraught with difficult choices. Lin's translators left no records of their work other than the manuscript itself, so any assessment of their thought process is inherently speculative. Phrases such as "appointed through deliberation" and "mutual guarantees of fitness for office" appear to be neutral descriptions that do nothing more than aggregate the basic meanings of the characters involved. However, a description of "public appointment" was an implicit analogy to the preexisting, indigenous Qing administrative appointment practice. This bottom-up, recommendation-based practice did not resemble voting, but it also differed from the standard method of Qing appointments via centralized and competitive written examinations. Lin's translators did not settle on a single strategy for explaining elections in Chinese, instead vacillating between offering descriptions and analogizing to specific Qing practices.

Other options for the translation of "elections" existed, too; a look at the potential choices these authors did not make is also illustrative. People unaffiliated with Lin's translation group favored at least two alternatives. Manchu nobleman Qiying (1787–1858), the Qing negotiator at the war's end and Lin Zexu's political foe, stated in an 1844 confidential report that "the leader of the American barbarians is [determined by] the support [*yongli*] of the people and is changed every four years."[24] Qiying's word of choice, strictly speaking, referred to support given to a monarch ascending a throne. This was description by very rough analogy: despite his rhetoric, the rest of Qiying's missive indicates that he understood that the U.S. president was not a monarch. Lin's team of translators, by contrast, seems to have deliberately avoided terms associated with a monarchy. Subsequent writers typically did, too.

A second option can be found in the writings of a foreigner. One of the most prolific Chinese-speaking Christian missionaries of this era, the German Karl Gutzlaff (1803–51), coined a neologism to explain elections, describing U.S. presidents as being "chosen by the people [*minxuan*]," in his 1838 introduction to world history.[25] Although Gutzlaff appeared to be nearly everywhere on the China coast in the 1830s and 1840s (among other tasks, he helped translate for the British during the 1841–42 Treaty of Nanjing negotiations that concluded the Opium War), others did not adopt this translation in his lifetime, and the phrase was rarely repeated in any nineteenth-century Chinese work. This is surprising given Gutzlaff's other influential translations (including an early translation of the Bible) and the seeming simplicity of this particular two-character compound, whose full meaning is clearly and directly derived from the root meaning of the two characters. Was the populist implication of this term perhaps too radical?

Though there was clearly a fascination with describing how foreign leaders were chosen, no single translation emerged in the years during and just after the Opium War. Instead, the two strategies favored by Lin's translators—explanatory description and analogies to Qing administrative practice—became the norm in subsequent decades. They completed their translation work just as a disgraced Lin was banished (only temporarily, it turned out) to the empire's remote Inner Asian frontier. As he began his long trek westward, Lin traveled through the Yangzi delta region and passed his manuscript to Wei Yuan, his protégé and an increasingly influential writer who in 1842 had just completed a well-received study of the dynasty's military history.

Wei's decision to edit and print Lin's text preserved the work of Lin's translators. Their writings became the foundation for his *Haiguo tuzhi* [Illustrated Gazetteer of the Maritime Countries], first published in 1844 and revised and expanded in 1847 and again in 1852. This compendium ultimately shaped understanding of the West within the Qing empire and throughout East Asia, although appeals for a government-sponsored printing went unanswered in the 1850s, and circulation remained limited for a further decade. His depictions of foreign politics, once the *Illustrated Gazetteer* gained a readership in the 1860s, enjoyed currency for decades. The *Gazetteer* itself was reprinted twice in the 1880s, once in the 1890s, and twice again in 1902.[26] Wei adopted the strategies used by Lin's translators to explain elections in foreign countries—neutral descriptive terms and analogies to public appointment—but his choice of vocabulary did not become the standard within the emerging Chinese discourse on Western political systems.[27] Other major geographical texts from the 1840s used different terms for elections.[28]

The decade after these scattered descriptions of elections were first printed witnessed the near-collapse of Qing power. Foreign aggression intensified, and the Taiping, a rival proto-dynasty claiming legitimacy through an amalgamation of Christianity and anti-Manchu sentiment, seized much of southern China. Against this backdrop of persistent crisis, Feng Guifen (1809–74), another Lin Zexu protégé, a friend of Wei Yuan's, and an early reader of Wei's *Illustrated Gazetteer*, began to think about these descriptions in a more systematic way. Possessed of a legendary intellect, Feng's extraordinary performance on the civil service examinations attracted public notice and ensured him an official career. It also brought him to Lin's attention during the latter's tenure as governor of Feng's home province, thus connecting him to a patronage network within the bureaucracy—and an intellectual lineage that emphasized local governance. The slow disintegration of Qing power nudged his life in unexpected directions, however. During the Taiping Rebellion, Feng spent the better part of a decade organizing the defense of his home, Suzhou; when the city fell to the rebels in 1860, he fled southeast to the foreign-ruled treaty port of Shanghai.

Exiled and in poor health, Feng penned a program for political reform titled *Jiaobinlu kangyi* [Essays of Protest] during 1860–61. Although it enjoyed limited circulation in manuscript form, Feng's writings were not published in their entirety until 1884, long after his death. Once published, his text quickly found an audience and was republished at least ten times over the next two decades.[29] The radical nature of his thought accounted for this delayed publication: among other ideas, Feng proposed the selection of certain official positions through a consideration of public opinion. Although this concept may have been inspired by descriptions of voting in Wei's *Illustrated Gazetteer* and by his own observations of foreign life in Shanghai, Feng remained silent about such influence—with one potential exception. Feng's "clean handwritten copy" of *Essays of Protest*, now lost, reportedly referred to descriptions of U.S. elections he found in "various barbarian books." These explained that presidents "pass [their position] to the virtuous, not to [their own] sons [*chuan xian bu chuan zi*]." He must have soon thought better of printing such anti-monarchial sentiments, as he appended a notation that this phrase should be excluded from the finalized version of his work. This wish was honored and these comments do not appear in published editions of his essays. For good measure, he also attempted to erase the characters for "the virtuous" and "sons" in the handwritten edition.[30] In the surviving version of his work, Feng created an intellectual genealogy for his ideas grounded solely in the Confucian canon and in the institutions and scholarship of the late Ming.[31]

Regardless of the precise origins of his ideas, Feng's essays hold an iconic status as the earliest concrete proposal for voting in Chinese history. His most stunning innovation, highlighted by Chinese and foreign historians alike, was his insistence that "public opinion" could be measured by counting the number of supporters for each potential office holder.[32] Such a system was a radical break from the normative route to the bureaucracy via competitive examinations and the standard path to promotion based on the assessment of superiors. The substitution of popular selection for those processes is indeed a remarkable feature of Feng's thought, but other, often overlooked aspects of his proposals tempered it significantly. All but one of his proposals for voting-like systems came balanced with a mechanism for official control over the results. In this sense, his vision was not of Western-style elections but of a dramatic expansion of the long-established practice of public appointment.

Feng suggested two different uses for election-like methods of selection: by the upper bureaucracy to fill vacancies within existing government institutions and by local elites for a newly created series of local offices. His vision for voting within the bureaucracy was composed of several distinct proposals, all of which call for the implementation of what he called "yearly appointments [*suiju*]."[33] At the central level, he envisioned two systems. First, all officials ranked as secretaries or higher in the Grand Secretariat would nominate one person annually for each of a dozen or so powerful institutions of the central government. Should an opening occur in an agency during that year, the Board of Personnel would be obligated to appoint the person who received the most nominations for that position. This intrabureaucratic election of officials by officials was Feng's purest vision of elections—the government would be compelled to abide by the results of this nomination system. The second set of elections to be held at the central level allowed for the same group of selectors to nominate individuals annually for the highest leadership positions in each government institution. Feng explicitly left open the possibility that those with fewer supporters could secure appointments ahead of those with more supporters: "When there is a request to fill a vacant official position, then [the Board of Personnel] should appoint he who has received the most recommendations [*ju*]. If a person who has received fewer recommendations is appointed, then the reasons for this must be stated."[34] Both proposals applied to only a very elite electorate, numbering no more than a few hundred of the empire's highest officials. Yet the choice of even this elite could be overturned in some instances. In many ways, this proposal called for a form of public appointment to be applied at the highest levels of the state.

In the same essay, Feng turned his attention to the appointment of the lowest members of the national bureaucracy, offices ranging from subprefectural magistrates to subcounty police officials. A limited group of locals, numbering perhaps several hundred people in each county—including current officials serving elsewhere, retired officials, holders of the county-level *shengyuan* degree, village headmen, and village elders—would be empowered to nominate individuals for these positions. These nominations would be collected by the prefect and forwarded to the provincial governor, who would evaluate them while "broadly making use of public opinion." The governor was empowered to remove names from the nomination list but could not add them. If a vacancy arose, the person with the most nominations on the revised list would get the position.[35] This was a form of selection in which the results were subject to scrutiny and veto from above, not unlike public appointment as it had been practiced for centuries.

Similar opportunities for official oversight can be found in Feng's proposal for the creation of new offices at the local level—assistant headmen (one for every 100 households) and headmen (one for every 1,000 households)—to be selected by a process he deliberately called "public appointment [*gongju*]."[36] Feng proposed that "each person in the village will write the name of the person that they have nominated on a piece of paper [*yi pianchu shu xingming baoju yi ren*] that will be collected and examined at a government office, and the person who received the most nominations will be selected for office [*ze qi de ju zui duo zhe yong zhi*]." This was Feng's closest approximation of majority voting.

Buried at the end of the proposal, however, was a significant caveat: "[officeholders] who err can be dismissed at any time."[37] This power presumably would be in the hands of the county magistrate, a central government appointee. Elsewhere he suggested an election-like alternative to the civil service examination system for entry into officialdom. The same group of local elites as in the above proposal could nominate a morally exemplary individual for a career in the bureaucracy once every three years. The county magistrate would forward the names of one or two people who had received the most nominations to the provincial government, which would conduct an investigation into these potential candidates. Those who passed this process would then be eligible to bypass the lower rungs of the examination system and sit directly for the national *jinshi* examinations in Beijing.[38] Public opinion would be counted, but the state would still play the pivotal role in evaluating it.

These ideas clearly bear the mark of Lin Zexu's and Wei Yuan's interest in expanding the portion of the population that could legitimately participate in politics; Feng shared their concern that current systems of selection and appointment overlooked a substantial number of talented people. He was animated by the fear that the Qing polity had grown increasingly fractured. He saw a number of divisions that weakened the state—"between the monarch and his ministers, between the center and the localities, between higher-ranking and lower-ranking officials, between officialdom and the general population, and between the government and the people," in the words of one scholar.[39] Voting procedures, he believed, could bridge some of these chasms in a systematic manner. Yet Feng's notion of selection through counting processes was not exactly an "unadulterated theory of elections."[40] Choice had its limits; his vision allowed the government (in most cases) to veto any electoral result it disliked. Feng shared Lin's and Wei's commitment to expanded literati political participation and reinvented the concept of voting to fit within the parameters of this particular philosophical tradition.

Feng's proposals, although only read by a few before the 1880s, directly tied the emerging notion of elections to critiques of the late imperial political system. His insistence on voting for a multitude of newly created offices neatly captured existing descriptions of elections and reimagined voting as a tool for reform based on the expansion of current practices. Missing from his proposal—and from the descriptions that may have inspired it—was any sense of what elections in the West actually looked like. Campaigning, competition between political parties, and electoral fraud were unmentioned. Such a lacuna is congruent with Lin's and Wei's writings and the tradition of public appointment. It is not surprising that Feng would base his assumptions on such sources: no matter how erudite, sincere, or committed he was, he had never witnessed an actual election take place.

Imagining Elections from Up Close

Officials stationed overseas after the construction of Qing diplomatic infrastructure from the late 1860s onward, however, had the opportunity to observe foreign political systems firsthand. As diplomats in government employ, they were enjoined to keep official diaries that were regularly submitted to authorities in Beijing. Within a decade, such accounts were joined by letters written by students at overseas schools to their state sponsors. The observations of diplomats and students, like the writings of early scholars in China, were unsystematic: there was no unified term used for "elections," and discussions about elections were buried within much longer chronological accounts of life overseas. Many of these accounts were ultimately published for public consumption, some decades after they were written.

The timing of publication critically affected the invention of Chinese ideas about elections. The texts that were published the earliest—between the 1870s and 1895—typically included detailed information about the structure and composition of elected legislatures, and even enthusiastic (if vague) endorsements of legislatures as tools of state strengthening, yet did not provide accounts of elections.[41] Their rhetoric mirrored that of the neutral descriptions and historical allusions that appeared in Lin, Wei, and Feng's works. This was largely the result of happenstance—there were only a few diplomats, and they endured frequent transfers; consequently, few had the opportunity to witness an election in progress. The bulk of writings published before 1895 by Qing China's earliest official envoys to the West, including the widely circulated and influential work diaries of Xue Fucheng (1838–94), contain few ideas not already apparent in domestic discourse.[42] Elections were not observed, they were imagined—at least in the materials that circulated publically.

A handful of early envoys did witness elections in progress and recorded their thoughts, but their reactions remained either unpublished until the very end of the nineteenth century (or later—some were not published until the 1980s) or published but not widely read. Although this seems to be the result of coincidence rather than design, the result was that a large body of critical observation existed in Chinese but was never incorporated into the broader discourse of elections in the late Qing. Only a few privileged officials would have had access to some of this material; other portions remained in private hands. As a consequence, these scattered accounts never provided a unified foundation to critique the dominant, optimistic folk theory that originated in Lin, Wei, and Feng.

The overall impression that emerges from these criticisms—which offer a moral condemnation of the competition, ambition, and corruption that accompanied nineteenth-century elections—foreshadowed popular complaints about Chinese elections in the early twentieth century. Zhi-gang (1819–ca. 1890), a diplomat of Manchu descent appointed to accompany the 1867–70 Burlingame Mission, visited Paris during a period of political instability following the disputed parliamentary election of 1869. Candidates, he heard, had bribed voters with "a bottle of wine and a pound of meat." Zhi-gang concluded that this "Western method of appointing officials through recommendations [*Xi fa yi baojian she guan*]" could not identify or appeal to those of true moral rectitude.[43] Despite being published twice before 1900, Zhi-gang's account does not appear to have attracted an audience during his lifetime.[44]

Zhang Deyi (1847–1919), a Han bannerman who eventually wrote a total of eight chronicles covering his multidecade career in the service of Qing diplomacy, accompanied Zhi-gang on that 1869 trip but left only a scant account of the election in Paris.[45] A fluent English speaker, Zhang was noticeably less reticent in assessing a vote he and Zhi-gang had observed several months earlier in Great Britain. While in London during the November 1868 general election, Zhang claimed that "bribery was openly practiced." He asserted that the power of the state, through relief for the poor and other "benevolent policies," had been perverted to "capture the people's hearts" and thus influence the election. Elections might appear similar to the recommendation-based system of "local selections and appointments [*xiangju lixuan*]" supposedly used to pick leaders in ancient China, but were actually "corrupt means to earn fame." Zhang offered little evidence for these conclusions; perhaps they reflected his personal observations, but they might have derived from the newspaper accounts he read the morning after the election.[46] His account was not published until after the dynasty he served had perished and its impact was correspondingly limited.[47]

Even Huang Zunxian (1848–1905), a diplomat famous for his sympathetic and influential account of Japan's political reforms in the 1870s, offered a particularly pointed poetic critique of the 1884 U.S. presidential election, which he observed from his new position at the Qing consulate in San Francisco:

Fellow countrymen angrily drew weapons on each other,
while [candidates] furiously struggled for office . . .
Private interest has perverted the public good,

the excessive [search for] advantage has produced corruption.
And even if a worthy man is selected,
Can he hold this elevated position with a clear conscience?
If only they could eliminate factional strife,
Then the Golden Age would follow close behind.[48]

Despite this text's vividness, evidence suggests he may have composed the poem almost a decade after the election it depicts.[49] At most, this poem would have enjoyed only limited circulation during Huang's lifetime; the first published version dates to 1911.

Informal observers expressed sentiments similar to those of these accredited envoys. Reformist officials deliberately sponsored overseas students in hopes of gaining direct insight into the nature of China's foreign adversaries. The most powerful such official, Li Hongzhang (1823–1901), dispatched Ma Jianzhong (1845–1900), a scion of a prominent Catholic Jiangsu family and a member of Li's staff, to France in 1876. While earning a law degree in Paris, Ma corresponded with Li, sharing his insights and knowledge of Western politics. One letter offered an unappealing depiction, apparently derived from secondhand accounts, of U.S. elections: "In America, the president is selected by the people themselves, seemingly as if everyone acts out of public, rather than private, interest. But when it is time for each 'selection and appointment [*xuanju*],' corruption is practiced openly."[50] Upon his return to China in 1879, Ma served with distinction on Li Hongzhang's staff but focused his energies on the technological aspects of reform. This dovetailed with Li's predilections. An able administrator and astute politician, the imposingly tall Li, whose very features "betoken inflexible determination," invested his energy in constructing modern arsenals, establishing of business enterprises, and promoting study about (and in) the West.[51] The abstract "constitutional crisis" that engaged the passions of Lin, Wei, and Feng was not central to Li's worldview. While Li's collected writings are filled with references to foreign legislatures, they reveal no interest in these institutions as potential models for China.

Unlike the line of thinking developed by Lin Zexu, Wei Yuan, and Feng Guifen, no evidence suggests that the critics who wrote scattered firsthand observations of elections saw their writings as containing a cohesive ideology, and it may be that these authors were entirely unaware of each other's observations. Some areas of spontaneous agreement emerge, however: a distaste for partisan competition, a belief that elections lent themselves to bribery, and a fear that elections subverted the public good in favor of private interests. In time, these themes formed a widely shared critical response to Feng's optimistic assertions that elections could create unity and dialogue between the state and the people.

A (Temporary) Rectification of Terms

Until the 1890s, neither admirers nor critics of elections embraced a consistent term to name elections. Instead, a variety of terms, phrases, and descriptions circulated. This linguistic plurality was reflected in a number of places, including the earliest English–Chinese bilingual dictionaries. One of first of these, missionary Walter Henry Medhurst's 1847–48 *English and Chinese Dictionary*, equated the English verb "to elect" with three different Chinese compounds. Two of these compounds, *xuanze* and *jianze*, simply mean "to choose" or "to select"; the third, *jianxuan*, carried the additional meaning with the Qing bureaucracy of "appointment to office."[52] Nearly two decades later, missionary William Lobscheid's 1866 *English and Chinese Dictionary* used variants of Chinese words for "choosing" or "appointing" as the equivalent for English-language notions of election.[53] One of the first bilingual dictionaries authored by a Chinese person, Yale-educated Kwang Ki-Chaou's 1887 *English and Chinese Dictionary*, proposed three translations for the verb "to elect": "select and appoint [*xuanju*]," "choose [*jianze*]," and "public appointment [*gongju*]."[54] The mixed strategies pioneered by Lin's team of translators—neutral descriptions paired with words drawn from Qing administrative practice—remained the norm for discussions of elections well into the final third of the nineteenth century.

By the 1890s, the use of "public appointment [*gongju*]" as the term for elections became more common, more systematic, and more purposeful than any other alternative. Ultimately, the rhetoric of public appointment came to be most strongly associated with those who advocated the adoption of electoral systems as a tool to reinvigorate the Qing polity. Linking the character compound "public appointment"—which had a specific history within Qing countryside administration—with foreign practices of majority voting represented the first successful systematic attempt to reinvent the concept of voting within Qing China's distinctive political culture. No particular event marked the widespread embrace of "public appointment" as the standardized Chinese-language term for elections. Instead, the word was suddenly everywhere in the months before the 1894–95 Sino-Japanese War. If it had its origins anywhere, however, it was in Shanghai mass circulation media outlets such as *Wanguo gongbao* [Chinese Globe], founded by U.S. missionaries in 1868, and *Shenbao*, a newspaper established under British ownership in 1872. Although both had used the term as early as the 1870s, it was two 1894 books linked to the intellectual environment created by these periodicals that spread discussion of public appointment across the empire that year.

The first of these best-sellers was Timothy Richard [Li Timotai] (1845–1919) and Cai Erkang's (1851–1921) translation of Robert Mackenzie's popular tome, *The Nineteenth Century: A History—The Times of Queen Victoria*. Richard, a Baptist missionary from Wales, had resided in China since 1870 and had acquired an impressive level of competency in the Chinese language. Though he had spent the previous twenty years in various locations in north China, Richard relocated to Shanghai in 1891 to manage the Society for the Diffusion of Useful Knowledge, a missionary organization that promoted the spread of Western scientific, political, and social thought. Cai, a pioneering Shanghai journalist conversant in English, had collaborated on the translation and editing of missionary tracts for decades.

Mackenzie's history identified the "progress of liberty in Europe" as the century's central theme. "Sixty years ago," he argued, "Europe was an aggregate of despotic powers, dispensing at their own pleasure of the lives and property of their subjects . . . To-day the men of western Europe govern themselves." The spread of elected representative institutions had made the difference: "Popular suffrage, more or less closely approaching universal, chooses the governing power, and by methods more or less effective dictates its policy." The revolutions that had created these institutions, he suggested, had become inevitable once Europeans had come to understand the value of liberty and self-government. Despotism "exists only by sufferance; it cannot continue when nations have determined that it shall cease." Such a system of government was doomed to fail because "it thwarts and frustrates the forces by which providence has provided for the progress of man; liberty secures for these forces their natural scope and exercise."[55]

Richard and Cai began working on their Chinese edition in 1892–93 and excerpts from the translation, titled *Taixi xinshi lanyao* [A New Historical Overview of the West] appeared in the *Chinese Globe Magazine* (then edited by Richard himself) between March and September 1894; a complete translation was published in book form the following year. They retained Mackenzie's chapter and subchapter structure and virtually all of his content. Mirroring the emphasis of Mackenzie's original, Richard and Cai's translation placed the history of Great Britain at the center of their narrative and took the expansion of suffrage rights in the 1832 Reform Bill as the key turning point in recent British history. Voting, elections, and the franchise were thus the pivotal mechanisms for the "progress of liberty" in Europe. Almost without exception, Richard and Cai adopted the character compound "public appointment [*gongju*]" to represent this central notion.[56]

Richard and Cai's translation circulated widely, in both authorized and unauthorized editions. Richard estimated that a million copies existed in print.[57] Although that number is almost certainly a wild exaggeration, the translation did attract a substantial number of readers. Richard noted that a "director of the China Merchants Steamship Company" purchased 100 copies to be distributed to officials in the capital.[58] Some of these may have found an audience at the highest levels of the Qing state. Leading officials, including Li Hongzhang, Zhang Zhidong (1837–1909), and Prince Gong (1833–98) reportedly read Richard and Cai's translation. Sun Jia'nai (1827–1909), the imperial tutor, claimed that he had read the text aloud to the Guangxu emperor (1871–1908; r. 1875–1908) over the course of several months.[59] Soon-to-be-famous reformist intellectuals Kang Youwei (1858–1927) and Liang Qichao (1873–1929) also joined this readership.

Mackenzie said little about the meaning of his thesis beyond western Europe, although his universalistic language implied that it could be applied elsewhere, too. Richard certainly embraced this interpretation, claiming that he embarked on this translation project "in order to give the statesmen of China information regarding the recent progress of the world and to point out that if they adopted the reforms of the West there would be hope for their country."⁶⁰ Richard and Cai hinted at this in a preface, suggesting that Chinese leaders should reflect on the Western historical experience. Beyond that general claim, the two made only modest policy recommendations: that a question about Western history be added to the civil service examinations and that Chinese officials be sent on overseas study missions.⁶¹

This reticence was probably wise. Richard harbored a number of views that Chinese readers might have found objectionable. At times, he proved unable to restrain himself in expressing these notions. In a February 1895 interview with reformist governor-general Zhang Zhidong, for instance, Richard argued that "God demanded reform on the part of China, and that if she neglected it God would appoint some other nation to reform her, as had been the case in India, Egypt, and other nations."⁶² Later that year, he met with Weng Tonghe (1830–1904), a powerful figure in the central government, and proposed that two "foreign advisors to the Throne" and a cabinet composed "half of foreign officials who would know about the progress of all the world" be appointed.⁶³ The connection between these proposals for foreign domination and the "progress of liberty" must have been difficult for these proud officials to discern.

Mackenzie's essential argument, nonetheless, was inspiring to a Chinese audience. One reader, moved to draft a poem reflecting on the book's message, exclaimed, "Autocracies require deluding the people/deluding the people is self-limitation . . . Republics desire popular knowledge/popular knowledge increases sagacity and ability."⁶⁴ By coincidence, this particular reader, prominent Guangdong-born, Shanghai-based businessman Zheng Guanying (1842–1922) published his own collection of political essays in March 1894, the same month Richard and Cai's translation began serialization. Although Zheng did not collaborate with them, he had not been working in complete isolation from them. Zheng had long-standing ties with the Shanghai foreign missionary community, corresponded with many of them, and may even have been the Richard's unnamed "director of the China Merchants Steamship Company" who purchased copies of the translation for distribution to the politicians in Beijing.

Zheng's tract, titled *Shengshi weiyan* [Words of Warning to a Prosperous Age], proved to be even more influential than Richard and Cai's translation. His essays attracted immediate attention for their emphatic call for specific and detailed political, social, and economic reforms. The first edition gained such prominence that a sympathetic official presented a copy to the emperor, who soon ordered 2,000 copies be distributed among high-ranking officials in 1895. Zheng produced an expanded edition (nearly twice the size of the first edition) that year and, in 1900, another substantially reorganized edition. Beyond these three versions, over a dozen other "unofficial" editions of the work circulated during the same period.[65] The total number of books this represented is unknown, although clearly considerable. The contents of these editions varied, but the work retained a level of thematic consistency.

One of these continuities was Zheng's insistence on establishing a new form of political infrastructure: deliberative assemblies [*yiyuan*]. This idea was not original; in 1890, reform-minded scholar-official Tang Shouqian (1856–1917) called for creating such institutions in an influential collection of essays titled *Wei yan* [Words of Warning]. Tang's text, an inspiration for Zheng's similarly named treatise, contained only a brief discussion of deliberative assemblies. At the central level, they would comprise members of the regular bureaucracy; at the local level, no selection method was specified.[66] Zheng's more fully fleshed-out proposal, by contrast, placed elections (for which he generally, although not exclusively, adopted the term "public appointments [*gongju*])" at the center of his program for political change. Zheng wrote comprehensively about voting and organized several essays specifically around notions of voting and elected legislatures. Unlike earlier writers, he provided a detailed comparative account of the specifics of Western election laws (including those in Great Britain, France, Italy, Prussia, Denmark, and a host of others), including restrictions on suffrage. More important, he sought to promote elections as an institution that could be adopted in China.[67]

Despite his focus on the phrase "public appointment," Zheng did not claim earlier Qing dynasty practice as a precedent—and, curiously, he denied that anything resembling this practice still existed. In "Public Appointments," an essay added to the 1895 edition of *Words of Warning*, he instead linked his proposal to the institutions of the Han dynasty, 2,000 years earlier:

> The method of "public appointment" is similar to the legacy of "local selections and appointments [*xiangju lixuan*]." During the Han, this method was widely used to pick people [for office]. It probably caused the literati

class to aspire to act in a moral manner, rather than to emulate fancy literary skills. People devoted themselves to statecraft, rather than argumentative words.[68]

The establishment of deliberative assemblies, filled with literati chosen by their peers rather than by written examination, would change the incentives for particular forms of behavior and learning. Deliberative assemblies of this sort, Zheng argued, had been a part of China's political culture in antiquity. Reestablishing it in the present day would be a reconnection with a lost piece of China's political traditions and would provide the court with a potent tool for harmonizing the interests of the government and the people. Zheng's emphasis on this point helped spread the foundational ideas of Chinese elections to a broad audience of reform-minded people.

These sentiments echoed Feng Guifen's, although Zheng remained silent about his sources of inspiration in this essay. Other writings included in Zheng's 1895 edition, however, do cite Feng's *Essays of Protest* directly; by 1895 (if not earlier), Zheng certainly had read Feng's work. The congruence in thought between the men is particularly noteworthy given their very different backgrounds. Zheng was no mandarin: having abandoned the examination system after an early failure, he devoted himself to a career in business. Sent to live with an uncle in Shanghai at age sixteen, he spent the rest of his life immersed in that port city's burgeoning foreign trade. Soon after arriving in Shanghai, he began studying English, first with his uncle (who was a comprador with a foreign firm) and later at a missionary-run institution. His linguistic skills, coupled with his keen business sense, allowed him to enrich himself as a middleman between Chinese and foreign merchants. This personal experience formed the foundation of his call for political change in Qing China. In the preface to his *Words of Warning to a Prosperous Age*, he explained, "I interact with [foreigners] daily. I have observed their habits, inquired about their politics and religions, and examined the strengths and weaknesses of their customs."[69]

Zheng's interest did not spring from an uncritical admiration of the West. He ascribed his interest in Western learning "to anger over foreigners' demands and to despair at the failed policies of the Chinese throne." He had a comprehensive set of new policies, based on the belief that, contrary to what self-strengtheners like Li Hongzhang thought, "the roots of wealth and power lie not only in strong ships and powerful guns, but also in the unification of the hearts of the high and the low through deliberative assemblies [*zai yiyuan shang xia tongxin*] and effective education [*jiaoyang defa*]."⁷⁰ Elected assemblies could bind the talents and loyalties of all people (especially those who, like him, had become successful outside of the examination system) with the needs and priorities of the state. This magic tool could harmonize the interests of the rulers and the ruled and would ultimately create a wealthy and powerful China.

Despite his sustained experiences with foreigners, bilingual education, and career outside of the official bureaucracy, Zheng's proposed elections ultimately differed little from the scholar-official Feng Guifen's—both mirrored traditional practices of public appointment more than any Western system of voting. Zheng agreed that the state should proactively manage elections to ensure their success. He proposed limiting suffrage to individuals with a "good family background" and either "a certain amount of property" or an "official salary." Further restrictions would apply to those who could be elected to office.⁷¹ In 1895, Zheng voiced concerns that Chinese people lacked the necessary enlightenment to participate effectively in Western-style assemblies, but in subsequent personal correspondence he entertained the possibility that elections could be held successfully if the state performed a proper supervisory role. The government should require that those elected to office be "conversant in Chinese and in foreign languages, possessed of experiences and prestige, and adherent to proper moral conduct." Such people would be "nominated by local gentry and merchants" and report to local officials. Critically, he assigned veto power to the state in the enforcement of these norms: "those who do not meet the standards cannot be elected."⁷² His frequent pairing of elections and education, evident in the preface to *Words of Warning* and the essay on "Public Appointment," suggest a fundamentally Confucian vision of the state as an educator: the teacher of appropriate behavior and the final arbiter of that behavior. This was a more elaborate version of Feng's proposals from a generation earlier. In this vision, the state disciplines the voters as much as, if not more than, voters discipline the state.

Conclusion

Soon after the publication of the Mackenzie translation and *Words of Warning* in March 1894, fighting broke out between Chinese and Japanese soldiers in Korea. Many observers thought the two sides to be evenly matched, but this view proved to be profoundly mistaken. In a succession of decisive land and sea battles, Japanese forces routed the Qing military in the Korean Peninsula and on the Yellow Sea, ultimately threatening northern China itself. Its armies vanquished and its navies sunk, the Qing throne had little choice but to sue for peace in 1895. The price was steep: Beijing ceded territory, paid an immense indemnity, and accepted greater foreign control over the treaty ports. The Qing government's acquiescence provoked a national debate over China's future.

The combination of a young emperor eager to make his mark and an elite angry over China's humiliating failure created an environment in which proposals for change flourished. The building blocks for this situation had existed before the war: some officials surrounding the emperor had a taste for radical suggestions and in 1889 had presented a copy of Feng Guifen's complete *Essays of Protest* to the then-eighteen-year-old Guangxu emperor. Tang Shouqian's reformist essays also soon reached the imperial court. By the opening stages of the war in 1894, Richard and Cai's translation and Zheng's *Warnings* had become objects of discussion within the highest ranks of officialdom. After the 1895 peace treaty, a few people at the highest levels of government began discussing the possibility of elections in earnest. Hunger for information about these systems spread far beyond the government, too. Booksellers published and republished works on foreign countries at an unprecedented rate. Wei Yuan's four-decades-old *Illustrated Gazetteer* was republished in 1895; six different private firms published Feng Guifen's *Protests* between 1892 and 1898; and a Shanghai bookstore printed the enormous *Xiaofanghuzhai yudi congchao* [Historical Writings from the Xiaofanghu Studio], a major collection of diplomatic diaries, records of foreign travel, and descriptions of foreign geography, between 1891 and 1897. Intellectuals urged the curious to read these disparate texts as a group; one reading list on "Western governance," printed in early 1898, recommended readers peruse Wei's compendium, Feng's essays, and selected writings from a variety of diplomats including Guo Songtao, Xue Fucheng, and Zhang Deyi.[73] The view of elections in all of these works reflected the optimistic foundational expectation that elections could serve as tools for state-strengthening.

Kang Youwei, an iconoclastic scholar from Guangdong, responded to this new political environment and sought to capture the emperor's interest with a series of reform proposals submitted to the throne in 1895. Among other ideas, he proposed that localities should use public appointment to identify "ministers for deliberation" from among the degree-holding population; these ministers would advise the government. Kang envisioned these positions being renewed on annually.[74] Though less detailed than Zheng Guanying's proposal for an elected legislature and significantly less radical than Feng Guifen's concept of elections within the bureaucracy, Kang's plan had an immediate impact due to his direct line of communication to the emperor. As a formal adviser to the Guangxu emperor in the summer of 1898, Kang channeled Zheng's vision and called for the establishment of a "national parliament." He asked the emperor to promulgate "election regulations" based on the experiences of other countries, though he did not specify the nature of the election process. Facing resistance even at the height of the reformist tide in July 1898, Kang felt obligated to abandon any hope of immediate elections, suggesting instead an interim period in which affairs of state were debated openly by a select group of literati recommended by government officials.[75]

The same month that Kang made his proposals, the emperor ordered Feng Guifen's essays distributed to several hundred officials in the central bureaucracy for commentary.[76] Perhaps the best informed recipient was Li Hongzhang, the giant of midcentury reform. Feng had served on Li's staff as an adviser in the 1860s, and Li had written a funerary inscription on his passing in 1874. Though out of political favor in the summer of 1898, the seventy-five-year-old Li—his imposing features now marked by a scar under his left eye, the result of an assassination attempt in 1895—could draw on decades of experience with foreigners and foreign policy when commenting on Feng's writings. Much of what Li knew about elections was unfavorable; as early as the 1870s, his subordinate Ma Jianzhong had sent him a negative account of Western elections. He may have had access to some of the unpublished diplomatic accounts of elections. Rereading Feng's essays in 1898, Li immediately linked Feng's concept of elections within the bureaucracy to U.S. congressional elections.

This was not meant as flattery, for "[in that system], those below seek their private advantage, those above protect their clients. At its worst, the system amounts to seeking office through bribery. Perceptive people in that country are already well aware of this."[77] Few other Chinese would have had access to the documents and the information that allowed Li to draw such a conclusion.

Even those sympathetic to Feng's program echoed the complaints of diplomats that representative institutions and elections were inherently corrupt. Censor Huang Junlong (dates unknown) remarked after reading Feng's proposals for voting within the bureaucracy that "employing people on the basis of public discussion certainly is a method from antiquity; the deliberative assemblies of Westerners also follow this idea. This method can be enacted and its defects of improper partiality and bribery can be eliminated."[78] Yet few shared Huang's optimism that corruption could be so easily dispensed with, even among Kang Youwei's closest allies. Liu Guangdi (1859–98), a reformer whose support for the Guangxu emperor cost him his life, believed that contemporary Chinese people lacked the proper moral character to participate in representative institutions (which, he noted, were also problematic overseas).[79]

A palace coup on September 21, 1898, orchestrated by Guangxu's aunt, Empress Dowager Cixi (1835–1908) ended these nascent discussions of "public appointment" for political office. Kang and other reformers fled to Japan, where they remained in exile for over a decade. The following year, Cixi threw the throne's support behind a ragged group of anti-foreign rebels known as the Boxers. This desperate attempt to reclaim the initiative against Western and Japanese imperialism resulted in both disaster and, paradoxically, a final chance for dynastic renewal. The disaster came first: a multinational invasion force defeated the Boxers, occupied Beijing, and extracted a humiliating peace treaty in 1901. As a result of this catastrophe, the dynasty publicly committed itself to a fundamental reorganization of the political order. In this new environment, many of the ideas that had seemed radical in the 1890s, such as the implementation of public appointment, came to be embraced even by those who had opposed them when they were first proposed.

Discussion of these ideas emerged slowly, only truly getting under way in 1905. By then, the vocabulary adopted by observers and reformers in the nineteenth century had already begun to be abandoned. Although the first government-sponsored elections occurred in 1909, barely more than fifteen years after the publication of Zheng Guanying's *Words of Warning*, his language had already become anachronistic. By 1909—and continuing to the present day—yet another character compound, *xuanju* or "selection and appointment," emerged as the dominant and standard term for voting and elections.

That final linguistic transformation marked official state legitimation of voting as a method of political selection—yet it did not bridge the divisions that had emerged in the nineteenth century between those who idealized elections as an easily controllable tool for the creation of a Confucian paradise and those who saw them as a path to a Confucian nightmare. The tension between these beliefs—that elected institutions are necessary to be modern (and hence strong), but elections themselves are corrupt and unpalatable—was never openly acknowledged in the nineteenth century. These cracks in the foundational expectation that Chinese elections were a path to national strength only gradually become apparent in the twentieth century, as control over the narrative of Chinese elections passed into the hands of leaders who had the political power, social prestige, and imagination to move them from the realm of ideas into the world of policy.

CHAPTER 2

Transmission and Re-Creation

Writing Laws for Voting, 1898–1908

The war between Japan and Russia that broke out in February 1904 inadvertently catalyzed the creation of the first Chinese election law. That conflict, which ended with Japanese triumph in 1905, laid the foundations for Japan's empire on the Asian mainland, reordered the balance of power in East Asia, and affected strategic calculations in capitals around the world. At least one early observer believed that the conflict had implications more profound than geopolitics. Writing to an acquaintance on June 26, 1904, in the aftermath of several Russian battlefield defeats, Zhang Jian (1853–1926) urged his recipient to see that "Japan's victory over Russia is the victory of constitutional government over autocratic rule."[1] No longer could states thrive without an engaged public—the time had come to build institutions that would create such a public in China.

Zhang's opinion carried real weight; few others were as prominent in public life during the final decades of the Qing dynasty. Born into a family of farmers and small merchants, his intellectual gifts led him to prepare for the civil service examinations in hopes of winning government employment. Overcoming narrow odds, he ranked first among those who passed the final, national level of the examinations held under the emperor's direct supervision in 1894. He remained in Beijing for six months afterward, participating as a member of the prowar faction in the intense intrabureaucratic political struggles precipitated by the 1894–95 Sino-Japanese War. His time in the capital, however, was suddenly interrupted by his father's death. Returning home to Nantong, Jiangsu, for the mandatory period of mourning, Zhang soon decided to break from the conventional path in the imperial bureaucracy. Within a few years, he reinvented himself as an industrial entrepreneur, social reformer, and advocate of political change. Despite this choice, he was never an outsider to those in power: he retained the status and connections to influence politics at the highest level.

Initially, the political ideas he advocated were quite conventional, similar to many other "self-strengthening"–inspired appeals for greater state investment in the military and the economy.[2] Although sympathetic to the reformers in 1898, Zhang largely stood aside from the Guangxu emperor's abortive "Hundred Days of Reform," believing that institutional change would only come at a more deliberate pace.[3] He embarked on a new direction in the aftermath of the Boxer defeat. Responding to the empress dowager's contrite January 1901 plea for policy suggestions, Zhang submitted a lengthy memorial in March listing forty-two specific proposals. These included the establishment of an appointed deliberative chamber at the national level and elected county and prefectural assemblies. The electorate for the latter would be limited to those of "wealth or moral prestige." These small institutions (each numbering no more than five members), he believed, would suffice to "link the affections of ruler and ruled [*tong shang xia zhi qing*]."[4] His plan attracted little interest from government officials, but Shanghai's *Shenbao* newspaper published it in its entirety over the course of nine days in May, ensuring it was not forgotten.[5]

Zhang's proposals broke little new ground. Kang Youwei had recommended an appointed national assembly at the height of the 1898 summer of reform; decades earlier, Feng Guifen had suggested a similar vision of local elections. Zhang was aware of these precedents: he had read Feng's *Essays of Protest* and followed the course of Kang's political career closely in the press. Yet his plans for local and national assemblies differed from these precedents in one crucial respect: he specifically cited Japan's recent historical experience as his inspiration for these (and other) innovations. Zhang's fascination with Japan grew over the next few years. He visited Japan for seventy days in 1903—the only overseas trip he took in his life—and wrote an effusive, detailed account of his journey. Upon his return home, he sponsored a mid-1904 publication of the Japanese constitution in translation and a book on Japanese representative institutions. He arranged for a copy of this translation to reach the Forbidden City, where it was reportedly read by Cixi herself. Her vaguely positive reaction—she commented that "the existence of a constitution has benefited the state in Japan"—resulted in at least one high official's hasty attempt to read up on constitutionalism.[6]

For Zhang Jian, the outcome of the Russo-Japanese War confirmed his preexisting belief that national strength could be unleashed through fundamental reform and reinforced his idea that Japan was an appropriate model. Such restructuring, begun in Japan during the reign of the Meiji emperor (1852–1912; r. 1867–1912), had transformed that country into an actor of global significance in the space of just a few decades. During this period, reformers replaced the decentralized Tokugawa shogunate with a strong national government, complete with a constitution and an elected legislature, centered on the symbolic power of the Japanese emperor. This new government embraced a radical program of comprehensive change, resulting in the rapid development of Japanese political, economic, and military power. The country's new strength had been vividly revealed to China a decade earlier; the war with Russia was further proof. Spurred to action, Zhang and other reformers outside the government seized the initiative to push for a Qing constitution. As they had been in Japan, elections and elected assemblies would necessarily be the critical elements of a constitutional reform process that would strengthen the Qing state.

The true historical value of Zhang's 1904 claim that Japanese military victories demonstrated the superiority of constitutional governments, however, derives from its context as much as its rhetoric: the acquaintance to whom he wrote was Yuan Shikai (1859–1916), at the time a high-ranking official in the Qing government. No communication had passed between the men for twenty years, but they had once been close. Both had been employed by the same military unit in the early 1880s, during which Zhang tutored Yuan in the texts of the classical tradition. Zhang abruptly severed ties in 1884, believing that Yuan's careerist ambitions had disrespected the commander who had acted as their patron. Zhang's accusations were only the first of many that Yuan eventually faced. In the summer of 1898, Yuan had appeared to ally with the Guangxu emperor's reform efforts, only to switch allegiance when the tide turned against the reformers. Even more shocking, acts of opportunism and duplicity lay in the future. These accusations obscure as much as they reveal, however—Yuan's contributions to the early twentieth-century reshaping of Chinese governance, which had only begun when Zhang reached out to him after decades of silence, cannot simply be dismissed as the by-product of his all-too-real lust for power.

Little resulted from this initial correspondence, but an unlikely partnership between these ambitious and powerful men ultimately developed. Over the following months and years, Yuan took the leading role within the government in organizing the agenda for late Qing China's constitutional reforms, including elections. On the outside, Zhang worked to create public pressure in support of this program. Their collaboration deepened over time, shaping the fabric of late Qing politics and establishing a pattern for Chinese elections that endured for decades.[7] Together, they had the prestige, power, and organizational ability to move elections from the realm of ideas into the real world.

During the final decade of Qing rule, Yuan sat at the center of a broad process that transformed the vague ideas of Feng Guifen, Zheng Guanying, and other nineteenth-century intellectuals into concrete legal and institutional forms. It would be an exaggeration to title him (even ironically) the "architect of Chinese elections," but his fingerprints appeared on almost all of the important developments that led up to the first authorized elections in Chinese history. Yuan played a decisive role in the 1905 abolition of the civil service examination system, in the 1906 push to investigate foreign political systems and commit the throne to adopting a constitution, and in the decision to experiment with local elections in 1907. Zhang Jian stood with him throughout these reforms, using his prestige and resources to organize in favor of constitutionalism outside the ranks of officialdom. Although neither man personally drafted the first nationwide election laws in 1908, they did more than anyone else to shape the contours of China's first system of elections. Their wholehearted embrace of foundational ideas synthesized by late nineteenth-century essayists and theorists meant that these concepts came to be embedded in the genetic code of Chinese election law and practice.

Examinations as "Selection and Appointment"

Despite its prominence in the writings of Zheng Guanying and others in the 1890s, the phrase "public appointment" as the preferred Chinese term for elections was abandoned in the first decade of the twentieth century in favor of the compound "selection and appointment [*xuanju*]." This two-character phrase appeared in the election laws advocated by Yuan Shikai and Zhang Jian and is still used in the twenty-first century as the standard term for elections. However, it was not consistently used in this sense until after 1900 and was not exclusively used in this way for more than half a decade beyond that. The emergence of this new term normalized elections and placed them within a continuum of traditional Chinese political thought and institutions.

This compound was not a blank slate for constitutional reformers to etch new meanings on to—there was already a meaning attached to it. "Selection and appointment" had long been a precise term for legitimate, regulated recruitment procedures for government officials. Examples of this abound in the written record. Each official dynastic history, from the *New Tang History* (completed in 1060) to the *Ming History* (finished in 1739), contained a "Treatise on Selection and Appointment [*Xuanju zhi*]" that detailed civil service examinations, military examinations, and other systems of bureaucratic selection. "Public appointment," by contrast, referred to an informal (but government-sanctioned) system; it was something that happened beneath, rather than within, the government and was consequently not discussed in these chapters of the various dynastic histories. The change in terminology that took place after 1900, from voting conceptualized as a type of informal, unregulated public appointment to voting understood as a variety of legitimate selection and appointment was a significant conceptual shift.

As a result, the compound for "selection and appointment" only slowly became the standard term for elections in Chinese, whereas it quickly became so in Japan. In Japan, where elections had been introduced in the 1870s, "selection and appointment" [*xuanju*, pronounced *senkyo* in Japanese] had been an accepted and perhaps even preferred translation for "election" since the mid-nineteenth century. Fukuzawa

Yukichi (1835–1901), the influential Meiji-era intellectual and the creator of much of modern Japanese political terminology, exclusively used the compound *senkyo* to represent the concept of elections in his copious writings.[8] Japan's first election law, the 1878 code for prefectural assemblies, also consistently used this compound when referring to voting and elections, as did the 1889 election law for the lower house of Japan's new national legislature.[9] Unlike China, where the examination system existed as the normative institutional form of selection and appointment, Meiji Japan lacked any preexisting institution with this title. There was thus no barrier to the appropriation of this character compound.

There is little evidence that educated Qing onlookers, despite their ability to read the character-based portions of written Japanese, felt influenced by this linguistic shift in Japan before the 1890s. China's unexpected and humiliating defeat in the 1894–95 Sino-Japanese War led some in the Qing government to consider the lessons that might be learned from Japan's post-1868 restructuring. Japanese-inspired political concepts—as well as leaders such as Itō Hirobumi (1841–1909)—influenced the Guangxu emperor's 1898 reform effort. After the suppression of that movement, a number of sympathetic officials were executed. Others fled to Japan, where they played a pivotal role in introducing Japanese terminology to China. These exiles adopted "selection and appointment" as their preferred translation for elections. This is evident in the prolific writings of Liang Qichao, the Guangxu-era reform leader destined to be one of early twentieth-century China's most prominent intellectuals: the compound "selection and appointment" appeared in his writings on elections only after he began his involuntary sojourn in Tokyo in 1898.[10]

Liang and Kang Youwei, the mentor he soon eclipsed, spent their decade of banishment introducing Japanese adaptations of Western political philosophies and institutions to the Chinese through various publishing and educational ventures. Textbooks published by people associated with them, such as a 1902 introduction to political science authored by future Jiangsu provincial assemblyman Yang Tingdong (1879–1950), were among the first Chinese texts to consistently use "selection and appointment" to refer to elections.[11] Translations of Japanese texts on elections, reprinted in Shanghai during the century's first years with little or no added commentary, circulated at the same time and further solidified the identification of

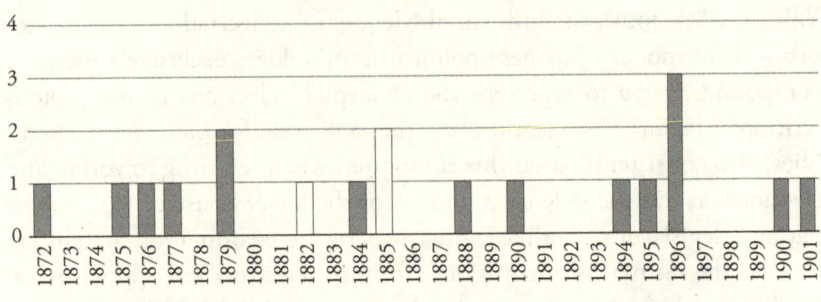

FIGURE 1: Frequency of terms *gongju* and *xuanju* to mean "election/voting" in *Shenbao* headlines, 1872–1901. The data are derived from a count of terms found using the headline search function in Green Apple Data Center's *Shenbao, 1872–1949* database. Each occurrence was examined to eliminate mistakes or false positives.

elections with this character compound.[12] Likewise, the influential 1903 Chinese encyclopedia of new political and scientific terms, the *New Erya Dictionary*, used "selection and appointment" to refer to elections.[13] One of this work's authors, Wang Rongbao (1878–1933), a returned student from Japan, later helped draft Qing local election laws; after the revolution, he held a seat in the Chinese Republic's first parliament.

The Japanese-inspired preference for selection and appointment had gained a foothold in China by the first years of the new century. The change can be roughly measured by comparing the use of this term and "public appointment" in the Shanghai press. Between 1874 and 1901, "public appointment" appeared in the headlines of *Shenbao*, one of Shanghai's most prominent daily newspapers, infrequently—but "selection and appointment" almost never at all (see figure 1).

By 1905, as the newspaper restructured itself to focus more specifically on political issues, use of both terms became more frequent. As elections and political reform found a place on the paper's editorial page and ultimately in the news of the day, writers became far more likely to use the term "selection and appointment" in their headlines (see figure 2).

A similar shift in frequency between the two terms can be observed in the headlines of the forty-one weekly, monthly, and semi-annual publications founded before 1899 and indexed in a major bibliographic finding guide (see figure 3).

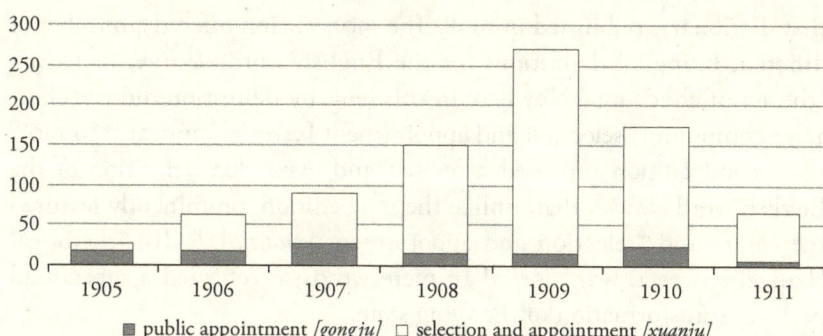

FIGURE 2: Frequency of terms *gongju* and *xuanju* to mean "election/voting" in *Shenbao* headlines, 1905–1911. Note that neither term appeared in any headline during the years 1902–4. The data are derived from a count of terms found using the headline search function in Green Apple Data Center's *Shenbao, 1872–1949* database. Each occurrence was examined to eliminate mistakes or false positives.

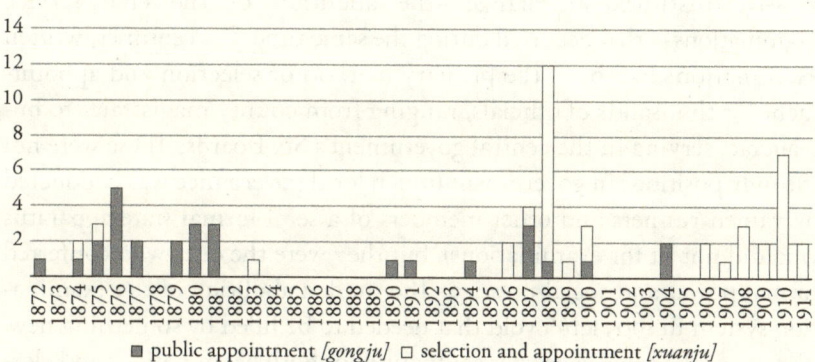

FIGURE 3: Frequency of terms *gongju* and *xuanju* to mean "election/voting" in headlines of forty-one Chinese periodicals, 1872–1911. The data are derived from a machine count of the headlines contained in Shanghai tushuguan, *Zhongguo jindai qikan bianmu huilu*, vol. 1. Each occurrence was examined to eliminate mistakes or false positives.

The shift in relative frequency of the terms "public appointment" and "selection and appointment" was matched by a transformation of meaning. One illustration of this comes from the differences between the Commercial Press's 1902 English–Chinese dictionary, the first such reference work published by a Chinese company, and the second edition of that dictionary, published in 1908. The 1902 version offered a number of different bilingual definitions for the English word *election*, including "the act of choosing." Nowhere in this lengthy definition did the character compound "selection and appointment [*xuanju*]" appear.[14] In 1908, the second edition provided a revised and expanded definition of the English word *election* that, unlike the 1902 edition, prominently featured the compound "selection and appointment [*xuanju*]."[15] This rhetorical change, however, was more than mere words; it reflected a substantial political transformation of the Qing state.

The End of the Civil Service Examination System

The linguistic shift from *gongju* to *xuanju* was only possible because of a massive institutional change—the abolition of the civil service examinations—that occurred during the same time. For centuries, written examinations had been the primary method of selection and appointment for thousands of officials, ranging from county magistrates to bureaucrats serving in the central government's Six Boards. These were not the only positions in government (much local governance was conducted by yamen runners and other members of a semi-formal state apparatus who did not sit for examinations), but they were the ones who conferred formal power and social prestige. The sudden abolition of the examination system in 1905 left a void that needed to be filled by something new. The use of the same character compound for both examinations and elections created the opportunity for mental slippage between the systems. It helped create a space in which elections would implicitly be compared with examinations as a method for selecting political leaders.

Late imperial China's complex civil service examination system had one primary goal that remained constant despite substantial administrative and curricular changes during the Ming and Qing dynasties. That goal, in the words of an authoritative mid-Qing compendium of laws and precedents, was to "obtain true talents for the use of the state [*de zhen cai yi wei guojia zhi yong*]."[16] Written examinations, based on the explication of canonical Confucian texts, were seen as tools for talent selection. This belief coexisted with a long tradition of criticism that mocked the shortcomings of the examinations and those who took them, but association between the examinations and the Confucian injunction to "select the worthy and the able [xuan xian yu neng]" remained fundamental until 1905.

The examinations fulfilled other roles, too, although these were less obvious to contemporary observers. The centralized system that administered them brought a level of unity to China's diverse local cultures during late imperial times. Through a study of common texts and participation in a common act of exam-taking, examinations helped "harmonize" the culture of elites across the vast territories controlled by various dynasties and impose on those elites an ideology that emphasized loyalty to the state.[17] This gentry class—dedicated to the study of the Confucian classics, trained to view themselves as leaders of local society, and possessed of a certain amount of wealth—totaled somewhere between 1 million and 1.5 million men by the nineteenth century.[18] A substantially larger number of people lived at the margins of this class as unsuccessful examination candidates. As the focus of political ambition and the ultimate guarantor of social status, participation in the examination system inculcated the values and norms of the state-determined classical curriculum into generation after generation of local gentry. The examination system acted as an "educational gyroscope" that tied "imperial state, gentry society, and neo-Confucian culture" together by allowing elites to exchange loyalty for access to political power, thus providing an avenue for dynastic legitimacy.[19]

Examinations retained a high degree of popular legitimacy as the path of "selection and appointment" for positions in the central government even as late as the 1890s.[20] Criticism of the system, though always present, grew dramatically in the wake of Japan's military victory over China in 1895. The curriculum and highly stylized form of writing required for the examinations came under increasing attack as the bureaucracy produced by the examinations appeared to be unable to govern effectively.[21] Reformers first aimed to revise the contents of the exam to emphasize historical and political knowledge rather than classical erudition. These proposals received imperial approval in mid-1898 as part of the Guangxu emperor's Hundred Days of Reform.[22] Although they were reversed after Cixi's late summer coup that ended the reform era, these changes would have altered the incentives to study particular texts and types of knowledge, without disrupting the examination system's role as a linchpin connecting the gentry class to the central government.

Weakened and chastised in the aftermath of the Boxer Rebellion, Cixi publicly committed her dynasty to a fundamental reorganization. She exhorted the people in early 1901 to "seek out how to renew our national strength" through, among other reforms, a reconsideration of "how to produce men of real talent."[23] Initially, this seemed not to threaten the examination system's role as a tool for talent identification. The empress dowager authorized another round of examinations at the local, provincial, and national levels in 1901, although most provinces deferred them to the following year. Yet at the same time, the throne ordered substantial revisions to the examinations, similar to those Cixi had voided in 1898: the long-mandated formalistic style of writing was abandoned and the questions were reorganized to focus on history, governance, and policies (both Chinese and foreign), as well as a selection of the Confucian classics.[24]

The examination system never regained its equilibrium. Consensus over the its continued relevance had already started to break down, led by the some of the high officials who had embraced Cixi's 1901 call for reform. These officials and their supporters began promoting a Western-style school system as an alternative. Although some rhetorical effort was made to construct a school system compatible with the preexisting examination system, most recognized this new infrastructure as a competitor to the examination system. On March 12, 1903, two of the most powerful officials in the empire, Yuan Shikai, then less than eighteen months into his tenure as Zhili governor-general, and Liangjiang governor-general Zhang Zhidong floated a proposal to reduce the number of exams offered each year based on the idea that "the examinations are an obstacle to [the development of] schools."[25]

Official opinion had begun to turn, but for the gentry elite as a whole, examination success still seemed to be a reliable indicator of talent and a path to social status and official appointment, while the value of an education at a new school was less clear.[26] Faced with a widespread unwillingness among the gentry to abandon the system that had defined their class for centuries, on September 2, 1905, the empress dowager and the emperor abruptly approved a proposal from Yuan Shikai and other leading officials to immediately discontinue the examinations and create a national school system based on foreign models. National survival was at stake, the throne claimed: "the present situation is dire, thus gathering talented people is an urgent need." The examination system, rather than training this talent, was merely producing "empty words." The emperor and his aunt assured the populace that the new system would be "essentially [the same as] the ancient schools [of the legendary period of sage kings]" and, more important, in their "awarding of degrees" would "be no different than the examination system."[27]

This earthshaking order immediately attracted considerable public attention, and major newspapers reprinted the edict in full.[28] Through this and other means, news of the cancellation and the transition toward a school system spread throughout the country during the final months of 1905. The newly invigorated urban periodical press, already beginning to exert a role in shaping an emergent public opinion, greeted the decision with applause.[29] Soon at least one *Shenbao* editorial developed this into a call for "general education" made available to the populace at large through the new school system. The goal of this education would be to "manufacture citizens [*zhizao guomin*]" and to "cause everyone to know that they have the responsibilities of a citizen."[30]

In addition to unsettling existing educational practices, the abolition of the exam system created profound and sudden ruptures in the social and political fabric of elite life.[31] The hundreds of thousands (if not millions) of men who had continued to sit for examinations until the very end—and who derived meaning and status from doing so—were cast adrift. The throne was aware of this, even if it had few answers. Soon after abolishing the system, the empress dowager and the emperor spoke to these former exam candidates directly, explaining the choices now available to them. However, these were limited to participation in the new school system or in a new, yet-to-be-designed, government examination system.[32] This was a manifestly insufficient response. The new school system was geographically fragmentary and incomplete and remained so for decades. Such efforts could only absorb a tiny fraction of the population of displaced examination takers. The new civil service testing regime proved to be even more piecemeal and limited. The throne did ultimately design and hold a variety of new examinations for specific groups, such as students returned from abroad, but these examinations never replicated the size and scope of the pre-1905 system, nor did success necessarily result in appointment to office.[33] Together, these institutional "paths out"—regardless of any ideological factors that may have made them less attractive to some—were too small, too disorganized, and too ill-funded to absorb the bulk of the examination candidates.

This was the true crisis created by the examination system's abolition. Two and a half decades later, the editors of the Suzhou, Jiangsu, local gazetteer recalled the void that opened in the wake of the 1905 edict: "The literati had nothing to orient themselves toward and the country was thereupon thrown into clamor and was disturbed."[34] The old system allowed local elites to exchange loyalty to the dynasty for social prestige and political influence in their home areas—even if most never advanced very far. The system had ordered and disciplined their lives; without it, many were disoriented. Given the limitations of the fledgling school system and new testing regime, Yuan Shikai, Zhang Jian, and other reformers sought a replacement for the sociological function of the exam system in Japanese and Western forms of "selection and appointment" via voting and elections. These elections, rather than the new school system or a modernized examination system, would inherit the now-vacant title of "selection and appointment." Certain expectations would come with this, including an often repeated claim that, like the old examinations, elections should function as mechanisms for identifying the talented and morally upright. The legacy of the informal system of public appointment, however, never disappeared. Consequently, elections were also expected to be consensual and noncompetitive, all under the watchful eye of appointed state officials. These foundational expectations came to undergird the election laws developed after 1905.

Importing Foreign Methods of Selection and Appointment

Advocates of political change had clamored for the creation of elected deliberative assemblies since the 1890s. Only after the 1905 abolition of the examination system, however, did this idea become a critical part of the national agenda. A small group of high officials in Beijing and the provinces ultimately determined the precise nature of the Qing constitutional arrangement and the place of elected assemblies within it. This group included Manchus such as Duan-fang (1861–1911), a high-ranking civil official who had briefly taken part in the Hundred Days of Reform (and who, as governor of Jiangsu in 1904, developed a close relationship with Zhang Jian), and Zai-ze (1876–1929), an imperial kinsman with ties to the ruling empress dowager; Han Chinese holders of the highest civil service examination degree, such as governor-general Zhang Zhidong and Dai Hongci (1853–1910), a bureaucrat in the central government; and the unclassifiable Yuan Shikai, still governor-general of Zhili. Working alongside other interested constituencies—local elites, newspaper editorialists, students returned from abroad, and exiled participants in the 1898 reform movement, among others—these officials labored to build the foundations for an eventual Qing constitution.

The process began with a series of overseas investigatory trips for high officials. Two initial groups were organized in July 1905 but were delayed by an assassination attempt and ultimately departed in December. Both teams circumnavigated the globe. One visited Japan, Great Britain, France, and Belgium, while the other traveled to the United States, Germany, Russia, and a number of smaller European countries. The travelers watched the proceedings of legislatures, talked political theory with monarchs and presidents, and listened to lectures on constitutional principles from foreign scholars. In these places, the visiting group analyzed the national legislative body and reported on its functions and structure. The commissioners noted the legislative body's method of election—which was nearly uniformly rendered as "selection and appointment [*xuanju*]" in their records, in a further indication of the ongoing vocabulary shift. The missions returned bearing official diaries covering the journeys in the summer of 1906.[35]

These reports, portions of which were later published for public consumption, did not decisively break from earlier literati or diplomatic depictions of election systems in the West or Japan. Organized chronologically rather than thematically, the diaries provided a welter of information on the structure, power, and composition of the various legislative bodies surveyed. Commissioners focused on the legal infrastructure of election systems without analyzing how those systems functioned in practice. Indeed, they could have hardly done otherwise—none of them witnessed an election in progress. Permeating these descriptions was the assumption that elected deliberative assemblies strengthened central governments, reinforced the power of monarchs, and bound the affections of the people to the state. Thus the work of the overseas investigatory missions reconfirmed the already well-established foundational expectations for elections in China.

Soon after the missions returned, Cixi announced imperial support for a constitution. Her September 1, 1906, declaration intensified, rather than resolved, debates over the future of the Qing state. The nature of the constitution had yet to be determined and the words "election" and "parliament" were conspicuously absent from her proclamation.[36] The notion of constitutional government may have been embraced, but the struggle over what it meant had only just begun. The next day, the throne appointed fourteen officials, Yuan Shikai among them, to begin preliminary work on a detailed plan. Meanwhile, Dai Hongci, Zai-ze, Duanfang, and the other members of the recently returned missions worked to organize their observations and the substantial amount of printed materials they acquired into lengthy reports organized by theme. These formed a framework for the discussions that followed.

The commissioners' efforts produced a hefty tome titled *Oumei zhengzhi yaoyi* [Essentials of European and American Politics]. Presented to the throne on October 23, 1906, and published for the public soon after, Dai and Duan-fang's report reinforced the reformers' conventional wisdom: a written constitution could strengthen monarchical rule. Their priorities can be crudely but accurately measured by the organization of the report's eighteen chapters: the first chapter focused on the ruling house, the second on the constitution, and the discussion of the "rights of the people" was relegated to the seventeenth. Establishing elected bodies that would consult with the government on issues of state should be a priority inasmuch as they would advance the agenda of dynastic renewal through the strengthening of the state. Such institutions would "link the sentiments of the rulers and the ruled [*tong shang xia zhi qing*]," thus creating the conditions under which the state would invest itself in improving the lot of the people, while the people would devote themselves to strengthening the country.[37] This notion would have been immediately recognizable to readers of Feng Guifen, Zheng Guanying, and Zhang Jian, who saw elections as a tool for strengthening the state.

Despite this endorsement of constitutionalism in general, *Essentials of European and American Politics* did not advocate the specifics of a constitutional system. Instead, it shaped the debate over those particulars by putting foreign practices in a comparative context. This strategy was evident in the commissioners' taxonomy of election systems. They classified voting laws according to two pairs of opposites: universal or restricted suffrage, and direct or indirect methods of voting. Though they claimed that the "trend of the world" was moving toward universal adult suffrage and direct elections, they suggested this might not be a model for China to follow:

> China's circumstances are very different from those of Western nations. Thus, when establishing a parliament, its election law should not rigidly adhere to the old practices of foreign countries, and indeed it is possible [for China] to devise methods of election for its own institutions.[38]

The authors did not detail what elections with Qing characteristics might look like.

Their sentiment highlighted a central conundrum of many Chinese reform efforts: the desire to follow "global" trends while also devising a system that was still fundamentally "Chinese." Left unaddressed in the report, however, was any indication of which foreign practices would provide the best model for Qing election law. Further public disclosures from the commissioners provided little additional direction; in 1907, they submitted a massive encyclopedia of translated political documents to the throne that included elections laws from the United States, Prussia, the German Empire, Italy, Austria, and Russia—without recommending any one in particular.[39] Despite the time commissioners had spent in Japan, Japanese laws were not included in this compendium.

In a pair of mid- and late 1906 memorials to the throne, former commissioner Duan-fang advanced a series of detailed proposals that took Japan as the model for Qing constitutionalism. The suggestion that Meiji Japan should serve as an inspiration for the Qing state was not new in 1906 (Zhang Jian had raised it five years earlier), but Duan-fang's insistence that "China's situation today is no different from Japan's [at the beginning of the Meiji era]" held particular ramifications for elected assemblies.[40] In the 1868 Charter Oath that outlined his government's aspirations for political reform, the Meiji emperor had promised the establishment of deliberative institutions and the expansion of the right to political participation. These promises were gradually implemented, culminating in the first national parliamentary elections in 1890. The Qing throne had yet to make a similar pledge.

Duan-fang proposed that Qing deliberative institutions follow this Meiji roadmap. In the early years of the transitional period, public discussion offices would be set up at the local and ultimately provincial levels; these institutions would provide the people with a forum for practicing the skills needed for the parliamentary system established at the end of the constitutional preparation period.[41] Duan-fang outlined several aspects of these transitional institutions, including an embryonic national institution composed of eight members from each province "elected provisionally by public appointment through the casting of ballots [*xuanju shi zanxing toupiao gongju*]," along with an unspecified number appointed by the court.[42] He further proposed that provincial assemblies with real (rather than just advisory) powers be opened in advance of a national parliament as an additional training ground for future legislators; members of these institutions would be representatives selected by county-level legislative bodies.[43]

Duan-fang and the other commissioners succeeded in shaping the debates about Qing election laws. Most significantly, by deriving inspiration from a variety of overseas models while simultaneously arguing for the importance of adaptation to Chinese circumstances, they ensured that the resulting election laws would be an amalgamation of several different foreign models, leavened with a measure of Qing innovation. Second and secretly, Duan-fang began the process of reintroducing the ideas of Liang Qichao, the exiled 1898 reformer, into the highest councils of state. Although his name did not appear in the documents Duan-fang submitted, Liang almost certainly had penned the memorials himself and passed them to Duan-fang clandestinely.[44] Perhaps because of their boldness, Duan-fang's plans were not acted on. By late 1906, discussion within the central government seemed to slow, and grand schemes for the wholesale adoption of Meiji institutions appeared to lead nowhere. Over a year of relative inaction in Beijing passed before Cixi and her nephew authorized the creation of national and provincial consultative institutions, and even more time was required before national election laws were issued.

During those months of drift, the locus of constitutional activism shifted outside of the Forbidden City. Much of this action even took place outside of the state per se. As early as the summer of 1906, the returning commissioners had used their informal networks of connections among the gentry elite to sow the seeds of constitutional thought widely. Both overseas investigative groups—Zai-ze's in early July and Dai Hongci's at the end of the month—stopped in Shanghai before continuing to Beijing. While there, they took part in a series of public meetings with local notables, including Zhang Jian.[45] One such meeting, held in Shanghai's Foreign Affairs Office, drew members of the merchant and student communities. Zhang commented in his diary that the audience favored a constitution. Yet he tempered his observation with the cryptic warning that "truly, few among them understood the benefits of constitutionalism."[46] He remained silent about the exact origin of his unease in his diary but soon began searching for a way to ameliorate it.

Zhang Jian found his answer in a new type of civic organization: the Shanghai-based Yubei lixian gonghui [Public Association for Constitutional Preparation]. This activist group, comprising elites with one foot in officialdom, had been conceptualized by Zheng Xiaoxu (1860–1938), a socially well-connected calligrapher living in Shanghai who had once served as a Qing diplomat in Japan. Zheng began the basic organizational work just days after the throne issued its edict in support of constitutionalism on September 1, and Zhang Jian joined his efforts before the end of the month.[47] Zheng's diary reveals months of work behind the scenes, including several meetings with Di Baoxian (1873–1941) editor of the newly founded reformist newspaper *Shibao*, before the association was announced to the public.[48] Nearly 300 people attended the Public Association's inaugural public meeting at Shanghai's Yuyuan garden on December 16, 1906, where Zheng Xiaoxu was elected the association's first leader and Zhang Jian an associate leader.[49] Most of the group's early members were similar to Zheng and Zhang; all had extensive contacts in government and most had had official careers. They included Tang Shouqian, the early proponent of deliberative assemblies who inspired Zheng Guanying's *Words of Warning* in the 1890s, and Wu Guangjian (1867–1943), a member of Zai-ze's constitutional study mission.[50]

For the following eighteen months, the Public Association dedicated itself to organizational and educational work, engaging in politics only to petition the government for the early opening of a national parliament. Zheng himself seemed despondent at times over the slow pace of the group's efforts, complaining in March 1907 that the "flame of constitutionalism is extinguished!"[51] His concerns proved unwarranted in the long run. Despite its benign name and seemingly apolitical activities, the Public Association became the embryonic form of China's first real political party.[52] It soon had elections to participate in, too. Even as the move toward elections seemed to stall at the central level, tentative experimentation with local voting began under Yuan Shikai's auspices.

Creating the Late Qing/Early Republican Election System

As the central government debated constitutionalism, some officials serving in the provinces were authorized to experiment with different kinds of local elections. These trials, though linked to the overall Qing constitutional project, were independently designed and implemented. The first attempts at creating popularly selected subcounty governing bodies began as early as 1902 in northwest China's Shanxi Province. Comprehensive and organized experimentation, however, began in August 1906 with the throne's authorization of similar experiments in Zhili, the province that surrounded the capital at Beijing and encompassed the major port city of Tianjin. Yuan Shikai, the governor-general entrusted with this critical territory, interpreted this mandate broadly and proposed an entirely new system of local government that included several elected institutions. This reinterpretation fit with Yuan's broader enthusiasm for institutional reform.

Reformist officials and representatives of different groups of local elites, working under Yuan's general supervision, devised election laws for Tianjin county over the course of nineteen meetings during the first months of 1907. Although inspired, in part, by Japanese election law, Yuan's subordinates—some of whom had been students in Japan—took particular pains to adapt these laws to Qing realities.[53] The resulting system was not a hybrid but a unique attempt to reconcile Qing political values and social structures with the global norms of elections. In spirit, this resembled Duan-fang and Dai Hongci's exhortations from the previous year.

Yuan's law restricted the franchise to a small portion of the population—but even this represented an expansion of the number of people allowed to legitimately participate in politics. Men over twenty-five years of age and native to Tianjin county could vote if they "had an occupation," were "not reliant on local public relief funds," and able to write their "name, age, occupation, and address." Nonnatives who had lived in the county for more than five years could vote if, in addition to meeting the above requirements, they owned more than 2,000 *yuan* of "commercial capital or real estate" in Tianjin. Convicted criminals, debtors, the mentally unsound, opium users, and those with "an illegitimate occupation" were disenfranchised. Noticeably lacking were any educational restrictions (beyond literacy) or financial limitations (other than solvency) on the right to vote for locals. Being elected to office required, in addition to the requirements for the franchise, either an educational credential (a primary school diploma or an examination degree), ownership of more than 2,000 *yuan* of commercial capital or real estate (or management of someone else's real estate or commercial capital in excess of 5,000 *yuan*), experience managing a school or other local public service, or having held official appointment in the bureaucracy.

The Tianjin system embraced a complicated mechanism for determining winners. Voters cast ballots for a smaller group of electors, who gathered to elect the membership of the deliberative body. Tianjin county was divided into eight electoral districts for the primary-stage election. In each district, the four highest vote getters, regardless of the actual number of votes received, automatically became primary-stage winners. The remaining ballots from all eight districts would then be combined and the top 103 vote getters, regardless of district, would also be named primary-stage winners. This yielded a total of 135 people empowered to cast votes in a secondary-stage election that would elect the 30 members of the county deliberative assembly, without reference to the original eight elections in the districts.[54]

Three aspects of this law proved to be influential for subsequent election laws. First, Yuan's subordinates strictly limited the size of the electorate by implementing significant restrictions on the right to vote. These educational, property, and status limitations had never previously been encoded in such detail, but they had been discussed in the abstract by many early promoters of Chinese elections, including Feng Guifen and Zheng Guanying. Second, they acted in concert with the spirit of the overseas commissioners' reports by implementing indirect elections. The particularly complicated form of indirect voting they settled on does not appear to have a foreign precedent, leaving it something of a mystery. Finally, despite the detailed nature of the law, little was said about the candidates for office themselves, or what types of campaigning they could legitimately engage in.

After Yuan signaled his approval for these election laws, Tianjin became the first Chinese county to hold central government–sanctioned local elections in July 1907. Yuan offered a somewhat terse report on the results to his superiors in Beijing that described the process of drafting and implementing this system. The report claimed that 12,461 eligible voters had been identified and registered (slightly less than 3 percent of the local population), of whom 2,572 possessed the necessary qualifications for election to office. Both stages of voting were completed successfully and a thirty-member county assembly [*xian yisihui*] was seated on August 18.[55]

News about the Tianjin election spread throughout the country quickly. One of Yuan's subordinates mailed an early form of the county assembly's organic law to Zheng Xiaoxu at the Public Association in Shanghai in December 1906.[56] A major Shanghai journal had published a more complete draft of its election law in July 1907, giving the text of this law national circulation.[57] Months after elections were held, an official from distant Guangxi Province cited them approvingly as a model for national institutions.[58] Some localities proactively adopted this system. The Chinese-controlled portions of Shanghai, which as early as 1905 had created its own deliberative council [*zonggongchengju*, lit. "Office of General Works"], transitioned to an indirect voting system similar to Tianjin's in 1907. Unlike Tianjin, franchise in Shanghai was restricted to taxpayers.[59] Although no other locality adopted the Tianjin system in its entirety, it had caught the attention of many across the empire. Despite the excitement generated by the law, few evinced much interest in the actual election itself, which was not reported on in any detail in the major Shanghai newspapers.

The real influence of Yuan's Tianjin system would be on provincial— and ultimately national—election law. In the wake of Tianjin's election,

Yuan Shikai proposed on July 28, 1907, that the central government "guide the situation by successively establishing county level deliberative councils, provincial assemblies [*ziyiju*], and a national deliberative council."[60] Yuan's timing and his choice of terms were notable. Other than approving the experiment in Tianjin, Cixi and the Guangxu emperor had done little to satisfy elite demand for political participation since its embrace of constitutionalism the previous September. Yuan now pushed for national policies to do this. His language aligned him with another powerful official (and bitter political rival), Liangguang governor-general Cen Chunxuan (1861–1933), who also advocated creation of a provincial-level deliberative institution a month earlier.

Cen, who gained influence with the throne by providing a military escort for Cixi during the chaotic final stages of the Boxer Rebellion, had been an early advocate of constitutionalism. In 1903, he had dispatched his associate Zheng Xiaoxu to Shanghai to make connections with like-minded elites; this bore fruit years later, with the founding of the Public Association. In June 1907, Cen called for the establishment of a new organ he called "offices of inquiry and deliberation [a literal translation of his phrase *ziyiju*, which is more commonly translated as 'provincial assemblies']" in each provincial capital. Unlike most other self-government institutions of the New Policies period, such as the one Yuan had built in Tianjin, this office's name did not include any indication of its geographical scope or its precise function. Rather than being labeled an "assembly [*hui*]," as Yuan had done in Tianjin, Cen designated it as an "office [*ju*]," a term that typically referred to locally organized gentry initiatives. The name seemed to indicate a limited role for this institution. In its original concept, this institution had nothing to do with elections—instead, it would be a formalization of the advisory role of the gentry class that had so excited a certain strain of reformist officials from Lin Zexu down to the end of the Qing. To this end, Cen suggested that the office be staffed by "gentry and merchants who understand governance" and "expectant officials who are not gentry of that province but understand its affairs." Members would be selected by the governor, not elected.[61]

Cen's institution retained its curious name but evolved over the course of the following fourteen months into something quite different from his original proposal: the first popularly elected institution to be implemented nationwide. Yuan's appropriation of Cen's term in his July 1907 proposal marked the first step in this process. On October 19, 1907, the throne authorized the establishment of these institutions. Governors were directed to "speedily set up a provincial assembly" through the "public appointment [*gongju*] of the worthy and the able [*xianneng*]," thus combining in one phrase constitutional reform, the talent selection purpose of the examination system, and the long-established semi-formal "public appointment" method for choosing local leaders.[62] The terse edict provided no further guidance, nor did it set any deadlines. It lacked an election law; thus the critical terms "public appointment" and "the worthy and the able" remained undefined.

Surprisingly, this vague order for the creation of a strangely named body with unspecified powers through a method yet to be determined immediately attracted enormous public interest. Some decided to construct this institution on their own authority. The elected council of the Chinese-governed portion of Shanghai held a meeting for this purpose on October 20, 1907, the day after the throne issued its authorization. Between forty and fifty delegates discussed a fifty-eight-article locally produced draft election law.[63] This Shanghai proposal envisioned an institution comprised of members elected by the various county assemblies, with each county being allowed three representatives.[64] At least one other local proposal circulated in Jiangsu at the time, too.[65] Behind the scenes, Zheng and Zhang's Public Association was involved with these efforts, but precise details are vague.[66] None of this activity had any apparent impact on the law that was ultimately adopted, but its existence attested to the excitement generated by the October 1907 edict. At the provincial level, scattered preparation work began, and by May 1908, at least seven provinces had begun designing their own provincial assemblies.[67]

For nine months, this public interest was not matched by any visible official action at the central level. The Constitutional Reform Office remained mostly silent, perhaps wracked by internal debate over what precisely the throne had just authorized.[68] The long pause broke briefly in late March 1908, when the office issued "provisional" election guidelines. No guidance was given on implementation, however, and these guidelines generated little public reaction.[69] As late as June 1908, almost eight months after provincial assemblies had received imperial approval, one frustrated memorialist complained directly to the throne about the lack of specific regulations for these bodies.[70] More worrisome, from the government's perspective, organized groups—including the Public Association—filed repeated petitions beginning in March 1908 demanding the opening of an elected national parliament, something the government had no immediate plans to do.[71]

Presumably prodded by these stimuli, the throne suddenly promulgated the first national election laws in Chinese history on July 22, 1908. These laws, the Provincial Assembly Regulations and the Provincial Assembly Election Regulations (hereafter referred to collectively as the 1908 Regulations), were historically unprecedented in scope.[72] They mandated the creation of elected provincial assemblies in all Qing provinces—this included not only the Han Chinese heartland south of the Great Wall but also the majority Muslim western territory of Xinjiang (made a province in 1884) and the Manchu homeland in the northeast (organized into three provinces in 1907). Tibet and the Mongol regions, dependencies that had yet to be organized as provinces, were excluded from the order.

The 1908 Regulations marked the throne's first attempt after the end of the examination system in 1905 to implement an empire-wide system for selecting political leaders of any sort. Similar to the examination system, elections for the provincial assemblies were governed by a code of rules established in Beijing and overseen by an office in the central bureaucracy. The system of elections was organized hierarchically; those who reached the highest deliberative body, the yet-to-be established National Assembly [*zizhengyuan*], passed through elections at the county, prefectural, and provincial levels. Each level had fewer elected seats than the one beneath it, and the lower ones functioned as repositories of talent for ones above them, mirroring the examination system. Unlike tests, which rested on a supposedly objective assessment of literary talent conducted by outside examiners, elections would be based on the opinion of one's peers—an idea that had been idealized in the writings of Zheng Guanying, Feng Guifen, and other originators of the foundational concept of elections.

By setting a relatively broad definition for who could participate, the system provided an opportunity to expand membership in the gentry class and transform that class into a proto-citizenry. The 1908 Regulations defined the parameters of this proto-citizenry in detail. It limited the right to vote to men over the age of twenty-five who were living in their province of ancestral residence and met at least one of the following five qualifications:

> 1. had "managed a school or other public service institution located within the voter's area of residence, for three years or more, with demonstrable success,"
> 2. had earned a diploma from either a Chinese or a foreign middle school (or equivalent institution),
> 3. had earned a county-level *shengyuan* degree or higher from the defunct civil service examination system,
> 4. had once held a civil office of grade seven or higher, or a military office of grade five or higher, without having been dismissed from office,
> 5. currently owned 5,000 *yuan* or more of real estate or "commercial capital [*yingye ziben*]," located within the province of residence.

The court also granted suffrage rights to men over twenty-five living outside of their province of ancestral residence who met the additional criteria of having lived in the location for ten or more years and possessing more than 10,000 *yuan* of real estate or commercial capital.

In addition, the law stipulated several disqualifications that led to automatic disenfranchisement. These were grouped into two categories. The first focused on behaviors and disenfranchised those who demonstrated "absurd moral conduct or who selfishly seek to make judgments about right and wrong," had been sentenced to imprisonment, held an "improper occupation," had gone bankrupt and not yet paid restitution, had used opium, had a mental illness, came from an "impure background," or were illiterate. The second focused on occupations and prohibited currently serving government officials, police, active-duty soldiers, monks or other clergy, and enrolled students from participation. Primary school teachers, though granted the right to vote, were prohibited from being elected to the assembly.

The size of each province's assembly was set in proportion to its old quota for successful examination candidates, with modifications for provinces that had unusually strict quotas. In total, the law authorized the creation of twenty-three provincial assemblies, comprising 1,679 representatives (not counting several dozen additional positions created specifically to represent Manchu garrison communities) elected for three-year terms. Elections would be indirect, as had been in the case in Tianjin, although the system was structured differently. During the preelection voter census, each county was assigned a quota of primary-stage election winners and each prefecture a quota of secondary-stage winners; these quotas were established on the basis of the total proportion of a province's voters in each county or prefecture. The law stipulated ten secondary-stage electors for each assembly seat, creating some 16,790 primary-stage winners across the empire (this number rises by several hundred when Manchu quota spots are included).

The complex vision outlined in the 1908 Regulations amalgamated foreign ideas and domestic concerns, indicating—as Duan-fang and the other commissioners suggested in their 1906 report—that the throne intended to adapt foreign voting practices to meet the political and social conditions of the late Qing. The resulting system bore surface similarity to a number of the foreign legal codes that inspired it, including Japanese and Prussian election laws. However, it resembled more closely its domestic predecessor, Yuan Shikai's 1907 Tianjin election law, but differed even from that in substantial ways. Although it is not possible to reconstruct the logic that undergirded every aspect of the law, clearly many contemporaries believed that the 1908 Regulations spoke to the needs of the times. Every election law adopted in China between 1908 and 1920 began with the 1908 Regulations as its basis. The fundamental legitimacy of this unique product of Qing lawmaking was not challenged for almost a decade after the 1911 Revolution.

The law's treatment of suffrage revealed the complex interplay of foreign and domestic ideas. The Qing deliberately imitated the contemporary practice in Europe, North America, and Japan of limiting suffrage to adult men. Imposing more requirements beyond age and gender also drew on foreign precedents. Many early twentieth-century states—Japan and Prussia being the most influential of these for Qing lawmakers—mandated that voters meet a wealth requirement. The Qing standard (itself only one of five separate paths to qualifying for the vote) differed from those models; instead of requiring payment of a minimum amount in annual taxes, as in Japan and Prussia, the law mandated a minimum cash value for owned real estate or commercial property. Although this proved excruciatingly difficult to implement in practice, the particular phrasing of this requirement suggested not only a recognition that the Qing taxation system was broken (making it an impossible standard to use for suffrage) but also the deliberate desire to enfranchise merchants. Though never cited, perhaps this was an instance in which Zheng Guanying's influence was felt.

The decision to allow four additional, nonfinancial paths to the franchise had no equivalent in Japan or Prussia; the only possible precedent was the 1907 Tianjin system's list of qualifications for being elected to office. These qualifications were clearly linked to the history and traditions of the Qing state. Automatic enfranchisement for holders of pre-1905 examination degrees and for civil or military officials of a certain rank provided continuity with the traditional ruling stratum and the examination system. There was no overseas precedent for this idea—the early Meiji Japanese government had not made a similarly explicit commitment to enfranchise the samurai, who made up the ruling class during the Tokugawa era. The Qing decision to extend the franchise to the holders of the county-level *shengyuan* degree represented an incorporation of all gentry into what was previously a narrower political class. Under the old examination system, holders of this degree (by far the most numerous of all degree holders) were ineligible for appointment to office and had been a source of anxiety for centuries.[73] Enfranchisement of this stratum reflected the long-standing interest of reformers, dating back to Lin Zexu and Wei Yuan, in integrating this class into active political life. Zhang Jian's 1901 musings on local elections had stated this premise bluntly—"Voters and those elected to office must all be gentry"—and it remained relevant seven years later.[74]

Likewise, the stipulation that enfranchised graduates of modern schools grew from the throne's hope that a modern school system could function as a successor to the exam system. The clause that allowed managers of "schools and other public service institutions" to participate in elections can be understood as a way of enfranchising members of the gentry who lacked degrees but still had engaged in the traditional tasks of managing local society or had helped create local institutions associated with the New Policies reforms. The various behavioral disqualifications excluded many who had been barred from participation in the examination system (such as Buddhist and Daoist clergy, as well as those with "improper occupations"). Following the precedent set in the Tianjin election law, the 1908 Regulations specifically banned opium users from participating in elections. As a practical issue, "opium user [*xi shi yapian zhe*]" was an exceptionally vague and difficult category to define, given the prevalence of occasional opium use among large segments of the population.[75] This denial of suffrage indicated both the symbolic power of opium, which was identified with Qing military weakness and social ills, as well as the reach of the late Qing's anti-opium campaign.[76]

In addition to defining a proto-citizenry, the 1908 Regulations demarcated the boundaries of a complex two-stage, indirect voting system. During the primary-stage election [*chuxuan*], all registered voters cast paper ballots at designated polling locations in their county of origin. Each county functioned as a single electoral district in the primary-stage election and was assigned a quota of multiple primary-stage election winners, ranging from several to two dozen or more. From a purely structural perspective, the decision to design primary-stage election districts in which multiple winners were chosen by voters who could cast only a single vote (referred to by political scientists as "single nontransferable voting in a multimember districts") necessarily meant that winning a seat might require only a tiny percentage of the vote cast. To make sure this percentage did not sink too low, the law established a formula for determining the minimum number of votes needed to win a primary-stage election:[77]

$$\text{Minimum number of votes to win} = \frac{\text{Number of valid ballots cast}}{2 \times \text{county quota of primary-stage winners}}$$

The winners of this election gathered together with winners from other counties in the same prefecture, which formed the secondary-stage election district, and held a secondary-stage election [*fuxuan*]. The winners of this secondary-stage election then became the new provincial assemblymen.

This mechanism bore only limited similarity to the 1907 Tianjin system and even less to foreign models. Although other nations used similar forms of indirect, two-stage elections, none combined this system with multimember electoral districts. The 1908 Regulations did not resemble Japanese election laws, which Duan-fang had proposed as an inspiration in his 1906 memorials. Japanese elections at all levels, beginning with the first prefectural elections in 1879, were direct elections in which the winner was the candidate (or, in the case of multiseat districts, the candidates) who received the highest number of votes, regardless of whether a majority was reached. Lawmakers revised election laws several times, most notably in 1900 when the format for lower house elections was changed from single-member to multiple-member districts to ensure greater representation for cities and to stall the development of a two-party system. This was reversed in 1919, and debates over the best way to structure Japanese elections continued throughout the early decades of the twentieth century.[78] Adherence to the principle of direct elections even amid these changes was a hallmark of the Meiji political system.

The Prussian system, another frequently cited model for the Qing, likewise contained only a few points of similarity. The 1850 Prussian constitution established a system of indirect elections for the House of Deputies and assigned voting rights on the basis of the amount that voters paid in taxes. The electorate was divided into three classes, with the highest taxpayers receiving proportionally greater voting rights. Each class elected one third of the electors in the primary stage; the electors then held a secondary-stage election to select representatives to the House of Deputies. The crucial difference from the Qing system, however, was that in Prussia each class of voters in the primary election functioned as an independent constituency that was required to choose one elector (or in some instances, two electors) by plurality voting.[79] This system remained intact in Prussia until the end of World War I, but it was not copied by any other German state. Nor was it necessarily popular in Prussia itself: even Otto von Bismarck (1815–1898), chancellor of Prussia (and later the German Empire) and a foe of parliamentary politics, believed that "a crazier, more contemptible electoral law had never been thought of in any country."[80] The Constitution of the German Empire, adopted in 1871 under Bismarck's direction, opted for a system of direct elections for the newly established Reichstag.

Qing officials in 1908 had access to detailed knowledge of the Prussian system. Dai Hongci and his commissioners had reported these election laws in 1906, and a Shanghai journal published a translation of the Prussian constitution that same year.[81] Qing regulations for county and municipal elections, issued over the course of the following eighteen months, derived from this Prussian system, although they divided taxpayers into two, rather than three, classes.[82] Circumstantially, this indicates that the Prussian system was rejected for provincial-level elections in 1908, but does not shed light on the reasons for this. Although it is safe to assume that the system of multimember districts coupled with indirect elections mandated by the 1908 Regulations was selected for specific reasons, those reasons are not directly spoken to in surviving documentation.

The apparent consistency of the philosophy undergirding the system devised in 1908 and the foundational expectations for elections embedded in the thought of Wei Yuan, Feng Guifen, and Zheng Guanying helps these unusual election laws begin to make more sense. Elections were to be a tool for unity and state-building; they were not meant to resolve conflicts within the elite or apportion power between different interest groups. The designers of the 1908 Regulations, much like those who influenced them, did not accept factional competition as natural, legitimate, or unavoidable. Elections were meant to be a tool of unity; voting was not supposed to be a means of contestation. Whether intentional or not, the complex system of voting could not work effectively without elite consensus, which became apparent once these election laws were put to use.

The hope of early twentieth-century Qing policy makers that elections could be a spark for the spontaneous generation of consensus was encoded in the design of the ballots themselves. When casting their ballots, voters did not choose from a preprinted list of names; instead, confronted with a blank space, they were invited to write the name of any eligible person in a rectangle on the back of the ballot. The structure and form of the ballot, which transformed every registered voter over thirty years of age into a write-in candidate for office, reveals a worldview that did not envision elections as an either/or choice between a limited number of preselected candidates but as an opportunity for men of good moral character to anonymously nominate their neighbors for public office. For those disgusted with the literary and stylistic emphasis of the examination system, this may have seen like a chance to ensure that men of talent and integrity, measured by the esteem of other gentlemen, would no longer go unnoticed.

It is not surprising that Qing officials understood elections as an opportunity for harmonious conversations, not clashes of competing interests. The goal of Qing constitutionalism—more specifically, the election laws that were one of its distinguishing features—was to strengthen and clarify links of communication between the people and the government. In their preamble to the 1908 Regulations, the drafters reiterated the optimistic assessments of Feng Guifen and Zheng Guanying:

> Despite differences in the nature of their basic political structures and variations in legal systems, all constitutional governments—both Western and Eastern—have established parliamentary bodies and have allowed the people to elect members in order to represent public opinion. By these means, constitutional governments link the sentiments of the rulers and the ruled [*shang xia zhi qing tong*] and reduce the harm caused by alienation.[83]

The identity of the "ruled" and the "rulers" was predetermined; the "ruled" did not have the right to select the "rulers." Instead, elected bodies were intended to harmonize, regularize, and strengthen the communications between rulers and those they ruled. More than anything else, this undergirded the structures of limited franchise and indirect voting that the 1908 Regulations created.

The goals of these drafters mirrored the expectations of the Qing dynasts themselves. Empress Dowager Cixi, acting on behalf of the captive Guangxu emperor, had endorsed the plans of constitutionalists in 1906, although rumors of the tentativeness of her commitment circulated for the remainder of her life.[84] Even as late as August 1908, after the 1908 Regulations had been released, she revealed in a court audience with Cao Rulin (1877–1966) that her support for constitutionalism was predicated on its ability to achieve unity between ruler and the ruled. Cao, a returned student from Japan who served in the still-new Ministry of Foreign Affairs, wrote his account of this audience half a century later; although some aspects of his account are confusing or mistaken, there is no reason to doubt that his memory of his only audience with the imperial pair is correct in substance. As he knelt before the two rulers, Cixi quizzed him about the nature of Japan's constitutional system. What were the origins of Japan's constitution? How were members of the Diet elected? Did conflict erupt between different political parties?

Cao, who had been seconded to the Constitutional Drafting Commission in December 1907, replied by arguing that Japan's constitution, inspired by the constitutional monarchies of Europe, enhanced the power of the throne and created a solid basis for national unity. Midway through his exegesis, the empress dowager slapped her hand on the table that lay before her throne, sighed, and exclaimed: "The weakness of us Chinese is that we are not able to come together in unity!" Cao took this yearning for political harmony as an indication that the empress dowager could be convinced to embrace constitutionalism as a tool for enhancing dynastic power.[85] Perhaps, however, her questions (which were almost certainly designed to prompt Cao to discuss his ideas, rather than as innocent requests for factual information) revealed a more realistic assessment of constitutionalism: the appreciation that elected bodies, rather than acting as a vessels for imperial will, might factionalize or even challenge the throne's prerogatives. A wily survivor of countless intrigues, she may have found the optimistic attitudes embedded in the widely shared foundational expectations for elections difficult to embrace. Her reaction to elections is ultimately unknowable; Cixi died soon before the elections she authorized were held.

Conclusion

Soon after the "selection and appointment" of the "talented and worthy" through civil service examinations ended in 1905, government officials began designing a system of selection and appointments via elections. Writers then and in subsequent decades categorized elections as a successor to the examination system. The *Draft History of the Qing Dynasty*, an early attempt at a comprehensive description of the institutions and personalities of the dynasty a decade after its demise, placed its discussion of elections at the end of the "Treatise on Selections and Appointments." As in the case of similar sections in previous dynastic histories, this was largely devoted to a discussion of the examination system. The compilers of the *Draft History* characterized these elections as "new-style selections and appointments [*xin xuanju*]," thus distinguishing them from, yet linking them to, the previous system.[86] Local gazetteers likewise listed those elected to public office in the final years of the Qing alongside the winners of the highest examination degrees.[87] A variant of "public appointment," recrafted by central government officials inspired by foreign election laws, had become the legitimate form of "selection and appointment."

In theory, elections shared much in common with examinations. Both were held to select the talented, the former through the considered opinion of peers (itself seen as a return to systems of selection believed to be the norm in antiquity) and the latter through the supposed impartiality of the examiner. Through participation and sometimes success in the examination system, local elites across the empire earned credentials from the central government that reinforced the place of these elites within local society; in turn, elites who had their status legitimated by this system offered a measure of loyalty and support to the state. This alliance between local elite families and the central imperial state characterized the political arrangements of late imperial China; the end of the examination system meant that for that alliance to continue, it would need to do so on a very different basis.

Deliberative assemblies were intended to provide that foundation. Elected institutions, unlike the small modern school system or semi-functional new examination system, could be large enough to supply such opportunities to a significant percentage of the gentry. The provincial assembly elections alone would generate over 16,000 election winners every three years; county and city elections, had they been established according to plan, would have produced tens of thousands more. The 1908 Regulations, through a carefully calibrated set of suffrage restrictions and indirect voting procedures, had been designed to ensure that men of intelligence and moral integrity would be elected to these positions. The exchange of prestige for loyalty that had characterized the examination system could be replicated on a larger scale, and the link between an expanded gentry elite and the dynasty maintained. This would fill the vacuum at the heart of the Qing political compact created by the abrupt end of the examinations.

Neither Yuan Shikai, who had been promoted to the Grand Council in September 1907, nor Zhang Jian, who busied himself with his various political, economic, and social ventures, left any indication that they foresaw what would happen after the implementation of the 1908 Regulations. Before balloting for the first election held under the Regulations began in March 1909, Empress Dowager Cixi had passed away (suspiciously preceded a day earlier by her much younger nephew) and the regent of the new child-emperor forced Yuan into retirement. He could only watch from the sidelines as the experiment he had helped set in motion was expanded across the empire. His ally Zhang, however, immersed himself deeply in the election. Zhang and the Public Association, working in an uneasy partnership with the increasingly powerful Shanghai periodical press, had to grapple with the reality that their elections had created opportunities for the competitive, ambitious, and opportunistic to seek office alongside the upright and worthy.

CHAPTER 3

The First Elections and the Last Emperor

Voting and Campaigning, 1909–1911

High officials in Beijing had drafted the 1908 Regulations, but a much broader cross-section of Chinese society assumed responsibility for the law's interpretation, implementation, and evaluation. The new election system attracted immediate attention and generated genuine excitement outside the capital. Within days of their promulgation, the regulations were reprinted in their entirety in major newspapers.[1] The eight months that passed between the regulations' announcement and the casting of the first ballots in March 1909 witnessed an explosion of local activism and media interest. An unprecedented combination of gentry elites, journalists, students returned from abroad, and reformist leaders collaborated to lay the groundwork for China's first nationwide election. Despite their differences in background, all drew on the foundational expectations for elections that had developed over previous decades as motivation for holding an election—and as inspiration for criticizing the election results.

Nowhere did these disparate groups mix more than in Shanghai. The offices of the reformist daily newspaper *Shibao*, founded in 1904, became a particular center for such interactions. The publisher, Liang Qichao's associate and Public Association affiliate Di Baoxian, formed the hub of an extensive social network. A club room above Di's office, dubbed the "Mansion of Repose," was set aside for the express purpose of entertaining reform-minded visitors, who came to gossip and snack on a regular basis. Many who spent time there—including Shen Enfu (1864–1944),

Yuan Xitao (1866–1930), Huang Yanpei (1878–1965), and Shi Liangcai (1880–1934)—became the nucleus of Shanghai's nascent elite.[2] Over the next several decades, they collectively dominated Shanghainese politics (Shen), education (Huang), and publishing (Shi and Yuan). In the first decade of the twentieth century, however, these men paled in influence, authority, and prestige to another visitor to the Mansion of Repose: the venerable Zhang Jian.[3]

Shibao writer Bao Tianxiao (1876–1973) recalled this club room as a place for politics as well as relaxation. Bao had little direct interaction with Zhang Jian—who was two decades older and affected a significantly sterner demeanor than the playful Bao—but had a deeper relationship with one of Zhang's lieutenants, Yang Tingdong, a scholar of law, politics, and philosophy. Both Bao and Yang hailed from the area near Suzhou and had been acquainted before moving to Shanghai. Bao's memoirs, written decades later, conveyed a curiously ambiguous description of his friend:

> Once I began working at the *Shibao*, [Yang] often came to visit me and became a frequent guest at the Mansion of Repose . . . At that time, there was a group of "men of high purpose" in Shanghai who called themselves the reform party. They organized the so-called Public Association with the goal of urging the Manchu Qing government to speedily adopt a constitution. . . . When they came to the Mansion of Repose, the speculative talk, the theorizing, the energy, and the enthusiasm had no equal in the world.[4]

The contrast between the idealistic-sounding Yang and the seemingly jaded Bao neatly encapsulated the divergent reactions that these influential men had to the elections held in 1909. Yang and many like him appeared to have been empowered by the provincial assembly elections; others, Bao included, were disgusted by what they beheld. While the former group included some of late Qing China's most distinguished individuals, the latter category contained many—like Bao—who had the talent, wit, and public platform to shape perceptions of the election. In many ways, these men's reactions reflected the divergent trends evident in the foundational expectations for elections—an idealistic belief in the ability of elections to strengthen the state via talent selection and a disdain at the messy nature of electoral competition.

Surveying an Electorate

Together, Yang, Bao, and other members of the Mansion of Repose group shaped the course of the 1909 election in the thirty-seven county-level political units that made up the southern portion of Jiangsu Province—and by extension the outcome and perception of the election across the empire. Conditions in southern Jiangsu were more favorable for the success of elections than anywhere else in Qing China. This wealthy region on the southern bank of the Yangzi, supervised by a provincial governor in Suzhou, contained not only the heartland of late imperial China's cultural and intellectual elite but also—in Shanghai—the core of China's newly emerging financial and industrial establishment. The political leadership was supportive of elections: from 1906 until 1909, Duan-fang, the former constitutional commissioner and architect of Qing reform, was governor-general in Nanjing, with oversight of northern and southern Jiangsu as well as two neighboring provinces. Semi-official reformist groups, Zhang Jian's Shanghai-based Public Association most prominent among them, flourished and enjoyed tight connections with Duan-fang's administration. The general social environment was conducive as well. Southern Jiangsu had a high concentration of literate, educated people with relatively easy access to information through Shanghai's mass media. Many of those periodicals loudly proclaimed that southern Jiangsu was a model for the rest of the country and devoted significant column space to the propagation of what they considered best practices for elections.

Unusually, the 1908 Regulations had authorized this subprovincial region to establish its own provincial assembly in Suzhou; the remainder of Jiangsu Province, encompassing the larger but poorer region north of the Yangzi, was assigned a separate provincial assembly that would meet in Nanjing. No other province had a similar arrangement, and Jiangsu's two assemblies would be unified into a single, Nanjing-based entity before either opened session. Yet this development occurred only in mid-1909, after separate votes had been held in the two halves of the province. If the 1908 Regulations were to succeed anywhere in the Qing state, it would be southern Jiangsu.

Qing authorities ordered the creation of Provincial Assembly Preparatory Offices in each province in early August 1908.[5] Within weeks, activists in Jiangsu—some of them affiliates of the Public Association, such as Shen Tongfang (dates unknown), who had earned the highest civil service examination degree alongside Zhang Jian in 1894—began organizing a bewildering variety of associations, meetings, and research societies.[6] These in turn spurred the province to establish official Preparatory Offices. A Suzhou office for southern Jiangsu opened its doors on October 10, 1908.[7] A similar office in Nanjing, focused on northern Jiangsu, formally commenced work November 4.

Zhang Jian, although a powerful force in both portions of Jiangsu, hailed from a county in the north and was most directly involved in the Nanjing Preparatory Office. He attended that office's opening and conferred with its staff.[8] Over the next several months, he continued his engagement with the northern elections, ultimately selecting the site of the assembly building in Nanjing. Although he personally remained at a distance from the southern elections, his allies gained high positions within the Suzhou Preparatory Office. These included Yang Tingdong, who was appointed to lead the Preparatory Office's division of elections.[9] Yang did not remain in that specific position—the Preparatory Office's final report in 1909 listed him simply as an "adviser"—but regardless of title, he played a powerful and influential role in shaping southern Jiangsu's election.

Although much of Yang's early life is unaccounted for (even the year of his birth is uncertain; some sources report it as 1861, others as 1879), he became politically engaged during the tumultuous 1890s. In 1898, he left his home near Suzhou to become one of the first Chinese students to embark on a formal course of education in Japan. He developed an interest in political philosophy and, based on a Japanese edition, made the first complete Chinese translation of Rousseau's *Social Contract* in 1900. This was the start of a prolific writing career. Over the next several years, he worked for several newspapers and penned a number of introductions to foreign political systems. One of these, a 1902 political science textbook, revealed a familiarity with election laws in France, the German Empire, Prussia, Switzerland, Austria-Hungary, Sweden, Norway, England, and the United States.[10] Sometime shortly after his return from Japan, Yang began teaching at a school Zhang Jian had founded in his hometown of Nantong; the two men developed a rapport and, within a few years, Yang became one of Zhang's closest companions. No one in Zhang's entourage was better suited than the educated, politically minded Yang to develop the infrastructure to implement the 1908 Regulations in southern Jiangsu.

Someone like Yang could exercise such power because the 1908 Regulations had left much to local initiative. The Preparatory Office, charged with coordinating the work of various ad hoc county-level preparatory offices, did not simply execute orders emanating from the Constitutional Reform Office in Beijing. Instead, it acted with considerable independence. Instructions from the center often proved useless. In December 1908, Bao Tianxiao opined that Beijing's directives were "riddled with omissions and often conflicted with other portions of the [1908] Regulations . . . this sort of explanation drives people crazy and leaves them without a clear route to follow."[11] Yang shared Bao's concerns, although he expressed himself with greater tact:

> Our country is only just beginning to hold elections and many affairs still need to be organized. Some of those responsible [for managing the election] have not yet learned what they need to. Few of the stipulations set forth in the Regulations are precisely defined.[12]

Unlike Bao, he proposed to remedy this lack of clarity. Following the publication of the Election Regulations, Yang invested himself in reading and commenting on this new voting system. This resulted in a manual for conducting elections, published by Shanghai's Commercial Press in September/October 1908, which was advertised heavily in Shanghai-based newspapers.[13] Yang's manual was ultimately a private endeavor, but it must have defined some aspects of the election work in southern Jiangsu simply by virtue of his position.

The need for definitions and direction was pressing. Even before the Preparatory Office formally opened in mid-October, some areas of southern Jiangsu had organized their own local version. Representatives from the "gentry, education, and business communities" of Changzhou prefecture, the first to organize, had begun planning for the election in September. They selected office leaders, raised contributions, and planned to print 5,000 voter registration forms. The Changzhou office drafted its own manual that anticipated initial voter registration would be conducted by village headmen and only then rechecked and revised by election officials.[14] Two of Changzhou prefecture's counties, Wujin and Yanghu, even began the voter registration process on October 10, the day the provincial Preparatory Office began work.[15]

Although this level of community initiative may not have been unwelcome by those trying to establish a provincial Preparatory Office—Bao Tianxiao initially praised the Changzhou efforts in his column—it represented a challenge to any enforcement of uniform standards.[16] The first draft of Changzhou prefecture's voter rolls, submitted for review on October 24, soon after the provincial Preparatory Office opened, was found to be riddled with unspecified errors and omissions.[17] In an attempt to regularize the process, the Preparatory Office announced a slower pace for county-level work, mandating that a voter census be conducted between November 3 to December 22, with the results verified by the county magistrate before January 1, 1909, and submitted to higher authorities before January 20.[18]

Yang's manual and similar texts revealed how provincial authorities hoped this more deliberate process of voter registration would proceed. This was a complex undertaking; the regulations specified myriad qualifications and disqualifications, all of which would need to be accounted for in voter registration. It would also need to be accomplished speedily, given that the elections had already been scheduled for late March 1909. Yang Tingdong suggested that local preparatory offices begin by asking "established organizations in the locality" to submit lists of people they thought would meet the qualifications to vote. These organizations ranged from organs of the county government (such as the Office of Rites and the Office of Education, which together held information on holders of examination degrees and diplomas from modern schools) to quasi-governmental bodies such as the local chamber of commerce, which was thought to be able to provide information about people who met the property requirements. Lists generated from these processes would form a first draft, which census takers could use as a rough plan for a door-to-door census.[19]

In addition to suggesting sources of information about the local population, Yang proposed a series of criteria for determining whether any given individual had met the qualifications to vote. For most of the five potential qualifications for suffrage, this process involved very little interpretation; for others, particularly the wealth requirement, more explanation was required. The text of the requirement was deceptively simple: men with 5,000 *yuan* or more worth of "real estate or commercial assets" were qualified to vote. Yet no precise definition was attached to any of those terms. These problems had been pointed out soon after the law was promulgated. Editorialists in the *Shibao*, for instance, claimed that determining the fair value of assets would be impossible, given the differences between urban and rural properties. They suggested that there was no logical reason to choose these two particular asset classes to the exclusion of others, such as cash savings or annual income.[20]

Yang proposed his own definitions without citing any justification or origin. Real estate, he opined, consisted of "fields (either wet or dry), mines, forests, pools, and houses, including the land that the house sits on." His definition of "commercial assets"—a phrase that did not previously exist in Qing law—was "capital that is used to seek profit, such as the inventory or equipment of a shop or a firm."[21] He explicitly excluded stocks, bonds, or personal valuables such as jewelry from this definition. Others, however, reached different conclusions. In Anhui Province, for instance, "commercial assets" were defined as the "wealth of those engaged in trade or industry" and included the value of stocks from railroads or mining companies, as well as interest-bearing bonds. Real estate was broadened to include boats.[22] Stocks and bonds counted as commercial assets in Jiangxi Province, but boats were excluded as real estate.[23]

Determining the value of real estate or commercial assets proved to be as difficult as defining the terms themselves. Yang offered no guidance on this thorny issue in his manual, and each region adopted its own standard. In Jiangxi, the value of real estate or commercial assets was to be determined by testimonials from local "gentry or public associations" with input from the county magistrate.[24] In southern Jiangsu's Jiading County, by contrast, a standard value was deduced for all land in the jurisdiction. During the construction of the Shanghai-Nanjing Railway between 1905 and 1908, affected landowners had been compensated according to a scale of set rates: fifty *yuan* per *mu* (the equivalent of slightly more than 0.15 acres) for the best fields, forty-five *yuan* for fields of secondary quality, forty *yuan* for those of middling quality, and thirty-five *yuan* for those of the poorest quality. Averaging these four values together, the county preparatory office reasoned that each *mu* of fields in Jiading should be valued at 42.5 *yuan* and, thus, "if a person of our county doesn't meet any of the other suffrage requirements, then as long as he owns 119 *mu* of land [approximately 18.3 acres], he should have the right to vote."[25] Other areas presumably adopted their own expedients, too.

Consequently, the property requirement—stated so precisely in the text of the regulations—functioned as no more than a vague yardstick. Other paths to the franchise, such as "managing a school or other public service institution" for three years, were also implemented inconsistently. Even the exclusion of "illiterates [*bu shi wen yi zhe*]" proved tricky to define—how, after all, would literacy be measured? Most problematically, the regulations specifically disenfranchised otherwise qualified voters who "consumed opium." Did this refer to addicts? To anyone who had ever used opium? Despite the seeming unenforceability of this clause, many were vociferous in demanding that it be implemented. Indeed, one of Bao Tianxiao's primary complaints about the botched Changzhou prefecture voter registration effort was that registrars had not paid enough attention to the exclusion of opium users from the franchise.[26]

Most southern Jiangsu counties successfully compiled voter rolls during the winter of 1908–9, and final figures for the electorate were released in March 1909, only a few weeks before the election was held. The Southern Jiangsu Preparatory Office had identified and registered 59,643 voters out of a total population of approximately 11.5 million in its area of responsibility. This enrollment rate, slightly less than 0.52 percent of the population, represented perhaps a little more than 1.7 percent of all adult men in the region.[27] Although a few provinces enrolled a somewhat greater percentage of their populations, southern Jiangsu's rate noticeably exceeded the national average, which was approximately 0.39 percent of the entire population, or about 1.2 percent of all adult men.[28] Although these numbers may appear small, the nationwide figure matched the size of the entire degree-holding population, estimated at 0.38 percent of the population, in the late nineteenth century.[29] The 1908–9 voter registration process thus produced a body of voters equal in size to the pre-1905 elite class. In all likelihood a greater proportion of the population met the qualifications set in the 1908 Regulations—Bao Tianxiao lamented in November 1908 that registrars had been neglecting qualified "farmers" and "artisans"—but such suspicions are difficult to substantiate empirically.[30]

The composition of this electorate differed from the old class of examination elites, however. The differences can only be sketched impressionistically using the small number of voter registration lists that have survived. These include voter lists for three counties in Jiangsu Province, two prefectures in Zhejiang Province, and partial lists for several prefectures in Guangxi Province.[31] Although most of these lists may have been government file copies, at least one appears to have been a commercial publication—advertisements appear along the margins of each page. Surviving lists lack information about the conditions under which they were created and do not explain which interpretation of the 1908 Regulations was used. Consequently, the voter rolls provide only a rough insight into how qualifications to vote were understood in practice.

Within this limited sample, the single largest bloc of voters in almost every county earned the franchise on the basis of wealth. In Yang Tingdong's native county, Changzhou (not to be confused with Changzhou prefecture, a different jurisdiction written with different characters), 1,184 people—Yang included, although he actually resided in Shanghai—appeared on the rolls; of these, 55 percent qualified on the basis of wealth, 32 percent on the basis of degrees from the imperial exam system, and the remainder from other qualifications.[32] In the nine counties that comprised Hangzhou prefecture in Zhejiang Province (lying just across southern Jiangsu's southern boundary), 13,360 voters were registered, of whom 69 percent qualified on the basis of wealth and 24 percent on the basis of examination degrees.[33] Incomplete data from Guangxi Province in the far south also indicates that probably the majority of voters there qualified to vote on the basis on wealth.[34]

For a few counties, it is possible to make more precise claims, because their voter rolls listed multiple qualifications per voter (for example, an examination degree-holder with a house worth 5,000 *yuan* would be listed as having met both the wealth and the educational requirement). Among these was Shanghai County, which fell under the purview of the Southern Jiangsu Preparatory Office. Of the 3,819 voters listed on the rolls, fully 86 percent met the wealth requirement—and 88 percent of those (73 percent of all voters) qualified because of wealth alone.[35] Shanghai did not report whether this represented real estate or commercial asset wealth. The election commissioners in southern Jiangsu's Wu County provided a level of detail in their voter rolls that does touch on this issue. The Wu County voter registration lists included information on 1,734 voters, of whom about 46 percent qualified because of wealth and 32 percent qualified because of exam degrees. Uniquely, the Wu County rolls provide a breakdown of the types of wealth, differentiating between real estate and commercial assets, for five of the six electoral districts (this missing district was the most populous one—the city of Suzhou). Each electoral district indicated this information in a different way on the voter rolls, suggesting that they may not have used the same criteria for measuring wealth. Even so, roughly 30 percent of all voters who qualified on the basis of wealth in these five districts did so because of commercial, rather than real estate, wealth. This represents 18 percent of all eligible voters in the five districts for which data exist.[36]

Given the small number of voting rolls available and the inherent vagueness of the 1908 Regulations, only limited conclusions can be drawn from the seeming preponderance of voters who qualified on the basis of wealth. It is suggestive of a deliberate attempt to incorporate the Chinese business community—the "merchants" traditionally denigrated in some versions of Confucian thought—into the body politic. This newly inclusive attitude accorded with the vision expressed in the writings of Zheng Guanying and Zhang Jian, who specifically discussed the civic role of merchants; the emphasis of local preparatory offices on registering the wealthy also reflect this interest. Such laws matched practices in the West and in Meiji Japan, in which wealth and property ownership had been seen to be prerequisites of active participation in politics.

The variations in the standards for counting voters proved less important than the message that the very act of counting was meant to convey: voter registration was ultimately a form of ideological work meant to identify a proto-citizenry. The census aimed not just to register voters but also to create them by inculcating them with a particular set of state-oriented values. This was openly acknowledged by organizers in southern Jiangsu, who advocated that educational activities, such as public lectures, accompany voter registration.[37] Other provinces provided even more detail about the contents and goals of such activities. The Jiangxi Preparatory Office's manual, for instance, explained that:

> The social customs of Jiangxi have only just begun to be enlightened. Few understand the rights of citizenship. Families of great wealth and prosperous countryside households are particularly likely to make a principle of closing their doors, focusing inward, and avoiding external concerns. The voter registration process is intended to use clear language in order to dispel their great confusion. It also should let them know that the throne's purpose in adopting the foreign practice of granting suffrage based on wealth . . . is to encourage the spirit of enterprise and to wash away ancient notions of "emphasize the roots [i.e., fundamental pursuits, such as agriculture], repress the branches [i.e., derivative occupations, such as trade]" and "value the literati, demean the merchants."[38]

The concern that wealthy families would isolate themselves from political participation was not limited to Jiangxi. During the preparations for the election in southern Jiangsu's Changzhou Prefecture, for instance, speakers were dispatched to the local chamber of commerce to argue, "the more wealth that one possesses, the more significant [the provincial assembly] is."[39]

The completion of this complex and unprecedented process rested on the backs of thousands (if not tens of thousands) of self-selected election organizers working in their own communities. They were left to their own initiative to a surprising extent—guidance emanating from the national government in Beijing had little impact on provincial level coordinating bodies. Guidance in the form of manuals, such as the one authored by Yang Tingdong, may have helped alleviate some of this. Even Yang's highly promoted manual, however, was ignored at times; none of the surviving voter lists (including the one from Yang's home county) were compiled in the precise format he recommended. While Yang and others in the Preparatory Office were active in generating rules, norms, and expectations, the reach of their small office was ultimately limited.

During the last weeks of September, the Changzhou Prefecture Preparatory Office embarked on a significant publicity campaign. At a mid-September public meeting, each attendee received a printed copy of the 1908 Regulations, and plans were made for a variety of events to publicize the upcoming voter registration process. These included a large public gathering devoted to "the nature of, and preparations for, the provincial assembly," which was to be advertised through printed handbills. That meeting, held on September 23, 1908, reportedly attracted "no less than one thousand people." A thousand people also attended a similar event on October 2.[40] In addition to holding rallies, it commissioned the printing of "several tens of thousands" copies of an introduction to the provincial assembly and planned for an additional series of public speeches.[41] Even those who could not vote were drafted for this effort: the principal of a women's school in Changzhou delayed a vacation to speak to students about the provincial assembly and the women's suffrage movement in England. The point of this lecture was to "arouse the political thinking of the students and so that they could tell their families after returning home, thus preventing any misunderstandings during the voter registration census."[42]

At its most extreme, the voter registration process was literally an investigation into the lives and personal practices of potential voters. Even the voters' names did not escape scrutiny. Under dynastic law, Qing subjects were not allowed to use characters that appeared in the personal name of the emperor. Thus, new characters suddenly became taboo whenever a new emperor ascended the throne. The unexpected death of the Guangxu emperor on November 14, 1908, and the subsequent elevation of the two-year-old Xuantong emperor (1906–67; r. 1908–12) meant that names already collected for the voter registration lists contained characters that were now prohibited. According to the southern Jiangsu Preparatory Office, by late December "an extremely large number" of voter names were still in violation; the office issued an order for voters to revise their names to avoid the taboo—and, to expedite the process, authorized local preparatory offices to preemptively change the names of those who could not be contacted in a timely manner.[43]

The registration survey was an act of control: performed properly, it would result in the compilation of a detailed list of each county's wealthiest and most educated inhabitants, organized according to address. Although the Qing government already maintained similar records (of dubious accuracy, particularly for property ownership), none approached this level of comprehensiveness. Potential voters understood this clearly, and many were wary; it was not unusual for Preparatory Office officials to pepper their speeches with claims that the voter census was not a "precursor to additional taxation," so those qualified to vote should not hide their property holdings.[44] Such efforts were necessary; as late as December 1908, "many merchants" in Wujin and Danyang counties who had been registered clamored to be removed from the rolls for fear that they had become targets of tax collectors.[45] This electoral survey, a precursor to the Qing population census of 1909–11 (which had been announced on July 23, 1908—one day after the 1908 Regulations), marked a dramatic shift away from previous dynastic practices of surveying the population to measure tax obligations or to count potential soldiers. Instead, this voter census measured individuals—not all, but the select few who would be trained to be China's first citizens.[46]

Election Day(s) and the Failure of Spontaneous Consensus

In the weeks before the election, newspapers remained silent about particular candidates but loudly endorsed voting as an activity. One writer for *Shibao* exhorted readers to:

> Pay attention! Pay attention! [March 22] will be the first day for the primary-stage election for provincial assemblymen throughout southern Jiangsu. I hope that all those with voting rights in this area treasure this extremely important, extremely valuable first day. Don't forget this first day! Don't forget this first day![47]

The task of voters on that first day would be simple: an anonymous editorialist writing in *Shenbao* called on primary-stage voters to "vote for [electors] who can select the talented and the moral [*cai de jian bei*] [in the secondary-stage election]."[48] The author gave little sense that he expected this process of selection to be anything other than uncontroversial and harmonious.

Such advice from journalists was intended to create the "public opinion" necessary for a modern nation. Reflecting a long-standing assumption among Chinese journalists, the exiled Liang Qichao explained that newspapers should construct, not reflect, public opinion: "Although public opinion arises from many sources, the most powerful among the organs that produce it are newspapers." The existence of a "healthy public opinion" was a necessary prerequisite for constitutional governance.[49] This concept guided the work of editors at *Shibao* and other publications in the newly emergent political press; it also appealed to those at preexisting newspapers such as *Shenbao* (founded in 1872 and originally focused on business news), which soon began to adopt overtly political stances. Journalism inspired by this directive found an audience, too: by the summer of 1909, *Shibao* printed 17,000 copies a day, *Shenbao* 14,000, and several other Shanghai papers had similar print runs.[50]

Journalists and editors claimed the right to pass moral judgment on the elections, based on their understanding of the now widely shared fundamental expectations for elections. Although they lacked the power of government officials, the evaluations of the electoral process printed in their pages created lasting impressions and shaped public discussion of elections. This judgment could be manifested in various ways, including the selection of topics to be covered in articles and the arrangement of articles within the paper. The most eye-catching strategy, however, was a particular genre of writing, newly invented for the early twentieth-century press: "timely commentary [*shiping*]" editorials.[51] These brief but incisive critiques provided instant analysis on the events of the day. Often they were positioned near relevant news articles, transforming *Shibao* (and other newspapers, which soon copied this popular style of writing) into a repository of not just news but also proper attitudes toward that news.

Bao Tianxiao, chronicler of the Mansion of Repose and acquaintance of Yang Tingdong, was one of this genre's early masters. Reading and writing had been Bao's consuming passions, even during his youth. Like many of his generation, he had been trained in the exacting, formulistic style of writing required for success on the civil service examinations, which he passed at the county level as a seventeen-year-old. Yet new forms of mass media captured his passions. He recalled first encountering newspapers as a child in Suzhou during the 1880s, when they were a relative rarity. Later, he practiced his literary skills by punctuating the lead editorials of *Shenbao*—which, he reported, bored him. In the wake of the 1894–95 Sino-Japanese War, he began to consume periodicals with fervor, including an early reformist newspaper and a Shanghai pictorial magazine.

At the turn of the century, the twenty-something Bao had abandoned pursuit of an examination degree in favor of a literary career. He translated foreign novels (typically working from Japanese translations of European works), founded a small publishing house, and spent several years teaching Chinese literature at a new-style high school. By 1905 he relocated to Shanghai, where a connection with Di Baoxian landed him a job writing opinion and fiction at the still-new *Shibao*. Soon, he came to write "timely commentary" pieces, focused on provincial politics, on a regular basis. He found a home at the paper and remained there until 1919, long after Di and many of the other original editors and writers had left.

In a general sense, Bao's politics aligned with those of the reformers affiliated with *Shibao*, ranging from Liang Qichao to Zhang Jian. Although not himself a member of the Public Association, he moved in similar social circles and was a leader in another pan-provincial reformist group, the Jiangsu Education Association, which was also linked to Zhang. Bao supported the idea of a constitution, advocated for political activism at the local level, and had no love for the civil service examination system or other reminders of the old order. Such attitudes were evident in the timely commentaries he contributed during the months-long voter registration process in late 1908: though sharp-tongued, he pushed for faster, more thorough, and more accurate registration to make the elections successful. He appeared to be someone receptive to the optimistic claims of election advocates.

However, Bao cannot be simply classified as a "pro-reform" journalist. Other inclinations played an equally powerful role in constituting his worldview. These soon led him away from the messages of earnest reformers such as Yang and toward a different depiction of elections. Rather than reflecting an ideological commitment, however, these attitudes grew, at least in part, out of artistic devotion. More than anything else, Bao made clear in his memoirs, he was a writer who wrote from the gut. As he later explained, "When I write, I don't polish or revise a second draft; all that I've written in the past, both creative and narrative, has been like this."[52] Although he was speaking specifically of his fiction writing (for which he is best known today), this basic instinct—a self-assured desire to tell a clear story quickly—also influenced his timely commentaries.

The primary-stage elections, once they began on March 22, 1909, furnished Bao with ample source material. That day had originally been the mandated date for the whole empire. Only the Preparatory Office in charge of managing southern Jiangsu had been able to keep to the original schedule. Thus, unexpectedly, southern Jiangsu's election became the first provincial assembly election held on Qing territory. Others, including northern Jiangsu and neighboring provinces such as Zhejiang, held elections soon afterward. All remaining provinces (excluding remote Xinjiang, which failed to hold elections) followed, and elections everywhere were concluded by late summer 1909. As the first region to hold this first national election in Chinese history, southern Jiangsu's experiences, as reflected, shaped, and amplified by newspaper opinion makers such as Bao, held an outsized influence in forming the historical narrative of the meanings of this unprecedented event.

Initial voting for the primary-stage election in southern Jiangsu was held from morning to late afternoon on the appointed day. Each county was divided into several polling districts, and each district was assigned one polling station. Upon arriving at the polling station and presenting the voter identification cards distributed during the census, voters received a blank ballot. Then, in a secluded part of the polling station, voters had the opportunity to write the name of a single individual on the ballot and cast it into a sealed box. At the end of the day, election workers forwarded their sealed ballot boxes to the county seat, where the magistrate oversaw the counting. Participation varied from place to place but was significant. Vote totals for twenty-seven of southern Jiangsu's thirty-seven county-level jurisdictions are extant. In seventeen of those, more than half of the registered voters cast ballots—in some jurisdictions, nearly three-quarters of eligible voters participated. Even in low-turnout counties, two out of every five voters still made it to the polls.[53] The first newspaper accounts emphasized the orderliness of the balloting, although (surprisingly) no photographs of this historical occasion appear to have survived.[54]

Once the ballots were opened and the votes tallied, however, a different image emerged—one that challenged the dominant optimistic narrative of elections. The outcome of the election in Wu County, Bao Tianxiao's ancestral home, illustrates this. Eleven people in Wu County met the minimum threshold to be anointed primary-stage winners on the basis of the March 22 vote. The first announcement of the vote tallies in the *Shenbao*, which simply listed the names and their vote totals without any additional biographical information, concluded with a disapproving line of commentary: "only four of them are from the city [of Suzhou]; most of the rest are local office holders from rural areas and some are opium users."[55] The veracity of this claim (which is unknowable—one of these winners was later criticized by name in the press, five others were famous scholars or officials, and no information is available about the remaining five) is less important than the newspaper's judgment that the voters had picked the wrong people.

The question of opium use haunted the legitimacy of the primary-stage elections throughout the region. In Wuxi and Jinshan counties, unnamed individuals accused three primary-stage winners of being opium users; one resigned his position, but the other two denied the charge.[56] Over a month after the election, as similar claims continued to circulate, a frustrated Bao Tianxiao grumbled that the opium users among the primary-stage winners in southern Jiangsu were "too numerous to count."[57] Opium use was not the only problem. One of the original eleven winners in Wu County was accused of having "oppressed countryside residents."[58] Others even had their voter qualifications challenged; one primary-stage winner in Wujin County was accused of having falsely claimed to meet the 5,000 *yuan* property qualification for voting.[59]

Just as important, the results of this first vote in Wu County revealed that voters could not spontaneously generate a consensus about who had the talent and integrity to serve in office. The county's 1,734 registered voters, Bao among them, had been asked to select nineteen primary-stage election winners, but had only been able to elect eleven. On election day, 703 Wu County voters cast ballots (it is not certain whether Bao voted), and 686 of the ballots were counted as valid. According to the primary-stage election formula—the minimum number of ballots to win had to equal the total number of ballots cast divided by twice the number of open seats—a winning candidate needed a minimum of 19 votes [686 / (19 * 2) = 18.05, rounded up to the nearest whole number to yield 19]. This was a difficult threshold to reach; no names appeared on the ballot, rendering every candidate a write-in candidate. Kong Zhaojin (1865–1936), a holder of the highest examination degree who had helped managed the local voter registration effort, received more votes than any other candidate on the March 22 election—and he only received forty-eight votes, or 7 percent of those cast. Many of the others elected that day received far fewer votes, one receiving only nineteen—the minimum to qualify for election.

After all of the ballots were counted, it became clear that the Wu County vote had not produced nineteen winners each with the minimum nineteen votes. Beyond the eleven who had reached this threshold, an additional sixteen named individuals had received between five and eighteen votes, while an unknown number of people received four or fewer votes. While unknown, that number is presumably not small: newspaper reports, which listed only those who received more than five votes apiece, only account for 505 of the 686 valid ballots cast in Wu County.[60] This was not an unanticipated phenomenon; the drafters of the 1908 Regulations had included provisos for a revote in cases like this. The revote also failed to generate enough additional winners. So did the second one; only a third revote—a fourth trip to the ballot box—allowed Wu County to fill out its quota of nineteen (see table 1).

The law stipulated that only voters who participated in the original vote could cast ballots during the revote, and participants in the revotes could only vote for people who had received more than a certain number of votes in the original election. Each subsequent vote thus attracted fewer

Table 1
Primary-Stage Voting and Revoting in Wu County, 1909

Round	Date	Ballots Cast	Minimum Votes to Win	Seats to Be Filled	Number of Candidates Earning Minimum Votes
Election day	March 22	686	19	19	11
First revote	March 30	548	35	8	5
Second revote	April 4	95	16	3	2
Third revote	April 7	69	35	1	1

SOURCES: The data are calculated from the following newspaper accounts—for March 22 election: "Zhuan dian [Special Cable]," *Shibao* jiyou/run 2/5 (March 26, 1909), 2, and "Difang xinwen: xiang ji Wuxian kaipiao qingxing [Local News: A Detailed Account of Counting Votes in Wu County]," *Shibao*, jiyou/run 2/6 (March 27, 1909), 3; for the March 30 first revote: "Difang xinwen: Chang Yuan Wu chong toupiao dangxuanren mingdan [Local News: List of People Elected During the First Revote in Changzhou, Yuanhe, and Wu Counties]," *Shibao*, jiyou/run 2/13 (April 3, 1909), 3; for the April 4 second revote: "Suzhou Chang Yuan Wu san xian xuanju jishi [Report on the Election in the Three Suzhou-Area Counties]," *Shibao*, jiyou/run 2/17 (April 7, 1909), 3; and for the April 7 third revote: "Jiangsu Sushu (Suzhou Wuxian) [Southern Jiangsu (Suzhou's Wu County)]," *Shenbao*, jiyou/run 2/19 (April 9, 1909), 18.

and fewer voters, who had fewer and fewer choices. Far from revealing a consensus, this first primary-stage election revealed a multiplicity of viewpoints. Newspapers, the self-proclaimed voice of public opinion, saw this as a deeply troubling manifestation of the election system's weaknesses. Bao Tianxiao, writing in the *Shibao* soon after the first revote, wondered what would happen if it did not produce enough winners. How many ballots, he asked, would be enough?[61]

It was a prescient question—and not just for Wu County. Thirty-three of the thirty-seven county-level jurisdictions in southern Jiangsu held at least one revote. Sixteen counties required a second revote; two more, including Wu County, needed a third; and two others, including Shanghai County, had to hold a fourth. Nor was this phenomenon limited to southern Jiangsu. One revote was required in twenty of the twenty-seven jurisdictions in northern Jiangsu for which results can be found, and a second was needed in the remaining seven. Of the thirty-five jurisdictions in neighboring Zhejiang Province for which data survive, thirty-one needed one revote and four had a second.[62] Less comprehensive data from elsewhere suggest this was a nationwide phenomenon. In Hunan Province, only one county reported filling its quota on the first vote, and six reported reaching the quota on the second vote. One jurisdiction reported that no one received enough votes on the first ballot to be elected.[63]

Paradoxically, the commonality of revoting suggests that these elections were generally free and fair. Any government attempt to dominate or control the election process (by intimidating voters or systematically stuffing ballot boxes, for instance) would presumably have resulted in easy victories for the preferred candidate. Likewise, dominance of elections by a specific faction of local elites would hardly seem likely to result in a situation in which so few received enough votes to win. The election of primary-stage winners who offended the sensibilities of Bao and other Shanghai-based writers is more troubling, yet it demonstrated that powerful entities—in this case, a media outlet tightly linked to some of the province's most powerful political figures—could not dictate the outcome of local elections. No observer in 1909 advanced these hypotheses. Instead, they saw in the messy, inconclusive results a profound challenge to the optimistic narrative of elections as state-building, talent-seeking mechanisms. Perhaps the problem was that voters were being misled?

"A Single Word from a Campaigner"

As early as February 1909, Bao had begun to fixate on the behavior of those vying for office. He felt they had resorted to crude and dishonorable conduct in their quest for office. This behavior, which he called "campaigning [*yundong*]" deserved nothing other than condemnation:

> "Campaigning" is, to state things bluntly, nothing more than currying favor, or seeking help from others, or making use of personal connections. When this new phrase emerged, it seemed that "campaigning" was some sort of extremely just and honorable thing. The political world and the scholarly word both took to it as a pet phrase. Alas! It has lost all credibility.[64]

Bao was not being pedantic by defining his term. Campaigning for elected office was a new phenomenon, and the word for it was, to cite the title of an early twentieth-century dictionary of neologisms that included it, one of many "new terms for new ideas" circulating at the time.[65] Moreover, the Chinese compound used to represent this term, *yundong*, simultaneously had a variety of other, unrelated meanings, including "movement [of an object]," "exercise," "[political] movement," and "to persuade somebody." The use of this term in the sense of election campaigning predated the 1909 elections by a few years but was still a relatively rare term (for obvious reasons) before voting began in March 1909 (see figure 4). It only survived a few decades; by the 1930s it fell into disuse and does not carry this meaning in twenty-first-century Chinese.[66]

"Campaigning" may have been a new term, but Bao's anxieties about it were not. It had been the basis for the pessimistic vision of elections articulated by nineteenth-century diplomats such as Zhang Deyi and Huang Zunxian and echoed by Li Hongzhang in his evaluation of Feng Guifen's proposals. These documents were not available to the general public in 1909, and there is no evidence that Bao had any knowledge of them, but similar attitudes had crept into mass circulation books and newspapers that he would have been able to see. As early as 1906, soon after the return of the overseas constitutional study commissions, an anonymous writer in *Shenbao* suggested that restricting electoral

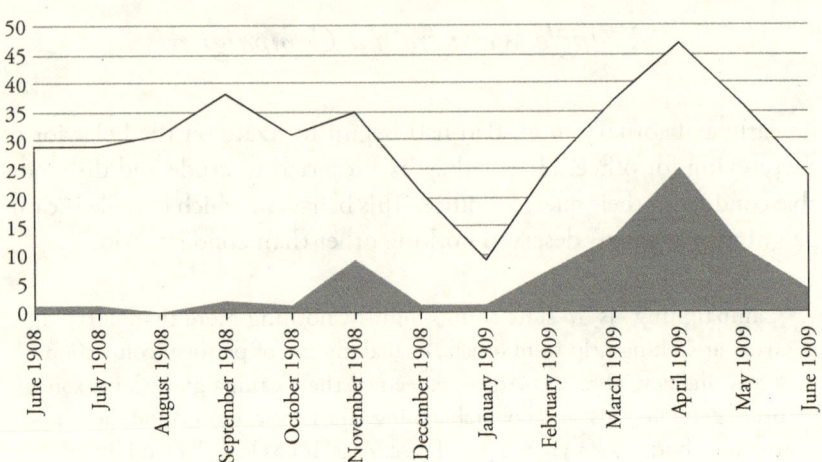

□ Total Articles Using *Yundong*   ■ Articles Using *Yundong* as "Campaigning"

FIGURE 4: Relative frequency of the use of the term *yundong* to mean "election campaigning" as compared to all uses of the term in *Shenbao* during the period of the 1909 provincial assembly elections. The two spikes on the chart correlate with coverage of the November 1908 U.S. presidential election and the March–April 1909 elections for provincial assemblies in the region near Shanghai. The data are derived from a count of terms found using the full text search function in Green Apple Data Center's *Shenbao, 1872–1949* database. Each occurrence was examined to eliminate mistakes or false positives.

competition and campaigning were important considerations for the design of election laws.[67]

Although the designers of the 1908 Regulations may have shared the desire to limit such things, they did not incorporate any clear rules regulating them into the law. The regulations merely imposed penalties on "those who use money to entice voters, the voters who accept such enticements, and those who act as intermediaries" without defining any of those terms. Even during the registration process, some at *Shibao* felt these lines were being overstepped and that the "struggle for the right to *be* elected" (emphasis added) had begun to eclipse the more important task of "struggling for voting rights [of others]."[68] The worry about candidates competing to be elected became the primary lens through which Bao and other writers observed the election.

Campaigning for the provincial assembly did not involve large-scale public events, such as speeches or rallies. These events would not have been effective given the size of the electorate—what would be the point of drawing a crowd without being certain that most people in the crowd could vote? Moreover, there were no formal political parties; new Qing legislation on public meetings and the right of assembly, issued in March 1908, placed tight restrictions on any politically oriented groups.[69] Candidates thus would have relied on private, personal ties and relationships to garner the relatively small number of votes required by the 1908 Regulations. Although no specific account of campaigning for election survives, critical commentary from newspapers supplies some evidence for how it worked.

It would have been possible for campaigners to calculate approximately how many votes would be needed to secure election. Voter registration rolls were completed and approved for most southern Jiangsu counties in January 1909. According to the 1908 Regulations, lists of registered voters were posted in public places—and for at least some counties, published copies were circulated. The formula for determining the number of votes required in the primary-stage election was enumerated in the regulations. Although the final number of votes needed depended on election day turnout, ambitious campaigners could estimate the number of votes needed and target specific voters listed on the rolls. To a significant extent, the structure of the election laws had unintentionally incentivized this type of strategy.[70] Rather than seeking the support of strangers, successful campaigners identified eligible voters with whom they had existing social ties. A satirical (and perhaps fictional) commentary in *Shenbao* a month before the election depicted a scenario that fits this supposition: an eager campaigner, holding a birthday dinner for his aged mother, attempted to persuade five guests to each convince five others to vote for him.[71]

In the months after the election, one anonymous wit created a satirical "Campaigning for Beginners" handbook. Although some of the suggestions were clearly facetious—the author suggested candidates change their names to use only easy-to-write characters—others might have had a basis in practice. These included "winning over rural people" by treating them to meals, creating a personal network by making connections with village headmen, posting notices (and gifting wall scrolls to be hung by people's doors) that featured the candidate's name, and even making public speeches. Other sources highlighted the practice of distributing name cards, presumably to help voters complete their ballots correctly.[72] Other, less benign enticements were used in some instances—including plying voters with liquor and bringing them to brothels.[73] Some candidates may have used financial incentives, such as paying supporters' membership fees in a local educational association.[74]

Such actions were almost never ascribed to any specific individual or located in an identifiable place. Instead, the actors were typically identified as "a student," "a member of the gentry in a particular county," and the like. Newspapers implied that such campaigning, all of which was coded as distasteful, was prevalent and effective. This particular narrative became steadily more negative with each subsequent revote in southern Jiangsu's primary-stage elections. An unusual series of illustrations printed in Shanghai's *Shibao* highlighted this progression.[75]

The first illustration, "Election Campaigning in the Rain," depicted the first vote of the primary-stage election (see figure 5). Southern Jiangsu experienced heavy rains that day (some contemporary observers blamed the weather for a disappointing voter turnout) and thus that aspect of the cartoon was not allegorical.[76] The depiction of the bedraggled line of pleading men in scholar's gowns, however, hardly makes the first authorized election in Chinese history appear to be a dignified endeavor. The candidates were identified in the caption as "campaigning," yet if anything, voters seemed unreceptive to their entreaties. The candidates gesture toward a man with an umbrella who is walking away from them.

This second illustration, "Election Campaigning," appeared on the day of the first revote in Wu County (see figure 6). It depicted a candidate (on the left) wearing a traditional gentry outfit, begging for a vote. His hands are clasped, he leans forward, and seems ill at ease. The other figure, the presumptive voter (standing on the right) is more difficult to decipher. He is poorly dressed and engaged in manual labor, yet is upright and has a disdainful expression on his face. The candidate, engaged in campaigning, by contrast, has become a truly pathetic figure. The nature of campaigning is unclear in this illustration. How is he pleading his case to this potential supporter?

The third illustration, "Election Campaigning (2)" published after the first revote in Wu County, suggested an answer to that question (see

FIGURE 5: "Yuzhong xuanju yundong [Election Campaigning in the Rain]," *Shibao*, jiyou/run 2/2 (March 23, 1909), 2.

figure 7). The campaigning candidate, the well-dressed taller figure on the right, stands at the door of a restaurant (the sign on the right reads "Relaxed, Informal Dining" and the one on the left reads "Noodles with Quick-Fried Fish") and beckons to two other men to enter. Campaigning, in this depiction, was transactional: a meal for a vote. Two additional illustrations in the sequence depicted other aspects of election campaigning, including one candidate holding an opium pipe and another being carried in a sedan chair.[77]

Illustrations were only a small part of the increasingly critical discourse printed in the newspapers. On April 1, 1909—the day on which it was clear that a second revote (a third balloting, in other words) would be needed in many southern Jiangsu counties—Bao Tianxiao compared the elections to a decaying piece of fruit in a blistering timely commentary:

FIGURE 6: "Xuanju yundong [Election Campaigning]," *Shibao*, jiyou/run 2/9 (March 30, 1909), 2.

The works of Herbert Spencer tells us that when political leaders desire something, and set up a law for that end, what they hope for will not materialize—and what they get will not be what they expected. The provincial assembly election is an example of this. It's like a melon: before it's cut open, everyone wants to taste its sweet, sweet flesh; once it's sliced with a knife, though, [we find that the] insides are all rotten. However, although this fruit is rotten, I still hope that once it's cleaned out, there will be a few melon seeds left for us. Something, after all, is better than nothing.[78]

An anonymous timely commentary in the same issue of *Shibao* further elaborated that "under a system of elections, it is impossible to avoid all

FIGURE 7: "Xuanju yundong er [Election Campaigning 2]," *Shibao*, jiyou/run 2/10 (March 31, 1909), 2.

sorts of election campaigning; there is nothing that those who set the laws can do about this.... [In this election], campaigning has already gone well beyond being just a poor imitation of the practices of other countries."[79]

Later, a *Shibao* editor indicted not only those who competed for election but also the voters they influenced:

> Those influenced by campaigning [*shou yundong zhe*] are like blind men riding sightless horses. Out of a hundred of them, not even a single person understands what sort of thing an election is, or what it means to vote or to be elected. It only takes a single word from a campaigner and the crowd falls into line behind him.[80]

By the end of the primary-stage voting, enthusiasm for elections had been subsumed by contempt for election campaigning—and for the voters who allowed themselves to be swayed by campaigners.

Such stories about the primary-stage election in 1909 circulated long after the event ceased being news; distaste for campaigning became one of the enduring legacies of this first election. Authors gathered newspaper clippings, anecdotes, rumors, and stories together and published them in the form of booklets with titles like *Strange Tales from the Election*. The circulation of such materials undoubtedly solidified the emerging discourse of the depravity of election campaigning—and revealed the continued existence of deep-seated anxieties over the nature of elections. The skeptical take on elections evident in the scattered writings of nineteenth-century diplomats who had witnessed elections abroad, now channeled by Bao, was finding a mass audience.

Conclusion

More serious allegations of election fraud were leveled. Some of these, such as charges of ballot box tampering, threaten the legitimacy of any electoral system. Cases of that sort of fraud violated the language of the election law and triggered formal investigations. This could result in punishment and did so in at least one case in northern Jiangsu.[81] Yang Tingdong's Preparatory Office later claimed a role in adjudicating similar issues behind the scenes, exercising oversight exactly as Zheng Guanying had anticipated in the 1890s. In a confidential report after the primary-stage voting, the Preparatory Office claimed that "some of those elected have reputations for wickedness," and thus their victories would be "nullified without exception." It assured the state that only those with "upright personalities" who would "not harm the people" would ultimately be seated as assemblymen after the secondary election.[82] The report did not specify how many primary-stage winners it rejected, nor did it explain if this process would have been public knowledge. In spite of all of the attention these complaints received, publicly available material reveals the vast majority of primary-stage winners were acceptable: only three of the 660 primary-stage election winners in southern Jiangsu had their elections voided, and an additional twenty-seven refused to serve.[83]

The election process ended on May 4, 1909, when the southern Jiangsu primary-stage election winners, 660 in total, gathered in their respective prefectural seats for a secondary-stage election to select the sixty-six regular members and thirty-seven alternate members of the provincial assembly. Technically, they were not bound by law to select these 103 individuals from among the 660 primary-stage winners. In practice, at least ninety-six of the regular and alternate members elected in this secondary-stage election had also won the primary-stage election.[84] Several of those elected as regular members of the assembly in the secondary-stage election, including Kong Zhaojin, winner of the most votes in the Wu County primary-stage election, declined to serve in office.

The sixty-six people finally confirmed as regular members of the provincial assembly included many of Jiangsu's most respected individuals, although certainly not all assemblymen could be counted as such. A substantial number of those who advocated for and then implemented the election gained seats. This included Yang Tingdong, a primary-stage winner from Changzhou County who found himself with an assembly seat when another candidate declined election at the secondary-stage election. Many of his colleagues joined him: including Yang, four out of the twelve Jiangsu natives in the southern Jiangsu Preparatory Office won seats.[85] The proportion for the northern Jiangsu office, six of seventeen, was even higher. Zhang Jian, who was later elected the assembly speaker, was among those six.[86] The Public Association, based in Shanghai but with a nationwide membership, also succeeded in placing a surprising number of individuals into this combined Jiangsu legislature: of the 396 individuals listed on a 1910 membership list, eighteen had been elected to the assembly.[87] This number included Di Baoxian, managing editor of *Shibao* and employer of "campaigning" critic Bao Tianxiao. This would suggest that the right outcome had been achieved: many of the new assemblymen seemed to fit any definition of talent and morality current at the time.

The tension between the condemnations of voter and candidate behavior that filled the columns of Bao and other Shanghai-based journalists and the stature of those elected to the provincial assembly proved difficult to resolve. Some, such as an anonymous *Shenbao* editorialist who lamented that "few of [those elected in the primary-stage vote] are skilled at self-government," implied that the experiment had failed.[88] Others, including at least one journalist at *Shibao*, expressed pride at the outcome of the secondary-stage election.[89] Foreign observers left mixed commentary about the provincial assemblies as well; G. E. Morrison (1862–1920), a longtime journalist for the *Times* of London in Beijing, praised their operation in December 1909 while noting that his subordinate J. O. P. Bland (1863–1945) had nothing but criticism for them.[90]

Some held both views. Zheng Guanying, who did more to popularize elections than any other figure in late Qing China, remained uncharacteristically quiet during the vote in 1909. Although his wealth assuredly exceeded the qualifications to vote, either in his native Guangdong or in his adoptive Shanghai, there is no evidence that he voted. More surprisingly, there is no evidence that any votes were cast for him. His personal correspondence reveals that he was not indifferent to this experiment, even if he was not directly involved. In May 1909, after the primary-stage election in southern Jiangsu and the negative press it engendered, Zheng made a donation to Zhang Jian's Public Association—an entity that was essentially indistinguishable from those who managed and won the election.[91] Yet in an undated letter to an acquaintance in Macau, he grumbled,

> Half of the assemblymen in our country campaigned with cash and the other half made use of personal connections. Nothing needs to be said of their abilities or character. Such assemblymen have no morals, no learning, and no experience—how can they know how to make laws?[92]

Zheng's commentary cannot be easily reconciled with the types of people who actually won office. Many Jiangsu assemblymen had, it would appear, the morals, learning, and experience necessary to make laws; this is also the case in many other provinces. If Zheng resolved the tensions between being both a supporter and a critic of the 1909 elections, he did not leave a written record of it.

The problem raised by the corrosive nature of campaigning was thorny. Zheng Guanying spoke for a well-established reformist vision in which elections were understood primarily as a means to strengthen the Chinese state. Members of this reformist group also saw their work as bringing Chinese political institutions and practices into alignment with prevailing global norms. By 1909, this was no longer simply the speculative talk or theorizing that Bao had once ridiculed—it was the basis for state policy. Yet the distasteful campaigning that Bao had observed and excoriated seemed an inevitable by-product of those reforms. Elections were intended to allow local people to use their own judgment to select the most talented and most moral of their neighbors to be their conduit to the government. How could that be reconciled with the reality that many had voted instead for someone who had bought them a bowl of noodles?

One anonymous *Shibao* timely commentary writer recognized this in the weeks after the southern Jiangsu primary-stage election:

> It is right to say that campaigning cannot be avoided in elections, but it is not right to say that there can be no elections without campaigning. It is right to say that the countries of the world cannot prohibit election campaigning, but it is not right to say that election campaigning is a method China ought to adopt. Campaigning is a flaw of elections; it is not the essence of elections. If it were possible to have elections without campaigning, there might be great rejoicing in political circles. Today's voters take as their excuse the fact that election campaigning occurs in all nations; what other nations have, our country cannot lack. How is it they do not know what it means to act on their own?[93]

Elections and campaigning were intertwined phenomena, but campaigning was a defect rather than an integral part of the true purpose of elections. If elections were necessary, but campaigning intolerable, how could a system of elections make China a stronger country? Or could it be possible, somehow, to separate them—saving elections by eliminating campaigning?

Yang Tingdong's career as an elected official suggests that timely commentary essayists such as Bao might not fully have grasped the complexity of the situation. Yang was deeply involved in the election as an organizer—but also perhaps as a candidate. He made himself available in public on an increasing basis as the election drew near. In late February, he joined the teaching staff of a Shanghai-based lecturing society sponsored by the Public Association. A few days later, he was in Suzhou, his home, participating in a similar group. These may be relatively highbrow forms of campaigning but nonetheless suggested that he was trying to make the rounds in the final weeks before an election.[94]

During the primary stage election in his home county, Changzhou, Yang received seventeen votes, just three shy of the mark needed to be elected. He won twenty-eight during the second balloting several days later, enough to make him a primary-stage winner.[95] His experiences at the secondary-stage election were similarly mixed. Ten of eleven slots in the assembly were filled during the first attempt at a secondary-stage election in Suzhou prefecture; Yang—who only received one vote—was not among them. Six slots for alternate candidates also went unfilled. Thus at the second balloting, seven vacancies needed to be filled. Yang and one other person tied for third place, each with six votes (exceeding the minimum needed by a single vote), thus ranking them second and third on the alternates list.[96] Over the next few weeks, however, three of the eleven elected to the assembly refused office, as did the highest ranked alternate. An assembly seat thus fell in Yang's lap. Or was it caused to fall there?

Yang Tingdong's winding path to electoral office raises an unanswerable question: was his difficult route a result of the depredations of campaigners, who made it hard for a moral and talented man to reach office? Or was he a campaigner with a savvy understanding of the rules of the game who amassed just enough support to gain a seat in the provincial assembly, even though he never earned enough votes to win outright? Or—most disturbing of all—was there really no difference between the two in the end?

No answer to this riddle would be found while the Qing ruled. Elected officials, who were supposed to represent hope for China's future as a constitutional monarchy, thus became nothing more than one additional group for the newly emergent mass media to mock.[97] The next provincial assembly election was scheduled for the fourth year of the Xuantong emperor's reign (1912 on the Western calendar). Revolution intervened and by the time the appointed election year arrived, the boy emperor had abdicated. The Qing experiment with constitutionalism was over, yet Zhang Jian, Yang Tingdong, and many others who had guided it remained. The assemblies (now transformed into legislatures) and the 1908 Regulations that structured their elections survived to a significant extent into the new Republic. So did Bao Tianxiao's critical assessment of the behaviors that elections encouraged. The continuity of Qing election laws under the Republic ensured that China's new government would also inherit the worry about campaigning. The foundational expectations for elections that had evolved during the Qing proved a challenging legacy for a republican government that sought to base its legitimacy on free, competitive voting.

CHAPTER 4

Free Elections and the First Republic

Parties and the Press, 1911–1913

A small, unplanned mutiny by elements of a Wuchang, Hubei–based military unit on October 10, 1911 set China's Republican Revolution in motion. Various anti-dynastic activists soon scrambled to assert control over events as the rebellion spread, but with little success. Some were entirely absent, including Sun Yat-sen (1868–1925), later immortalized as the "father of the Chinese republic." He learned of the uprising from a newspaper in Colorado, where he had been fundraising for the revolutionary cause. Sun returned to China at a leisurely pace, arriving in late December to be proclaimed president of the provisional republican government. Though often called an election in histories of the period, only a handful of revolutionary leaders participated in Sun's selection, casting votes on behalf of the seventeen provinces that had nominally joined the revolution by that point.[1] Not everyone was impressed by this process. Zheng Xiaoxu, a former Public Association leader who remained loyal to the Qing, scoffed in his diary a few weeks later that "calling this 'elected by the nation [*quan guo gongju*]' is a real joke."[2] Reflecting this inauspicious beginning, debates over elections proved central to postdynastic China's identity. The values and ideas that underpinned these debates grew out of the foundational expectations for elections laid in the nineteenth century. The Republican Revolution did not mark a discursive break in the concepts developed to justify and explain elections over the final decades of Qing rule.

The real work of establishing republican political infrastructure had begun weeks before Sun's return and had little to do with him or his followers. After the initial revolt in Wuchang, unrest spread to other major urban areas around the empire. Still-loyal elites, Zhang Jian among them, looked askance at these developments—and at the throne's slow and indecisive response. Zhang, elected to the Jiangsu assembly in 1909, had been at the forefront of a movement to push for continued constitutional reform. He and his supporters pressed for a national parliament but were repeatedly rebuffed. Ultimately, a disappointed Zhang resigned his assembly seat after a conflict with the provincial governor in May 1911. The next month, he traveled to Beijing for an audience with the regent who ruled in the name of the child emperor; along the way, he stopped to visit Yuan Shikai, who had been dismissed from his offices in 1909. His renewal of ties with Yuan in the end proved more important than his visit to the Forbidden City, where he proposed yet another laundry list of reform policies destined to be ignored.[3]

Returning home, Zhang busied himself with his expanding business empire. One journey to visit a factory brought him to Hankou, across the Yangzi from Wuchang, on October 4. Six days later, he watched fires spread through the city on the opposite bank as the mutiny began. He and his companions escaped downriver to Jiangsu, stopping in Nanjing to urge the Manchu military commander and the governor-general to send aid. Neither acted on this advice. Continuing to Suzhou, he met with Jiangsu governor Cheng Dequan (1860–1930), Yang Tingdong, and several other close political associates.[4] Together, they drafted appeals to the throne, calling for a dismissal of the unpopular cabinet and the early adoption of a constitution.

By November 3, revolutionary groups had seized power in Shanghai. Two days later, Governor Cheng in Suzhou—who had been so trusted by the throne before his 1910 transfer to Jiangsu that he had been one of the few Han Chinese to hold office in the ancestral homeland of the ruling Manchus—defected to the rebels.[5] Zhang now joined the new government, too. Belatedly, loyalist officials in Nanjing decided to resist the crumbling of dynastic power, and fighting soon engulfed the city's immediate environs. In the heart of southern Jiangsu, however, enough stability existed that Cheng, Zhang, and other elites could begin constructing a postmonarchical regime.

A week after siding with the revolution, Governor Cheng convened a provisional legislature. Seventy-eight members of the 1909 assembly responded, including a number, such as Zhang Jian, who had resigned from that body before the revolution. They gathered on November 21, anointed Zhang as speaker, and heard an impassioned speech from Cheng. Speaking with the sincerity of a new convert, the governor began with a paean to the will of the people as explained by philosophers as diverse as Mencius, the seventeenth-century anti-Manchu theorist Huang Zongxi, and Jean-Jacques Rousseau. More pointedly, he asserted that the "false constitutionalism" of the Qing had now "created a real revolution."[6] The provisional legislature remained in session until December 8, dedicating itself to laying the foundations for popular government.

Even as some of the revolution's bloodiest fighting occurred in Nanjing, legislators in Suzhou began writing election laws for the province. The priority placed on these laws by the new government indicates the extent to which its creators took seriously the notion of popular sovereignty and embraced elections as a tool for expressing it. In quick succession, the legislature adopted election laws for county magistrates, county legislatures, and local legislative councils.[7] They preserved substantial elements of the Qing election system while introducing changes that would expand participation. In these laws, suffrage was limited to male Chinese citizens over the age of twenty-one who had lived in a locality for more than three years and paid two *yuan* or more in annual "direct taxes" to any level of government. Voters could be disqualified for the same reasons as under the Qing, including opium use, illiteracy, and immoral conduct. In a departure from precedent, local and county legislatures would be directly elected. Two-stage indirect elections, using rules very similar to those of the old provincial assemblies, would be used for county magistrates, thus transforming an appointive office into an elective one. In total, these November/December 1911 laws reflected the deeply felt democratic impulses of the moment.

The passage of these laws reflected the revolution's aspirations, rather than its actual position: the emperor's regent still ruled from the Forbidden City, the Qing government still functioned, and armies loyal to the throne still fought revolutionary forces. Desperate to maintain their position, the Qing rulers recalled Yuan Shikai on October 14 to lead efforts to suppress the revolution. Yuan dithered, waiting to see how the situation would develop. On November 8, a few days after his own transformation into a revolutionary, Zhang Jian reached out to Yuan (on one occasion using Yang Tingdong as an intermediary) to sway him to the republican cause. For weeks, Yuan remained unwilling to commit fully to either side. Although in contact with the revolutionaries, he also masterminded a counteroffensive that reclaimed several rebel cities for the dynasty at the end of November. Pushed by Zhang's words, tugged by his ambition, and shoved by the increasingly visible collapse of Qing legitimacy, Yuan agreed to a cease-fire in December and negotiated a February 1912 deal for imperial abdication. In exchange, Yuan secured his elevation as provisional president of the Republic in place of the recently "elected" Sun Yat-sen.

After assuming office, Yuan sanctioned the existence of self-constituted provincial legislatures, such as Jiangsu's, under local authority until such time as the central government developed a replacement.[8] Although subprovincial local election laws were not mentioned, Yuan's order appeared to endorse the democratic shift of late 1911. Local elections, based on the winter 1911 laws, occurred with increasing frequency in the spring and summer of 1912. Jiading County, slightly northwest of Shanghai, elected its magistrate in early July 1912.[9] Local legislative elections were also held: Shanghai County's legislature was elected in mid-July, and Jiangdu County, on the north bank of the Yangzi River, held similar elections in October.[10] As late as September, provincial governor Cheng continued to push counties to hold elections under the province's own laws.[11]

This spurt of elections reawakened the complaints of 1909. At the end of August 1912—only slightly more than six months after the emperor's abdication—the editor of *Shenbao* opined that public behavior during the Republic's summer of elections was an unwelcome reminder of the old regime:

> In the old Qing elections for local self-government bodies [i.e., county or township legislatures], those who campaigned did not have upright motives and those who were influenced by campaigning did not have a fixed point of view. Corruption and fraud knew no limits. The ugly appearance of today's city and village elections are no different from those of the past.[12]

This editor blamed the character of the people, ending his column with the plaintive cry: "What happened to that which was supposed to be 'new' about these 'new citizens'? What happened to that which was supposed to be 'harmonious' about this republic? Alas!" Even as China's republican experiment began, some feared it would not escape the tensions that had rendered Qing-era elections unpalatable.

Pushing the Boundaries of the 1908 Regulations

The temporary constitution adopted in early 1912 defined voting as a fundamental right and committed the new government to elect a parliament by January 1913. Meeting this deadline required the Provisional Senate, which relocated to Beijing in April 1912, and Yuan Shikai's administration to design new election laws. Parliament finally selected a drafting committee in early July and tasked it to have a proposal ready for debate by July 14. The committee of eleven included many former members of Qing provincial assemblies, Yang Tingdong among them.[13] Whether due to the pressure of time or to ideological predilections, the committee's proposal bore a striking resemblance to the 1908 Regulations. From very early in their deliberations, the majority of senators supported the retention of a two-stage, indirect election process in which only a restricted electorate could participate.[14] Though heir to an anti-monarchical revolution, the Republic maintained the institutional arrangements of the imperial era; Qing election laws were tweaked, not rejected.

The adopted revisions expanded the scope of the elections. Similar to the 1909 elections, each county was its own district for the primary stage of the election process, and the quota of primary-stage winners was apportioned on the basis of number of registered voters. The formulas used to determine primary-stage winners, however, were modified to reduce the total proportion of votes needed for one to be elected: in 1909, the number of ballots needed to win was equal to half the number of ballots cast divided by the number of open spots, but in 1912, this was revised downward to one-third of the ballots cast for the provincial legislative and national parliamentary elections.[15] Thus, the new formula was:

$$\text{Minimum number of votes to win} = \frac{\text{Number of valid ballots cast}}{3 \times \text{county quota of primary-stage winners}}$$

The total number of primary-stage election winners was dramatically increased at the same time. In 1909, it had been ten times the size of the provincial assembly (in the southern Jiangsu election that year, the 66-member assembly required 660 primary-stage winners): in 1912, the multiple was raised to 50 for the lower house parliamentary elections (Jiangsu, with a delegation of 40, was to elect 2,000 primary-stage winners) and 20 for provincial legislative elections (Jiangsu's new legislature of 160 seats thus needed 3,200 primary-stage winners). This was not mere fiddling; although the shell of the 1908 Regulations remained, the stage was set for a much larger election than the one held in 1909.

The revised electoral formulas suggested an intent to expand opportunities for participation, as had been pioneered in Jiangsu's postrevolutionary election laws; the loosening of suffrage requirements demonstrated that this was a matter of deliberate policy. A fierce, albeit ultimately lopsided, debate over the appropriate boundaries of the electorate occurred in the Provisional Senate. Some argued at length for the enfranchisement of all literate adult males. Li Fang (dates unknown), a senator from Jilin Province with ties to Sun Yat-sen's anti-Qing Revolutionary Alliance, claimed in a July 3 speech in the Senate chamber that the Chinese people had fought their revolution out of a desire "to expand popular rights and to demand political reform." Any attempt to limit those now by imposing strict limits on the franchise would represent "a betrayal of the revolution's meaning."[16] Five days later, when proposals on voter qualifications came to a vote, few of Li's colleagues concurred with his vision: only eight of the eighty senators in attendance voted in favor of "universal suffrage [*putong xuanju*]" for men.[17]

Virtually all agreed, however, that any new restrictions should be looser than those used in 1909. As one representative from Yuan Shikai's government testified in a Senate session, "[We] cannot all at once adopt a system of universal suffrage, but also cannot restrict suffrage too strictly."[18] The details of this had to be settled. The basic concept was enunciated early by Senator Wang Xinrun (1878–1959), a trained lawyer. Wang noted that according to international practice, two principles governed restricted electorates: the laws should be designed to enfranchise "those of independent means" and "those with learning."[19]

"Independent means" was defined in economic terms. The original proposal enfranchised taxpayers who paid at least two *yuan* a year in direct taxes, reflecting the phrasing of the November/December 1911 Jiangsu laws. Later an alternative qualification based on the ownership of at least 500 *yuan* of real estate [*budongchan*] was added. Together, these standards clearly paved the way for an increase in the electorate. Compared to the 1908 Regulations, the property requirement had been reduced by three-quarters and a new path, tax payments, had been added. Given that the vast majority of voters in 1909 qualified on the basis of the property requirement, these changes alone should have led to a dramatic expansion of the electorate.

Yet these reworded clauses, as some senators noted, had the perverse effect of potentially disenfranchising merchants who stored much of their wealth in assets other than real estate. In response to this issue, Hubei senator Zhang Bolie (1872–1934) moved to amend the property requirement to the more general standard of "capital [*ziben*]." Although this would have done nothing more than align this law with the phrasing of the 1908 Regulations, the chamber did not adopt his suggestion.[20] The Parliamentary Preparatory Office, charged with implementing and interpreting the election law, later defined "direct taxes" in the most restrictive manner possible. The office considered only two specific types of taxation, the land tax and the grain tax, to be "direct." The exclusion of commercial taxes, such as the internal tariff, from this narrow definition completed the disenfranchisement of merchants—including potentially some who had voting rights in 1909. Thus, although the new property requirements laid the groundwork for a sizable growth of the electorate, this expansion skewed toward the traditional rural elite rather than the emerging urban professional and business classes.

Enfranchisement of "those with learning" formed the second path to the ballot box. The initial proposal granted the right to vote to graduates of Western-style elementary schools, a lower standard than had been used in the 1908 Regulations. In response to objections that very few people had degrees of this sort, the Senate extended the franchise to those who held credentials "equivalent" to an elementary school degree; this was understood to mean the holders of any degree from the old civil service examination system. These degree holders, still numerous in 1912, had been enfranchised in 1909; their reenfranchisement in 1912 ensured another connection between the new elected government and the traditional gentry class.

The list of disqualifying characteristics was also largely inherited from the 1908 Regulations. As in 1909, people who used opium, were unable to write Chinese characters, had a mental illness, or had gone bankrupt, were disenfranchised. The law, however, did not provide a mechanism to determine the boundaries of such groups. The disenfranchisement of "opium users [*xishi yapian zhe*]," approved by the Senate without discussion, exemplified this.[21] As in 1909, authorities put special emphasis on the enforcement of this disqualification; during the registration process in October, Governor Cheng in Jiangsu specifically reminded registrars to exclude opium users.[22] Unlike 1909, the overtly moral disqualifications—such as those that disenfranchised on the basis of "impure" family backgrounds or occupations—were dropped. Beyond these, voting rights for people in certain occupations were restricted. Among these were occupations that had the potential to intimidate voters (such as judicial officials, police, and soldiers) or those who might have undue power over voters (such as ministers, Buddhist monks, and Daoist priests; elementary schoolteachers, who were allowed to vote but not run for office, were also in this category). In provincial elections, contractors who engaged in business with the government were excluded from the franchise; this prohibition, which the national law lacked, was the only significant difference between the voter requirements at the national and provincial levels.

After a series of deliberations in August 1912, the Provisional Senate adopted a set of three interlocking laws (the Republic of China Parliamentary Organizational Law, the Lower House Election Law, and the Provincial Legislature Election Law) that together specified the structure of and means of selection for the government's new legislative branches. The election laws for the lower house of Parliament, published on August 11, 1912, and those for provincial legislatures, printed on September 5, 1912, differed from each other only slightly.[23] These 1912 laws in turn were the basis for the subsequent national and provincial elections held during the following decade. Although the national government changed several times between 1909 and 1927, the legal architecture that undergirded elections remained stable throughout much of this period.

Signaling the democratic tenor of the moment, a variety of groups challenged these restrictions. The significantly more restrictive 1908 Regulations, by contrast, had not engendered a similar reaction. Women's suffrage groups, which had begun organizing themselves in late 1911 and early 1912, launched the most sustained protests. In March 1912, months before the Provisional Senate began drafting election laws, some of these groups surrounded the Senate's temporary chambers in Nanjing, demanding that the provisional constitution be revised to clearly affirm the equality of the sexes. Because voting had been specifically listed among the civil rights in the constitution, this would have created a strong legal foundation for women's suffrage. This first protest lasted several days and at times became rowdy; it did not, however, result in changes to any law.

When an enlarged, Beijing-based Senate took up the issue of election laws in July, activists resumed their push. Early that month, they petitioned the body on behalf of women's suffrage, although no senator proved willing to introduce the petition in session.[24] The debates over the election laws in the Senate resolutely ignored the issue of voting rights for women. Senators barely mentioned it during their discussion of "universal suffrage" and raised it only sporadically thereafter. The release of the election laws in mid-August sparked another round of protests, many of which was directed at the newly formed Nationalist Party for its unwillingness to invest political capital in the quest for women's suffrage.

That party's predecessor, Sun Yat-sen's Revolutionary Alliance, had negotiated a union with four other parties in August that resulted in a larger, but more moderate political party. One price of the merger was the abandonment of the Revolutionary Alliance's stated commitment to gender equality. This outraged female Alliance members, a number of whom had fought in the revolution. Two of these activists, Tang Qunying (1871–1937) and Shen Peizhen (dates unknown), charged the speaker's platform at the newly created party's first convention and, in the ensuing mayhem, slapped party leader Song Jiaoren (1882–1913).[25] This very public assault was widely reported in the press. Male columnists gleefully mocked Tang and Shen for weeks afterward.[26]

Despite the unveiling of the election law and the Nationalist Party's unfriendly platform, activists continued to push for suffrage. As late as November, activists brought another petition for women's voting rights to the Senate floor. The Senate angrily rejected it, with only six voting in its favor, and a Senate leader issued a strongly worded public condemnation.[27] Although no women legally voted in the first Republican elections, held only a month after the rejection of this final petition, a foundation had been built for a vibrant suffrage movement.[28]

Merchant groups also organized to object to their exclusion from the election. In early November 1912, representatives of business groups filed a petition, complaining that:

> A person with only 500 *yuan* worth of real estate gains the right to vote, but a merchant with commercial assets of several tens of thousands, several hundreds of thousands, or even several million *yuan* does not enjoy equal political rights with that person ... most of those [with only 500 *yuan* worth of real estate] are from remote villages and are not open-minded. If you compare [such people] to merchants and artisans who have lived in the cities for a long time, you will naturally see whose capacity [*chengdu*] is superior.[29]

If their demands for the franchise were not met, the petitioners threatened to withhold future tax payments. Despite this threat, merchant political activism proved no more successful than that of the women's suffrage movement.

Other groups had more luck. In October 1912, several Nationalist Party senators sought the disenfranchisement of men who still wore the queue, a hairstyle imposed by Manchu rulers in the seventeenth century and a hated reminder of their deposed imperial regime. One proponent of the measure argued that only "the ignorant" remained unwilling to change their hair. The only way to rid the country of this "evil custom," he averred, was to take the right to vote away from those who refused to cut their hair.[30] An outside pressure group of natives from one of the provinces that would be most affected by this change organized in opposition. In its petition to the Senate, the group claimed (implausibly) that although the queue itself might have "a connection to issues of hygiene, or to the ease of movement," the hairstyle itself was absolutely not "connected to politics."[31] Yuan Shikai mooted this senatorial debate with a presidential order that prohibited any restrictions on suffrage rights beyond those enunciated in the August law.[32]

Students also challenged aspects of the law. In July, senators had heatedly debated the enfranchisement of otherwise qualified voters who were currently enrolled as students. Such individuals had been denied suffrage rights under the 1908 Regulations. Proponents of ending this ban asserted that voting would provide students a valuable opportunity to engage with the political system. Others feared it would be disruptive, believing that "if students are given voting rights, then before elections it will be unavoidable that people will visit them and campaign for their votes" with the result that some students will leave school.³³ The August law ultimately enfranchised students, but it precluded them from being elected to office themselves. The opponents of this notion had anticipated correctly what would happen once voting began—students wanted to return home to vote, but some institutions refused to excuse them from class. In the northern cities of Tianjin and Baoding, affected students threatened to boycott classes in response.³⁴ The Ministry of Education backed school administrators but also sought guidance from the Provisional Senate. Legislators split the difference by mandating the continuation of regularly scheduled classes but allowing students to petition for leave (with any missed classes counted as absences).³⁵

The Provisional Senate's voting laws delineated the boundaries of acceptable attributes for citizens in the new Republic. The participation of disparate groups—educated women, merchants, queue-wearers, and students—in challenging these boundaries suggests that many of those excluded saw participation as a full citizen to be meaningful. This should not be overidealized; most if not all of these groups were motivated by self-interest as much as democratic zeal. The leaders of these groups engaged in self-aggrandizement, and it is uncertain how many people they actually spoke for. Yet none of this diminishes the value they assigned to voting.

Building Republican Voters

The Ministry of Internal Affairs ordered all provincial governments to begin the voter registration process in early September 1912 and to have completed voter rolls by October 10, the first anniversary of the revolution.³⁶ The Jiangsu government issued detailed instructions for registering voters soon after the national orders were circulated.³⁷ County governments established their own procedures and deadlines for conducting voter censuses. Shanghai County, for instance, set October 1–10 as its registration period for the national parliamentary elections.³⁸ As in 1909, county-level election preparation offices appointed registrars, who then conducted a door-to-door census to identify and enroll eligible voters. This was a complex process, but only a relatively short period of time was devoted to it. Numerous problems resulted.

Two days after voter registration began in Shanghai County, *Shenbao* editorialists wrote a damning critique of the census work in an unnamed county. They complained that "nearly every man with Chinese citizenship" in this county was being entered into the voting rolls, including habitual opium users, illiterate farmers, and even "mute orphans who sell fried-dough snacks." This process of unrestricted registration, the writer warned, would lead to charges of electoral fraud.[39] Officials in Shanghai County reported a preliminary voter total by the October 10 deadline, identifying 16,375 residents (about four times larger than the 1909 electorate, but still a surprisingly small number) eligible to vote for the lower house of parliament and the provincial legislature. It is suspicious that the two numbers are identical, given that the election laws specified slightly different criteria for the two electorates. The likely explanation is that only one survey was completed, using one set of criteria, and was declared acceptable for both.

The Jiangsu government submitted the entire province's voter rolls, listing approximately 1.2 million qualified voters (7.5 times larger than the 1909 electorate), to the central government in late October.[40] Revisions to these numbers were made constantly during a special reporting period in late October; these changes resulted in substantial modifications in the total number of voters. In Shanghai County, for instance, the county magistrate reported an astonishing 34,667 voters who had been left off the initial rolls, thus bringing the total number of registered voters in the county to 51,042.[41] A revised count issued on November 2 indicated that the provincial voter rolls held 1.8 million voters, or 50 percent more than just a few weeks earlier.[42]

The demands of surveying such a large group strained the capacity of local governments. As late as November 3, Governor Cheng was still pleading with counties to submit finalized lists by November 5.[43] Over a week after that deadline passed, five Jiangsu counties, including Wu County, had yet to comply, and as a consequence the civil magistrates of these counties received official demerits on their records.[44] Voter rolls in Wu County, which had been expanded earlier in 1912 by absorbing

Changzhou and Yunhe counties, were still not completed for several more weeks. On November 22, the county government posted the names of the approximately 63,000 registered voters (6 percent of the population) and invited citizens to check for mistakes, oversights, and omissions.[45] In 1909, slightly fewer than 6,000 voters had been registered in the same area. Not all counties could keep pace with this expanded electorate. Voter rolls were only barely finished before the election, but even then some areas of Jiangsu, such as the region around Nanjing, complained that they were severely underrepresented in terms of registered voters. At the end of November, six counties surrounding Nanjing unsuccessfully applied to the governor for another ten days to register additional voters, claiming that over 200,000 eligible people had been left off the rolls. The petitioners explained that "conducting the voter census is not easy work—there were no [preexisting] records of wealth and property, no thorough population census on record, and the [records] of educational qualifications are extremely misleading."[46]

Statistics reported by the national government in January 1913 indicated that Jiangsu's final tally reached 1,939,368 registered voters.[47] A later report, compiled by the Jiangsu provincial government in 1914, gave the total number of registered voters in the province as 1,950,368.[48] Some of this difference might reflect different speeds at which localities complied, edited, and submitted their voter registration lists; the rest could be the result of fraud, incompetence, or indifference. Such issues were not limited to Jiangsu; nearly every province reported multiple problems in conducting the voter census, and none finished before the original deadlines. Nationwide, approximately 10 percent of the population—nearly 41 million people, based on the statistics released in January 1913—was registered to vote, a twenty-five-fold expansion from 1909; in Jiangsu, registered voters comprised around 6 percent of the population, a twelve-fold increase.[49]

Some critics charged that the voter registration process was little more than fraud on a mass scale. Localities competed to have more registered voters on their rolls in an effort to gain additional representation in the provincial and national legislatures. An editorialist at *Shenbao* claimed that this impulse grew out of an overabundance of "localist sentiment" that drove people to seek advantage for their home area at the expense of the greater good. This ultimately was a "village mentality" that presented "a great obstacle to the election process."[50] While inflated voter rolls undoubtedly occurred everywhere, the comparatively small number of registered voters in Jiangsu—only 6 percent of the population in this relatively educated and wealthy province—suggests that it was not prevalent there. In other provinces, overenrollment clearly occurred: Zhili, for instance, reported a registration rate in excess of 20 percent of the population, an astounding figure given the restrictions on the franchise and almost certainly the result of fraud.[51] Like its Qing predecessor, which it resembled, the Republican voter census was designed to be an instrument of control and state-building—but serious institutional and procedural weaknesses made this an aspiration, rather than a reality.

As had been the case under the Qing, a combination of official agencies and nonofficial associations, including newspapers, worked together to educate the public about the election process. Election laws circulated in pamphlet form, sometimes with explanatory commentary, sometimes without. Some of these were commercially printed and then sold; newspaper ads for these pamphlets ran frequently and even offered discounts for bulk purchases.[52] Newspapers published the complete text of the election laws as part of their regular issues.[53] The government sponsored the printing and distribution of leaflets that explained the election and its importance.[54] The central government ordered Jiangsu Province alone to print over 60,000 copies of the presidential and ministerial statements on elections for distribution to eligible voters and to dispatch public lecturers to the counties to explain the election process.[55]

The goal was not merely to inform but to create and disseminate attitudes. State administrators and private reformers used public lecturing as a critical tool to spread ideas and information in a society where literacy was limited. Although references to public lectures abound in government orders, the relative paucity of records from the 1910s makes it difficult to determine the scope and content of public lecturing activities. Materials in Jiangsu are particularly lacking, despite the provincial legislature's allocation of funds for public lecturing. A 1912 lecturing manual from Hunan Province contains drafts of speeches that provided basic information about the new election laws and admonished voters to cast their ballots only for "a person you know to be reliable," rather than allow themselves to be distracted by "feelings" that would cause them to instead "vote, without any thought, for a friend or relative."[56] Collectively, these methods of public persuasion promoted the notion that voter preferences should be founded on a transcendent, universal concept of the public interest.

Even as they were critiquing the Republic's summer of elections, editorialists in early September 1912 proclaimed great hopes for the newly enunciated national and provincial legislative election laws. In a two-part masthead editorial in *Shenbao*, "A Message for Voters," the newspaper emphasized the talent-selection aspects of voting. Voters, the editorialists cautioned, must take their newfound "right to employ government leaders" seriously:

> If our country cannot make use of the truly talented, then it will be very difficult to strengthen ourselves. The truly talented are those who simultaneously possess the four qualities of scholarly ability, experience, trustworthiness, and fortitude. If our country has people who are truly talented, then voters must not fail to select them merely because of some personal opinion [*sijian*] that the voter might cling to.[57]

Voters were not electing people to represent them, nor were they being asked to select people who are similar to themselves; instead, they were expected to use their powers of discernment to identify people who were talented in an objectively measurable sense and then select those people for state "employment." This line of thinking was not limited to the relatively nonpartisan *Shenbao*; even Bao Tianxiao, the *Shibao* essayist who had mocked the process in 1909, now exhorted voters to select people who "understand law and politics, are eloquent in argument, are just and upright, and do not lust after empty glory."[58] The hope for political renewal sparked by the Revolution allowed even the most cynical to embrace the optimistic foundational expectation that elections could function as state-building rituals.

Political Parties and Political Coordination

The inability of most areas to elect a full slate of primary election winners on the first ballot in 1909 revealed a serious communication gap between candidates and voters. Without any formal organization, most candidates could not attract enough votes; even within a single county, few people had webs of personal connections and relationships extensive enough to provide the dozens of votes required. The dramatic expansion of the electorate in 1912 made organized structures, in the form of political parties, even more of a necessity. Without them, virtually no candidate would have been able to earn the hundreds of votes now needed. As in 1909, winners in multimember constituencies were determined by a formula, rather than by a plurality; thus, a party would have to have been concerned about making sure that enough party-affiliated electors received more than the minimum number of voter required to win. Voters would have to be managed.

The prohibition on political parties ended with the fall of the Qing. Even before the February 1912 abdication, various Jiangsu groups had organized proto-political parties, including one centered on Governor Cheng and Zhang Jian. The next several months witnessed a flowering of political parties; more than 300 were established that year, although only a handful were truly influential.[59] Later some of these parties began coalescing into larger units, but in an unstable and haphazard manner. Cheng and Zhang's initial party merged with another in Shanghai in early March, and then split to ally with a different party in May. The resulting party, now called the Republican Party, in turn absorbed several other parties in September to form one of the nation's larger parties. A substantial portion of the now-defunct Public Association's members, including Yang Tingdong, followed Zhang from party to party. The Republican Party; its rival, the Nationalist Party; and others functioned openly and freely in this period: they had offices, held meetings, wrote platform documents, and even advertised in the newspapers.[60] Most of all, they promoted candidates for election.

Some of this promotion occurred in public. Wang Shao'ao (1888–1970), a native of Wujiang County in southern Jiangsu and successful Republican Party candidate for the lower house of parliament in 1912, recalled years later the speaking tours he went on in his home region:

> As for election campaign activities [*jingxuan*] at that time, other than a few [candidates] who secretly engaged in bribery, most made use of open public speaking events. During the period when I was working for the Jiangsu military governor's office, I found the time to take over forty trips to [several areas in southern Jiangsu] to make campaign speeches.[61]

Wang, the scion of a literati family fallen on hard times, had studied in Japan during the final years of the Qing, only returning on the eve of the 1911 Revolution. Though earnest and diligent, the young Wang was hardly likely to draw a crowd on his own. To attract popular and press attention, major leaders of the political parties traveled around the nation, holding public rallies. In early November 1912, for instance, Democratic Party leaders Tang Hualong (1874–1918), former speaker of the Hubei provincial assembly, and Liu Chongyou (1877–1942), former vice speaker of the Fujian provincial assembly, journeyed through Jiangsu on a lecture tour. In Yangzhou around November 6, they reportedly attracted a crowd of "several thousand" to hear them explain "their political principles and their party's plans."[62] Two days later, Tang and Liu continued on to Nanjing, where they spoke to a crowd of 600 to 700.[63]

Much more occurred behind the scenes. In Yangzhou, Tang and Liu's arrival coincided with internal party elections for leadership positions, suggesting that their trip had an organization-building aspect to it as well.[64] Few details about such activities survive, but crumbs scattered in memoirs suggest that senior party leaders used occasions like this to recruit candidates. In the late spring 1912, for instance, Yang Tingdong traveled to the home of novelist Zeng Pu (1871–1935), a long-standing acquaintance of Zhang Jian's circle, to encourage him (successfully) to run for the provincial legislature.[65] Zheng Xiaoxu, the Public Association founder who remained a monarchist at heart, was privately approached by another Zhang Jian associate for a similar purpose in December. He bluntly refused.[66] Wang Shao'ao also had powerful patrons who almost certainly encouraged his run for office.

Once recruited, candidates spoke to voters directly. Wang Shao'ao recalled:

> The overwhelming majority of these speeches were held at teahouses or other public locations. The candidate would lead a group of people, who alternated between banging gongs and loudly shouting: "Such-and-such person from such-and-such party has come to give an election speech! All are welcome to attend!" When a crowd gathered to listen, the speech started. Sometimes, candidates from different political parties would come to the same teahouse at the same time; when this happened, they would divide the teahouse into two sections, and each would [simultaneously] give his speech.[67]

Unfortunately, Wang's evocative description of dueling speeches in a Wujiang teahouse provided no hint of content or rhetorical style. His emphasis on the significance of party labeling, however, suggests that identification with parties—many of them only a few months old—proved an effective strategy for gaining attention and support. Yet parties had limits to their organizational and ideological power in 1912. Though a member of the Republican Party, Wang had vocally opposed the party's convoluted strings of alliances with pro–Yuan Shikai parties. As a consequence, representatives from the party office asked him to withdraw from his race; after he refused, they attempted to "buy votes" away from him.[68] The local favorite, he won anyway.

Details from other localities suggest how "vote buying" might have been accomplished—or what it might have meant in practice. On election day, parties opened "rest stations" near the polls to interact with voters heading in to cast ballots. In Songjiang, party officials at the Nationalist Party and Republican Party rest stations "allocated ballot totals [*zhipei e piao*]," presumably spreading the support of party voters across the party's ticket. These offices also offered food, liquor, train tickets, and even a small cash bounty to those with voter identification cards.[69] Although universally deplored by newspaper writers, such coordination was a necessity, given the unforgiving nature of the ballot design. The ballots, similar to those used in 1909, provided only blank spaces in which voters could write any three characters they wished (see figure 8). The prevalence of homophone characters in the Chinese language meant that chaos could result in the absence of deft management. In Jiangyin County's provincial legislative election, for instance, some voters who intended to vote for one Zhang Mingchu (who wrote his name with the "ming" character meaning "brightness") accidentally voted for a different Zhang Mingchu (who wrote his nearly identical name with the "ming" character meaning "to engrave").[70] Similar instances of name confusion arose elsewhere.[71]

Attempts at fraud, effective or not, did not doom the election in Wang Shao'ao's eyes. His own experiences notwithstanding, he suggested that bribery was not the norm. Instead, he concluded sadly, the election itself was disconnected from the realities of Chinese society:

> The audience [for election speeches] was generally made up of local gentry or other people in the middle and upper levels of society. Rarely, a few

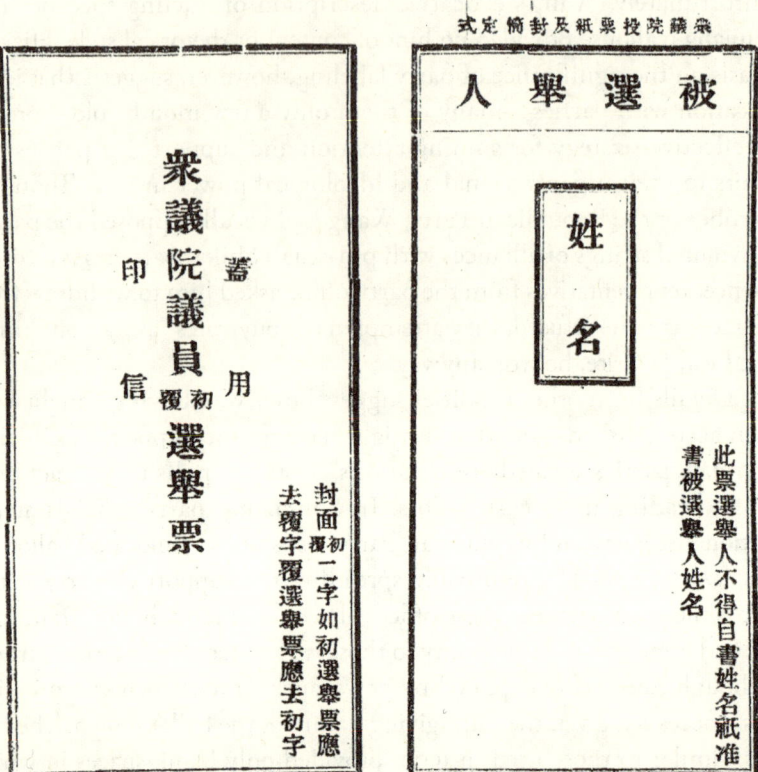

FIGURE 8: A model ballot for the 1912 parliamentary election. The front of the ballot (on the left) reads: "Lower House of Parliament Primary/Secondary-stage Election Ballot" and notes that the ballot should be stamped with an official chop. The back side of the ballot (on the right) has "Person Being Voted For" written across the top, provides a rectangle in the middle (in this version, marked with the characters for "family and given name") for the voter to write his choice, and reminds the voter in the lower right corner to write only the name of the candidate, not the voter's own name. Source: *Zhengfu gongbao*, September 21, 1912, mingling 3–14.

peasants would come to listen, but because the content of the speeches never interested them, some would just sit for a while before leaving, while others would sit but not listen.[72]

Wang's account of his run for office is unique; no other similarly detailed reminiscence exists. Yet the published version is dated 1961, well into the communist era, and concludes with the claim that real political change could only come under the leadership of the Chinese Communist Party. He could hardly have believed otherwise. Wang had joined the party in 1933, although his membership remained a secret to facilitate his political career in the pre-1949 era. It remained so after the establishment of the People's Republic, too. Even when persecuted during the Cultural Revolution, he maintained party discipline and continued his silence. Long after his death in 1970, his children discovered his real political allegiance; in 1981, Wang was eulogized in the *People's Daily*.[73] Wang's account of the first Republican election, particularly his emphasis on class politics, reflected the political realities of the Maoist era as much as those of the early 1910s.

Wang filtered his account of running for office through not only party ideology but also the specific complexities of his political position. He painted his younger self as an idealistic agent for change who had been deluded by bourgeois electoral politics. The reality suggests a much greater willingness to cooperate with existing power structures. Despite his self-proclaimed independence from the pro–Yuan Shikai Republican Party (as well as that party's final incarnation as the Progressive Party after May 1913), little evidence of his defiance remains in the historical record. In late 1913, after a failed Nationalist Party armed uprising against Yuan, the president purged hostile members from parliament. Wang's name did not appear on that list. Although he explained that he avoided this due to his refusal to cooperate with the Nationalists, perhaps more was at work. In May 1914, long after Yuan's dictatorial tendencies had become manifest, Wang was appointed to a Beijing-based court that investigated official corruption.[74] It is difficult to imagine such a position offered to an obstinate critic of the regime. Wang was undoubtedly an idealist, but perhaps the circumstances of his election did not reflect this—and in this sense, perhaps his career reflects the compromised nature of electoral politics.

Wang's Wujiang County and most others in southern Jiangsu held primary-stage elections for the provincial legislature on December 6, 1912. Election day reports for Wujiang are missing, but newspapers estimated that in Shanghai County over 20,000 people cast ballots out of the more than 50,000 registered to vote. Polling stations were packed with people, but initial reports do not mention fraud or abuse.[75] Unfortunately, no photographs of the scene on election day appear to have survived. Following days brought disturbing news from around the province. On December 8, *Shenbao* printed a long letter on its front page, with a big, bold headline, purporting to give the "inside story of the primary-stage election" in nearby Huating County. Using a pseudonym, the writer described a number of fraudulent activities that he claimed to have personally witnessed in Huating: single voters casting multiple ballots, people filling out ballots before entering the polling station, crowds of thousands damaging ill-prepared polling stations. He suggested that in the future, elections needed more of everything—more sign-in books, more tables, more ballot boxes, and more poll supervisors.[76]

Similar events were reported elsewhere. In Zhenjiang, many "strange phenomena" were observed, including voters who brought name cards with their candidate's name written on them into the polling booth. The magistrate in Yangzhou had to tear down fake government decrees that purported to cancel the election. In Changzhou city, citizens destroyed eight of the nine polling stations. Hasty election preparations (including a postponement of the election announced—and then rescinded—at the last minute), inadequate sign-in facilities for voters, and a mysterious plot by someone to deliberately crowd the doors of a polling station were cited as contributing factors.[77] The governor punished the new magistrate with an administrative demerit.[78] Wujin County, which encompassed Changzhou, ultimately had to redo its primary-stage election for the provincial legislature on December 12, although that spawned its own controversies, resulting in a court case that still had not been adjudicated two days before the secondary-stage election.[79]

Although the situation in Wu County, where over 20,000 people were initially reported to have voted in Suzhou city alone, seemed calmer, reporters on the scene noted that political parties had set up "rest stations" near the polls to provide voters with tea and snacks.[80] *Shibao* provided a very different account of the same election; it claimed widespread voter fraud that involved 20 percent to 30 percent of the people who turned up at the polls attempting to use someone else's name to vote. Noting the presence of "rest stations," the paper decried the "shameful conduct of behind-the-scenes campaigning" that happened there, concluding that "it is really unbearable to discuss." A subsequent article reported that 12,000 people came to vote at the Suzhou city polling station, but 4,500 of them were not allowed to vote because they failed the age or residency requirements or were using false names, so only 7,791 ballots were cast, not counting 13 invalid or spoiled ones.[81] These two accounts are not easy to reconcile with each other, nor with the administrative commendation that the governor later gave the Wu County magistrate for his "diligent" management of the election process.[82]

Officials opened the ballot boxes for the Jiangsu provincial assembly election beginning on December 9. In Shanghai County, 12,329 votes were cast for the eighty-three primary-stage elector spots; this was both noticeably less than the 16,000 to 20,000 votes that newspapers had estimated on election day and significantly less than the 56,000+ registered voters in the county. According to the primary-stage election formula stipulated by law, a minimum of fifty votes was required to win. In Wu County, 16,583 votes (representing approximately 25 percent of registered voters) were cast in the election for 104 primary-stage winners; a minimum of fifty-four votes was required to win. Wu County filled all 104 of these positions on the first ballot, with the highest vote getter receiving 637 votes and the lowest winner receiving sixty-four. Beyond these 104, an additional twenty-two people received more than fifty-four votes; they became alternate primary-stage winners.[83] The absence of run-off elections, which had been the norm in 1909, is evidence of the success of parties in coordinating the 1912/1913 elections.

Primary-stage elections for the lower house of the national parliament were held just a few days after the provincial legislative elections. Similar to the provincial elections, initial media reports from Shanghai were positive.[84] Shanghai County's second polling district, for example, reported that the election was orderly and the process was much better than for the provincial elections.[85] Other counties, such as Huating, reported problems.[86] In Wu County, 25,584 ballots were cast in the primary-stage parliamentary election. All sixty-three elector seats were filled, with a minimum of 136 votes required for each seat. In addition, seven alternates were selected.[87] No newspaper account of the election in Wujiang County, where Wang Shao'ao ran for his parliamentary seat, survives. The province's civil commissioner reported in late December that primary-stage elections for the national and provincial elections had been completed, but that "in several counties, there were one or two balloting districts in which the election results were invalidated," thus necessitating revotes.[88] The last of these was completed by the first week of the new year, bringing the freest election in mainland Chinese history to a close.

Nearly two years after the December 1912 primary-stage elections, Jiangsu's Internal Affairs Bureau compiled county-level data from the elections. The information was far from complete: ten counties, out of sixty, were missing some or all of their information. Many reported a substantial turnout of registered voters—Jiangning County, which included the city of Nanjing, reported that over 75 percent of registered voters voted in both elections—but in many others, such as Wujiang County, only 20 percent of eligible voters cast ballots in the provincial election and just 30 percent did so in the national parliamentary election. Province-wide, almost 1,172,000 valid ballots (representing 60 percent of the registered voters) were cast during the provincial election and approximately 1,150,000 (59 percent of registered voters) in the parliamentary election. Statistics reveal the chaotic side of the election, too; some counties reported extraordinarily large numbers of invalid ballots. In the mismanaged Wujin County provincial legislative election, nearly one in every nine votes was counted as invalid. In a handful of counties, more "invalid" than "valid" ballots were cast.[89] It is not easy to know what these numbers represent—in some localities, when combined with available government reports and newspaper articles, they suggest that the election failed to meet any minimally credible standard for fairness; in other places, they reveal a fairly successful (but not flawless) election. This muddled record of success and failure might appear to a twenty-first-century reader as normal, if not promising, for a nation transitioning from autocratic to democratic rule. In early twentieth-century China, however, few (if any) held such views.

Talking Freely about Elections

Writers at major Shanghai newspapers built a narrative out of the more disturbing of these statistics, buttressed by anecdotes of electoral misdeeds. These writers were typically not reporters, as the term is generally understood, but essayists, editorialists, and even fiction writers. The pithy

"Timely Commentary" essays that decoded the 1909 elections remained an important source for analysis, but images of this election were predominantly created by a new genre of newspaper writing: *Shenbao*'s "Free Talk" page. First introduced in the August 24, 1911, edition of that paper, "Free Talk" soon became an engine of the Shanghai literary scene. In the beginning, "Free Talk" page editor Wang Hui (1888–1950), better known by his pen name "Blunt Root [Dungen]," focused on cultivating writers with a particular ethos. Writers worked in a variety of styles—lengthy serialized short stories, poems, witty epigrams, and cultural commentary—but strove to maintain a distinctive "Free Style" voice in each. That voice could be jaded and cynical, although at times also strikingly naive; it both mocked and embraced the foibles of contemporary urban life. It was not necessarily a political voice, but it was not entirely apolitical, either—and the spectacle of the Republic's first election quickly proved to be irresistible to these skilled writers.[90]

Even during the Republic's first tentative experiments with elections in the summer of 1912, "Free Talk" writers expressed unease about voting. One of "Blunt Root" Wang's earliest colleagues, Xu Tai (ca. 1880–?), incorporated this sense of ambiguity in a pair of witty September 1912 essays written under the playful pen name "Skinny Butterfly [Shoudie]." First came "Skinny Butterfly's Ten Delights," a list of enjoyable activities that included reading "without seeking deep comprehension," getting "a little rowdy" after drinking, and discoursing with "famous scholars and beautiful women." He ended on a more serious note, explaining that he also "delighted in freedom and equality within the bounds of the law" and of course "reading and writing for 'Free Talk.'"[91] A second essay, "Skinny Butterfly's Ten No's," immediately followed:

> No smoking (either "Chinese" or "Western"), no infidelity, no gambling, no joining political parties, no "Go" or guessing games, no making the wrong friends, no false speech, no religion (of any kind—Confucian, Buddhist, Daoism, Protestantism, Islam, or Catholicism), no betraying morality, and no voting (I willingly give up my rights).[92]

This odd menagerie of likes and dislikes mixed the sublime and the frivolous, yet cohered into a rough portrait of an aspiring urban sophisticate. Skinny Butterfly, despite the traditional scholar's robes he favored, was not a reactionary: he welcomed the Republic and its values, but put elections is the same category as opium and lying. This proved to be a difficult balancing act.

This attitude infused "Free Talk" discussion of the Republic's unfolding electoral experiment in late 1912 and early 1913. "Free Talk" provided some of the most sustained and intellectually consistent discussion of these elections anywhere in print. The combination of fiction and commentary, both anchored in current events, found on the "Free Talk" page attempted to paint a larger picture. Writers like Skinny Butterfly found much to mock in the behavior of voters and candidates. By writing stories and semi-fictional essays inspired by real events, they universalized the import of particular incidents. The power of these interpretations is difficult to measure, but it was real; over the next years, many of these same writers defined the mental universe of the "petty urbanites" who made up urban China's new middle class.[93]

As a whole, "Free Talk" authors channeled much of the same critical tradition as "Timely Commentary" writers had in 1909. They also (if unknowingly) reflected the discomfort with campaigning evident in the writings of nineteenth-century Qing diplomats. They added to these a whiff of the fantastical and the derisive. Just before the first elections in early December, for instance, a "Free Talk" writer drew up a set of satirical "rules and regulations" for a fictitious Research Association for Election Campaigning. This institute, devoted to "the general diffusion of knowledge about election campaigning" was open to any willing to donate large sums of money and offered to run educational courses on subjects such as "bragging, flattery, fraud, currying favor with authorities, secrecy, and spending money."[94] This parody evidently amused readers; another author wrote a similar one just after the December elections concluded.[95]

Postelection writings further refined and reinforced these images. A "Free Talk" satire published the day after the official ballot counting began in Shanghai, titled "A Record of Many Laughable Scenes from the Election," gave snapshots of the comic failings of all participants—voters, election officials, and candidates—in the Jiangsu provincial legislative election. Like all such commentaries, this text did not mention any specific places or people; the intention of the author (about whom nothing is known) was to point out election archetypes. Among these are the backward voters ("Villagers arriving at the polling station, wearing queues and dressed in traditional clothing—Laughable!"), opium-addicted voters ("Entering the polling station with the wan and sallow face of an opium smoker—Laughable!"), and voters casting ballots for candidates of high social status ("Villagers going to the polling station and asking one another in a flurry, 'Who will you vote for?' Some say, 'Old Master Such and Such'; others say, 'Young Master Such and Such,'—Laughable!"). Those who campaigned were mocked for bribing voters ("Campaigners buying train tickets for voters—Laughable!") and bringing voters to the polls ("Enticing people to vote in the same way pimps find clients for whores—Laughable!").[96]

As primary-stage votes for the national parliament were counted across Jiangsu, pointed criticism of "campaigning" continued in the Shanghai press. In a "Free Talk" rumination on election campaigning, self-proclaimed nonvoter Skinny Butterfly repeated the by-then-standard complaint that although voting was important "for the future of the nation," voters had "treated it like a child's game." This, he hinted, was not necessarily a failure of elections as a system but a result of the corrupting influence of Chinese election campaigners. In a breathtaking display of naiveté, he claimed that election campaigners in other countries, such as the United States or France, were "generally enthusiastic for benefiting their countries and people." Chinese election campaigners, by contrast, "made their sole goal the search for personal fame and profit." Although some might also be men of talent, the majority, Skinny Butterfly assured readers, merely coveted "the title of legislator" and "the benefits of being a legislator."[97] Beneath his world-weary exterior, Skinny Butterfly held idealistic expectations for how elections should work and found observing voting in practice to be profoundly disillusioning.

These attitudes were no longer limited to newspapers published in Shanghai. The dramatic expansion of newspapers since 1909 created a lively press culture in the smaller cities of southern Jiangsu that produced their own "Timely Commentary" essays and "Free Talk"–style satires. After primary-stage elections for the national and provincial legislatures were held in Changshu, the lead editorial in one local paper claimed that the election had been marred by "campaigning by banqueting and cash payments." All of this, the editorialist claimed, created a situation in which "morality and proper human relationships were ruined by the election."[98]

Other local newspapers such as *Xibao*, published in the industrial city of Wuxi, carried similar commentary. A *Xibao* political cartoon depicted a voter selling his vote; the caption bemoaned voters susceptible to "campaigning by money [*jinqian yundong*]," who would "vote for anyone, regardless of whether he's an upright man or a thief, as long as they get paid."[99]

Secondary-stage elections in Jiangsu were originally scheduled on January 6, 1913, for the provincial legislature and January 10, 1913, for the national parliament. Given the disruptions of the primary-stage elections, a number of regions postponed these votes. In Jiangsu's second district, which included Shanghai County, the secondary-stage election was postponed five days, until January 11, after it was discovered that three of the provincial legislative primary-stage winners were not registered voters.[100] As preparations for these elections began, they were also mocked; one "Free Talk" essay created parody advertisements from primary-stage election winners looking to sell their votes in the secondary-stage election to the highest bidder.[101] Nonspecific allegations of vote buying appeared in the *Shenbao*, with one editorial even quoting alleged prices for different seats.[102] Short fictional pieces mocking elections filled the "Free Talk" page in early January, all following similar themes. In "Auctioning Primary-stage Election Winners," "Blunt Root" Wang reimagined the secondary-stage election as an auction for Republican- and Nationalist-brand goods.[103]

"Free Talk" and "Timely Commentary" writers alike pointed to campaigners as the proximate cause of electoral corruption, but many also identified a more fundamental origin: the moral flaws of voters themselves. One *Shenbao* commentator, writing in the wake of the second district's election postponement, provided his own analysis of "voter psychology":

> Although I am not a voter, I can basically understand the psychology of the average voter. The best voters have their own beliefs, are not dominated by political parties, and are not swayed by campaigning. Fundamentally, they think their own thoughts. The next best kind of voters are those who adopt the ideas of a political party as their own ideas. Beneath them are the kind of voters who are immersed in a "village mentality" and who take on a localist mindset. Worse than these are those who are greedy for

friends ... and place personal relationships at the center of their worldview. The worst are voters who have no thought at all, and are only in it for the money. Based on the current situation [i.e., the just-concluded elections], voters with no thought of their own make up 60 to 70 percent of all voters, and not even one out of every hundred voters follows their own thoughts. For those who don't believe this, just look at today's voting in the Jiangsu second [provincial legislative] electoral district secondary-stage election.[104]

This piece was unsigned, rendering the author's claim to have not been a voter uninterpretable (did he refuse to vote, like Skinny Butterfly? Or did he fail to qualify?), but his psychological profile of the electorate resonated with much in the "Timely Commentary" and "Free Talk" traditions, as well as with the foundational myths both drew from.

Jiangsu's elections concluded by early February 1913; around that time, all elected provincial and national legislators from the province met for informal discussions in Nanjing.[105] After the election, the Jiangsu provincial government evaluated the performance of county magistrates, who had responsibility for managing primary-stage elections; magistrates in twelve of Jiangsu's sixty counties received administrative commendations, while magistrates in six other counties received demerits.[106] The *Shenbao* writing staff's assessment was much more negative. Observing the results of the voting, the paper claimed that all those who had been elected were either partisans of a particular political party or a specific locality or were merely the adherents of the "principle of money [*jinqian zhuyi*]."[107]

Whether such accounts were exaggerated or not, some strange things had clearly been afoot in this election. Yang Tingdong, who lived in Shanghai but hailed from Suzhou and had been sent to the Qing provincial assembly from Suzhou prefecture, was elected to the lower house of parliament from an entirely different part of the province. The circumstances around this event were particularly suspicious. The three lowest vote-getters (Yang among them) had tied, so the election supervisor was compelled to select one for the last remaining seat by drawing lots. Yang won this game of chance to the approval of the crowd observing the election. Was it just a coincidence that Yang's patron, Zhang Jian, was another winner in the same secondary-stage election and that the election was held in Zhang's home region?[108] Was Yang's election the result of fraud? Of cunning planning? Or did it reflect the community's appraisal of his intellectual suitability? The vision of elections idealized by reformers for decades emphasized that elections would result in communal harmony—in this instance, however, they only resulted in confusion. As in 1909, Yang Tingdong's career presents an unsolvable conundrum: did his success represent a fulfillment or a violation of the fundamental expectations that most held for elections?

Conclusion

Before the elections had even concluded, Yuan Shikai offered a bleak assessment of the election process. On December 15, as reports of disturbances during the primary-stage elections reached him in Beijing, he issued a public statement condemning people who, in "competing for election," created public disturbances, seized ballot boxes, damaged polling stations, or otherwise disrupted the election. Yuan claimed the origins of this could be found in the conflicts generated by the "different opinions of the political parties" and the "divergent ideas of the localities." Such narrow interests, he warned, could not be allowed to interfere with "the sacred and momentous task of building the Republic of China."[109]

High-minded pronouncements notwithstanding, competition between political parties dominated the election. In the contest between parties, the Nationalists emerged early with an organizational and ideological edge. That party's nationwide election efforts had been tirelessly coordinated by Song Jiaoren, the slight, mustachioed native of Hunan Province who had been slapped by suffrage activists in August. A hardened veteran of the anti-Qing revolutionary movement who was entranced by the notion of elected government, he enjoyed electioneering in a manner thoroughly unlike many of his contemporaries. At the Nationalist Party's founding convention in August, he had proposed that the party create an "Election Department [*xuanju shiwuke*]" for the upcoming contests, modeled after similar structures in Western political parties. Nothing came of this suggestion; it was opposed by another party founder, who reasonably claimed that "Chinese society views election campaigning by political parties as distasteful."[110] This rejection did not dampen

Song's enthusiasm for "campaigning," however; unique in his era, he embraced that term. As late as February 1, 1913, after weeks of "Free Talk" mockery of the term, Song publically exhorted Nationalist Party activists in Hubei to: "Stop all other activities and focus everything on election campaigning [*yundong*]. Competing for election is an open thing, an honest and upright thing. There is nothing suspicious to hide or to speak carefully about."[111] With the completion of secondary-stage elections across the country in the weeks following this speech, it became clear that his strategy had succeeded in making the Nationalists the largest party in the national parliament. Song had long made known his intentions to assert the authority of the legislative branch to restrict Yuan Shikai's power as provisional president. The thirty-year-old Song looked forward to using his newfound authority to restructure the central government, perhaps as prime minister.

This was not to be. An assassin shot him at the Shanghai railway station on March 20, 1913, and he died two days later. Though a Nationalist-dominated parliament was seated that April, conflict between the Nationalist Party and Yuan's government escalated into warfare as it moved from the legislative chamber to the battlefield by late summer. Nationalist armies were defeated, party members were expelled from parliament and the provincial legislatures, and many fled into exile in Japan, vowing to return. It seemed that the bullets that felled Song brought down Chinese democracy, too.

Significant, serious, and sustained challenges to the legitimacy of the 1912 elections, however, were widespread before the assassination of the much-mythologized dapper young campaigner. Newspaper editorialists were dismayed by the number of voters who were willing to cast ballots for reasons they considered illegitimate; campaigning of all sorts, as an activity that persuaded voters to select candidates for reasons other than an objective assessment of the public good, was seen as anathema to the health of the republic. As "Blunt Root" Wang opined in "Free Talk," "Elections based on campaigning [*yundong*] are incompatible with the truth."[112] His pithy statement reflected a long tradition of anxiety about voting, yet it was becoming increasingly apparent that campaigning was necessary for and inseparable from elections.

That tension—visible in newspaper editorializing intended for a mass audience, yet rarely mentioned by the elite intellectuals who shaped (or hoped to shape) the structures of government, was evident in both the Qing elections in 1909 and the Republican elections in 1912. It carried more troubling implications in 1912 than it had three years earlier; the Qing court had actively resisted the idea that sovereignty lay with the people, but the Republic had embraced the notion. As a consequence, the successful operation of elections had become crucial for the new government's legitimacy. This new purpose was grafted onto a continued expectation that elections could provide a conduit through which the state could guide and transform the people—and the belief that electoral competition would undermine this.

CHAPTER 5

Warlord Democracy

Coercion and Coordination, 1913–1921

After Yuan Shikai quelled the 1913 Nationalist-sponsored mutiny, a nervous and chastened parliament gathered in the capital. It formally passed a presidential election law on October 4 and, under the watchful eyes of soldiers, elected Yuan to that position two days later. Three ballots were required before the provisional president received the necessary support to become the first formal president of the Republic. Yuan soon retaliated. On November 4, he ordered the dissolution of the Nationalist Party's organizations and expelled party members from parliament. He issued a lengthy justification for these actions, pointing to the summer uprising and the party's conduct during the election. Yuan accused the Nationalists of "competing for election [*jingzheng xuanju*]" through the use of "enticements," "intimidation," and even "guns and bombs." In several southern provinces, the president claimed, the party stole control of the election process from "the will of the citizens." Those elected thus "knew their party rather than the nation, the individual and not the collective."[1]

An undersized parliament met again on November 10, but that proved to be the last session during Yuan's lifetime.[2] A formal presidential order for dissolution came two months later. Yuan charged the legislature with an inability to confront the serious problems facing the new Republic. The root cause for this could be found in the "beginning of the selection of members of parliament," during which those who "struggled for power, hewed to their party's line, and were heedless of the fate of the nation or the well-being of the people" seized the advantage from those more able to serve the public good.³ In the following weeks, Yuan used similar justifications to disband elected provincial and local legislatures across China.⁴ By the end, as one *Shenbao* writer well known for his political activism lamented, everything necessary for "a republican state"—political parties, a parliament, an independent cabinet—had "all been overthrown."⁵

Yuan's dismissal of the Republic's earliest representative institutions, however, was not a rejection of elected bodies entirely. Even as he dissolved the legislature, he promised the creation of a better one. Many allies linked to him through long-standing ties solidified during the constitutionalist struggles of the late Qing remained at his side. Despite the Nationalist Party's standing in the national parliament, the mutiny of Nationalist-affiliated military units in summer 1913 was not a popular rebellion, nor did it reflect widespread discontent. Many supporters of constitutionalism (and, by extension, elections) remained in Yuan's cabinet during this revolt, from Zhang Jian to the ubiquitous Liang Qichao. Liang and several others resigned from their cabinet positions in February 1914, but they retained other positions in government.

Zhang, appointed minister of Commerce and Agriculture in September 1913, remained in office until April 1915, despite misgivings about Yuan's increasingly autocratic tendencies. Nonetheless, Zhang held on to one national office, director of water conservancy, until nearly the final months of Yuan's rule. His associate Yang Tingdong also lingered in Yuan's orbit for years. Claiming "spiritual distress," Yang had attempted to resign his parliamentary seat on September 23, 1913, the same day he joined other Jiangsu representatives in complaining about the ongoing military occupation of the Nanjing region.⁶ This would seem to align him with Yuan's opponents, as the army had seized Nanjing earlier that month only as a result of the Nationalist uprising. Yet in November, Yuan appointed Yang to an advisory body meant to replace parliament; Yang left that position in December to become the national director of mines, where he again worked closely with Zhang Jian until his resignation (for unknown reasons) in late July 1914.⁷ Throughout this period, proponents of voting persisted in thinking that elections could play an important role in building the state. Surprisingly, Yuan Shikai was among them.

Elections for a Dictatorship

Initially, such expectations may have seemed far-fetched. By early 1914, Yuan had restored a measure of fiscal, administrative, and military unity to the country that no other regime before 1949 was able to equal. This came at a cost: he freely used press and mail censorship, the secret police, and martial law to maintain a hold on power.[8] To cloak his government in legitimacy, he issued hastily written election laws for a constitutional convention at the end of January; these laws, he claimed, were "consistent with our country's tradition of selecting the worthy and the able [*xuan xian yu neng*]," harkening back a foundational expectation for Chinese elections. Despite the facade of balloting, these laws broke with immediate past precedent by empaneling tiny electoral colleges—made up of as few as twenty voters per province—to select convention delegates.[9] Delegates selected at these minuscule meetings gathered in Beijing on March 18, less than two months after the laws were issued, and produced a constitution on May 1.

Although the new system of government was designed to radically strengthen central power, this constitution still outlined a recognizably republican form of government. The right of the people to vote and be elected to office continued to be listed among the guaranteed rights of Chinese citizens, and legislative power was assigned to an elected national Legislative Yuan. In June, the convention began deliberating an election law for that body, but would not issue a final law until late October. The government representative charged with introducing draft legislation alluded to the experiences of previous elections, arguing that "if [a legislative body's] organic laws are not appropriate to our national conditions, or if elections [for that body] excessively depart from the will of the people, then not only will this not help solve national affairs, it could cause hidden problems to grow."[10]

In practice, this vague philosophy meant the restoration, in large measure, of the 1908 Regulations, with specific modifications based on the experiences of the 1912–13 elections. The electorate was reduced to those who met the 1908 standards, thus cancelling the expansion of suffrage introduced after the revolution. The two-stage, indirect voting system was maintained with a few modifications. Although the size of elected delegations was greatly reduced (Jiangsu was slated to send only ten representatives to the Legislative Yuan, compared with forty to the old parliament), the expansion of primary-stage winners and the reduced formula for election encoded in the 1912 parliamentary election law remained. Curiously, the prohibition on opium users was rescinded.[11] Subcounty election laws, operating on similar premises, were announced at nearly the same time.[12] Given the continuities between these laws and those of the late Qing, it is not surprising that Yuan retained the support of so many former constitutionalists well into 1914.

His election laws, however, broke with precedent in the adoption of "open ballot voting [*jiming toupiao*]," in which the name of the voter was recorded on the ballot. In previous elections, during the Qing and in the early Republic, balloting at the primary-stage level was secret [*wujiming toupiao*], in keeping with a global norm that had emerged from 1850s Australia. Fang Shu (1884–unknown), Yuan's representative at the convention, explained that voters would behave better if their names were recorded:

> With an anonymous ballot, there is absolutely no responsibility. If Person A campaigns with money, then Person A will be elected; if Person B campaigns with money, then Person B will be elected. [Voters] are not free in this kind of election. . . . If an open ballot is used, however, then there are things that the self-respecting will not do.[13]

Though only one part of a broader series of changes, this proposal was the first to attempt to check the prevalence of campaigning. To be sure, the transition to an open ballot was a form of control imposed by a strong-arm ruler—but it also drew on an idealistic conception of voter behavior. If forced to make their votes public, voters would be ashamed not to select the talented and virtuous.

Yuan's constitution required ratification by an elected Citizens' Conference. For the provinces, the just-drafted Legislative Yuan elections laws were adopted wholesale to elect this separate body.[14] Preparatory work for elections to both institutions began in mid-1915, and a slow, careful electoral census got under way. Survey work in Jiangsu started on July 18 and continued until September 15, with the finalized voter rolls certified by the provincial government around October 7.[15] The electorate identified in these surveys was much smaller than that of 1912–13. In Nanjing, it was reduced to one-tenth of the previous number, essentially the size of 1909.[16] In Yangzhou, only 300 people were registered, although many others believed that they met the requirements and petitioned for inclusion on the electoral rolls.[17] Tentative and limited as it was, the advent of registration represented a renewal of elections as a political system.

However, Yuan Shikai hijacked these elections for a different goal: by mid-1915, he had resolved to claim the vacant imperial throne.[18] As a first step, he repurposed the Citizens' Conference elections of late October and early November 1915 into a referendum on the nation's form of government. By the time voting began, his intentions were hardly a secret. Primary-stage elections for the conference, held on October 20 in Jiangsu, attracted only a small number of voters. In Shanghai County, for instance, a minuscule 407 votes were cast.[19] Primary-stage winners of the Citizens' Conference elections assembled in their respective provincial capitals, where they were asked to elect a Congress of Citizens' Representatives, a previously unheard-of body. Newly elected members of this congress received preprinted ballots with two options for China's future form of government: constitutional monarchy or republican government.

Jiangsu's delegates met in Nanjing on November 1 and unanimously voted in support of monarchy.[20] Similar scenes were mirrored in provincial capitals across the country; reportedly, no delegate anywhere cast a vote in favor of maintaining the Republic. This was unsurprising: Shanxi diarist Liu Dapeng (1857–1942), a representative to his province's congress, recorded that he and the other delegates had received specific instructions from supervising officials to vote for a monarchy.[21] Leaked telegrams revealed that such deliberate manipulation occurred nationwide at the behest of central authorities.[22] Once the results were collated in Beijing, the national government offered the crown to Yuan. After modestly declining at first, Yuan accepted and declared his intention to ascend the throne on January 1, 1916. Technically, he was not "elected" emperor—electors (although acting with no autonomy) selected a form a government, not the identity of the emperor. That Yuan felt the need for such a process, however, reveals the importance voting had acquired in the Chinese political imagination.

The would-be emperor, adopting "Abundant Constitutionalism [Hongxian]" as the title for his reign, ordered the previously scheduled elections for the Legislative Yuan and the Citizens' Conference to continue. In some areas, voting occurred, although the political situation had already become unstable. Even these elections attracted campaigners and their detractors. Liu Dapeng, recalled to the capital of Shanxi Province in December 1915 to fulfill his obligations as a secondary-stage elector for the Citizens' Conference, wrote disparagingly of the many campaigners, who, "shameless in the extreme," infested the city. Though his descriptions of campaigning focused largely on ostentatious banqueting and obsequious flattery, he noted that someone did attempt, unsuccessfully, to buy his vote. In the end, he was moved to lament: "Who says the election laws are equitable? All I see is campaigning."[23]

The institutions elected in December 1915 never met and they—like the rest of Yuan's agenda—were destroyed in a firestorm of opposition to his imperial pretensions. Yuan abandoned the throne in March 1916, but even this retreat failed to calm the situation. As armed rebellion erupted in China's southernmost provinces, Yuan's allies in the military and intellectual classes fled from him. He had not formally relinquished the presidency by the time he died suddenly in June 1916, but his regime had already crumbled. Although he rejected the institutions of the Republic of China, his vision of monarchical governance anticipated ruling through elected assemblies of talented and moral citizens. These legislatures would expand, rather than check, the power of the state. Yuan's autocratic instincts did not conflict with his vision for elections and in fact were compatible with the idealistic notions of late Qing constitutional thinkers.

Manipulation as Coordination

Yuan also created a new tradition of centralized electoral manipulation, targeted voter fraud, and organized intimidation; like the advent of political parties in 1912–13, these tactics attempted to solve the problems of coordination that had plagued voting since 1909. These stratagems outlasted him, although this was not apparent immediately. As Yuan's rule unraveled in 1916, pressure to reconstitute republican institutions grew. Beijing authorized the recall of the pre-1914 provincial legislatures in early April, during the twilight period between Yuan's March abdication and

June death. Many provinces dawdled through these chaotic months, only organizing the return of those elected in 1912–13 after the situation settled in Beijing. The coalition of former Yuan supporters that took power there quickly renewed the institutions of the early Republic. They reinstated the 1912 constitution, gaveled parliament to session on August 1, and rehabilitated the Nationalist Party members purged in 1913. Wang Shao'ao and Yang Tingdong reclaimed their seats in the lower house of parliament. The provinces followed, and the Jiangsu legislature opened its own session on October 1.

The reinstatement of the institutions created in 1912–13 and the recall of the specific people elected during those years was an attempt to repair a line of legitimacy that had been severed during Yuan's rule. At the local and provincial levels, this policy proved largely successful until the early 1920s. At the national level, however, this restoration quickly foundered. By the early summer of 1917, a dispute over China's participation in World War I—Premier Duan Qirui (1865–1936), a former Yuan subordinate, favored entering the war on the Allied side, but the Nationalist Party–led majority in parliament blocked attempts to declare war—led to a second forced dissolution on June 13.[24] Taking advantage of the chaos at the highest levels of the Republic, General Zhang Xun (1854–1923), whose anti-Republican political sympathies were manifested by his retention of the Qing-mandated queue hairstyle for the forces under his command, seized the capital. On July 1, Zhang proclaimed that the deposed boy emperor of the Qing, still living with a vestigial court in the Forbidden City, had resumed his role as China's proper ruler. This final attempt at an imperial restoration was crushed within two weeks, but Duan's returning regime opted to elect a new parliament rather than recalling the 1912 parliament for a third time.

To ensure a pliable legislature, Duan ordered a revision of existing parliamentary organizational and election laws in September 1917. The nature of the changes this government expected, as well as the reasoning for them, remained vague in these official statements.[25] Duan's decision split the country. Several provinces refused to participate in elections for a new legislature, which they considered illegitimate. Members of the old parliament, who had been summarily disbanded only a few months earlier, reconvened in Guangzhou on August 25, 1917, and elected Sun Yat-sen as president of China. The two governments, one in Beijing in the north and the other in Guangzhou in the south, each claimed constitutional sanction to rule the whole nation. As a result, no national-level institution was seen as fully legitimate for nearly another decade.

A Beijing-based Provisional Senate, convened at the end of 1917, debated and adopted revisions to the 1912 election laws in February 1918. The essential architecture of the 1912 parliamentary laws was maintained: a restricted electorate, voting indirectly, would select the lower house of parliament. Several adjustments were made. The election of members of the upper house of parliament, originally a prerogative of the provincial legislatures, was now entrusted to small groups of extremely wealthy voters. For the lower house, the financial requirements for voting rights were raised: in 1912, they had been set at either payments of 2 *yuan* in annual direct taxes or possession of real estate valued at 500 *yuan*, but in 1918 these values were doubled, to 4 *yuan* and 1,000 *yuan*, respectively.[26] Many of the other paths to enfranchisement, including the educational requirement, remained the same in the revised law. The size of legislative delegations was reduced; Jiangsu's shrunk from forty to twenty-seven. The clause excluding opium users from the franchise, a major feature of the 1909 Qing law and the 1912 Republican law, was dropped from the 1918 revision.[27]

The purpose of these changes is difficult to gauge, although it has been reasonably suggested that in total, they would make parliament easier to control (by reducing it in size) and disenfranchise supporters of the Nationalist Party (by raising suffrage requirements).[28] One practical implication of these cumulative changes was to create a difference between those who qualified to vote in national elections and those who were enfranchised for provincial legislative elections. In 1912–13, those electorates had been virtually identical; in 1918, the revision of the national parliamentary election law was not matched by parallel changes in the provincial election laws. The provincial legislative elections, scheduled for the month following the 1918 parliamentary elections, thus continued to use the 1912 election law. As a consequence, those who viewed the national election as illegitimate were still able to claim that provincial elections had a valid, legal basis. Election law at the provincial and the national levels would henceforth no longer move in lockstep.

The real difference from previous elections had nothing to do with the law. Weeks after the election law was issued in February, one of Duan Qirui's most trusted subordinates, the crafty military officer Xu Shuzheng

(1880–1925), transformed an existing "political club" located in Beijing's Anfu Alley into an unparalleled patronage machine. More organized, better financed (reputedly through Japanese loans negotiated by the old Qing constitutionalist Cao Rulin), less ideological, and significantly less scrupulous than the political parties of 1912–13, Xu's Anfu Club [*Anfu julebu*] set about to systematically steal the election on behalf of Duan's government. The meticulous Xu, working with parliamentarian and Duan ally Wang Yitang (1877–1948), constructed a nationwide network of offices and branch parties, building an unprecedented infrastructure for competing in the upcoming elections.[29] Anfu's liberal use of cash to purchase votes during secondary-stage elections has made its name a synonym for political corruption. The taint of this was so strong that in later years even core members of the organization disavowed any association.[30]

Neither a secret conspiracy nor a formal political party, Anfu existed on the edges of public consciousness as election preparation work began. *Shenbao* began reporting on the Anfu Club's activities only on May 7, nearly two weeks before the primary-stage election, noting that the club's "campaigners," flush with stipends of 3,000 *yuan* each, had departed the capital for their home areas.[31] Two weeks later, the paper reported that a dozen or so Anfu agents had arrived in Jiangsu, stocked with cash for the election campaign.[32]

The exact activities of Xu's Anfu agents before May remains hidden, but they must have at least observed the work of the legitimate authorities. In Jiangsu, a province-wide preparatory office for the national elections appears to have been established only in late March, but informal planning at the local level began earlier in the month.[33] Some registration work, conducted by local elites who held formal leadership positions in town and neighborhood governments, was completed by early April.[34] During the later portion of this period, candidates began actively seeking support; as early as April one source in Wujin claimed that "those who are bent on becoming members of the national parliament or provincial legislature are campaigning everywhere."[35] The lines between the local elites who managed elections, the "campaigners" who sought election, and the Anfu machine cannot be drawn precisely; it is easy to suspect that they had already begun to blur.

Some unknown portion of this voter registration process was fraudulent. Several incentives existed for the registration of nonexistent voters.

First, apportionment of legislative seats was based on the number of registered voters, not the entire population, in a county. Thus inflating voter rolls could result in allocating more positions within the legislature, to the potential benefit of local elites. Second, and of greater potential interest to an organized entity like Anfu, the number of blank ballots provided to a county was based on the number of registered voters. Excess ballots created for voters who did not exist could be stolen, filled in, and fraudulently cast. This strategy was employed with tragic consequences in northern Jiangsu's Funing County, where gentry, merchant, and student leaders conspired to inflate the roll of registered voters. On the day of the primary-stage election for the lower house of parliament, they attempted to cast these extra ballots, filled out with the name of the person to be elected, at the county's ten polling stations. One polling station manager refused these ballots and was subjected to abuse, humiliation, and threats. He later hung himself.[36] It is presumably not a coincidence that Funing was home to Jie Shuqiang (dates unknown), a provincial organizer for Anfu who was elected to Parliament.[37]

To curb voter roll inflation, the Preparatory Office ruled in late April that registrars could only enroll voters who could provide documented proof of their land holdings, tax payments, or education.[38] Amid continued complaints, the office soon ordered provincial governors to dispatch officials to selectively examine voter rolls and punish those involved in fraud.[39] In Jiangsu, Governor Qi Yaolin (1862–1949) attempted in early May to reevaluate each county's voter rolls.[40] On May 15, Jiangsu reported a final total of 2,779,600 registered voters for the lower house of parliament elections, approximately 800,000 more than in 1912.[41] On the surface, this figure (approximately 8.25 percent of the provincial population) does not appear unreasonable, given the specifics of the election law, but some portion of this expansion was certainly the result of fraud.

Despite the inflated voter rolls and the presence of Xu Shuzheng's Anfu machine, most newspaper accounts of the May 20, 1918, primary-stage election for the national parliament sound no different from similar accounts from 1909 or 1912. As in those previous elections, focus was directed on anonymous campaigners. In Wuxi, a local paper reported boisterous election day campaigning that included the "widespread distribution of name cards," exuberant greetings of people barely known to the candidate, and an accusation of cash campaigning.[42] Some candidates with "the fever to become a legislator," established "reception centers" near the polls, providing snacks and, in one case, entry tickets to an entertainment center. This supposedly proved incentive enough for one inventive person to vote thirty times. Wuxi's reports were not unusual for southern Jiangsu; similar ones can be found in Suzhou, Songjiang, and Yangzhou.[43]

After the primary-stage elections, the Anfu Club took an increasingly active and visible role. Within days of that vote, a local Wuxi paper diplomatically noted that a "certain club that has recently become famous" and had taken an interest in a few of Wuxi's primary-stage winners. This interest almost certainly took the form of cash. At the beginning of the summer, the Anfu Club distributed a total of 1.5 million *yuan* nationwide to influence voting; by the time parliament convened in August, it had spent a total of more than 9 million *yuan*.[44] Weeks in advance of the secondary-stage election, club representatives offered primary-stage winners in Jiangyin up to 700 *yuan* each for their votes in the secondary-stage election.[45]

Perhaps in response to such reports, unofficial "election monitoring teams" sprang up in some southern Jiangsu localities, ostensibly to observe and expose campaigning, corruption, and fraud. The earliest known team announced its presence in Wujin city on June 5 by an open letter in the local newspaper. As its first task, the team investigated rumors that secret agreements to buy and sell votes had been reached during the parliamentary primary-stage election.[46] It engaged in an active publicity campaign over the next weeks, arguing that "the quality of elections is connected to the survival of the nation," but also admitting that they had yet to "obtain evidence" of their accusations of vote buying beyond rumors.[47] A newspaper offered support, claiming that primary-stage ballots were selling for 200 to 300 *yuan* each, the result of a coordinated action to create a market in ballots.[48] Later articles alleged that campaigners, including "Mr. Liu from a certain company, the secretaries from certain guilds and organizations, and certain village headmen" had been involved, and they were planning on expanding their activities for the secondary-stage election to be held in Suzhou on June 10.[49] Were such monitoring efforts partisan in nature, thinly veiled in the rhetoric of adherence to the law? Or were they honest attempts at popular oversight of an election process corrupted by Anfu machinations?

The activities of such groups notwithstanding, corruption, vote buying, and fraud permeated the secondary-stage elections for the lower house of parliament. In some provinces, Anfu leaders circulated secret lists of their preferred candidates to provincial governors just before balloting began. A pair of June 7, 1918, communications from Xu Shuzheng to governors in Shanxi and Shaanxi provinces listed Anfu's preferred candidates for both houses of parliament, as well (in Shaanxi) as a list of people who should not be allowed to win a seat.[50] Xu did not intervene as brazenly in Jiangsu, but he did attempt to intercede there on behalf of at least one candidate.[51] Instead, Anfu affiliates within Jiangsu simply sought to buy the votes they needed. Jie Shuqiang, among other candidates, was accused in the press of bidding up ballot prices to over 300 *yuan* (as well as using other unspecified "base tactics") at the secondary-stage election held in Qingjiangpu. Other dramatic stories of electoral corruption circulated widely in the local press throughout June.[52] Unsurprisingly, the election resulted in a Jiangsu parliamentary delegation dominated by Anfu members.

Some had derided these national elections as illegitimate from the very beginning; the abrupt dissolution of parliament and the precipitous changes in the election laws deprived them of constitutional basis long before Xu Shuzheng set his Anfu agents in motion. This logic did not apply to the provincial legislative elections that occurred weeks later. They were held in accordance with the original 1912 legislation and occurred at the end of a legislative term. Newspapers, particularly those most critical of the "illegality" of the national elections, drew a strong contrast between that vote and the July elections for provincial legislature. One Wuxi editorialist writing in early June urged readers to participate in the provincial elections, stressing that they were "legal."[53]

Although the 1912 standards for registering voters remained in place, Chinese society had changed: inflation had changed the value of property, and a larger modern school sector had increased the number of people with degrees. Rather than being virtually identical, as they had been in 1912, the provincial electorate was now substantially larger than the electorate for national elections. Reports filed in May 1918 indicated 4,087,066 voters registered for Jiangsu's provincial election, over 1.25 million more than were registered for the parliamentary election.[54] This number was also distorted by fraud. A month later, the provincial governor postponed the election and dispatched investigators to northern Jiangsu in search of fabricated voter rolls.[55] These agents removed 196,000 names in four northern Jiangsu counties alone; tactfully, the governor attributed the enfranchisement of these voters to "misunderstandings about the law."[56] Even so, Governor Qi soon certified a provincial electorate of 4,015,717 people.[57] Though slightly less than the previously reported total, this final number was still more than twice the size of the 1912 electorate.

In the weeks before the elections for the Jiangsu provincial legislature, trepidation grew. In response, additional election monitoring teams organized. In northern Jiangsu's fraud-plagued Funing County, a team announced its existence on June 9.[58] Another, based in rural Anshang township, declared itself to the Wujin community through the newspapers on June 30. In an appended statement, a reporter from the paper noted that such organizations, strictly speaking, were not legal—but then went on to say that these groups, given their laudable goals, were very different from truly illegal organizations.[59] On July 8, Wang Qing (dates unknown), a Wuxi merchant who chaired the local chamber of commerce in the 1920s, called for volunteers to monitor that city's elections.[60] Wang's advertisement joined that of Jiang Zengyao (dates unknown), a Wuxi lawyer, on the front page of the local newspaper. Jiang promised to take, without fee, cases from provincial election voters who did not receive voter identification cards on the legally mandated date.[61] Jiang's policing effort may not have been entirely innocent; it is likely that he was a relative of Jiang Zengyu (ca. 1883–unknown), the founder of the newspaper that carried his advertisement, an elected representative to the 1912–13 parliament, and a member of the Nationalist Party. This hints that monitoring groups were not simply innocent expressions of public outrage but were themselves shadowy partisan organizations.

Complaints about the legislative elections filled newspapers across the province. In Wujin, one newspaper described cases of people casting other people's ballots and voters being plied with food and drink all coordinated by "lackeys and running dogs," one of whom, during a final burst of work, was "sweating like rain."[62] In total, 132,094 ballots were cast in Wujin County for 110 primary-stage winner spots; a minimum of 401 votes was needed to win. All 110 positions were filled, and 7 alternates selected, on the first ballot.[63] In Wuxi, large voter turnout in the city polling stations was reported, as were the usual reports of fraud, including the charge that one person had been buying "polling station entry tickets" cheaply from indifferent voters and selling them for a profit.[64]

Accusations and complaints about the primary-stage election for provincial assembly continued until the end of July. Of the ninety-four primary-stage winners in Wuxi, *Xin Wuxi* reported that more than ten of them had already been accused of failing to meet the legal qualifications to hold office; the paper asserted that even more had yet to be uncovered.[65] The most common reason for disqualification was the suspected use of opium; although the disenfranchisement of opium users had been deleted from the national parliamentary election law used in 1918, it remained in force for provincial elections. Wang Qing, initiator of the Wuxi election monitoring group, charged three primary-stage winners with opium use. At least one would later be exonerated by a local hospital.[66] Most of these challenges probably went nowhere; as one editorialist opined, "seeking a resolution to these disputes is truly a fantastic delusion."[67]

Within a week of the election, citizens from over forty of Jiangsu's sixty counties had complained to the provincial governor of irregularities.[68] The character of the complaints was generally local and particularistic. Focus was squarely on the candidates' and voters' moral failings. No linkage was drawn between national groups such as Anfu (or its smaller, less successful competitors) and this provincial election. Once assembled, the newly seated legislature bore little resemblance to the one elected in 1912. Only 25 members of the 160-member body had also served in the first legislature, a proportion even lower than the national parliament.[69] Unlike the 1912 parliamentarians, many of whom refused to recognize the legitimacy of the 1918 elections and thus still considered themselves to be China's true elected representatives, no one challenged the 1918 provincial legislative elections. Despite this, few were returned to the chamber's new session.

Money, perhaps, had made the greatest difference to the results. One editorialist at *Wujin* recorded the thoughts of "a certain political theorist," who claimed that

> In 1912–13, Chinese people had only the word "election" on their minds. They did not yet know that elections could be used to get filthy rich.... [Now] voters take making money as their goal, and those who seek office use money as bait... although the words "legislature" and "legislator" still exist, in reality there is only the bewitching power of money.[70]

Never before had a Chinese election been so thoroughly dominated by money. Earlier rounds of voting in 1909 and 1912–13 had experienced episodic, disorganized incidents of voter bribery, but nothing on the scale witnessed in 1918. Even more notable than the power of cash, however, was the emergence of two new organizational forms. The Anfu Club, although the source of much of this corruption, also represented a form of nearly nationwide coordination unmatched by any previous political party. This feat was not repeated for decades. At the opposite end of the spectrum, the seemingly spontaneous organization of local monitoring teams, even if perhaps colored by partisan associations, signified a continued belief that elections could be made to function as talent-selection mechanisms.

Idealism as Manipulation?

The parliament elected in 1918—referred to as either the "new parliament" to distinguish it from the "old parliament" seated in 1913 or as the Anfu parliament in recognition of the political club that dominated it—served only until July 23, 1920, when it was dissolved in the wake of renewed warlord conflict. A few weeks later, the Anfu Club was banned by presidential decree and its organizers dispersed to their various fates.[71] Some, such as financier Cao Rulin, left politics forever; others, such as mastermind Xu Shuzheng, soon met violent ends. After its overthrow, Anfu became a byword for greed and immorality, and its national infrastructure collapsed.

The new authorities that took power in Beijing during the summer of 1920 confronted the same problems of parliamentary and constitutional legitimacy that previous governments had faced. Like their predecessors, the leaders of the new government felt compelled to embrace elections as a strategy for solidifying their rule. Newly appointed President Xu Shichang (1855–1939; no relation to Anfu's Xu Shuzheng), a longtime Yuan Shikai lieutenant, issued a terse order in October for yet another round of parliamentary elections. This would restore the 1912 election laws but not allow members elected in 1912–13 to automatically reclaim their seats.[72] In mid-November, Xu directed authorities nationwide to prevent abuses that might undermine the election's goal of ensuring that "people who are whole-heartedly admired" by the public are elected to office. Through such efforts, the government hoped to avoid a situation in which "the structure of elections remains, but the spirit is lost."[73] Dates for the upcoming election, to be held in spring 1921, were set in late November 1920.[74] Xu's attempt to buttress his government by resetting the clock to 1912 was doomed from the beginning. Members of the first parliament still sat in Guangzhou, where they vigorously disputed the legality of a new election. Many southern provinces simply ignored Beijing.

Jiangsu, controlled by a warlord allied with Beijing, complied. These elections coincided with the long-planned triennial elections for the provincial legislature. The body elected in 1918 had continued to sit in Nanjing, despite the chaos at the national level, and discussion about the imminent expiration of its term had already begun in fall 1920. Preparation work for both elections began at the same time. Wuxi voter registration efforts began in late 1920, and the government was already revising and rechecking the voter rolls in January 1921.

Parallel with official preparation efforts, "election monitoring teams" began to reemerge. Though bearing a similar name to the entities that existed in 1918, these teams seemed more purposeful, better organized, and more tightly connected to the interests of Sun's Nationalist government in Guangzhou. As early as November 10, even before the dates of the national elections had been announced, Yangzhou native Xie Xiaoxian (dates unknown) issued an open call in *Shenbao* for a province-wide monitoring team.[75] The motivations of Xie, an early leader of the Boy Scout movement in China who was never elected to public office, are obscure. Those who took up his call had linkages to preexisting political parties. Yuan Xiluo (1876–1962), working with some two dozen allies, sponsored a late November meeting in Shanghai to organize the team Xie had proposed.[76] Writing as a "citizen" a few weeks later, Yuan petitioned the Ministry of Interior in Beijing to authorize his activities. The ministry responded coolly; monitoring elections was a prerogative of the government, not the citizens.[77] Yuan was much more than a disinterested citizen, however. He had joined Sun's Revolutionary Alliance in 1906, been present for Sun's inauguration as provisional president in 1912, and maintained strong enough ties to the Nationalists that once that party seized national power in 1927, he was appointed to a variety of county magistracies. He had personal ties to Jiangsu's constitutionalist elites, too: his elder brother, Yuan Xitao, was a prominent educator and one-time frequenter of *Shibao*'s Mansion of Repose.

More than forty people, representing fifteen different Jiangsu counties, gathered at the China Vocational School in Shanghai for Yuan's meeting on November 28. Copies of Xie's article and several responses printed in later issues of *Shenbao* were distributed, after which Di Fuding (1895–1964) led a discussion of the group's fundamental aims. Di had grown up near Shanghai, participated as a teenager in the 1911 Revolution, and graduated from Beijing University in 1919—and had taken part in that year's famous May Fourth protests in Tiananmen Square. In the mid-1920s, Di joined the Nationalist Party and served in a number of high offices both before and after 1949. At this meeting, Yuan, Di, and their associates attempted to place themselves above politics. Di listed "refusal to take elected office" as one of the group's two founding principles. The manifesto adopted at the meeting sounded a note of idealism, arguing that "if citizens want to save the country, we must rectify elections."[78] To prevent the abuses seen in every election since 1909, which had grown to epic proportions in the Anfu era, the manifesto suggested that rigorous monitoring by moral individuals was all that was needed. The problem was not with the lofty expectations many held for elections but with the boorish behavior of campaigners.

Despite the frosty reaction of the central government, the Jiangsu Citizens' Election Monitoring Team expanded throughout the province. By December 7, at least four counties had established affiliates, and many others had expressed interest. Attention turned to policing the voter registration effort, already under way, to prevent the falsification of voter rolls prevalent in 1918. Campaigning came into focus as a target; a newly formed monitoring team in Kunshan proclaimed its desire to "smash cash campaigning" in its first correspondence with the provincial team.[79] Weeks later, a local branch placed advertisements in a Wuxi newspaper, announcing that it would ensure the election "expresses the true will of the people and avoids the disasters of the last election." It noted that similar groups now existed in forty of Jiangsu's sixty counties.[80]

Election monitoring teams increased the pace of their activities in the new year. The provincial team sponsored a January 1921 publication of an election law handbook that included both the text of the election law and laws that specified the punishments for various types of election fraud; presumably this was designed so that members could carry it on their persons as they visited polling stations.[81] Public meetings, including one sponsored by the Wuxi team in a city park on February 12, 1921, occurred at the local level.[82] Despite such efforts, some observers remained skeptical the problems with elections could be fixed either by the government or through the efforts of the private groups. Instead, as one Wuxi newspaper opined, elections depended on the "good conscience of the voters themselves." In practice, this meant that voters should think of the interests of the nation, rather than allowing their vote to be swayed by money, food, or relationships with friends or relatives.[83]

It was to little avail. On the day of the election, one Shanghai observer claimed that falsified voter rolls had become the norm.[84] Anecdotal evidence supports this. The Wuxi County voter rolls listed 174,171 eligible voters (out of a total population of approximately 800,000) for the 1921 elections, 100,000 more than had qualified either under the more restrictive laws of 1918 or under the first voter census in 1912.[85] An astounding 171,305 ballots were cast in that county's March 1, 1921, primary-stage election for the lower house of parliament. Some of these were deliberately spoiled, such as those cast for the twice-deposed Qing emperor.[86] Total registration numbers from Wu County (with slightly more than a million residents) do not survive, but 223,332 ballots were reportedly cast in that county's primary-stage election; this number alone was nearly four times greater than that county's 1912 electorate.[87] Only two explanations are possible: either localities quietly decided to embrace universal male suffrage in violation of the law, or they engaged in fraud on a scale that eclipsed even the 1918 elections. The latter presumably is far more likely than the former. Voting in both counties manifested the same series of problems as previous elections—the vote in two of Wuxi's seventeen districts was declared invalid, and newspapers were rife with speculation about fraud, misdeeds, and electoral manipulation.[88]

Monitoring teams remained vigilant during the March 1 primary-stage election for parliament, filing complaints with the provincial government over observed improprieties and complaining about irregularities in fifteen different counties. Some monitors even attempted to intervene to prevent fraud; one, in northern Jiangsu's Taixing County, received a beating for his efforts.[89] Although the Shanghai-based provincial monitoring team included both Wuxi and Wu counties in its complaint to the authorities in Nanjing, it remained curiously silent about the election in Shanghai County. There, 77,368 votes had been cast on election day, a number that may seem small given the size of this highly urbanized area (population around 1.2 million in 1912) but seems reasonable in comparison with the 1912 electorate of 51,000.[90]

Within days of the election, however, Shanghai lawyer Yang Chunlü (ca. 1887–1932) filed suit against several members of the city's political establishment, alleging election fraud on a massive scale. Yang's background is obscure; there is no record of his activities before this lawsuit. He was not connected to the monitoring team in any apparent way, although the team later trumpeted the results of his suit in public telegrams to the national and provincial governments.[91] Much like the monitoring team, which had been prompted into existence in part by the platform provided by *Shenbao*, Yang may have derived inspiration from that newspaper's stance. The day after the election, one editorialist challenged "socially conscious individuals" to take up the task of cleansing elections by, among other means, filing formal complaints.[92]

He was not challenging the establishment alone. Yang's efforts were backed by the influential Shanghai educator Shen Enfu, a Mansion of Repose alumnus, affiliate of Zhang Jian's Public Association, and then-current member of the powerful Jiangsu Education Association.[93] Shen was no stranger to electoral politics. As early as 1909, he had been a candidate for the provincial assembly in his native Wu County; despite winning votes at the first several rounds of that election, he ultimately was not a primary-stage winner. He was close to many who did win, however, including Yang Tingdong. Days before Yang filed suit, Shen wrote an account of witnessing voting irregularities that was reprinted in *Shenbao* and later cited in Yang's court filings.[94]

Yang's initial petition to the court laid out a narrative of his experiences on election day. Arriving at his assigned polling place, he witnessed three large groups, each made up of thirty to forty "suspicious-looking" people, rushing in and out of the polls. After these groups left for a break, Yang snatched up nearly 250 polling station admission tickets they had abandoned on the ground. Upset, he could not bring himself to cast his own ballot. He visited two other polling stations instead, where he collected several hundred more discarded admission tickets. Some of these tickets, which were supposed to be individually produced for voters at the time of registration, bore identical names; many more were found in sequential order according to their identification numbers (unlikely to happen naturally, as voters would presumably not appear at the polls in the exact order in which they had registered to vote). Together, these activities suggested to Yang a comprehensive effort to stuff ballot boxes and steal the election.[95]

His account, the cornerstone of the lawsuit, failed to mention two pertinent facts. First, Yang himself was a candidate in the primary-stage election and had garnered enough votes to be declared an "alternate winner [*houbu dangxuan ren*]," a position that Chinese election laws created in the event that the actual winners could not fulfill their role. Ninth on the list of alternates, he may have stood only a small chance of receiving a winner's seat; nonetheless his lawsuit did not mention his personal stake in the election's results. Second, although Yang cited Shen Enfu's account as corroboration for his own claims, he never divulged any personal connections with Shen. No evidence exists to show that the two men met before 1921, but Yang and Shen came to have overlapping membership and leadership roles in a number of political organizations thereafter. Although it is possible that Yang came to Shen's attention through this lawsuit, it is more likely that Yang, a relative unknown, filed his case only after securing approval from this influential civic leader.

The support of established figures like Shen was necessary, given that Yang deliberately targeted three of the city's most powerful men in his lawsuit. The first, county magistrate Shen Baochang (1880–1935), was *ex officio* the election commissioner for the primary-stage election; his inclusion in this lawsuit was thus expected. Shen Baochang (no relation to Shen Enfu) did not appear in court, complied with orders to turn over evidence slowly, and generally appears to have been indifferent to this case. The other two defendants, Yao Wennan (1857–1934) and Lu Wenlu (1855–1927), had served as registrars during the election preparation period. The two men had long been prominent leaders in Shanghai's early twentieth-century "gentry democracy."[96] They owed their status to traditional means; they were members of the old gentry class, deriving power from their participation in the civil service examination system and managing various community projects, such as the compilation of a local gazetteer and the repair of Shanghai's temple for the city god. One or both had served on every Shanghai local government council that had ever been seated. Yao had been elected to the first Republican parliament and had won primary-stage elections a number of other times in following years. Both Yao and Lu, significantly, were among the Shanghai County primary-stage election winners this time, too.

Yang's case took weeks to resolve in March and April 1921. Several additional hearings were held, during which a series of technical questions about the election laws arose. After a lengthy correspondence with the national Supreme Court, the Shanghai local court ruled on April 15 that the county's primary-stage election was void. The thirty-one winners of that election, including Yao and Lu, were stripped of their victories. The court justified this invalidation on the basis of improper voter registration practices and sloppy voter sign-in procedures, leaving Yang and Shen Enfu's claims of deliberate fraud unaddressed.[97] Regardless, this verdict was remarkable, perhaps even unprecedented. Qing and Republican lawmakers had drafted procedures for electoral disputes and the invalidation of electoral results, but this may have been the first time that such codes were used by a court of law to cancel the entire outcome of a particular vote.

Given its unusual nature and dramatic result, public attention in Shanghai focused on this trial and its verdict. Some found the whole affair distasteful—one *Shenbao* essayist, Yang Yinhang (1878–1945) (unrelated to Yang Chunlü, but a former classmate and lifelong friend of the politician Yang Tingdong), commented derisively on the crowds that flocked to the courtroom to listen to Yang Chunlü's case. For his own part, Yang Yinhang claimed he avoided the case because he preferred "fresh air" to the "stench of politics."[98] After the verdict was announced on April 15, the Nationalist Party–backed Shanghai newspaper *Guomin ribao*, which had long characterized the election as illegal in accord with the party line emanating from Guangzhou, celebrated the result. Defendants Yao and Lu were predictably less enthused and accused Yang Chunlü and the judge of conspiring to deny them election. Other critics would later claim that jealousy and a desire for mischief motivated Yang's suit. Many mocked those who had presumably won elections by bribing voters, only to find that their purchased positions had been seized by the court system.[99]

The secondary-stage parliamentary election for the region that included Shanghai was briefly postponed during the early phase of the trial, although primary-stage winners (including those from Shanghai whose election was about to be invalidated) continued to gather in Suzhou, where the secondary-stage vote was to take place. On April 4, over a week before the Shanghai verdict, these electors cast their votes for Jiangsu's parliamentary delegation. Perhaps this would have led to a second legal confrontation (as it was, Yang and the defendants continued to file motions well into the summer of 1921), but soon after the initial verdict was announced, the balance of forces in Beijing shifted again, ensuring that this just-elected "New New Parliament" would never be seated.

Some hopeful would-be parliamentarians gathered in Beijing anyway, where they repeatedly petitioned in vain for someone to pay attention to their plight. Despite this tragicomic ending to the 1921 national parliamentary election, few realized that it would be the last one ever for that institution. Even the Chinese Communist Party, founded in the same year as this failed election, adopted a plan in July 1922 for fielding parliamentary candidates in future elections, albeit with the notion that any communist parliamentarian would help in "instigating, or supporting, major revolutionary uprisings."[100]

Elections for the Jiangsu provincial legislature, however, continued; this institution of government, still deriving its legal foundations from the 1912 constitutional settlement, maintained a level of legitimacy even as the authority of the national government crumbled. As in previous elections, newspapers attempted to prescribe correct voter behaviors. A month before election day, the *Shenbao* urged election participants to:

> Vote by going to the polls yourself and writing the name of a person who you admire. Refuse, in no uncertain terms, relatives and friends who campaign for your vote [*yundong*] or those who say they will cast it for you [*baoban toupiao*].[101]

Even after two elections rife with fraud, some still believed that moral exhortation would be enough to influence voters and candidates to act appropriately. By election day itself, however, *Shenbao* editorialists had dropped the pretenses of hope evident in earlier editorials. The primary-stage election, one claimed, was nothing more than "a first chance to sell people's political rights."[102]

Incidents around the province illustrated this. In Wuxi's Huaixia township, one citizen alleged that a local leader had taken home a large number of ballots before the July 1 primary-stage election, hired people to fill them out, and then attempted to cast all of them on election day. This person lost some of the ballots on the way to the polling station, which were then found and his plot exposed.[103] Others with hopes of being elected resorted to fraud; a candidate in Yangming township reportedly cast 1,400 ballots for himself, only to be disappointed to find he had fallen short. Some voters spoiled their ballots in apparent protest, writing critiques such as "cash campaigning" instead of a candidate's names on their ballots.[104] Across the province, more than 180 election complaints were filed with the governor's office after the primary-stage election.[105] Separately, Yang Chunlü returned to the courtroom to challenge this election's results in Shanghai, although this time his complaint was rejected.[106]

None of the efforts to police the election, from the monitoring teams to Yang's lawsuits, had fundamentally altered its nature. At least for the moment, cynicism became the default coping mechanism. One Wuxi editorialist proposed getting rid of balloting altogether, and simply "giving the prize [of elected office] to the person who spends the most money." Voting, after all, "was not necessarily fair and has many defects."[107] Others proposed variants of this vision: one writer in a Suzhou newspaper suggested that the government select future legislators through a lottery—the money raised from the sale of tickets, after all, could be a useful revenue stream for the government.[108] A few weeks later, another writer in the same paper proposed the establishment of an "election auction company" to sell seats in the provincial legislature, snidely commenting that:

> In the secondary-stage election for the provincial legislature, calls for a "focus on talent" have been everywhere. Our company, however, relies on the fact that people in Jiangsu lack understanding of elections. We desire

to break this "focus on talent" in order to achieve the goals of cash campaigning [*jinqian yundong*].[109]

In between the national and provincial elections, an editor in Wujin simply opined that "given the level of the people in today's China, it is impossible to expect a good result from elections."[110] The people, in other words, had repeatedly failed to live up to the role that the designers of Chinese election laws had assigned them.

Conclusion

Despite these complaints, an elected legislature was seated in the provincial capital at Nanjing later in 1921. Its three-year term was due to end in mid-1924 and election preparations began in the early months of that year. The process was never completed. Questions about which set of election laws to follow—the original provincial election laws of 1912, which had been used in 1918 and 1921, or new ones devised in 1923 as part of a proposed provincial constitution—led to an indefinite suspension of the planned elections.[111] The provincial legislature, a body "long abhorred by the whole province" seemed to one editorial writer "to be doing its best to commit suicide."[112] According to the *Shenbao*, "average people . . . did not have much feeling" about the impending discontinuation of the legislature. This lack of emotion was, in the newspaper's analysis, caused by the fact that "members of this legislative session have paid no attention to popular sentiment."[113] On August 1, 1924, the legislative session expired, and Jiangsu was left without a legislature for the first time since the Yuan Shikai era.

Jiangsu's problems were not unique; provincial legislatures across China had begun to disappear in the mid-1920s. On March 27, 1925, the national Ministry of Interior in Beijing issued one last ruling on the system of elected provincial legislatures that had been in place since 1912. By then, a handful of provinces retained the system as it was envisioned in the early days of the Republic, a few embraced alternate systems, and many had no system at all. The ministry ratified this existing situation, pending the enactment of a new constitution: provinces that currently lacked legislatures did not need to re-create them, provinces that had legislatures in session—regardless of when the last election had been held—did not need to hold any further elections, and provinces that had held elections in 1924 should convene those new legislatures.[114] In response, the Jiangsu legislature elected in 1921 gathered for one final session, in April 1925, before finally passing from the scene. The late Qing/early Republican electoral laws and the institutions they authorized were not resurrected in Jiangsu again.

This was mirrored at the national level, too. Undermined by internal divisions and challenged by a rival regime based in Guangzhou, the Beijing-based government struggled to maintain a level of legitimacy and control after the failed parliamentary elections of 1921. No further elections were called under the 1912 constitution, nor would multiprovince elections be held again in China until the 1930s. Instead, in spring 1922, the authorities in Beijing recalled the parliament elected in 1912 to act as the nation's legislature for a third and final time. In the summer of 1923, after a complex series of maneuvers by military commanders, Cao Kun (1862–1938), a former subordinate of Yuan Shikai's, seized power in Beijing. Hoping to use the 1912 provisional constitution to legitimate his position, Cao bribed members of the 1912–13 parliament who had fled that capital to return and elect him to the presidency. Not all proved receptive—the redoubtable Wang Shao'ao, for instance, helped direct a boisterous opposition movement in parliament (and had an inkpot thrown at his head for his troubles). However, enough cooperated for his gambit to work.

As president, Cao oversaw the ratification of a "permanent" constitution for the Chinese Republic on October 10, 1923. Along with this new constitution, he called for new elections to be held in April 1924.[115] The system of voting was to be a near-replica of the indirect, restricted system in use since the 1908 Regulations. Planning for this election may never have advanced much beyond this initial announcement, and no vote was ever held. Cao served in office until October 1924, when he was ousted by rival military commanders.[116] That act destabilized what was left of the early Republican government. Fatally weakened, the nation spun into civil war.

The experiences of elections since 1909 had already convinced some that voting—at least as currently designed—could never reliably select the talented and virtuous. Instead, elections merely aggregated private interests, which could be manipulated by unscrupulous campaigners for personal benefit. Out in the provinces, this line of thinking would lead to experimentation with new, different styles of election even as chaos reigned in early 1920s Beijing. New provincial election laws, significantly different from any previously used in China, reemphasized the aspects of the foundational expectations for elections that took voting as a vehicle of public education and enlightenment—and accomplished this by removing competition from elections.

CHAPTER 6

Elections as Education

Political Tutelage, 1921–1987

When Hu Shi (1891–1962) returned to China in July 1917 after nearly a decade abroad, he made one commitment to himself before taking up a teaching position at the new Beijing University: he would abstain from direct involvement in politics for twenty years. Instead, this formidable Cornell- and Columbia-educated intellectual turned his scholarly gaze to the reconstruction of Chinese culture through promotion of the vernacular language, among other projects. The allure of political commentary never faded, however, and he took an increasingly active role in opining on current events. By spring 1922, during a particularly intense bout of warlord conflict near the capital, he engaged in the "tiring work" of writing his "first piece of political commentary" to offer fundamental solutions to the nation's most pressing issues.[1] It was the start of a political career that made Hu one of twentieth-century China's most famous intellectuals. Despite his foreign education, Hu championed the educational potential of elections celebrated by the late Qing constitutionalists and others. His writings came to embody the tensions between pedagogical aspects of the foundational expectations for elections and the lived experience of voting.

Hu's 1922 manifesto, "Our Political Proposals," was printed that May in his own newly founded journal, *Nuli zhoubao* [Endeavor Weekly], and several other major Beijing periodicals. He organized fifteen other prominent figures from across the political spectrum, among them Communist Party founder Li Dazhao (1888–1927), Nationalist Party stalwart

Wang Chonghui (1881–1958), and Confucian modernizer Liang Shuming (1893–1988), to endorse his statement. Given the diverse range of political views held by his cosigners, Hu spoke at a broad level of generality, aiming to articulate areas of elite consensus. He called for a "good government" that could police itself, provide for the national welfare, and allow a measure of individual freedom. Building such a government would require the active participation of "good people" in politics. Society's "best elements," Hu claimed, had immersed themselves in political activism in the years immediately following the 1911 Revolution but had recently abandoned the field to the unfit. His call for reengagement remained an influential statement of liberal political thought in China for decades.[2]

To pave the way for a "good government" of "good people," Hu and his cosigners proposed six policies. Most focused on defusing immediate crises, such as calling for a national peace conference, demobilizing warlord armies, or recalling the "old" parliament elected in 1912–13. Others focused on broader structural issues. Notably, these included the "urgent need for the reform of the current election system." Such reform would require the "abandonment of indirect elections and the adoption of direct elections," tough laws against election fraud, and reductions in the size of national and provincial legislatures. Despite their fixation on the current moment of unrest, Hu and his allies evinced an interest in building the long-term institutions and systems necessary for republicanism.[3]

Hu's advocacy of direct elections was a challenge to the indirect two-stage voting first implemented under the 1908 Regulations. Though modified several times since the fall of the Qing, the core of the 1908 Regulations had survived the change in regime, and indirect elections continued to be the only nationally sanctioned standard. Hu and his cosigners were not alone in rejecting this system in the early 1920s. Less famous intellectuals had complained about it for years before Hu published his "Proposals." Writing in Shanghai, the relatively obscure essayist Lou Mingyuan (dates unknown) had argued in October 1920 that indirect voting systems encouraged the people to adopt a "lackluster sense of responsibility" toward elections.[4] Activists involved in provincial reform had already sponsored direct elections for legislative positions in Hunan and Guangdong months before Hu Shi's proposal. Hu's essay did not create a new discourse about elections, but it functioned as a powerful endorsement of an idea that had been slowly gaining currency.

Although Hu did not outline in this statement what he thought electoral reform would accomplish, he almost certainly would have agreed with Lou's assertion. In other writings, Hu spoke forcefully about the educational effect he believed elections would have on voters. "We must recognize," he claimed in 1923, "that democratic institutions are an important instrument for the training of good citizens." Pointing to the slow development of representative government in Great Britain, he emphasized that time would be required for experience with democratic processes to reshape Chinese people into citizens. Yet, as he explained, "educators all know that the best teacher is practical experience." Hu claimed to have seen this process at work while studying in the United States. Visiting the polls during the presidential elections of 1912 and 1916, he found himself perplexed by the information included on the sample ballots and sought explanations from ordinary voters:

> I purposefully picked voters who did not appear to be upper class—people chewing tobacco or with foreign accents—and was shocked that they all were able to offer detailed explanations [of the items on the ballot]. Did these tobacco-chewing, foreign-accented American voters need to read [a political science textbook]? They were simply born under a republican system and grew up in a democratic environment. Because they experienced the training of this system, they naturally acquired the knowledge that citizens of many democratic countries need to have—and, as a result, were much more enlightened than those of us who have learned about politics through reading at universities!

To manufacture "good citizens" for a Chinese republic, people would need to be "given an opportunity to practice citizenship."[5] Better elections, with better election laws, the implication went, had to be a key part of this.

At times, Hu was willing to push this idea to its logical extreme. Writing in August 1922, he claimed that

> Popular politics itself is a kind of citizen education. Give someone a ballot and he might go sell it today, but some day in the future that person will not be willing to sell it. If you never give that person a ballot, there will be no chance to sell it now, but also no chance in the future *not* to sell it.[6]

Similar ideas bubbled up in his later writings, including his characterization of democracy as "the most basic school of politics" and the "kindergarten of politics" that provided opportunities for otherwise uniformed, unexceptional, and unmotivated people to learn about issues of national importance. "The advantage of democracy," Hu maintained, "is that it causes the broad majority of the people—those who 'follow sports in the news and read detective novels'—to go to the polls from time to time and think for a minute or two about affairs of state."[7] Elections forced people to concentrate on their duties as citizens of a state.

Hu's interest in direct elections as a pedagogical device reflected a boisterous discussion about the defects of the existing voting system that began around 1920. The visceral disappointment felt by many observers found expressions far more radical than those offered by Hu and his co-signers. In late 1922, Hu Shi's Beijing University colleague, the UK- and French-trained legal scholar Wang Shijie (1891–1981), summarized many of these trends in the pages of Shanghai's influential *Dongfang zazhi* [Eastern Miscellany]. Wang relayed detailed descriptions of new innovations, included voting by occupational (rather than geographic) constituency, systems of proportional voting, women's suffrage, and the increased use of plebiscites. Some of these ideas already exerted an effect on Chinese politics. The women's suffrage movement, victorious in the United Kingdom in 1918 and the United States in 1920, had long attracted attention, as did Japan's movement toward universal male suffrage in the mid-1920s. Similarly, the establishment of the Weimar Republic in Germany meant the abrogation of the limited, indirect Prussian electoral system that had inspired the 1908 Regulations. Wang refrained from commenting on the Chinese political system, but his essay helped create a sense that a Chinese quest to fundamentally revise the country's system of elections would be part of a global movement.[8]

All of the reforms Hu Shi demanded, and many of the options Wang Shijie introduced, were tried in China over the next several decades—indeed, several had already been attempted in certain provinces. The slow-motion collapse of the early Republican constitutional order had discredited any notion that elections alone could be a tool for identifying talent. Consensus had proved impossible; citizens had been manifestly unable to recognize, much less select, able and worthy leaders. In this vacuum, the belief that voting could be part of a greater project of state-led ideological transformation assumed a renewed importance. Hu's U.S. experiences may have given his proposals a distinctive flavor, but earlier advocates of Chinese elections had argued in broadly similar terms for decades. Elections had been conceptualized since the late Qing as political rituals through which the government could inculcate a certain set of values in the people. This had been a central, if heretofore underemphasized, aspect of the foundational expectations for elections in China. The transformative effect of elections held under the 1908 Regulations and the subsequent Republican variants, however, had been limited by the restricted electorate and by an indirect voting system that only required the temporary mobilization of a small number of voters. To educate, elections would need to inspire a deep sense of involvement among the population at large, rather than "lackluster" feelings of limited commitment.

Electoral competition in the form of campaigning likewise had little relevance for this pedagogical process. If anything, the past decades had revealed that election campaigning combined with a relatively unrestricted press produced little more than embarrassing spectacles. As a result, the elite push for new election laws aimed at educating the populace also led to the end of open competition for office. Hints of this were apparent as early as 1920. A month after his column advocating direct elections, Lou Mingyuan proposed another change to Chinese election law (in an unconscious echo of ideas voiced by Yuan Shikai's government half a decade earlier): secret ballots, mandated under the 1908 Regulations and its Republican successor laws, should be abandoned in favor of open ballots that bore the voter's own name. Lou thought this procedure could help prevent the baleful influence of campaigning and thus allow elections to contribute to the growth of public knowledge and morality.[9] Whether or not Lou recognized it, his proposal would also have resulted in increased societal—and, in the end, state—control over the actions of voters. Although nothing came of Lou's particular idea before 1949, the state found other ways to exert significant control over elections in this era. The outcome of elections after the mid-1920s came to be predetermined, although the process took decades to perfect. The electoral systems devised by provinces participating in the "provincial autonomy movement" of the 1920s and those created by the Nationalist Party government in the 1930s and beyond, allowed more people to participate but gave them fewer—if any—choices. The expansion of the electorate coincided with the disappearance of electoral competition. This was also consistent with a concept of elections that emphasized primarily what voting could do for the state.

Provincial Autonomy and the Spread of Direct, Universal Elections

In the early 1920s, amid the collapsing legitimacy of the 1912 constitutional system, activists and intellectuals attempted to rebuild China from the provincial level up. Nation-building at the central level had already failed, they reasoned; perhaps provinces, many of which were already ruled as semi-independent entities, might provide a more promising basis. The loose movement these activists formed, variously called the "provincial autonomy movement" or the "provincial federalist movement" (both translations of the same Chinese term *liansheng zizhi yundong*) proposed that provinces convene independent constitutional conventions, which would draft and adopt fundamental laws appropriate to their own internal conditions. These new governments could then engage in state-building activities within their borders. Eventually they would knit themselves together as the foundation for a revived Republic of China.

Although the provincial autonomy movement took individual provinces as arenas of action—and appeared to emphasize the particular needs and characteristics of each province—it had a unified national set of policies, issues, and concerns. These emanated from a single center: Shanghai. Perhaps more than their counterparts anywhere else in the nation, the professional, educational, and media communities of Shanghai embraced this push to transform the Republic into a federation of self-governing provinces.[10] Communication between autonomy activists across China took place primarily in Shanghai-printed periodicals, and the constitutional drafting committees established in each province tended to draw in part from individuals affiliated with Shanghai-based networks. This was a national movement that embraced a particular rhetoric of local autonomy, not a series of distinct movements reveling in particularism. Thus, provincial activists, regardless of location, adopted remarkably similar sets of ideas about how to rewrite Chinese election law.

While Shanghai was the center of discussion, several southern provinces were the sites of action. The earliest and most dramatic of these actions, the October 10, 1920, march in Changsha, Hunan, ended with protesters—Mao Zedong among them—raising banners emblazoned with demands for provincial freedom and expanded voting rights when they stormed the provincial legislative chambers. Extended theorization of the linkage between autonomy and election law followed action in the streets. An early exposition, published the same day as the Changsha protests, by Shanghai educational reformer, political activist, and Zhang Jian associate Huang Yanpei (1878–1965), argued that two pairs of ideas defined the provincial autonomy movement. The first drew attention to the relationship between the province and the nation: the movement aimed to "smash centralized power" and "eliminate the warlords." The second focused on transformation of elections: "implement systems for direct popular expression" and "implement representation systems by occupational group."[11] Although Huang expressed significant doubt about the viability of direct elections in China and said nothing about the scope of the electorate, his essay further cemented the linkage between provincial autonomy and a radical transformation of the existing system of voting. It was codified again in Shanghai-based scholar Zhang Taiyan's (1868–1936) canonical formulation of the provincial autonomy movement's goals, aims, and methods. Zhang explained that the movement envisioned a China in which "the people of each province would create their own provincial constitution . . . [and] from county magistrates to the provincial governor, [all officials] would be directly elected by the people."[12]

Mao, Huang, and Zhang were the leading edge of a new mainstream consensus about elections. Proponents of provincial autonomy across south China quickly adopted this logic of redesigned election laws with surprisingly little detailed discussion. Before 1920, no organ of Chinese government at any level had supported either direct elections or universal suffrage; in years that followed, authorities in at least seven provinces—Jiangsu, Zhejiang, Hunan, Guangdong, Henan, Sichuan, and Fujian—circulated proposals for provincial constitutions that did.[13] Each of these stipulated that legislatures should be chosen through direct elections in which most adults could participate. Educational and property restrictions on suffrage were greatly reduced or eliminated. Even more striking, all proposed provincial constitutions extended the franchise to women.

Some accomplished this by including clauses that specifically mentioned women's voting rights, others by removing all gender references from the election law.[14]

The earliest attempts to draft such laws happened in Jiangsu, although ultimately the movement achieved its greatest successes elsewhere. Two long-term members of the provincial legislature produced the first public proposal for an autonomous Jiangsu in late November 1920. They did not act on their own; both were affiliated with Zhang Jian's newest political party, Sushe [The Jiangsu Society] (Huang Yanpei, who had written about the importance of direct elections a month earlier, was also a member). New political institutions, they claimed in their preface, should "adhere to global trends," "reflect an understanding of the nation's situation," and "cultivate the people's ability to be self-governing." To do so, the two argued in rhetoric that echoed the long-standing beliefs about elections that "the common people should be given an opportunity for equal political participation, [thus] allowing them to train and develop their abilities." Voting in provincial elections, the only form of potential popular participation mentioned in their draft constitution, of necessity would be the primary vehicle for this. The proposal called for direct election of legislators by a broad electorate, comprising all taxpayers who had received schooling (neither of which was defined in the proposal) without reference to gender.[15] This was the first serious proposal anywhere in China to contemplate something other than the 1908 Regulations as the basis for an election law, but little ever came of it in Jiangsu. Despite an active pro-autonomy movement, the province continued to operate under the old electoral system until 1924. After that, no further elections were held until the era of Nationalist rule.

The first Chinese political leader to move these ideas from the realm of drafts into the real world emerged in the far southern province of Guangdong. In late 1920, a former member of the Qing-era provincial assembly and early ally of Sun Yat-sen, Chen Jiongming (1878–1933) captured the provincial capital from Beijing-backed militarists. Although a political figure of note for decades, by 1920 he seemed little different from the other warlords occupying territory across the Republic. Yet Chen soon displayed a heretofore unknown infatuation with the provincial autonomy movement and attempted to govern in accord with its ideals.[16] At the end of December 1920, less than two months after formally assuming the governorship, Chen Jiongming forwarded two election laws to the provincial legislature that bore the unmistakable marks of the movement. One allowed for the popular election of county magistrates, and the other instituted a system of direct elections for local legislative office. County legislatures had previously relied on a complicated indirect electoral system similar to their provincial-level equivalents; Chen's legislation was the first anywhere in China to make these institutions directly elected by the people. Voter qualifications, though not abolished, were dropped to a new low: an annual commitment of three days of labor to the county government or the payment of an equivalent fee. No mention was made of gender under the voting qualifications section, itself a significant shift from earlier laws that invariably specified that only men could vote. The text of the law hinted, through its unprecedented inclusion of gender as a category to be recorded during voter registration, that Chen intended to enfranchise qualified women.[17]

Direct elections had become an accepted idea by this time; universal adult suffrage rights, however, still proved to be controversial. Chen Jiongming's failure to affirmatively stipulate that women had the right to vote opened a gap for opponents of universal voting rights. During the provincial legislature's March 1921 debate on Chen's system, some legislators attempted to add language that would restrict suffrage to men. In response, 700 women entered the legislative chamber to demand that the final version of the law uphold women's suffrage. A scuffle ensued, during which several protesters were injured. In the aftermath, the suffrage activists sought out Sun Yat-sen (now living in Guangzhou) and Chen Jiongming, each of whom voiced support for the protesters' goals. Believing themselves victorious, the women paraded through the streets of Guangzhou.[18] When the legislature met again in early April, however, a substantial majority voted against women's suffrage.[19] This revised law was overturned under pressure from Chen before the end of May, thus confirming women's right to vote in the summer 1921 county elections.[20] Newspaper coverage of municipal and county elections held in June and September 1921 report that some women did cast ballots.[21] One woman—Huang Bihun (1875–1923), an outspoken advocate of women's suffrage who had been physically hurt during the protests—won a seat in her county's legislature, making her the first Chinese women elected to political office.[22] Opposition to women's enfranchisement remained entrenched, Huang's election notwithstanding. The Guangdong provincial constitution, a draft proposal of which was passed in December 1921, specified direct elections but made no overt commitment to female suffrage, and at least one early version of the 1922 provincial legislature election law limited voting rights to propertied men.[23]

This debate was soon rendered moot. Chen's tenure in office proved brief and turbulent, factors not conducive to musing on the meaning of elections or retaining government records. By mid-1921, he was consumed by an increasingly tense relationship with Sun Yat-sen that resulted in the collapse of his regime in early 1923 and the abandonment of his election laws. Chen spent most of his remaining years in Hong Kong, penning a political manifesto marked by its critique of Nationalist policies and its insistence that unless the Chinese people had the opportunity to practice "self-government," real democracy would never develop.[24] To the end, he saw elections as an education for citizenship.

A broader and more detailed conversation occurred in Hunan, the only province to reach the apex of "provincial autonomy" by promulgating its own constitution. This constitution, announced to the public on June 1, 1921, passed a province-wide referendum in November and entered into force on January 1, 1922.[25] Referenda had not been part of previous Republican practice; the decision to hold one in Hunan marked a clear, dramatic break with the institutions of the early Republic. The November plebiscite supposedly involved more than 19 million voters, men and women, of whom only slightly less than 600,000 voted to reject the provincial constitution. Newspaper reports indicated that the vote was chaotic, even in the provincial capital of Changsha. Few voters came during the early days of the multiday vote, but a rush developed at the end after urgings from community leaders and the police.[26] Results from outlying counties were announced slowly, and even at the end of the month, some still had not reported their final tallies. It mattered little. Voters had been casting ballots for an outcome that had been predetermined; the referendum was a ceremony meant to create a bond with the new provincial government. The purpose of this activity was decidedly pedagogical. According to the text of a speech written as part of the official publicity campaign, "the meaning of this plebiscite is so that our thirty million [Hunanese] brothers and sisters can all know the contents of the constitution and can all speak about the benefits of enacting the constitution."[27] Education and assent, rather than a demonstration of popular will, had been this election's goal.

In March 1922, a second vote—a direct election, open to men and women, for the newly authorized provincial legislature—was held.[28] Adding the enfranchisement of women to the provincial constitution in spring 1921 proved as controversial as the nearly simultaneous suffrage proposals in Guangdong. As in Guangdong, public pressure forced the issue but did not end debate entirely; as late as 1924, an attempt was made to disenfranchise women.[29] During the 1922 election, some county magistrates refused to register women, violence broke out at least once over whether a women would appear on the ballot, and only a small number of women may have actually cast votes.[30] At least two women won election to the provincial legislature that year, along with several others to various county legislatures.

Races were competitive, perhaps more so than in any earlier election. A month before the vote, one report claimed thirty candidates were "campaigning furiously" for Hengyang County's five seats.[31] Supposedly as many as seventy candidates competed for as few as four spots in other counties, leading one writer to complain that "campaigners were as numerous as maggots in a bucket of manure."[32] The phenomenon of campaigning had not disappeared, despite the introduction of direct elections and universal suffrage. Newspapers complained of it, with the same term derogatory term, *yundong*, they had used since 1909. Residents of Hengyang and other locations organized monitoring teams similar to those during the 1918 Anfu parliament elections.[33] The persistence of campaigning, no matter how worrying to those who witnessed it, provided evidence that provincial authorities had not determined winners in advance of election day. The hasty process of voter registration and indifferent administration of polling stations, combined with pervasive allegations of fraud, make the election's official results impossible to assess. Supposedly over 910,000 ballots were distributed in Changsha County alone (some were stolen—but recovered—during the course of the election), of which nearly 700,000 were recorded for the top eight vote-getters. Yet the results of that election were challenged on the day they were announced, with an unknown result.[34] The existence of fraud does not mean these elections were a fiction; to an unknown extent, substantial numbers of real people voluntarily voted in Hunan's March 1922 election.

Despite the stated intentions of its organizers, there is nothing to indicate that this exercise had much in the way of a pedagogical effect on the population. Yet this ritualistic form of voting, particularly evident in the earlier referendum, pointed to a logical result of the marriage of mass participation in elections and a vision of voting as an educational experience. Writing for a Shanghai publication in September 1922, near the high-water mark of the movement, a participant in Hunan's autonomy movement explained:

> The 400 million people of China do not care about national affairs . . . if a federal system were enacted, then the opportunities for popular participation in government would be increased, and the government would be closer to the people. This could invigorate the people's interest in politics and inspire a sense of patriotism.[35]

The program of his fellow activists made clear that elections for legislative office and plebiscites would be the most significant of these "opportunities."

As was the case in Guangdong, the Hunan government soon fell victim to conflict and violence, rendering the province's constitutional structure meaningless. Although other provinces drafted constitutions, none came even as close as those two provinces to implementation. By 1923, the provincial autonomy movement had all but collapsed. The hope that elections could train the people to be citizens endured beyond this collapse. None of China's successive governments have openly sought to find aspects of this movement's legacy to salvage—yet all adopted the direct, universal system of voting pioneered in Jiangsu, Guangdong, and Hunan. Similarly, all saw elections primarily as a tool for educating a recalcitrant population. To make this work, governments after the early 1920s sought to exert more effective and thorough control over voting itself. Political parties had attempted to do this during the 1912 and 1918 elections by campaigning for support and at times by manipulating the electoral process through bribery, fraud, and chicanery. Under the auspices of the state, competition was essentially eliminated and elections came to be acclamations of predetermined results. Provincial autonomy elections were the first in Chinese history to be direct and universal, but the last for decades to offer voters a choice.

Voting and Political Tutelage in the Nanjing Decade and After

Commenting later on the chaotic politics of the mid-1920s, former Hunan provincial autonomy activist Li Jiannong (1880–1963) remarked that "the line of constitutional legitimacy was broken ... and the only new hope could come from the Nationalist Party."[36] As the Republic's foremost parliamentary party, Nationalist legitimacy in the 1910s was based on the existing election system. Nationalist-leaning members of the first national parliament sitting in session in Guangzhou had elected Sun Yat-sen as president (his second time) in April 1921. Sun specifically pointed to the rival Beijing government's manipulation of election laws as the source of its illegality.[37] In June 1922, however, the basis of his regime fell away once the first parliament was recalled to Beijing, and members in Guangzhou packed up and headed northward. Abandoned, Sun soon rejected the institutions of the early Republic in their entirety. His ouster later that year at the hands of Chen Jiongming, the most famous advocate of provincial autonomy, turned him decisively against that movement, too.[38] Yet the Nationalist Party would become the unlikely vehicle for the nationwide spread of provincial autonomy-style election laws centered on direct elections and universal adult suffrage.

In the wake of these events, Sun's rump Nationalist Party repositioned itself as a critic of the 1912 constitutional order and an opponent of the still-powerful provincial autonomy movement. It was unwilling to acknowledge any intellectual debt to either. A January 1, 1923, party declaration claimed that "the present system of representative government has already weakened democracy and the [current] class-based system of elections is easily controlled by a minority." To replace it, the Nationalists advocated universal adult suffrage, direct elections, and the use of initiative, referendum, and recall exercised through either plebiscites or mass meetings.[39] A similar call for universal suffrage (with the significant caveat that "traitors and dishonest people loyal to the imperialists or the warlords" would not be granted any rights) was incorporated into the resolutions made at the party's first national conference on November 25, 1923.[40] No acknowledgment was made of the similarities between these ideas and those of the provincial autonomy movement.

As part of this new bid for authority, Sun decided to scrap the structures and symbols of the old Republic. His new philosophy, encapsulated in the April 1924 manifesto "Fundamentals of National Reconstruction," committed the nascent Nationalist government to rebuild the Republic through a three-stage process, beginning with a phase of military rule [*junzheng*], during which the territory of each province would be pacified; transitioning to a period of tutelary rule [*xunzheng*], in which "trained [government] personnel who have passed examinations" would be sent to help achieve "self-governance" at the county level; and ending with constitutional rule [*xianzheng*] after the majority of provinces had reached "self-governance."[41] Elections were critical aspects of the final two stages of the process—county-level elections would be held at the end of tutelary rule and national elections at the beginning of constitutional rule. Little detail was provided beyond the stipulation that elections were to be direct and that candidates would need to pass state-sponsored examinations.

Rough forms of this idea had percolated through Sun's thought long before 1924. An abbreviated version had been included in the charter of his short-lived Chinese Revolutionary Party in 1914, and the concept of "tutelary rule" occurred with increasing frequency in his writings in the late 1910s.[42] Soon before arriving in Chen Jiongming's newly recaptured Guangzhou in November 1920, he lectured party members in Shanghai on the pressing need for tutelary rule: "The Republic has been in place for nine years, but the average person still does not understand the true nature of a republic." Tutelage under a firm government hand could accomplish this, although the task might require force—Sun concluded his lecture by comparing the tutelary task his party faced to the one undertaken by the United States in the Philippines.[43] In this swirl of ideas, texts, and speeches, the role of elections in political tutelage became ambiguous: elections were an aspect of tutelage but would occur only at the end of that era. Were they a tool for political tutelage or the culmination of that tutelage?

Sun Yat-sen died in 1925 without resolving that question, but his ideas became the guiding ideology for the Nationalist Party's decades of rule on the Chinese mainland. Beginning in 1926, Nationalist forces based in Guangdong launched a military campaign to subdue the regimes ruling northern China; by 1928, Chiang Kai-shek (1887–1975) had established himself as the dominant leader of a new Nationalist government in Nanjing. In October 1928, Chiang's government declared the end of military rule and the beginning of an era of tutelary rule that would "train the people to wield the power of government."[44] During this period, the people would be "trained" in the rights of election, recall, initiative, and referendum as detailed by Sun Yat-sen's writings. Despite this pronouncement, the new government—mired in factionalism, beset by foreign and domestic crises—took relatively little action to develop concrete plans for Sun's "political tutelage," although the phrase remained an important rhetorical device.[45]

Several national elections were held during the first decade of Nationalist rule, without any clearly articulated connection to the broader policy of political tutelage. In early 1931, the Nanjing government assembled a Citizens' Conference, which was tasked with drafting a constitutional compact to guide the period of tutelary rule. The election law for this institution assigned voting rights to members of formal social organizations, such as unions, farmer's associations, chambers of commerce, and of course the Nationalist Party.[46] This corporatist conception of a legislature that represented economic organizations, rather than geographical constituencies, had been discussed during the provincial autonomy movement but had never been a major aspect of that movement's election laws.[47] In Beijing and Nanjing, competitive elections under these laws did occur; in other locations, voters were instructed whom to vote for.[48] These elected delegates adopted a constitutional compact for the "tutelary" era that May. Among other things, it mandated that the exercise of voting rights would be "guided" by the Nationalist state.[49] The impetus for this whole process lay in tensions between Chiang and rebellious regional military commanders; once that crisis passed, this document was forgotten.

Five years later, the Nanjing government released another draft constitution after years of negotiation, revision, and controversy. The announcement of the constitution, coupled with the steady extension of Nanjing's authority into areas formerly dominated by regional regimes and a slow recovery from the Great Depression, was an aspect of a short-lived moment of optimism in China during 1936–37.[50] Ratification required the election of a National Assembly. In its most essential elements, the election law for this body incorporated the main elements of provincial autonomy–era systems. Voting would be "universal, equal, direct, and based on a secret ballot" with suffrage extended to all citizens over twenty years of age.[51] Detailed election regulations, issued several months later, stipulated a National Assembly of 1,200 members, to comprise 665 from geographical constituencies, 380 from occupational constituencies, and 155 from "special" constituencies (these included Tibet, Mongolia, overseas Chinese, Manchurian territories occupied by Japanese forces, and the military).[52]

In several major aspects, however, this law broke with past precedent. For the first time, an election law placed tools for pre-determining election results in the hands of the state. Voter registration would be government-run, rather than subcontracted to local elites. It mandated a nomination process for candidates that would be controlled by government officials. To help enforce this, ballots were to be preprinted with the names of candidates for the first time in Chinese history. Voters needed only to make a mark (literacy, a requirement to vote in the past, was quietly dropped from this new system). In addition to disenfranchising groups that had been prohibited from voting in earlier election laws, such as opium users, a new population was now disqualified: "traitors to the National Government."[53] Collectively, these changes suggest an interest in policing elections by exerting control over who could run and by selectively excluding opponents of the regime.

Moreover, a mandatory loyalty oath was now required of voters. The contents of the oath constituted a form of political education in the symbols, terminology, and ideology of the Nationalist government.[54] Oath-taking was a ceremony, during which presumptive voters faced the flag of the Republic of China, the Nationalist Party's flag, and an image of Sun Yat-sen and pledged to "protect the Republic of China" and help actualize the basic program of the Nationalist Party, including Sun's Three Principles of the People. Administration of the oath in advance of the election happened in some areas. In Shanghai, for instance, civil servants were scheduled to take the oath on August 14, 1936, and average citizens were asked to report to any one of 153 offices between 8 am and 5 pm on September 13 for the same purpose.[55]

Amid delays in the creation of voter lists and other preparation work, the whole process was postponed from 1936 until July 1937. In the weeks before the vote, a propaganda campaign replete with banners, posters, and radio speeches was held in Shanghai (if not elsewhere). Voting finally commenced in portions of the country in mid-July; in Shanghai over a million ballots were cast on July 16.[56] By then, however, events had intervened. A skirmish between Chinese and Japanese forces at the Marco Polo Bridge near Beijing on July 7 initiated the two countries' final slide into war. Though the fighting was contained to north China in July, it spread to the Shanghai region in August, morphing from a regional crisis into a general conflagration. By the end of the year, Nationalist forces were in full retreat, and their plans for the political, economic, and cultural rehabilitation of China were in ruins. The elections were abandoned in the midst of a fight for national survival.

Despite periodic discussion of enhancing the democratic credentials of the Nationalist regime, no further experiment would (or could) occur while combat continued. The members of the National Election Preparation Office who relocated with the government to Chongqing (legal scholar and writer Wang Shijie among them) could do little more than shuffle papers for the next eight years. Tellingly, one of their tasks was to maintain a list of the current status of those elected in July 1937, making note of those killed or collaborating with the Japanese.[57] Only after the Japanese surrender in September 1945 did Chiang Kai-shek's government squarely turn its attention back to the question of elected government.

Under pressure from domestic and foreign forces, the Nationalists were compelled to devise a path to the regularization and democratization of their rule. Events, rather than any clear plan, prompted these decisions. The sudden cessation of the war with Japan in 1945 led to a quick resumption of fighting between the Nationalist government and communist forces. The decision to declare an end to tutelary governance and the consequent enactment of a constitution were linked to United States–backed efforts to create a coalition government that could avert civil war, reduce the appeal of the Communist Party, and appease demands for democratic reform. Chiang's government, over the objections of the Communist Party, adopted a constitution on December 25, 1946, that outlined an election system generally similar to that of 1936–37.[58] Elections for the three different legislature-like institutions—the National Assembly, the Legislative Yuan, and the Control Yuan—were to be held from late November 1947 to early January 1948. The Communist Party rejected the legitimacy of the new constitution, refused to participate in any elections, and escalated its attacks on the Nationalists. Voting would occur in the midst of a civil war.

Although earlier ideas of elections as an educational process still percolated through the Nationalist Party and state-controlled media, the administration of the election was chaotic, and few received the lessons the state hoped to teach. Voter registration was supposed to have occurred during spring and summer 1947. Jiangsu authorities assigned responsibility to county governments, leading to a wide variance in actual practice. Some counties simply reported back, without explanation, a total number of eligible voters. Others filed reports indicating that little registration work had actually been done. Jiangyin County merely reported the number of inhabitants over the age of twenty, minus those who met one of the legal "disqualifications." Authorities in that county noted that although they had planned on administering the citizen's oath to these potential voters, they had yet to actually do so.[59] This was fairly representative of the state of election preparations in Jiangsu: the numbers reported to the provincial government may have had little basis in attempts to actually register voters on the ground.

Even if voter registration failed as an educational experience, Nationalist government agencies had still planned for a major publicity campaign to precede the election. In late September 1947, the Nationalist government's Executive Yuan issued a "Framework for Spreading Propaganda for Constitutional Government" that was transmitted to the provincial governments, which then forwarded it to the counties. In Jiangsu, this process took several weeks and localities received the Framework only a month before voting began. To explain the benefits of the new constitution and the process of constitutional activities such as elections, the Framework outlined an ambitious publicity plan. Suggested activities included holding large-scale events, such as speech contests, dispatching lecturing teams to villages and factories, and sending groups of students organized as "Constitutional Governance Propaganda Teams" to tour the countryside on weekends and holidays. In addition, the Framework envisioned the creation of folk songs, plays, and even movies about the constitution. Slogans were to be posted in "restaurants, teahouses, theaters, and other places of entertainment" as well as on trains, buses, and boats.[60]

Some counties complied or attempted to. The plan developed in Wujin County called for a "propaganda week," during which representatives from local schools, media outlets, Nationalist Party organizations, the Chamber of Commerce, and the Youth League would take turns making broadcast speeches. Leaflets with slogans such as "Everyone should follow Sun Yat-sen's Last Will and implement democracy," "Correct the corrupt practices of the past," and "Select the worthy and the able so that we can build a democratic new China," would be distributed. Student groups would engage in publicity efforts.[61] Mass meetings were held in Shanghai to promote knowledge of the election and particular candidates, and in nearby Nanhui County local elites participated in an "election education movement" to instruct voters on their rights.[62] Individual candidates similarly engaged in a variety of publicity activities, including several National Assembly candidates in Taipei, Taiwan who engaged in a vigorous schedule of public speechmaking.[63] Newspapers, now under firm state control, likewise published editorials urging the people to embrace the election process.[64]

These efforts left little evidence of having much impact on public consciousness. Foreign observers detected little popular enthusiasm. A *New York Times* reporter in Nanjing noted that "most voters were far more obsessed with the difficulties of life under conditions of civil war and inflation than with the new experiment in democracy. Just outside [of] [Nanjing], peasant families continued to search for weeds to fire their mud huts' ovens."[65] Chinese commentators concurred with some of this, although in less florid language. Pan Gongzhan (1895–1975), a prominent Nationalist leader and assembly candidate in Shanghai, explained that the people were "indifferent" due to an unfamiliarity with elections and a "reduced interest in politics" stemming from postwar economic difficulties.[66]

Despite this backdrop of deprivation and chaos, official Nationalist sources, both public and confidential, recorded significant voter participation in November. *Shenbao* reported that between 500,000 and 600,000 ballots were cast on the first day of voting in Shanghai.[67] After the third day of voting concluded, the Shanghai Election Office claimed that of 1,887,484 registered voters in the city, 1,041,234 cast valid ballots during the National Assembly elections.[68] Nationwide, the government publicly claimed that "about half of an estimated 250,000,000 qualified voters" participated.[69] These numbers are impossible to verify, but given the dire situation of the Nationalist state in late 1947, they are almost assuredly greatly exaggerated.

Women formed an unknown percentage of that total, although neither precise statistics nor even rough approximations survive. Female voters were highlighted in propaganda work. An English-language Chinese government periodical, *China Magazine*, interviewed several Nanjing voters, including "housewife Chen Chia-fang." Chen, who "decided to vote in order not to disappoint [her] daughter," cast her ballot for a female candidate, explaining that she "figured that women are always better balanced than men."[70] The same magazine documented the process by which Mei Lien-hua, a schoolteacher who "was one of 150,000 women" to vote in Nanjing, cast her ballot (see figure 9). As one of the earliest photographs of a Chinese person voting, the images of Mei were intended as striking documentation of universal suffrage in action. No man was similarly profiled in this particular propaganda display, but photographs of men casting ballots in this election appeared in other sources.

In all likelihood, only a small minority of voters experienced the election the way Mei purportedly did. Although the caption explained that she "picked" which candidate to vote for, many voters were probably instructed which name to write on their ballots. The valorization of women as voters—and by extension, the celebration of nearly universal adult suffrage—occurred simultaneously with a comprehensive state- and Party-led attempt to dictate the outcome of the election. Vote totals reflect the extent to which this election functioned as an acclamation, rather than a selection. All 61,600 votes cast in Huaiyin County for the provincial farmer's association seat in the National Assembly went to a single candidate, to cite one egregious example. Similarly unbelievable results were reported across the province for other occupational constituencies.[71] Some of this may have been due to ballot box stuffing, but much of it was also due to the actions of poll workers (some of whom were elementary school students!) completing ballots on behalf of illiterate and indifferent voters.[72] The same phenomenon occurred in the results from geographical constituencies. In Tongshan County, 390,553 valid votes were cast for the county's two geographical representatives to the National Assembly. Ten candidates received votes; the highest vote-getter earned 227,971 votes and the second highest vote-getting candidate received 83,914 votes.[73] The sizable gap separating the highest and second-highest vote getters was replicated across many other counties. These results are consistent with the notion that the elections were intended to be

FIGURE 9: "Miss Mei Votes in China's First General Election," *China Magazine*, December 1947, 17–18.

noncompetitive races in which anointed candidates would be acclaimed by the masses.

Races were deliberately structured to produce such results—unlike previous elections, candidates could not freely choose to compete. The law mandated that only candidates registered with the government could run for election, and registration would only be possible through a popular petition or party nomination. In practice, the second path predominated. The Nationalist Party tightly controlled the nomination process and issued lists of party-supported candidates in the weeks before the November voting began. Considerable social pressure was brought to bear on voters to ratify that choice. Wang Shijie, the legal scholar who wrote on electoral reform in the 1920s and later served on the Nationalists' election preparation committee, was selected to represent his home county, Chongyang, Hubei, in the National Assembly despite being "unable to find the time to take a trip there." "Local elites," he wrote in his diary, "appealed to the public, of their own accord, and advised others not to run against me. I am moved by their enthusiasm."[74] Hu Shi, now serving as president of Beijing University after spending most of the war years overseas, was also elected with little apparent effort to a National Assembly seat in a functional constituency reserved for the university sector.

In some locations, the party's will—or the will of local agents acting in the party's name—was enforced through voter fraud and intimidation. A November 25, 1947, telegram from the Wu County Nationalist Party organization to the Jiangsu provincial government, for instance, included allegations that one local official led "more than ten plainclothes police men, armed with three machine guns, to Xiangshan, where they forced the village headsman to surrender over two thousand blank election ballots." The party organization requested a halt to the counting of ballots while these acts were investigated.[75] Similar complaints from Wuxi, Songjiang, Rugao, Liuhe, and Huaiyin counties, among others, reached the provincial government through official reporting channels in December 1947. More can be found in other provinces.[76]

Elsewhere slightly subtler methods were used. Factionalism within the Nationalist Party at times resulted in electoral victory for candidates not preapproved by the party leadership.[77] Officials often attempted to force these successful but unauthorized candidates to decline the seats to which they had been elected. This did not always have the intended result. In northern Jiangsu's Suqian County, government-sponsored discussions were held before the election to "reduce disputes." During these, candidate Lu Xuanzhi (1911–93) agreed to decline the seat in the National Assembly if elected. He reneged once he learned that he had won more votes than any other candidate. To persuade him to honor the original agreement, the provincial government authorized the county magistrate to offer an unspecified reward; several weeks later, Lu issued a formal statement relinquishing his position.[78] Lu's interest in holding elective office was not extinguished by this experience; even as he agreed to abandon his claims to a seat in the National Assembly, he declared his candidacy for the Legislative Yuan. The Nationalist Party did not endorse him in that race, either, and he lost his election.[79]

Not everyone proved to be as amendable to persuasion as Lu: a significant number of unanticipated winners, particularly Nationalist Party members who had won in constituencies that Chiang had assigned to smaller, independent (but Nationalist-aligned) political parties, refused to surrender their seats. This dispute carried into 1948 and delayed the opening of the National Assembly, as some of the most intransigent of these office-seekers staged a hunger strike on the assembly floor.[80] These protests became a humiliating public symbol of the shortcomings and limitations of Nationalist rule.

Nonetheless, Nationalist authorities declared the election a success. Hu Shi, who had long ago been inspired by visits to U.S. polling stations, explained in an unguarded moment several months before the election that "democratic politics is educational training. Our country's first mass-suffrage election, both the good and the bad, will be an experience and a lesson."[81] After visiting several polling stations in Beijing, he asserted more positively that "public response to the call of election was spontaneous and widespread."[82] Apparently, education had worked. Once voting for the National Assembly concluded, *Shenbao* similarly enthused: "Undoubtedly, we the people have truly given ourselves 'political tutelage' during this mass suffrage election; we hope that this kind of political self-education or political self-training will only continue to get stronger in the future."[83] Little evidence exists to substantiate these claims.

Whatever hopes Hu Shi or others had that the election might confer domestic and international legitimacy on the Nationalist regime proved futile. The required Citizen's Oath and the planned propaganda campaign notwithstanding, the 1947–48 election did no more to reshape the attitudes and behaviors of the population than the provincial autonomy elections two decades earlier. Nor did the Nationalists' clumsy and often public attempts to dictate winners do much to endear them to the Chinese population or the international community. In this sense, the 1947–48 elections are easily seen as another example of the incompetence, arbitrariness, and venality of Nationalist rule during the party's last years on the mainland. This election and Nationalist ideas about voting, however, laid an important legacy for the future. It linked an older notion, that voting should be an educational ritual aimed to teach citizens about the state, with the belief that this pedagogical purpose could only be achieved by suppressing campaigning and other forms of electoral competition. These ideas continued to characterize elections in the mainland in the following decades—but were gradually abandoned on the other side of the Taiwan Strait.

Voting in "Free China"

The island of Taiwan, which fell under Nationalist authority only in 1945, was an unlikely spot to experiment with elections. A Japanese colony returned to Chinese control as part of the 1945 terms of surrender, it was virtually a foreign territory from Chiang Kai-shek's perspective. It had not been ruled by a Chinese government since 1895, and the majority of the native population had little reason to identify with the newly arrived Nationalist administration. Yet a provincial administration was soon established and, just as on the mainland, voters there participated in the 1947–48 National Assembly elections.

Taiwan's electoral culture had preceded the Nationalist administration. Under Japanese rule, some elective representative assemblies had been established, providing a basis for a tradition of voting, although with a highly restricted franchise.[84] The Nationalists built on this. Borrowing a little-used law for village and township assemblies first promulgated by Chiang's wartime government, the new provincial authorities announced Taiwanese regulations for the direct election of local assemblies by a fully enfranchised population. They scheduled the first elections to occur on a staggered basis in 1946. This was a striking decision. Taiwan had been under Nationalist rule for only a few months by that point; as a sign of the gap between the government and the population, authorities felt compelled to print both Chinese- and Japanese-language versions of the law.[85]

These elections attracted a surprising level of interest. In Tainan, 98,565 people (95 percent of those eligible) took part in the oath registration process, and 9,376 people registered as candidates for local assemblies, of whom 8,891 (84 of whom were women) were certified by local authorities to run for an unspecified number of assembly seats in jurisdictions throughout the county.[86] Races for a twenty-six-seat citywide council in Taipei attracted interest from more than 215 candidates, although apparently many did not complete the candidate enrollment process or actively campaign.[87] Candidates were required to register in advance, but the sheer numbers of those who did so suggest that the state did very little detailed vetting. Editorialists at nonstate newspapers had many complaints about the election, but none suggested undue party influence in determining the outcome. George Kerr, a U.S. diplomat stationed in Taipei and a harsh critic of Nationalist policies, observed that "the first elections were held and the Councils convened before the Party could get a firm grip on the machinery. Many men who later proved wholly undesirable from the Government's point of view were elected."[88]

Consistent with a long-standing theme, the 1946 local elections had an educational component. In advance of these elections, authorities administered the loyalty oath to approximately three million island residents. Elementary school students were enlisted to propagandize on behalf of the election and encourage adults to vote.[89] After the ballots had been counted, the provincial government planned three-day training classes for the newly elected local representatives, complete with lectures on state ideology (involving discussions of Sun Yat-sen's will, the Three Principles of the People, and Chiang Kai-shek's speeches), unspecified administrative matters, and a three-hour "spiritual lecture."[90]

This was a moment of calm before the storm. Unrest engulfed the island in 1947 after the February 28 Incident, during which government forces launched a violent crackdown on the local population. Elected institutions counted for little as unrest spread across the island and martial law was imposed. Within another eighteen months, battlefield defeats in the mainland forced Chiang and the Nationalist Party to flee to Taiwan and establish a rump regime in semi-exile. This government sought to demonstrate its continued claim to sovereignty over the mainland by retaining the National Assembly as constituted in 1948. Assembly members who relocated with the government, elected by mainland constituencies beyond Taipei's control, remained in office for decades. No longer subject to even theoretical discipline by elections, they came to symbolize the authoritarian and alien nature of Chiang's regime. Chiang buttressed his rule with tougher tools as well, including the continuation of martial law, the suspension of the constitution, and the pervasive use of political violence.

None of this halted the spread of local elections for long, although it marked a change in their purpose and structure. Elections in Taiwan, held using Nationalist laws written in the mainland, came to perform a profoundly different role on the island. From the early 1950s onward, the Nationalist government held elections in Taiwan with a consistency unknown in the pre-1949 period. Elections now became familiar, routine, and (mostly) predictably scheduled. Voters, in response to the regularity of elections, actually cast ballots, with over 70 percent consistently turning out to the polls from the 1950s to the 1970s.[91] Simultaneously, state authorities dropped many of the rhetorical claims made for pre-1949 elections, particularly those related to the tutelary or educational functions of voting. Instead, regularized voting was intended to solidify the rule of a semi-alien single-party state.

Control over competition remained, as it had in the pre-1949 period, a foundational aspect of the Nationalist approach to elections. Organized political parties, other than the Nationalist Party and several satellite groups, were banned, although races were still nominally competitive within that constraint. When the Nationalists felt their dominance truly threatened, other measures—including various forms of harassment and fraud—were brought to bear against some of the more popular independent candidates.[92] In the final analysis, the state did not hesitate to use the tools of political repression, ranging from arrest to worse, that it retained during the martial law era. Hard measures accounted for only one side of this structure, however. Softer methods often sufficed to maintain Nationalist dominance at the polling both. A "single vote, multiple-member" election system, which had characterized Chinese election law since the 1908 Regulations, was introduced in Taiwanese local legislative elections as part of the "local self-government" initiatives in the early 1950s.[93] Under this system, which limited voters to casting a single ballot in races involving multiple seats, coordination was required for allied candidates to win. In the early Republic, this system of voting had provided a powerful (if unintended) structural incentive for the formation of political parties; in post-1949 Taiwan, it meant that significant advantages accrued to the Nationalists.[94] Without a coordinating structure, candidates outside of the party could only score limited victories.

Unlike the heavy-handed intervention that characterized the 1947–48 National Assembly elections, the Nationalists now ensured favorable outcomes through astutely managing intraparty factions, coopting outsiders, and acceding to the occasional election upset. As a consequence, elections gave rise to vast patronage networks that enmeshed elected officials, party operatives, and people from all aspects of society.[95] Nothing like this had emerged in any earlier election in the mainland. Taiwanese elections thus became a consequential social phenomenon long before democratization in the 1980s. Now a "recurring mechanism," elections, argues Taiwan-based political scientist Hu Fu, would ultimately "transform both the nature and significance of the established authoritarian regime."[96]

Despite the constraints set by the Nationalist state, local elections became a site of resistance for activists seeking to end single-party rule; over the decades, they provided just enough space to challenge Nationalist authority that the opposition movement maintained an orientation toward the existing political infrastructure.[97] Political scientist Shelley Rigger concludes that

> the genius of Taiwan's electoral system was the way it used competition to encourage political participation and enthusiasm for a regime that imposed itself from the outside.... The key to this success lay in transforming the energy of grassroots conflict and interest-seeking into support for the ruling party. The mechanism for performing this alchemy was the electoral system.[98]

Enough activists embraced the notion that the Nationalists ultimately could be defeated at the ballot box, rather than in the streets (or on a battlefield), to forestall any more revolutionary alternative.

Contestation of elections increased after Chiang Kai-shek's death in 1975. The generational shift represented by Chiang's passing, as well as the pressures of international isolation (U.S. diplomatic relations with the Republic of China on Taiwan ended with the recognition of mainland China on January 1, 1979) and an energized civil society, resulted in the formation of an opposition party in 1986, the end of martial law in 1987, and the dissolution of the old National Assembly in 1991. By this time, free and fair elections had become the norm, culminating in the first direct election for president in 1996. Taiwan's Cold War moniker, "Free China," suddenly lost its irony as democratization transformed the island's political life. A lively culture of sometimes outrageous election campaigning, reminiscent of the early Republic, reemerged—and like decades earlier, inspired anxiety among observers.[99]

A history of elections may have conditioned people on Taiwan to demand an elected government, but familiarity with elections is not sufficient to account for the successful democratization movement of the 1980s.

Instead, several unique factors facilitated Taiwan's move to free elections: the need to manage ethnic tensions between a disempowered Taiwanese majority and an entrenched mainland minority, the strategic necessity of finding new sources of state legitimacy after the formal end of the U.S. alliance in 1979, and the legacy of a generation of widely shared economic prosperity. The personality of Chiang Ching-kuo (1910–88), son and successor to Chiang Kai-shek, also played a role in catalyzing these factors in the 1980s. Although he had inherited rule over a one-party state, the younger Chiang acquired democratic sympathies late in life. Rather than blocking opposition activists, he stood aside, ordering an end to martial law and endorsing the shift toward democracy.[100] Without these factors, it is hard to imagine that a tradition of voting alone would have been enough to transform the Nationalist party-state into a democracy. Voting has served as a method to release and redirect political pressures, not as the catalyst for systemic change.

Conclusion

Ironically, the end of martial law in 1987 and the democratic transition that followed had little to do with any belief that voting could serve as a form of state-sponsored education. Sun Yat-sen's concept of a tutelary government was not implemented on Taiwan (on the mainland, it had never amounted to much more than a slogan); Chiang Kai-shek had declared a nationwide end to political tutelage in December 1947, only two years after Nationalist forces occupied the island. The phrase disappeared from official government rhetoric after that point.[101] For decades, election planners from the Qing constitutionalists to the organizers of Hunan's autonomy movement assumed that elections could inspire the population to proactively identify as citizens of a particular regime. The theorists who promulgated the foundational concepts of Chinese elections had promised no less.

In pursuit of this goal, provincial autonomy activists and Nationalist Party theorists dramatically rewrote Chinese election laws. The system of indirect voting and a sharply restricted franchise, based on an exclusionary notion of talent selection, were replaced with direct elections and the universal franchise to invest more of the population more deeply in the process. Elections after the 1920s became a mass, not elite, experience—but to ensure that the unpredictable populace made the correct choices, the authorities sharply curtailed competition for office. It is not surprising, then, that complaints about campaigning declined dramatically after the Nationalists came to power in 1927. Despite all of the effort that governments devoted to the propaganda and ritual aspects of these larger, constrained elections, the experience of Nationalist-sponsored elections provides little evidence that voting contributed to the education of loyal citizens. The historical experience of what some have called the "first Chinese democracy" on Taiwan, therefore, stands at odds with the foundational expectations that Chinese election advocates had embraced since the nineteenth century.

CHAPTER 7

Voting without a Choice

Elections in the People's Republic, 1949–2018

In the summer of 1953, three of mainland China's foremost legal scholars penned a lengthy assessment of a newly released national election law, the first since the founding of the People's Republic in 1949. They gushed that:

> We are about to embark upon a historically unprecedented nationwide universal suffrage election. The development of history tells us that any election system that is marred by the manipulations of the reactionary ruling class, by hypocrisy, and by lies will inevitably go bankrupt. Instead, it is the election system of the new democracy, which truly belongs to the people, that will be victorious.[1]

Reflecting the relative discipline and efficiency of the new party-state, elections for these new institutions, the local People's Congresses, would be implemented more thoroughly and over a larger portion of Chinese territory than any previous election system. Over the next year, more people in China would vote than had ever voted before—in that sense, something new truly was about to occur.

However, the sharp contrast these scholars drew with earlier elections was not justified. They celebrated attributes of these elections, particularly universal adult suffrage, that had been widely accepted for decades. Provincial autonomy governments in Hunan and Guangdong, as well as the Nationalist state, had adopted them with at least the same level of sincerity as the communist state. An expanded electorate was not an innovation in 1953. Other aspects of the new law left unmentioned in the essay, such as the suppression of competition, were likewise carried over from the previous era. Before 1949, even as voting rights became universalized, voters were deprived of meaningful choices. This trend only intensified after the Communist Revolution. Some of this came through the exclusion of class enemies from the voting process, an expanded version of the Nationalist-era disenfranchisement of "traitors." The most significant change came from the deliberate suppression of alternatives. When asked to cast a ballot for the ratification of a provincial constitution in the 1920s or a National Assembly delegate in the 1930s and 1940s, voters were expected to approve a decision that had already been made, not make one for themselves. Any other choice presented the authorities with a defect to be remedied, not a decision to be respected. Yet in those elections, alternatives had appeared on the ballot, creating space for opposition. Elections for the local People's Congresses solved this paradox by nominating only one candidate for each elected position.

Thinkers across the political spectrum in the mid-twentieth century believed that politics could be pedagogical. Hu Shi, though his alliance with the Nationalist Party was sometimes uncomfortable, supported this notion just as much as Sun Yat-sen did. In his various writings, Hu implied that this learning process would be natural and intuitive, asserting that voters in the United States could understand elections because of the environment they lived in, not because it had been taught from a textbook. Sun's model emphasized the state, rather than experience, as the teacher. The Nationalist state proved to be a distracted teacher before 1949 and deemphasized that role thereafter. Could a more disciplined teacher wring educational results out of elections?

Participation in an election of this sort was intended to signal membership in the national political community and provide the state with an opportunity to educate the populace in a new set of citizenship values. Despite the immense efforts that went into such activities, little education actually occurred in most elections before 1949. Intellectuals from the end of the Qing to the fall of the mainland Republic complained repeatedly that ordinary people failed to understand the purpose of voting and, moreover, knew little about their status as citizens of a Chinese state. The idea that elections as a mass political ritual could rectify this ignorance remained alluring to many in the new communist state after 1949. Unlike their predecessors, they brought an unparalleled level of efficiency, organization, and brutality to bear on the administration of their new elections. The early People's Republic proved to be a stern and unbending teacher.

New China's "New" Elections

The early 1950s was not the Chinese Communist Party's first experience with elections. The party had begun writing election laws over two decades earlier, soon after it acquired its first semi-permanent territorial base in Jiangxi, under the leadership of a still youthful but now firmly communist Mao Zedong.[2] His system for worker-peasant-soldier soviet assemblies restricted the electorate by social class, with a large number of groups excluded—ranging from those who "exploit the labor of others" to "merchants," as well as anyone with a Nationalist Party affiliation. Voting would be conducted openly, with raised hands, and a plurality was required for victory. As the name suggests, this system was intended to evoke the Soviet Union as a model. The Jiangxi election law, enacted at the same time as a number of other major initiatives, including a constitutional draft and a land reform law, was just one aspect of a broader attempt to build up political legitimacy for a putative communist state in China. Mao used the late 1931 creation of this Chinese Soviet Republic to consolidate his own power within the party and the international communist movement and presumably saw the law as one of the trappings of a modern state, rather than as a tool for other purposes.

Around the time of the communists' forced relocation from Jiangxi to Yan'an in 1935, the party deployed an innovative form of elections, "bean voting," as a strategy to mobilize political support among the largely illiterate and rural population still under their control. Voters received beans, rather than ballots, and placed them in bowls located behind the candidates they supported.[3] Bean voting was a formalized and ritualized experience: voting occurred in public (the candidates themselves, facing away from their bowls, could not see how voters cast their beans; election supervisors and other voters could see quite clearly) as part of an elaborate ceremony. It is difficult to determine exactly how widespread such elections were, although the strategy proved effective enough at mobilizing the population and at burnishing the party's democratic credentials that they continued throughout the 1937–45 war against Japan.[4] Once that conflict ended and civil war with the Nationalist government erupted in full, bean voting for local offices was expanded to newly acquired territories. William Hinton, an American living in a communist-controlled village in Shanxi Province, recounted two elections in spring and summer 1948 as part of his sociological study of land reform in the Chinese countryside.[5] His descriptions of these elections, the first for a local supervisory group and the second for a village people's assembly, emphasized the extent to which the process of voting could bind ordinary people to a new and unfamiliar government. For some voters and candidates, the result was a subjective transformation; Hinton relayed the tale of one peasant farmer voted in to office, "Old Tui-chin," who came to embrace his identity as a "true proletarian" during the course of the election.

After proclaiming his new government from atop Beijing's Tiananmen Gate in October 1949, Mao appeared to lose interest in elections as a tool of either state consolidation or popular education. Previously, he had claimed in his 1940 blueprint for a new government, "On the New Democracy," that China needed both a class dictatorship and an elected People's Congress. Days before Mao's formal proclamation of the People's Republic, his new government committed itself to both of these in its Common Program, the state's first constitution-like document. The class dictatorship came immediately. The mass suffrage election was put off to the unscheduled future, once "military operations have ended, land reform is thoroughly complete, and people from all sectors of society have been organized." In the following years, elections receded from the national agenda. Mao himself appears to have directed little attention to the issue, but other political leaders at least toyed with the idea of using voting for the traditional purpose of binding the people to the state. The Party's North China Office (which supervised Beijing, Tianjin, Hebei, Shanxi, and Inner Mongolia) called for the speedy establishment of local representative assemblies throughout its territory via mass suffrage elections in late October 1949; elsewhere in the country, village elections on the model described in Hinton's book may have continued.[6]

External pressure forced the question of elections back to center stage. Soviet leader Joseph Stalin, in a series of conversations with Mao's lieutenant Liu Shaoqi (1898–1969) in October 1952, pushed Mao to incorporate voting into the structures of the People's Republic. Liu had traveled to Moscow seeking advice on a host of issues, including the promised People's Congress elections. In vague terms, Liu explained that the party leadership felt that China's interim (and unelected) political consultative body was held in high esteem. Few clamored for elections, so it would be best to postpone them for several more years. The aged Soviet leader disagreed. Holding elections, Stalin argued, could improve China's international image (even Albania had elections, he remarked) and consolidate Communist Party rule at home. Stalin won his argument; on December 25, 1952, officials in Beijing began work on an election law to be used the next year.[7] Mao had fallen into line, explaining to his colleagues in January 1953 that despite what the leadership claimed to believe only a few months earlier, "the conditions are ripe for a national election, now that military actions in the mainland have ceased, land reform is basically completed, and people from all walks of life have been organized." He made no mention of Stalin's role or the Soviet leader's reasoning; instead, Mao claimed that elections would identify incompetent local officials, increase economic production, and strengthen the ongoing war effort in Korea.[8] Whether he believed these rationales is unclear.

Notwithstanding the expectations for elections articulated by China's supreme leader, the authors of the People's Republic's election law accepted the traditional logic that voting could transform popular consciousness. As it had under previous governments, voting would become a tool for instructing the people on the goals and philosophies of their new rulers. Evidence of this began to appear soon after Mao provided his justification for elections to a meeting of party leaders. Two days later, the *People's Daily* editorialized on behalf of the new electoral system in terms that echoed Mao's remarks, including his assertion that voting would strengthen the state, stimulate the economy, and help the war effort. Yet the editors inserted an additional claim that Mao had not made: an election would "greatly raise the people's revolutionary enthusiasm."[9] Those involved in writing and implementing the law were even clearer: Deng Xiaoping (1904–97), a member of the law's drafting committee and (later) of the Central Election Commission, declared, "Undoubtedly our election law will greatly unleash the activism and creativity of the masses and tighten the linkage between the people and Chairman Mao, the

Chinese Communist Party, and the People's Central Government."[10] Such claims gestured toward the long-standing expectations for the effects of elections that had inspired voting in earlier Chinese regimes.

Although communist-era election laws confirmed and strengthened tendencies visible in previous Chinese election practice, the immediate model for these laws was not the Nationalist system nor that party's pre-1949 experiments with voting but the Soviet model.[11] The 1953 system's most profound break with earlier Chinese elections, the introduction of "single-candidate elections [*deng'e xuanju*]," was derived directly from Soviet election law. This particular innovation, in which only one candidate was nominated for each open office, completed the transformation of elections from a choice into an acclamation of a person already selected by other means. Although this would have been alien to the systems of voting used between 1909 and the mid-1920s, in which competition for office had been a central feature of the system, it had some resonance with the 1921 Hunanese constitution referendum and the Nationalist elections of 1937 and 1947. In those elections, the state had a preferred outcome, although it did not prohibit (or even fully control) opposition and competition. The party's new system, by contrast, virtually guaranteed a particular outcome in each election. It did not hide its dominance of the election process, but rather embraced it and publicized it as a new form of democracy—a logical conclusion, given the goal of voting.

To make this system work, the communist government mobilized an enormous number of people from party organizations and the general public. No previous system of election preparation had been so thorough. A major bureaucracy was created to manage the complex process of registration, propaganda, and publicity that preceded the election. In Jiangsu, 97,209 cadres were organized to run the process for the province's 40.8 million people.[12] Shanghai assigned 11,778 people to manage the election for this municipality's 6.2 million.[13] That city was divided into more than 800 election districts, each staffed by six people, drawn from party work teams, local police, activists, and, if necessary, "housewives, unemployed workers, and unemployed intellectuals." Election workers registered voters by door-to-door census taking, workplace registration in coordination with local employers, and voluntary voter walk-ins.[14]

The slow, methodical, and organized manner with which the party conducted elections stood in striking contrast to elections before 1949, which were all hastily organized within the space of a few months. The government and the party supervised the enrollment of voters and the conduct of voting down to the smallest minutia. Even in a place as remote as Hainan Island's Ledong County, for instance, voter registrars engaged in a detailed correspondence with their superiors about the necessity of registering inhabitants of villages known to be inhabited by lepers. Although these registrars were allowed to "temporarily" avoid those villages, the exchange is revealing: election workers, even those assigned to some of the most obscure areas of the People's Republic, were concerned that someone would notice if a few villages were skipped.[15]

The detailed census and registration activities mandated by authorities had a particular function for the election, of course, but they were also an aspect of a broader project to survey, measure, and define the population. This was not new—from the late Qing period onward, election laws had been used to classify the population into politically favored and disfavored groups. Typically the line between those categories was fluid and ill-policed, as in the case of the disenfranchisement of opium users during the Qing and early Republican eras. Moreover, election law fluctuated significantly in those eras: the electorate expanded and shrank too rapidly for any of these imposed categories to have a deep effect on the population.

This changed after 1949. Voter registration intersected with the other major social surveys of the early 1950s, including the 1953 population census and the 1954 ethnic classification project. These projects built off one another: specific guarantees for dedicated minority group representation in the People's Congress system, for instance, could only be fulfilled if the state could define membership in the various ethnic groups.[16] Election preparation work was similar to those projects in two ways. First, voter registration reinforced the categories created and shaped by those projects. Registration books had a standardized format that mandating that every voter be identified by a formal name, a gender, an age calculated according to the Western calendar, and an identified ethnicity.[17] Second, like the ethnic categories created or reified during that classification project, identities as "voter" and "nonvoter" acquired a life and a force of their own. These categories were entirely political: the law mandated the disenfranchisement of "unreformed elements of the landlord class" and "counterrevolutionaries who have been deprived of their civil rights." Being formally placed in one of these categories had serious consequences beyond exclusion from the election. Individuals remembered their status, internalized it, and incorporated it into their identity during the Maoist era.

This process sought to reinforce and redefine older categories as well. The role of women as citizens and voters, for instance, received particular prominence in the first People's Congress election. Most propaganda images and texts were careful to feature identifiable women voters, while some, such as the 1953 poster "We Have the Right to Vote and to Be Elected," specifically foregrounded women's participation in the election (see figure 10). In this poster, a vigorous rural woman with ruddy cheeks waves her voter identification card in the air. Seated at the registration table behind her is another woman managing the registration campaign. Women's participation was celebrated as the ultimate form of political liberation ushered in by the Communist Revolution. One fictionalized account from a village in Songjiang County ends with a scene reminiscent of the "We Have the Right" poster: an "ordinary middle-aged woman . . . whose difficult life had etched deep wrinkles on her face" raising her voter identification card in the air and exclaiming,

> This small piece of paper did not come easily. Now that we have it, we will not suffer again. Now that we have it, we can maintain today's happy condition. Now that we have it, we can live a better life and, step by step, become like the Soviet Union.[18]

Instances of women's suffrage before 1949 were downplayed and ignored; the incorporation of women into the electorate was presented as a hallmark of communist rule. Internal statistics later compiled by Jiangsu provincial authorities revealed that 45 percent of registered voters in urban districts and 52 percent of voters in rural areas were women and that they voted at approximately the same rate as men.[19]

Classification proved a frustrating task at times. Local cadres—much like their predecessors in Qing and Republican times—often had difficulties applying the abstract categories mandated by law to concrete situations. The 1953 election law specified that "landlord class elements" were ineligible for the franchise, yet left the definition of that group vague. The Huangpu District Election Committee in Shanghai queried higher authorities in October 1953 as to whether the adult sons and daughters of landlords who "stay and home and don't work, enjoying the fruits of exploitation, but have not themselves taken an active role [in that exploitation]" should have the right to vote.[20] Other vexing issues included former wives of landlords who later married a member of the "working masses"; the Jiangsu Election Committee decided such women could qualify for voting rights if they now worked and had relied on the income generated by this labor for at least a year.[21] These arbitrary decisions were not sanctioned by national law.

To make presumptive enemies of the new state an object lesson for the edification of the rest of the population, some people would need to be publicly excluded from the franchise. An election law for a nominally universal suffrage election, however, could not afford to exclude too many. Shanghai mayor Chen Yi (1901–72) highlighted the cleavages and the tensions inherent in this policy in his 1953 call for election cadres to "on the one hand draw a sharp line between us and the enemy, but on the other hand unite with the absolute largest number of people" while conducting election work.[22] This was a tough balancing act. Election officials saw their work as being the building block of a civil government and thus sought to distinguish it from the violent political campaigns of the 1950s, many of which actively persecuted individuals now targeted for inclusion in the electorate.

Elections were supposed to be guided by a gentler process that would build alliances across class lines, excluding only those deemed totally unreconciled to communist rule. In general, voting rights were supposed to be an enticement to people from suspect backgrounds. In this vein, the Jiangsu Election Committee suggested that giving voter identification cards to "rich peasants" would "draw them closer to the People's Government."[23] Local cadres, some of whom "lumped [the election] together with propaganda from the recently concluded 'Suppress the Counterrevolutionaries' campaign" understandably became confused, such as the Shanghai election workers who hung a politically incorrect banner proclaiming, "Voting rights are only given to good people, not to counterrevolutionaries."[24]

Despite the Election Office's seemingly sincere efforts to differentiate their purpose from that of other contemporaneous mass campaigns, some people naturally perceived exclusion from voter rolls as a final

FIGURE 10: Yang Xianrang, "Women you xuanjuquan he bei xuanjuquan [We Have the Right to Vote and to Be Elected]" (1953), Stefan R. Landsberger Collections, International Institute of Social History (Amsterdam).

symbol of their rejection from the new state. A number attempted suicide in response. One Shanghai man with a "complicated personal history" swallowed poison at home after being listed as ineligible for the franchise during the voter census. He had successfully appealed to the city Election Committee to reverse this decision, but his local committee had not adjusted his status. He was reported to be recovering in a hospital, but the Election Committee concluded that this situation had resulted from a "leftist error" in the classification of people and warned local committees to pay attention.[25] This phenomenon was nationwide. The Jiangsu Election Committee later reported that at least nineteen incidents of attempted or successful suicide were linked to the election. Other sources counted at least twelve in Hebei, five in Henan, one in Hubei, one in Jiangxi, fourteen in Liaoxi (a province until June 1954, when it was merged with Liaoning), and thirty-four in Anhui.[26]

These suicides reflected different circumstances. Sometimes a dispute over election rights was merely the final manifestation of other conflicts, as in the case of Zhao Shiqing (unknown–1953), villager from Jiangsu's Jiangyin County, who was driven to suicide by his local headmen. The two had previously clashed over irrigation rights, after which the headman nursed "feelings of revenge." As voter registration began, the headman told the local work team not to issue Zhao a voter identification card, on the basis of Zhao's brief membership in a Nationalist-era mutual responsibility organization. His involvement had already been investigated after 1949, and Zhao had been cleared of wrongdoing; still, the headman and members of the work team used it to threaten and intimidate him. Returning home from a confrontation, Zhao said to his wife, "The headman told me that it's either him or me, so I'd better just get out of his way." On the night of July 3, 1953, he killed himself.[27]

In its judgment on this and other incidents of suicide, the Jiangsu Provincial Election Committee urged all localities to be more vigilant in the future. It recommended better education for local cadres, some of whom persisted in using "inappropriate methods" drawn from "Land Reform, the Suppress the Counterrevolutionaries Campaign, and the Five Antis Campaign." Some, the committee feared, even believed that "deaths are unavoidable during political campaigns." This was condemned as a "careless and very incorrect way of thinking."[28] Yet it was all too common. One village headman in Wujiang County inquired of a visiting election work team, "During the election, how many landlords should we identify? How many people should we shoot?"[29] In another southern Jiangsu county, cadres asked, "Is this a second Land Reform Campaign? Who do we struggle against this time?"[30] The election and the propaganda campaign that preceded it were, despite pronouncements from the government, intimately linked to the climate of pervasive political violence that characterized the early years of the People's Republic. Although the election was ostensibly not intended as a mass political campaign that targeted "enemies," it is not surprising that many saw it as exactly that.

Leniency had its dangers, too. Some reports claimed that "landlord elements" had hidden themselves among the people. A few of these had registered as voters and, in the case of one "escaped landlord," had even managed to be nominated for his local People's Congress. The Jiangsu Election Committee warned, "this indicates that class struggle during the election is very intense."[31] To assist with this classification process, governments at various levels produced handbooks for work teams, filled with detailed criteria. One of these, written by the Nanjing Public Security Bureau in late July 1953, provided miniature biographies of several dozen real people with complicated backgrounds. For each person, the bureau offered a judgment about whether the person qualified to vote and provided brief justifications. Examples included former members of Nationalist military, intelligence, and police services, as well as adherents of the banned Yiguandao religious sect, gangsters, and those who had collaborated with the Japanese occupation. One subject of a biography was described as having served in Republican armies from 1918 to 1937 and in Chiang's security apparatus from 1945 to 1947. There was no evidence that he had committed any "concrete crime" during those final two years of service and since 1949 he had "proactively confessed his history to the government" and surrendered a telephone and a pair of binoculars to the government. He was given the right to vote.[32]

Eligible voters were issued identification cards, which some reportedly treasured. One eighty-four-year-old woman in rural Yixing County, known only as "Granny Han," supposedly "bought a red cloth to wrap her voter identification and property deeds, and stores [the bundle] in the bottom of a chest."[33] In some places, voter names were posted in public spaces as a means of building an interest in and a connection to the election process. One worker in Wuxi, after seeing his name on the publicly displayed voter rolls, supposedly exclaimed, "My name has never been up on a big red announcement board before; this has only happened because of Chairman Mao."[34] In later year, this tangible proof of inclusion in the electorate became a symbol of the rehabilitation of former undesirables. The deposed last emperor of the Qing, Puyi (1906–67), celebrated his voter identification card—issued in 1960, after long years of imprisonment—as proof of his inclusion in the new political order.[35]

Propaganda work extended beyond voter registration into a variety of other activities. In northern Jiangsu's Xuzhou municipality, neighborhood and work unit propaganda teams were established, and links were created with existing cultural institutions, such as amateur theater groups. These groups engaged in a variety of activities ranging from "calling mass meetings, small meetings, smaller meetings, and courtyard meetings," to conducting individual visits, holding classes in night school, "performing *xiangsheng* cross-talk, *kuaiban* clapper-talk, and short plays," creating blackboard announcements, and using the public broadcast system.[36] In Dongtai County, a village opera troupe performed works with names like "Voter Identification Card" and "Zhang Xiulan Looks at the Announcement Board."[37] No previous election had seen such an extensive outpouring of propaganda and educational materials.

Much of this propaganda proceeded from the assumption that the majority would need guidance through every step of this new process—starting with the definition of the word *election*. Authorities feared the terminology of the new regime might be incomprehensible to many, particularly the contraction for mass suffrage election [*puxuan*]. The term itself predated 1949, although it only came into general use after the 1930s. The Nationalists had used it to describe their election in 1947. Yet reports filed by work teams sent to run early elections in certain countryside counties reported in some cases that villagers confused the word with "selecting seeds for growing rice" or "selecting models [i.e., model workers, model cadres, etc.]."[38] To compensate, officials designed processes to educate the public. In one opera written for this purpose from south China's Guangdong Province, the first scene began with two peasants deep in discussion:

SHAN: All right, then you tell me—what is a "mass suffrage election [*puxuan*]"?

CHOU: "Mass suffrage election"? Well, the character *xuan* means "to choose", as in choosing seeds; the character *pu* means different kinds of seeds: seeds for beans, or seeds for greens, or . . .

SHAN: Oh, you! You're pretending that you know what you're talking about, when you really don't . . . (*bursts into song*)
This is an event of great importance to the people, no one should look upon it lightly.
Everyone from all across the country gathers for an election [*xuanju*], that will choose good representatives who will do good things.[39]

Thus the state sought to amuse and educate at the same time.

At the heart of the propaganda effort were small group meetings that work teams held with local residents; these occurred nationwide and are uncountable. These meetings aimed to explain the upcoming election to the population and provide the government with a view into the mindset of average citizens. After spreading word of the election, teams guided the people to select candidates through a process of conversational "comparison and assessment." Often, such candidates were people who had already been lauded by the new regime. A report from a meeting held at Shanghai's Putuo District Number One State-Owned Dyeing Factory in December 1953 concluded approvingly that "the average worker cares greatly about who becomes a [People's Congress] representative."[40] In an ideal situation, the work team then guided members of the electorate to nominate easily electable individuals, who had already demonstrated their worth to the regime. This vision was reflected in period artwork, such as that reprinted on this book's cover, in which the election of a representative is depicted as a moment of acclamation, consensus, and unity. "Elect good people," the slogan on that poster reads, "to do good things."

Nomination and election did not always proceed so smoothly in real life. In Shanghai, ordinary people complained openly about the party's tight control over the nominations. Organized groups in Beijing, such as the Catholics, who formed a significant proportion of one district's voters, disregarded the work team cadres and made their own nominations.[41] As unlikely as it might seem, campaigning for election reemerged in some places during the nomination phase, although details can be vague. In

Tianjin, official sources complained that "capitalists" held banquets, networked, and studied the election law in hopes of winning office in the new system.[42]

Even when the nomination phase appeared successful, latent popular dissatisfaction could lead to actual ballot box defeats. In one district in Nanjing, only three of the nine candidates originally nominated ended up winning election. According to the official report, during the nomination process seven peasants, one worker, and one member of a government organization had been chosen. Once the election meeting began, however, participants proposed to replace some of these previous nominees with new ones; the meeting chair assented, but when it was time to vote, he found that "the feelings of the masses were sluggish" and half failed to participate. As a consequence, only five people (three of the original candidates, along with two of the newly selected ones) received majorities. The work team concluded that the election had failed because leaders had not inserted themselves deeply enough into the details of the nominating process. If they had, they would have identified the particular issues that led to this problem (which included a general dislike of two candidates, and a widely shared feeling that another, an impoverished but respected single man, would not have enough time to earn a living if elected) and could have made adjustments.[43] Events such as this were relatively rare, however.

Voting, held in a staggered manner with localities voting at different times between late 1953 and early 1954, typically took the form of a mass rally held in a location specially decorated for the occasion. Anecdotal reports from the election meetings conveyed the sense of excitement and participation they were supposed to create: workers at Shanghai's Zhonghua Match Factory, for instance, broke into song and began dancing the revolutionary *yangge* folk dance.[44] After the voters gathered, a meeting chairperson was selected to explain the election procedures and introduce the prenominated candidates. Local People's Congress elections, unlike most earlier elections, essentially dispensed with the notion of a secret ballot. Although the 1953 law permitted written ballots, few election meetings used them. Most used other methods—raised hands or, in some cases, voice—allowed by the new authorities. Each candidate was voted on individually. Public voting of this sort, a departure from pre-1949 mainstream election law and from practice in the Soviet Union, was a concession to mass illiteracy and was a clear form of political control that dramatically increased the social and personal cost of opposition. It also completed the ritualistic aspects of Maoist era voting: elected delegates were literally acclaimed by the masses.

Overall, election officials judged their work a success. Jiangsu's eighty-one counties and cities had a total of 22,797,773 registered voters, about 55.81 percent of the entire population. Over 80 percent of those voters (nearly nineteen million people) voted. More than a half million people, or 1.28 percent of the provincial population, were "deprived of voting rights in accordance with the law," and an additional 39,205 people were excluded from the franchise on the basis of mental illness.[45] In terms of sheer number of voters, this was the largest election held in Jiangsu to date. Nationwide, supposedly 85.88 percent of eligible voters cast ballots in these grassroots elections.[46] In Shanghai, a January 1954 report claimed that the election propaganda campaign had succeeded in creating a "mindset of being [the nation's] masters" among this unprecedented number of participants. Other beneficial effects included an increase in group unity in neighborhoods and factories, the elevation of elected People's Congress members to the status of role models, growing confidence in local cadres, and the opportunity to "feel the glory of being Chinese and experience the happiness of being a member of the motherland's great family."[47] Some credited the election with economic benefits. Northern Jiangsu's Xuzhou City Xiukang Iron Wok Factory reported an increased daily production of 500 woks, thanks to a new spirit of unity among the workers.[48] Jiangsu provincial authorities concluded in 1954 that

> the achievements of the election were gigantic. It improved and raised the people's enthusiasm for politics and production, and also thoroughly educated and improved the cadres, allowing the connection between the Party, the government, and the masses to grow even closer.[49]

This was an overstatement. Confidential reports revealed apathy and confusion, including one Shanghai voter who did not raise her hand to vote for the slate of candidates, claiming, "I don't know what kind of meeting this is; I only know that I was told to be here." Other problems included cadres, rather than voters, filling out written ballots in the few precincts that used them.[50] This experience highlighted the limits of party control, even in such a tightly designed and monitored system. Such events never became widely known; given strict party control over the press, they became fodder for secret reports, rather than the "Timely Commentary"–type critiques or "Free Talk"–style satires of earlier decades.

For those at provincial or municipal election offices who had access to these confidential reports, there was plenty of evidence to disappoint those who hoped voting could create a new Chinese political culture. At a May 1953 "discussion meeting" in Shanghai, for example, participants offered politically incorrect sentiments, such as "The election has nothing to do with me—I'm too old," "I'm old and have no education, so tell us who to vote for," "There's no benefit to coming to meetings, because they don't solve anything . . . let them do whatever they want, it has nothing to do with me," and "Don't vote for women, because they have to cook and take care of children, so they have no free time." One even complained, "The election is for those who have already eaten their fill and still have nothing better to do—what sort of person has that much free time?"[51] This phenomenon occurred nationwide. In one Sichuan village, cadres concluded that even after two weeks of intensive election propaganda, residents still "either didn't know or didn't care how to vote, why to vote, or who to vote for." Bankers in Xi'an, farmers outside of Changsha, and many others reportedly held similar attitudes. Some had good reason for their disinterest. In food shortage areas in Hunan, residents simply told reporters from the party's restricted-circulation newspaper: "We don't have anything to eat. What are we going to do with an election?"[52]

The local People's Congresses were the first step in the creation of a chain of legislatures that culminated in the creation of a National People's Congress in September 1954. Unsurprisingly, Mao himself—along with many other major figures in the communist power structure, including Premier Zhou Enlai (1898–1976), military commander Zhu De (1886–1976), and Secretary General of the State Council Xi Zhongxun (1913–2002)—found themselves in that highest representative body. Despite the unprecedented mobilization of resources and energy that underlay this act of institution building, the pedagogical value of the 1953–54 elections is hard to assess. Although some voters were indifferent and a few reappropriated the official election rhetoric of choice and mastery to assert their own interests against the state, there could easily be truth in the state's claims that a substantial number of voters—who had never been reached by any election in previously decades—adopted (at least in part) an identity as citizens of a still-new state. Certainly, the local People's Congress elections had a much deeper and more intimate effect on the lives of ordinary Chinese than any earlier experience at the ballot box. The incidents of attempted and actual suicide, apparently nonexistent in pre-1949 elections, testify to that.

A Maoist Interruption

The election made little impression on Mao. He spent only ten minutes at the polling station, appeared expressionless and bored in the official photograph taken as he voted, and left without saying anything about the significance of the occasion.[53] The elections had not been his idea, and ultimately voting had no place in his vision for a revolutionized society. In this sense, Mao was the great exception among twentieth-century leaders. Apart from his participation in the 1920 Changsha protests, which called for the reform of provincial election law, nothing in his political career suggested that he either embraced elections as opportunities for talent selection and popular enlightenment or feared them as moments of manipulation. Consequently, he was essentially indifferent to the People's Congress system and the elections that created it.

The frequency and comprehensiveness of local People's Congress elections waxed and waned in inverse proportion to Mao's political fortunes in the following decades. The original plan had been to schedule such elections roughly once every two years. Local People's Congress elections in summer and fall 1956 were held on the same scale as those in 1953–54 and were also the subject of a substantial propaganda campaign. On the basis of the partial statistics available at the end of 1956, authorities claimed that 92.9 percent of enrolled voters cast votes in that year's election (as compared to 85.88 percent in the previous election) and that substantially fewer individuals had been deprived of their right to vote.[54] Within months, however, the environment changed completely. The Anti-Rightist Campaign, which began in the summer of 1957, marked the start of nearly two decades (with brief interruptions) during which Mao's personal power and political philosophy dominated the national scene. Elections played a diminished role until Mao's death in 1976.

Interruption characterized voting in this era. The scheduled third (1958) and fourth (1960) rounds of local People's Congress elections occurred during Mao's 1958–62 Great Leap Forward and the consequent famine. Substantially less documentation is available from these elections, but the relative paucity of coverage in the *People's Daily* reflects their limited significance in Maoist political culture. The 1958 election process took place over only a few months, concluding by the middle of May, and its apparent goal was to reinforce popular excitement for Mao's Great Leap Forward.[55] Even less was printed about the 1960 election, held during the depths of the Great Leap Forward famine. Voting occurred in the major cities, although seemingly with less fanfare than earlier elections.[56] Puyi, the now-rehabilitated deposed emperor living in Beijing's university district, voted for the first time in 1960 and included a copy of his registration card in his memoirs. His experience was probably exceptional. The *People's Daily* is conspicuously silent about voting in the countryside that year, suggesting that there may have been major disruptions outside of the cities due to famine.[57] After a brief (and unexplained) delay, local elections occurred next in spring 1963, this time throughout the country.[58] Perhaps reflecting Mao's weakened position in the wake of the Great Leap Forward's failure, the rhetoric of this election drew more from the language used in 1953–54 and 1956 than it did from 1958.[59] As late as the summer of 1965, local elections continued to be held in Beijing; one prominent Beijing University scholar who had been persecuted earlier (and whose sufferings only grew in the following years) later recalled his delight at seeing his name still listed among eligible voters that year.[60] These were among the last institutionalized elections held during Mao's lifetime.

The advent of the Cultural Revolution in 1966 and the consequent disruption of institutions across the nation forced the People's Congress elections into abeyance until Mao's death in 1976. The *People's Daily*, the party's official mouthpiece, provides graphic evidence of this: between August 1965 and July 1979, the phrase "grassroots elections [*jiceng xuanju*]"—used both before 1965 and after 1979 to refer to the local People's Congress elections—does not appear even once.[61] Those fourteen years were the longest stretch of time in the twentieth century that mainland China lacked formal procedures for government elections.

The Cultural Revolution did not lack for the rhetoric of elections, although it was a decidedly minor aspect of that movement's conceptual infrastructure. One early attempt to set goals for (and constraints on) the Red Guards, the Central Committee's August 1966 "Decision Concerning the Great Proletarian Cultural Revolution" (commonly referred to as the "Sixteen Points"), demanded elections for "members of Cultural Revolution small groups and Cultural Revolution committees, as well as and representatives to Cultural Revolution congresses." These elections, rather than being based on previous Chinese practice, were to use a "system of comprehensive elections [*quanmian de xuanju zhi*]" modeled after that of the 1871 Paris Commune.[62] The phrase "comprehensive election" had never appeared before in official discourse before the Sixteen Points and it had no particular set meaning—but it did have the virtue of being cloaked in the romantic revolutionary aura of the Paris Commune. In an effort to translate the "Sixteen Points" into a platform for action, the *People's Daily* explained that "who to pick and how to pick them must be the result of several days of consideration and repeated discussions among the masses."[63] Other attempts to flesh out the meaning of this ambiguous phrase appeared in print during the late summer and fall of 1966, but all celebrated, rather than described, "comprehensive elections."[64] In keeping with the anti-establishment impulses of the Cultural Revolution, virtually all authors emphasized that there would be no set terms of office under this system; recall and replacement could happen at any time. Mao's permanent revolution was to have been accompanied by a permanent election, albeit one unencumbered by fixed rules or procedures.

Despite this rhetoric, none of the violent seizures of power in workplaces, universities, and government agencies during 1966 had anything to do with voting. Some claimed the term "comprehensive elections" in this era to legitimate themselves, including a Red Guard group at Beijing University, but this is little more than a rhetorical claim.[65] Even as late as 1970, a visiting Italian communist was told of such an election (again, without any details) that supposedly took place two years earlier among Tianjin's dockworkers.[66] Such examples notwithstanding, the concept of a "comprehensive election" fell out of official favor, along with the idealization of the Paris Commune as a model, in February 1967 as Mao turned against the complete replacement of the party and government at all levels with ill-prepared, poorly understood opportunistic local organizers. This pivot, symbolized by his refusal to accept the declaration of a Shanghai Commune that month, lead to a dramatic decline in this rhetoric. Accordingly, authoritative publications such as the *People's Daily* and *Red Flag* slowly dropped the phrase "comprehensive election" over the course of 1967.[67]

Despite this tactical shift of rhetoric, Mao's philosophical distaste for voting was certainly sincere. He disliked procedures and formal structures, romanticized spontaneous action, and pined to make revolution a permanent condition. Voting had very little role to play in such a society. Very little of his writings from the Cultural Revolution era deal specifically with elections, leaving only crumbs to build speculations out of. Meeting with a pair of Albanian communists in February 1967, Mao offered a series of slightly disjointed observations about the progress of the Cultural Revolution that touched on his view of elections. Declaring "I am not a believer in elections," he explained that after victory in 1949, the party appointed officials to govern. Some of those officials were later "elected" to office, which appears to be a reference to the People's Congress system. This did not sit well with his view of political action. Given that China is too populous and its electoral districts too large, he asked:

> How could [a voter] know so many people? I was elected in Beijing, but many people have never even met me! How can [a voter] elect someone they have never met? . . . this is not as good as [how] the Red Guards [select leaders], because at least [ordinary members] have spoken with their own leaders.[68]

People learned through direct experience and personal interaction—mass elections, lacking in intimacy, could never provide that. Comprehensive elections may have proved too unruly, but the old structures of the People's Congress system were too stultifying for Mao's tastes. Although the word *election* was used to describe a variety of selection processes during the Cultural Revolution period, there was little attempt to attach any meaningful, coordinated activity to the term for over a decade.

Training Classes in Democracy

After Mao's death, as part of a process of institutional reconstruction, newly ascendant party leaders revived the local People's Congress system and elections have been held routinely since 1980. Some reform-era leaders, such as Peng Zhen (1902–97), who had helped write the original People's Congress election law in 1953, still held to the initial vision of voting as an opportunity for educational and propaganda work, as well as a tool for the expansion of state power by giving the center leverage over local cadres. Peng, the son of a poor peasant family who had joined the party at twenty-one and served as an underground communist organizer during the Nationalist era, governed Beijing in the early years of the People's Republic before becoming a prime victim of the Cultural Revolution. This now rehabilitated loyal soldier of the party wanted to put its rule on a firmer procedural basis, not plant the seeds of its demise.[69] Peng and his allies saw a return to elections as a signal that the Cultural Revolution was over—and with it, any lingering support for Maoist-style participatory "democracy." They found themselves attracted to the same myths that had intrigued authoritarian reformers since the late Qing: elections could foster communication between rulers and ruled, could aid in the selection of talent, and could be a valuable educational opportunity for the state to instruct its citizens.

To introduce a measure of competition—and give teeth to the center's ability to discipline local leadership—Peng's revised local People's Congress election law, issued in 1979, mandated that the number of candidates for local elections exceed the number of elective positions.[70] Over the following years, a nomination system that (in theory and sometimes in practice) allowed for non-party candidates to enter local races would also be developed. Although formally competitive, the number of seats contested by outsider candidates has remained extremely small. Dissident candidates, ranging from college students in the early 1980s to political activists such as Yao Lifa (1958–present) and others since in the 1990s, attract a moderate amount attention (not all of it welcome; Yao was detained in 2016) but only rarely win seats in local People's Congresses.[71] Such challenges are not the norm, however. At least through the 1990s, the local People's Congress system functioned as a relatively stable mechanism for funneling the "cooperation" of substantial elements of the population.[72] Ultimately, even the presence of multiple candidates on the ballot might provide the party with a sophisticated tool for controlling the election results without the appearance of heavy-handedness.[73]

After their resumption, local People's Congress elections ceased to play the educational role some had envisioned for them in the 1950s, even though their function as tool for reflecting public opinion to the party elite has arguably assumed a new level of importance and the ability of congressional representatives to act as advocates has increased.[74] Although the role of these elected assemblies to "connect the rulers and the ruled" (to use a Qing-era phrase) may be more vibrant than ever, the ceremonial aspect of voting disappeared since reinstatement of these elections. Rather than taking the form of mass meetings, in which voters signaled approval by raising hands in unison, elections after the 1979 law became a more individualized experience in which voting was conducted by written secret ballot. In terms of popular perception, the vast majority of the population evinces little interest in their existence. Despite claiming that typically 95 percent of eligible voters cast ballots in People's Congress elections, a major nationwide survey of Chinese political attitudes conducted in 2011 found that 15.7 percent of respondents had attended the candidate forums held before each local congress election, 21.5 percent could recall how they voted in the last local congress election, and, of those who remembered how they voted, only 37.4 percent remembered if the candidate they supported had won.[75] The elections occur without much fanfare or popular mobilization, although a vestigial propaganda campaign still accompanies each round of voting (see figure 11).

Peng Zhen and other reformers paired the restoration of local People's Congress elections with an expansion of voting into other situations. As one of the architects of the 1982 Constitution of the People's Republic, Peng ensured that in addition reasserting the right to vote for local People's Congress delegates (as had two of the three earlier post-1949 constitutions), this document would extend voting rights to two new domains: workers in "collective economic organizations" could elect "managerial personnel" and urban and rural residents could elect "residents' or villagers' committee."[76] The implementation of these new forms of elections after 1982, however, has been mixed. At least initially, some elections were held in "collective economic organizations," such as the semi-public "town and

FIGURE 11: "Use your democratic rights in accordance with the law/Cast a sacred ballot." Propaganda slogan posted on a building for the 2016 local People's Congress election in Changsha, Hunan. Photo by author.

village enterprises" that helped fuel China's initial economic boom in the 1980s, but they have been the object of little research or reporting.⁷⁷ Urban residents' committees have become a fixture across Chinese cities, yet most research suggests that elections for these bodies are little more than manifestations of party fiat and consequently generate very little public excitement or interest.⁷⁸

Village committee elections, however, attracted enormous interest—and, initially, opposition. It took Peng Zhen an additional five years after the 1982 constitution's enactment to gain support for a draft election law, a length of time that suggests a considerable amount of dissent at the top levels of government. The full contours of this debate are still unknown, but the portions that existed in public documents show that proponents claimed that elected leaders could improve administrative efficiency at the local level by allowing talented people to take office—and this would enhance the reach of the central state.[79] No one envisioned elected committees setting major policy initiatives, nor would Peng or other advocates have found such an idea attractive. Other echoes of old myths about elections surfaced in the rhetoric used to justify rural voting. In his final push for the authorization of election for village committees, Peng Zhen appealed to the trope of education: "Grassroots self-government organizations [i.e., elected village committees]," he claimed, would function as a "training class in democracy [*minzhu xuexi ban*]."[80]

Since the beginning of authorized village elections in the early 1990s, millions have been held all across the country. During the 2005–7 cycle alone, central authorities claimed that 624,252 villages (out of a national total of 637,279 villages) completed the election process for village committees and that 90.97 percent of eligible voters participated.[81] Although urbanization has reduced the number of villages, approximately 559,000 elected village committees were still reported to exist in 2016.[82] Over the course of the past three decades, procedures for voting (including use of the secret ballot) have become standardized across the nation, and in a formal sense, most elections appear to comply with the basic requirements of the law.[83] Village elections have been accompanied by debates over their meaning and significance, but a decidedly pessimistic trend has emerged in twenty-first-century scholarly literature.[84] One study concluded that even in the relatively relaxed political atmosphere at the turn of the century, informal institutions and activities in villages were better able to provide public goods than were formal elected bodies.[85] A rich (if unverifiable and anonymous) online commentarial tradition has emerged that conveys the sense of pervasive sleaziness, low-level fraud, and general nonsense that accompanies these elections in the present day.[86] The state, always leery of overly independent village leadership, has more recently demonstrated a hard line against elected village committees that challenge its interests too directly, as exemplified by the 2016 arrests of committee members in the famous "protest village" of Wukan, Guangdong. Contrary to early hopes, elections have not spread upward from the village level to higher jurisdictions, either.

This historical importance of village elections is not that they appear to mark a path to a democratic future, but that they harken back to long-standing concerns in Chinese political thought. The underlying vision of elections that they reflect, in which voting serves as a ritual for citizens to engage with the symbols of the state and in which elected officials (who are presumably the most respected and most talented members of their communities) are expected to be a node connecting the center to the locality, is well over a century old. These intimate elections, held within the natural unit of a village and under the tight scrutiny of party oversight, are a modernized version of the "public appointment"–style selection that late Qing reformers took as their model for elections. Communist cadres and Qing constitutionalists may have differed on many things, but on this they would agree: local elections and any representative bodies they produce are a "training class" from which voters are not supposed to graduate.

Conclusion

No government in mainland China has ever come to power based on the results of an election, but most twentieth-century regimes promised elections after consolidating authority through armed force. The 1911 Revolution began with a mutiny, but within weeks leaders began planning elections. Yuan Shikai's 1913 coup was followed by constitution writing and an imperial restoration based on a vote. Likewise, the various provincial autonomy regimes sought to buttress their legitimacy through new kinds of election laws. For all of its militaristic trappings and Leninist inclinations, the Nationalist Party of the late 1920s was formally committed to transition to an era of "constitutional rule" founded on popular voting—although the Nanjing government proved chary about sticking to a specific schedule.

The People's Republic began with this same promise. Mao, left to his own devices, probably had little philosophical or political investment in creating an election system, but other members of the elite of the early

People's Republic were dedicated institution builders. The People's Congresses, and the elections that produced them, fit neatly into their agenda. Their reasoning for this had Cold War aspects, certainly: the desire to emulate the Soviet Union and the wish to showcase Chinese-style "new democracy" to a decolonizing world. At the same time, aspects of the Chinese foundational idea of elections permeated their expectations and planning. The mammoth scale of the first two local People's Congress elections are a testament to this. During the height of the Maoist era, such thoughts were unfashionable (if not dangerous—many of those associated with the 1953 election law were victims in the Cultural Revolution), but they remerged after 1976 to color the return of local People's Congress elections and newly introduced village elections. Ideas about elections not only crossed the 1949 divide, they outlived Mao himself.

The post-1979 national and local election systems reflect the old expectation that elected institutions would function primarily as a node of communication between the state and the people. To a limited extent, these systems come closer to meeting this goal than any earlier iteration of mainland Chinese elections. Unlike their Qing or Republican predecessors, village committee elections and local People's Congress elections have become fully regularized and routine. The bodies they produce, particularly at the People's Congress level, perform important communicative functions (although, critically, not independent legislative functions) in the contemporary People's Republic. In the twenty-first century, state authorities and public intellectuals devote relatively little attention to the expectations for elections that had once excited such interest in China, particularly claims that elections can educate the populace and create opportunities for identifying the talented. Voting still exists as a state-building rite—and as such appears today to appeal mostly to those with other connections to the government, such as employment in the state sector—but it has undeniably acquired elements of being an empty ritual for the rest of the population.[87]

CONCLUSION

*Democratization and the Discourse
of Elections in China*

The Hunan provincial legislature building that Mao stormed in 1920 survives today. Located down a narrow lane in a Changsha neighborhood yet to be invaded by high-rise apartments, it sits within the enclosed compound of the Hunan Federation of Trade Unions. Although now a rarely used recreation center, the building's former elegance is still discernible (see figure 12). The old meeting chamber, once a vast space several stories high and lit by skylights thick enough to survive Japanese bombs, is now subdivided into small rooms filled with dusty table tennis tables. Visiting is not encouraged, but it is not prohibited, either. Similar structures survive in other cities. The Jiangsu provincial legislative building that Zhang Jian helped construct in 1909 is now part of the People's Liberation Army's garrison headquarters for the Nanjing military district. Although it is in a restricted zone, it is surrounded by a vibrant shopping district and is easily spotted from the street. Others, such as Hubei's, have been repurposed into museums. Even the old national parliament building in Beijing has endured the dramatic twenty-first-century reconstruction of that city. Located inside the state-run Xinhua News Agency's campus, it, too, is closed to visitors. At first glance, these buildings appear a perfect metaphor for the place of elections in contemporary China: half-ignored, disconnected from their surroundings and histories, and sometimes inaccessible. On the mainland, the local People's Congress elections elicit little public interest, while village committee elections seem increasingly formulaic. Only in Taiwan and Hong Kong—both

FIGURE 12: The former provincial legislature building in Changsha, Hunan. Photo by author.

exceptional cases—are elections inarguably central to the political and intellectual life of a Chinese society.

Like those forgotten legislative chambers, voting persists in mainland China. The government continues to run a vast network of elections even as it suggests that elected government is unsuitable for China. President Xi Jinping (1953–present) has highlighted this, listing in a 2014 speech all of the political systems that have failed modern China: "constitutional monarchy, imperial restoration, parliamentarism, a multi-party system and a presidential system—we considered them, tried them, but none worked."[1] With the partial exception of "imperial restoration," it is hard to ignore the fact that all of the forms he dismissed are inherently based on elections. Xi also points to a resolution for this contradiction, explaining elsewhere that "the kind of governance best suited for a country is determined by that country's historical heritage and cultural traditions, and its level of social and economic development, and it is ultimately decided by that country's people."[2] This echoes the ideas of other contemporary thinkers, most notably Yu Keping (1959–present), former deputy chief of the Communist Party's Central Compilation and Translation Bureau, who argued in an essay strikingly titled "Democracy Is a Good Thing," that Chinese democratic practices must be built on "the national tradition of political culture, the quality of the politicians and the people, and the daily customs of the people."[3] Elections do have a place in China, as long as they are elections with Chinese characteristics.

The foundational expectations for elections that developed in the nineteenth and twentieth centuries were an early part of this quest to domesticate a foreign political process. The translators, diplomats, reformers, writers, and politicians who contributed to the synthesis of this theory have all, knowingly or unknowingly, drawn on China's own traditions of political and institutional thought. Ballot boxes and the numerical counting of supporters may have been foreign inventions, but elections were analogized and conceptualized within a domestic cognitive framework. The rationale for elections offered by Chinese politicians and thinkers—emphasizing their meritocratic potential, capacity for popular enlightenment, and ability to harmoniously link the rulers and the ruled, all in the service of building a powerful Chinese state—drew from this framework. This was not the only possible way of conceptualizing voting within the vast, complex, and often contradictory reservoir of Chinese political thought, however. Instead, it was an interpretation tailored to provide actionable solutions during a long era of acute national crisis. This discourse was a consequence of the particularities of the nineteenth- and twentieth-century Chinese experience, not an inevitable product of what it sometimes referred to as "5,000 years of civilization."

The transformation of Chinese election law across the twentieth century, from limited, indirect yet competitive elections to mass suffrage, noncompetitive elections emerged from attempts to balance the various aspects of the particular foundational expectations set in the late nineteenth century. The spectacle of campaigners in 1909 and 1912–13 led to harsh critiques of voting as a system for selecting leaders even before elected legislatures were seated. This complaint stemmed from ideological concerns as much as anything else. Similarly, the expansion of the electorate in the 1920s and 1930s, culminating in nearly universal adult franchise, emerged as much from a renewed emphasis on the pedagogical value of voting as it did from the efforts of suffrage activists.[4] Changes in Chinese elections since then have been similarly driven by this same set of expectations, including the reemergence of voting as an educational tool in mainland China as part of the post-Mao "reform and opening" initiative. Emphasis on these ideas may be growing in the present, as intellectuals and leaders become increasingly concerned with tracing distinctive Chinese intellectual genealogies for the institutions of the contemporary state.[5]

To think about China's future, it is important to grapple with the implications of this long-established discourse on elections for the trajectory of Chinese political reform in the present era. The current government assumes no tension between properly conducted elections and the supremacy of the Chinese Communist Party. This aligns with the expectation that voting is a state-strengthening ritual and appears amply justified by over a century's worth of experience of Chinese elections. Even during periods when elections have been held regularly, there was never a transfer of power from the state to the people. Have these foundational expectations finally been fulfilled in the form of elections with Chinese characteristics that will buttress the power of history's most successful single-party state?

Elections do not equal democracy—but the link between them is undeniable. It is natural to ask: why have nearly 175 years of thinking about, and over a century of experimenting with, elections not led to democratization?[6] Does the persistence of these foundational expectations, even in a diluted form, help explain the routinization of elections without the formalization of popular control over political processes? Four major ways of thinking about the history of Chinese elections are worth considering in light of this question.

One solution is to declare that Chinese elections have never been elections in any meaningful sense of the word. Historian Feng Xiaocai makes this case by provocatively calling the political culture of early twentieth-century China "the politics of usurpation."⁷ This analysis could easily be extended past 1949 on both sides of the Taiwan Strait. Anything that appeared to be proto-democratic, including elections, civic organizations, and even the use of the word *citizen*, was simply an elaborate fraud. Although these terms were bandied about with great frequency in twentieth-century China, they never truly meant anything to most people—thus, associations with grandiose names but few members would claim to speak on behalf of large populations, powerful politicians would hide their identities behind the humble titles "citizen" and "comrade," and governments would assemble uncomprehending people to drop paper into a box and call it an election. There could be no contradiction between the presence of elections and the absence of democratization, therefore, because the elections that occurred were not real.

This overstates the case. Few elections were truly faked, although Nationalist-sponsored elections between 1945 and 1949 come close, and governments had a notable tendency to draft laws for elections that were never held. For many elections, considerable evidence survives in the form of newspaper accounts and printed government documents. Although these need to be examined critically (and Feng is absolutely correct to caution readers not to take "democratic" rhetoric in documents at face value), they demonstrate that elections occurred, that people participated in them, that a surprising number of them featured some form of competition, and that intellectuals and political leaders thought they were important enough to worry about and complain about. These elections, no matter how real, did not primarily seek to represent the "will of the people"; instead, they were intended to select talented officials and educate the populace. Although some rulers may have adopted this position cynically, many more were sincere in their expectation that voting could accomplish these goals. In this sense, Chinese elections were not all "counterfeit."

A second solution is to argue that meaningful democratic change did originate in the early twentieth century and carries legacies to the present day—but this change took place in the realms of culture and personal attitudes and was disconnected from electoral politics. Henrietta Harrison, who details the new beliefs and behaviors that emerged from the Qing/Republican transition in 1911, concludes that "men showed their allegiance to the Republic not by taking part in its political institutions, which for most was impossible, but by wearing short hair and felt hats, bowing to their acquaintances, shaking hands with their friends and taking part in the celebration of new holidays such as National Day."[8] Participating in these new ceremonies and rituals allowed Republican Chinese to forge a new identity, separate from that of the fallen Qing. In a similar vein, David Strand holds that the early Republican era generated a "republican repertoire" of freewheeling, passionate, and confrontational "speech making, political debate, and street protest" that still constitutes a powerful subcurrent of Chinese political culture today. This repertoire emerged in tandem with the failure of the earliest elected representative assemblies in the early 1910s and is all the more poignant because of it.[9]

The cultural and attitudinal transformations begun in the 1910s have been deep and lasting, as these arguments highlight. Harrison and Strand acknowledge that not all of these changes have moved in the direction of a democratic political culture. Paradoxically, elections contributed to the growth of this authoritarian system. Animated by a particular set of fundamental expectations, intellectuals and lawmakers complained bitterly about China's earliest elections, even though many were largely free and fair by twenty-first century standards. Voting had appeared to fail as an instrument of state-building through the selection of the worthy and the education of the people. The lesson that many observers took was that stronger measures would be needed to manufacture a citizenry that could build a strong and prosperous China. The early twentieth-century experience of voting was not marginal to Chinese political development; ironically, it served to promote antidemocratic trends.

A third notion that has currency, particularly in Chinese-language works, is that elections did not lead to democratization because of the nature of Chinese political culture. Historian Chang Peng-yuan's various works on Chinese elections contain an aspect of this line of thinking: he repeatedly and judgmentally highlights instances of fraud, confusion, and ignorance.[10] Overall he offers a complex multicausal argument for the persistence of elections without democracy in pre-1949 China, but the tone of moral criticism underlying it is unmistakable. Indeed, he concludes his magisterial 2007 history of Chinese elections with a rumination on "national character" and "elite personality."[11] Some of Chang's writings reveal a deep level of anguish at this state of affairs: "From [the first elections in 1909 until the 1947–48 elections], four elections were held.

People hoped that each would be better than the previous one and that progress would steadily be made . . . if China had become the first democracy in the East, it would have been the glory and pride of all East Asian peoples. Sadly, the elections became worse, each inferior to the one that came before. Where is Chinese democracy heading?"[12]

A similar message can be found in Chen Weijun's award-winning 2007 documentary on the election of a class monitor at a Wuhan elementary school, *Please Vote for Me*. The election was supposed to teach Chinese third-graders about democracy, yet these students manifested shocking behavior throughout the process, including bribery and character assassination of the sort that would not have appeared out of place in an early Republican "Free Talk" parody. The film ends with the winning candidate barking commands ("Quiet! Anyone who talks has to stand in front!") at his classmates. These children, by seemingly following their natural instincts (with only a little prompting from their parents and teachers), transformed the election into a disturbing and disheartening spectacle.[13]

It is easy to find countless examples of bad behavior during Chinese elections—but it is not clear that such behavior was worse than what occurs in elections elsewhere. The question that should be asked is: why have many commentators from the last years of the Qing to the present day held such high expectations for Chinese elections? The political sympathies of those who created *Please Vote for Me* are not entirely evident, but those of Chang Peng-yuan and many others working in this vein are. Implicit in Chang's writings is a real anguish at the failure of multiparty democracy to develop in China, thus his concerns are best understood as part of a long tradition of Chinese intellectuals "worrying about China," to use Gloria Davies's apt phrase.[14] Ironically, in expressing this worry, his line of thinking comes very close to mirroring the foundational expectations for elections established over a century ago. Yet the logical end result of those ideas is not democracy but something quite different. It is not surprising that many of those who participated enthusiastically in China's first elections came to embrace the People's Congress elections of the early People's Republic as the fulfillment of their vision, as parliamentarian-turned-secret-communist Wang Shao'ao almost certainly did.

A less fraught variant of this idea undergirds Tianjian Shi's work on political culture in mainland China and Taiwan. Arguing on the basis of social surveys conducted between 1993 and 2008, Shi proposes that despite the vast institutional differences between those two societies, a common political cultural defined by relatively communitarian and hierarchical values makes the population on both sides of the Taiwan Strait inclined toward a "guardianship" (rather than liberal) vision of democracy. This concept, which he derives from the Confucian tradition of statecraft, defined "democracy as government that produces good substantive results for the people rather than government limited by procedures that protect the rights of the people."[15] Voting for the purposes envisioned by the foundational expectations are compatible with this mindset—and indeed, tracing the justifications for voting to the eras before the public opinion surveys Shi relied on provides additional qualitative support for his quantitative argument. Yet the notion of political culture in both Chang's and Shi's works ultimately appear static and ahistorical; Chinese political culture is simply what it *is*, regardless of whether it is described in judgmental or neutral terms. This conceptualization seems to allow little potential for change in values or behaviors. Yet the foundational expectations that major thinkers and political leaders have held for elections in China did not just develop out of thousands of years of accumulated norms and ideas—they were also a historically specific response to a period of domestic turmoil and foreign invasion.

In the early twenty-first century, as a "rising" China has consigned that era of existential crisis to history, a solution worth considering emphasizes the potential for change to emerge from within preexisting political institutions and political culture. This line of thought holds that China's tradition of elections will ultimately create a foundation for democracy, but the transition might take generations, not years. Although this process might currently be blocked by the party-state in the mainland, Taiwan's unique political trajectory provides a potential model for this.[16] During its era of authoritarian rule, semi-competitive elections were held on a regular basis. Ultimately, elections became free and authoritarian rule ended. This progression seems to reflect Hu Shi's notion of learning through experience: once you give someone the right to vote, a day will come when that person will want their vote to count for something. The continuity of elections under the Chiang regime on Taiwan is so striking that it is natural to link it to the nonviolent transition to democracy in the 1980s and 1990s. Shelley Rigger, Linda Chao, and Ramon Myers have all done so, invoking versions of Hu Shi's idea by asserting a connection between semi-free elections and democratization over the long term.[17]

Cause and effect is difficult to tease out in the case of Taiwanese democratization, because they impinge so closely on factors unique to Taiwan—in particular, the enduring tensions between "mainlanders" who came after 1945 and "Taiwanese" whose ancestors' arrival long predated that. Under martial law, power was in the hands of the mainlander minority, an unsustainable situation that became increasingly fraught over the years. Elections became a strategy for dealing with that tension, and it is doubtful that a habit of voting would have led to democratization in the absence of that conflict. Rather than prioritizing a history of elections, it is more reasonable to see elections as a single factor amid a variety of interrelated and overlapping causes. J. Bruce Jacobs, for instance, lists ten causes for Taiwanese democratization. A tradition of voting is only one.[18]

To the extent that its history of elections helped lay a foundation for democratization, the Taiwanese experience differs significantly from that of the mainland. The foundational expectations for elections fashioned in the mainland had only barely begun to circulate when Taiwan fell under Japanese rule in 1895. As residents of a Japanese colony, Taiwanese did not experience the electoral experiments conducted by the Qing and Republican governments. By the time that Nationalist control over Taiwan began in 1945, the ideology of tutelary rule had already run its course. After 1949, despite its continued interest in propaganda and citizenship education, there is little evidence that the Nationalist government hoped elections could accomplish these goals. Taiwan is different from the mainland in many respects, and the Chiang leadership was subject to unusual pressures after 1949, but the willingness of that regime to continue to hold elections while abandoning the original rationale for voting suggests that change is possible. When the situation is right, leaders and thinkers will look for new justifications, concepts, and values.

Ideological constructs such as the dominant discourse on elections, grounded in what Xi Jinping called a "country's historical heritage and cultural traditions" or what Yu Keping referred to as "the national tradition of political culture," might prove remarkably durable but do not last forever. Chinese history is littered with once stable and powerful political concepts—ranging from the Confucian monarchy to Maoist notions of endless revolution—that have lost their ability to inspire. This, too, may be the fate of ideas about elections that have already endured for over a century. As long as the foundational expectations have been cited to justify voting in mainland China, there have been critics who have decried the tensions between the idealism of these expectations and the actual experience of elections. The relatively unsupervised elections of the late Qing and early Republic manifestly failed to transform the population into a state-oriented citizenry. Instead, those elections allowed voters and candidates to give free rein to their worst impulses toward competition, particularism, and (sometimes) avarice. Conversely, the increasingly controlled and micromanaged elections introduced by subsequent regimes, continuing to the present day, tended to bore rather than educate or mobilize ordinary people—except, as in 1953–54, in the few cases where violence was so pervasive that elections became terrifying. Today, few criticize the election system with the ferocity of their early twentieth-century forebears; instead, many simply quietly opt out. Although elements of the foundational mythology continue to be cited as a justification for elections today, the intellectual and emotional energy that once pulsed through this idea is almost certainly exhausted. Perhaps that opens space for a new framework for justifying elections—one that will open, rather than foreclose, paths to democratization.

No self-conscious planner masterminded the creation of the influential late nineteenth-century foundational expectations for elections, but they were fashioned by human hands nonetheless. Generations of Chinese political thinkers and actors blended observations of the world around them with lessons derived from historical experience to craft a broadly acceptable explanation for what elections would do and why it is important to have them. Tracing the 175-year history of these expectations reveals that these ideas did not arise organically from a primordial Chinese folk culture, nor do they express some sort of intrinsic, unchangeable essence of Chinese politics. Instead, they were the imperfect products of a moment of intense cross-cultural contact coupled with profound threats to the nation. Looking at these expectations as a product of history suggests that if the idea of Chinese-style elections could be invented once to meet the needs of a specific time, it can be reinvented again to meet today's different needs. Like the repurposed early twentieth-century legislative chambers that dot mainland China's major cities, voting is a rite that can be appropriated and reappropriated for a variety of ends. The question for the future is: what will those ends be?

Character List

Anfu julebu 安福俱樂部

Bao Tianxiao 包天笑
baoban toupiao 包辦投票
baojia 保甲
bu shi wen yi zhe 不識文義者
budongchan 不動產

cai de jian bei 才德兼備
Cai Erkang 蔡爾康
caifang gongping 采訪公評
Cao Kun 曹錕
Cao Rulin 曹汝霖
Cen Chunxuan 岑春煊
Chen Jiongming 陳炯明
Chen Yi 陳毅
Cheng Dequan 程德全
chengdu 程度
Chiang Ching-kuo 蔣經國
Chiang Kai-shek 蔣介石
chuan xian bu chuan zi 傳賢不傳子
chuxuan 初選
Cixi 慈禧

Dai Hongci 戴鴻慈
Daoguang 道光
de zhen cai yi wei guo jia zhi yong 得真才以爲國家之用
Deng Xiaoping 鄧小平

deng'e xuanju 等額選舉
Di Baoxian 狄葆賢
Di Fuding 狄福鼎
Dianshizhai huabao 點石齋畫報
Dongfang zazhi 東方雜誌
Duan Qirui 段祺瑞
Duan-fang 端方
Dungen 鈍根

Feng Guifen 馮桂芬
fuxuan 複選

gongju 公舉
Guangxu 光緒

Haiguo tuzhi 海國圖志
Hongxian 洪憲
houbu dangxuan ren 候補當選人
Hu Shi 胡適
Huang Bihun 黃碧魂
Huang Junlong 黃均隆
Huang Yanpei 黃炎培
Huang Zunxian 黃遵憲
hui 會
huxiang baochong 互相保充

Jiang Zengyao 蔣曾耀
Jiang Zengyu 蔣曾燠
jianxuan 揀選

jianze 揀擇
Jiaobinlu kangyi 校邠廬抗議
jiaoyang defa 教養得法
Jiaqing 嘉慶
jiceng xuanju 基層選舉
Jie Shuqiang 解樹強
jiming toupiao 記名投票
jingxuan 競選
jingzheng xuanju 競爭選舉
jinqian yundong 金錢運動
jinqian zhuyi 金錢主義
ju 局
ju 舉
junzheng 軍政

Kang Youwei 康有為
Kong Zhaojin 孔昭晉

Li Dazhao 李大釗
Li Fang 李芳
Li Hongzhang 李鴻章
Li Jiannong 李劍農
Li Timotai 李提摩太
liansheng zizhi yundong 聯省自治運動
Liang Qichao 梁啟超
Liang Shuming 梁漱溟
Lin Zexu 林則徐
Liu Chongyou 劉崇佑
Liu Dapeng 劉大鵬
Liu Guangdi 劉光第
Liu Shaoqi 劉少奇
Lou Mingyuan 樓明遠
Lu Wenlu 陸文籙
Lu Xuanzhi 陸選之
lunliu 輪流

Ma Jianzhong 馬建忠
Mao Zedong 毛澤東
minxuan 民選
minzhu xuexi ban 民主學習班

nianjiu lunchong 拈鬮輪充
Nuli zhoubao 努力週報

Pan Gongzhan 潘公展
Peng Zhen 彭真

Prince Gong 恭親王奕訢
putong xuanju 普通選舉
puxuan 普選
Puyi 溥儀

Qi Yaolin 齊耀琳
Qianlong 乾隆
Qiying 耆英
quan guo gongju 全國公舉
quanmian de xuanju zhi 全面的選舉制

shang xia tong 上下通
shang xia zhi qing tong 上下之情通
Shen Baochang 沈寶昌
Shen Enfu 沈恩孚
Shen Peizhen 沈佩貞
Shen Tongfang 沈同芳
Shenbao 申報
Shengshi weiyan 盛世危言
Shi Liangcai 史量才
Shibao 時報
shiping 時評
Shiwubao 時務報
shou yundong zhe 受運動者
Shoudie 瘦蝶
Shunzhi 順治
sijian 私見
Sizhou zhi 四洲志
Song Jiaoren 宋教仁
suiju 歲舉
Sun Jia'nai 孫家鼐
Sun Yat-sen 孫中山
Sushe 蘇社

Taixi xinshi lanyao 泰西新史攬要
Tang Hualong 湯化龍
Tang Qunying 唐群英
Tang Shouqian 湯壽潛
tong shang xia zhi qing 通上下之情
tuize 推擇

Wang Chonghui 王寵惠
Wang Hui 王暉
Wang Qing 王勍
Wang Rongbao 汪榮寶
Wang Shao'ao 王紹鰲

Wang Shijie 王世杰
Wang Xinrun 王鑫潤
Wang Yitang 王揖唐
Wanguo gongbao 萬國公報
Wei Yuan 魏源
Weiyan 危言
Weng Tonghe 翁同龢
Wu Guangjian 伍光建
wujiming toupiao 無記名投票
wulun nan nü pin fu dou you xuanjuquan
　無論男女貧富都有選舉權

Xi fa yi baojian she guan
　西法以保薦設官
Xi Jinping 習近平
xi shi yapian zhe 吸食鴉片者
Xi Zhongxun 習仲勳
xian yisihui 縣議事會
xiangju lixuan 鄉舉里選
xiangyue 鄉約
xianneng 賢能
xianzheng 憲政
Xie Xiaoxian 謝嘯儒
xin xuanju 新選舉
Xu Shichang 徐世昌
Xu Shuzheng 徐樹錚
Xu Tai 許泰
xuan 選
xuan min wei guan 選民委官
xuan xian yu neng 選賢與能
xuanju 選舉
xuanju shi zanxing toupiao gongju
　選舉時暫行投票公舉
xuanju shiwuke 選舉事務科
Xuanju zhi 選舉志
Xuantong 宣統
xuanze 選擇
Xue Fucheng 薛福成
xunzheng 訓政

Yang Chunlü 楊春綠
Yang Tingdong 楊廷棟
Yang Yinhang 楊蔭杭
Yao Lifa 姚立法
Yao Wennan 姚文枬

yi pianchu shu xingming baoju yi ren
　以片楮書姓名保舉一人
yi tuijian zui duo zhe wei ru xuan
　以推薦最多者爲入選
yiju 議舉
yingye ziben 營業資本
yiyuan 議院
yongli 擁立
you zhong gongju 由眾公舉
Yu Keping 俞可平
Yuan Shikai 袁世凱
Yuan Xiluo 袁希洛
Yuan Xitao 袁希濤
Yubei lixian gonghui 預備立憲公會
yundong 運動

zai yiyuan shang xia tongxin
　在議院上下同心
Zai-ze 載澤
ze qi de ju zui duo zhe yong zhi
　擇其得舉最多者用之
ze 擇
Zeng Pu 曾樸
Zhang Bolie 張伯烈
Zhang Deyi 張德彝
Zhang Jian 張謇
Zhang Mingchu 張明初 / 張銘初
Zhang Taiyan 章太炎
Zhang Xun 張勳
Zhang Zhidong 張之洞
Zhao Shiqing 趙士清
Zheng Guanying 鄭觀應
Zheng Xiaoxu 鄭孝胥
Zhi-gang 志剛
zhijie xuanju 直接選舉
zhipei e piao 支配額票
zhizao guomin 製造國民
zhong tui 眾推
Zhou Enlai 周恩來
Zhu De 朱德
Zhu Xi 朱熹
ziben 資本
ziyiju 諮議局
zizhengyuan 資政院
zonggongchengju 總工程局

Notes

Abbreviations

DG   Daoguang Reign
GX   Guangxu Reign
JQ   Jiaqing Reign
QL   Qianlong Reign
XT   Xuantong Reign
YZ   Yongzheng Reign

Introduction

1. Snow, *Red Star over China*, 154.
2. "Bensheng xinwen: guoqingri de youjie yundong [Provincial News: The National Day Street Protest]," *Dagongbao* (Changsha), October 11, 1920, 6; "Bensheng xinwen: Youjie yundong zhong zhi yiwen [Provincial News: Stories from the Street Protests]," *Dagongbao* (Changsha), October 11, 1920, 6; "Bensheng xinwen: Zuori shengshu dahuiyi jishi [Provincial News: Yesterday's Meeting at the Provincial Government]," *Dagongbao* (Changsha), October 13, 1920, 6; and "Bensheng xinwen: Shengyihui zi shengzhang wen wei shimin youjie dahui shi [Provincial News: The Provincial Legislature's Response to the Governor Regarding the Street Protests]," *Dagongbao* (Changsha), October 14, 1920, 6.
3. Platt, *Provincial Patriots*, 184–215.
4. Wang Wuwei, *Hunan zizhi yundong shi shangpian*, 84–85.
5. These essays are translated in Schram, *Mao's Road to Power*, 1:561–74.
6. Liang Chi-Chao [Liang Qichao], *History of Chinese Political Thought*, 150–52; Liang Qichao, "Xian Qin zhengzhi sixiangshi [History of Pre-Qin Chinese Political Thought]," reprinted in *Liang Qichao quanji*, 5:3619.

7. Chang Peng-yuan, *Zhongguo minzhu zhengzhi de kunjing*; Ye Lijun, *Minguo Beijing zhengfu shiqi xuanju*; Thompson, *China's Local Councils*; and Fincher, *Chinese Democracy*.

8. For example, see the articles printed as part of the "State of the Field: Assessing Village Elections in China" special issue of *Journal of Contemporary China* 18.60 (June 2009). In other works, a brief history of pre-1949 democratic thought coupled with a discussion of the Maoist era serves as a preface, such as Brown, *Ballot Box China*, 5–24, and Ogden, *Inklings of Democracy*, 60–79.

9. Rigger, *Politics in Taiwan*, and Edwards, *Gender, Politics, and Democracy*. There is a large body of literature in Chinese on elections or legislatures in specific provinces, too. Examples include Wang Shu-hwai, "Qingmo Minchu Jiangsu sheng," and Shen Xiaomin, *Chuchang yu qiubian*.

10. Achen and Bartels, *Democracy for Realists*, 1–20.

11. This is just one of a vast (and politically diverse) literature that explores the gap between the idealized notion of elections and the actual experience of elections held in the United States. Other recent examples include Brennan, *Against Democracy*; Caplan, *Myth of the Rational Voter*; and Somin, *Democracy and Political Ignorance*.

12. Kishlansky, *Parliamentary Selection*.

13. For example, elections occurred nearly simultaneously with the 1909–11 population census and the 1954 Ethnic Classification Project. See Lam, *A Passion for Facts*, and Mullaney, *Coming to Terms*.

14. A summary of the scholarship on this topic as it relates to early twentieth-century China can be found in Harrison, *Making of the Republican Citizen*, 2–4.

15. Hsiao, *Rural China*, 184–258. On community compacts, see Hauf, "Community Covenant," and for the Sacred Edict, see Mair, "Language and Ideology."

1. Rectifying Names

1. Chang Peng-yuan, *Zhongguo minzhu zhengzhi*, 1–49, and Ye Lijun, *Minguo Beijing zhengfu*, 16–44, contain very thorough summaries of nineteenth-century Chinese references to Western elections.

2. Kuhn, *Origins of the Modern Chinese State*, 2.

3. Liu, *Translingual Practice*, 26.

4. Xiong Yuezhi, "Difficulties in Comprehension," 2; *Yapian zhanzheng dang'an shiliao*, 1:20–21.

5. Giles, *Chinese-English Dictionary* (1892), 309. Giles listed this compound under the entry for its second character (*ju*, romanized as *chü* in his dictionary), not its first character. Other foreign obseverers described public appointment in action at the village level, although without using the term. Hsiao, *Rural China*, 271–75.

6. Elvin, "Gentry Democracy," 42, n. 9; Thompson, *China's Local Councils*, 23–35, 78, 188 n. 31.

7. Zhu Xi, *Zhu Xi ji*, 3903–13.

8. Hsiao, *Rural China*, 184–91.

9. *Qing huidian shili*, 5:422.

10. For community granaries, see *Da Qing lichao shilu*, entry for YZ 3/12/dingchou (January 16, 1726). Similar orders were issued in the nineteenth and early twentieth centuries. *Qing huidian shili*, 3:220 and Liu Jinzao, *Qing chao xu wenxian tongkao*, 8171–72. For salt production, see *Da Qing lichao shilu*, entry for YZ 6/7/jisi. For lineages, see *Da Qing lichao shilu*, entry for QL 6/2 yue xia. For water conservancy, see *Qing huidian shili*, 10:677. For self-defense groups, see *Da Qing lichao shilu*, entry for DG 23/12/jiyou.

11. *Qingmo-Minchu xianzheng shiliao jikan*, 1:171.

12. Huang Zunxian, *Huang Zunxian quanji*, 510–14; *Da Qing lichao shilu*, entry for GX 32/4/jisi.

13. *Qing huidian shili*, 1:959.

14. Huang Liuhong, *Juguan fuhui quanshu*, 450–52.

15. *Da Qing lichao shilu*, entry for JQ 5/1/jimao.

16. Lin Qingyuan, *Lin Zexu pingzhuan*, 227–31.

17. Lin Zexu, *Lin Wenzhonggong zhengshu*, jia ji Jiangsu zougao 5.5a–9b, yi ji Huguang zougao, 1.11a–22b, yi ji Huguang zougao 2.2b.

18. Lin Zexu, *Lin Zexu quanji*, 5:146–47.

19. For Wei Yuan's political thought, see Kuhn, *Origins of the Modern Chinese State*, 27–53. The broader ideological climate of the time is persuasively described in Polachek, *Inner Opium War*.

20. Morrison, *Dictionary of the Chinese Language*. Morrison defined *xuanju*, the compound now used in Chinese for *election*, as "select promotions in the government."

21. Lin Yongyu, "Lun Lin Zexu zuzhi," 118–37. See also Mosca, *From Frontier Policy to Foreign Policy*, 242–43; Wong, "Translators and Interpreters," 42–44.

22. Lin Zexu, *Si zhou zhi*, 30b–32b (for the British system), 20b (for the French system), and 38b (for the U.S. system).

23. Murray, *An Encyclopædia of Geography*, 1338.

24. *Chouban yiwu shimo (Daoguang chao)*, 73.19b–20a. The translation of this passage that appears in Teng and Fairbank's documentary reader—"the ruler of the American barbarians is established by the *campaigning* [emphasis added] of his countrymen, and is changed once in four years"—is misleading and adds a concept (campaigning) lacking in the original. Teng and Fairbank, *China's Response to the West*, 39.

25. [Gutzlaff], *Gujin wanguo gangjian lu*, 20.np.

26. Chen Qitai and Liu Lanxiao, *Wei Yuan pingzhuan*, 494–505.

27. For uses of "public appointment," see Wei Yuan, *Haiguo tuzhi*, 669, 1391, and 1379. Other descriptive terms for elections can be found on 669, 1391, 1408–9, 1422, and 1632–33.

28. Liang Tingnan, *Haiguo sishuo*. Liang used a variety of terms, including "selection and appointment [*xuanju*]," "choice [*xuanze*]," "choose [*xuan*]," and even "chosen by the people [*minxuan*]." Xu Jiyu, *Yinghuan zhilue jiaozhu*. Xu's terms included "push forward and choose [*tuize*]," "pick [*ze*]," and "choose [*xuan*]."

29. Xiong Yuezhi, *Feng Guifen pingzhuan*, 182–95. I follow Philip Kuhn's translation of Feng's title. Kuhn, *Origins of the Modern Chinese State*, 57.

30. This incident is related in Xiong Yuezhi, *Feng Guifen pingzhuan*, 189–90.

31. Wei, "Popular Opinion and Public Reasoning," chap. 3.

32. Kuhn, *Origins of the Modern Chinese State*, 61; Chang Peng-yuan, *Zhongguo minzhu zhengzhi*, 10; and Xiong Yuezhi, *Zhongguo jindai minzhu sixiang*, 91–92.
33. Feng Guifen, "Gong chuzhi yi," in *Jiaobinlu kangyi*, shang 1a–2b.
34. Feng Guifen, "Gong chuzhi yi," in *Jiaobinlu kangyi*, shang 2a.
35. Feng Guifen, "Gong chuzhi yi," in *Jiaobinlu kangyi*, shang 2a.
36. Feng Guifen, "Fu xiangzhi yi," in *Jiaobinlu kangyi*, shang 12a–14a.
37. Feng Guifen, "Fu xiangzhi yi," in *Jiaobinlu kangyi*, shang 13b–14a.
38. Feng Guifen, "Guang qu shi yi," in *Jiaobinlu kangyi*, xia 27a–27b.
39. Xiong Yuezhi, *Feng Guifen pingzhuan*, 197.
40. Chang Peng-yuan, *Zhongguo minzhu zhengzhi*, 10.
41. For one example, see the journal of Guo Songtao, China's first permanent ambassador overseas. Guo Songtao, *Lundun yu Bali riji*, 404–7 (entry for GX 3/11/18 [December 22, 1877]).
42. Xue Fucheng, *Chushi siguo riji*, 515 (entry for GX 18/2/18 [March 16, 1892]), 559–60 (entry for GX 18/5/3 [May 28, 1892]), and 802–3 (entry for GX 19/6/14 [July 16, 1893]).
43. Zhi-gang, *Chushi Taixi ji*, 318–19 (entry for TZ 8/5/1 [June 10, 1869]). See Huangfu, "Internalizing the West," 87–92, for a fuller discussion of Zhi-gang's account of Western political culture and 90–91 for this quote specifically.
44. Huangfu, "Internalizing the West," 66–113.
45. Zhang Deyi, *Ou-Mei huanyou ji*, 785–86 (entry for TZ 8/5/2 [June 11, 1869]).
46. Zhang, *Ou-Mei huanyou ji*, 714 (entry for TZ 7/10/5 [November 18, 1868]).
47. Huangfu, "Internalizing the West," 319, n. 9. Zhang's view of legislatures was significantly more positive. See Zhang Deyi, *Sui shi Ying E ji*, 374–75 (entry for GX 3/2/30 [April 13, 1877]).
48. Huang Zunxian, "Jishi [An Account]," in *Renjinglu shi cao*, 4.4b–6b. This translation is a modified version of Schmidt, *Within the Human Realm*, 247–52.
49. "An Account" does not appear in the 1891 copybook version of Huang's poetry collection, suggesting that it may have been composed later. Huang Zunxian, *Renjinglu shi cao jianzhu*, 365–78.
50. Ma Jianzhong, *Shikezhai jiyan*, 1.6b–7a. A partial translation of Ma's report is printed in Teng and Fairbank, *China's Response to the West*, 95–96, and a full translation is in Bailey, *Strengthen the Country*, 38–46.
51. The description of Li's features is taken from Thomson, *Illustrations of China*, 4:13–14.
52. Medhurst, *English and Chinese Dictionary*, 485.
53. Lobscheid, *English and Chinese Dictionary*, 711–12.
54. Kwang Ki-Chaou, *English and Chinese Dictionary*, 119.
55. Mackenzie, *Nineteenth Century*, 453–60.
56. Richard and Cai, *Taixi xinshi lanyao*. Examples of the use of this compound can be found on 5.2a (describing elections to the British House of Commons), 6 xia.5a (on the expansion of suffrage), and 24.2b–4b (summaries of various European election laws).
57. Richard, *Forty-Five Years*, 232.
58. Richard, *Forty-Five Years*, 233.
59. Richard, *Forty-Five Years*, 240–57.

60. Richard, *Forty-Five Years*, 230–31.
61. Richard and Cai, *Taixi xinshi lanyao*, yibenxu, 3b–4a.
62. Richard, *Forty-Five Years*, 235.
63. Richard, *Forty-Five Years*, 256.
64. Zheng Guanying, "Du Taixi xinshi gan yan [Thoughts on Reading *A New History of the West*]," in *Zheng Guanying ji*, xia ce, 1391.
65. Xia Dongyuan, *Zheng Guanying zhuan*, 265–69.
66. Tang Shouqian, *Wei yan*, 9a–9b.
67. Zheng Guanying, "Yiyuan, shang [Deliberative Assemblies, Part 1]," in *Zheng Guanying ji*, shang ce, 311–15. This essay appeared in the original 1894 edition under the title "Yiyuan [Deliberative Assemblies]"; later, a second essay with the same title was added, hence "Part 1" and "Part 2."
68. Zheng Guanying, "Gongju [Public Appointments]," in *Zheng Guanying ji*, shang ce, 328–30.
69. Zheng Guanying, "Shengshi weiyan zi xu [Preface to *Words of Warning for a Prosperous Age*]," in *Zheng Guanying ji*, shang ce, 233–36.
70. Zheng Guanying, "Shengshi weiyan zi xu," in *Zheng Guanying ji*, shang ce, 233–36.
71. Zheng Guanying, "Gongju [Public Appointments]," in *Zheng Guanying ji*, shang ce, 328–30.
72. Zheng Guanying, "Zhi Shengjing qing lun bianfa yi she shang, xia yiyuan shu [Letter to the Minister at Shenjing on How Reform Requires the Establishment of a Parliament]," in *Zheng Guanying ji*, xia ce, 291–92. Zheng's statement on restrictions is made in Zheng Guanying, "Zhi Yao Bohuai taishou shu [Letter to Yao Bohuai]," in *Zheng Guanying ji*, xia ce 295–99.
73. Cited in Chen and Liu, *Wei Yuan pingzhuan*, 501. Neither Zeng Jize's nor Li Fengbao's official diaries contains direct observations of an election.
74. *Wuxu bianfa*, 1:152–53.
75. *Wuxu bianfa*, 2:236–37 and 1:240–42.
76. *Da Qing lichao shilu*, entry for GX 24/6/wuzi (July 24, 1898). Some of these responses are published in *Qing ting qianyi "Jiaobinlu kangyi" dang'an huibian*.
77. Cited in Kuhn, *Origins of the Modern Chinese State*, 63. The original text of this document is not available.
78. Cited in Xiong Yuezhi, *Feng Guifen pingzhuan*, 269.
79. Cited in Xiong Yuezhi, *Feng Guifen pingzhuan*, 271.

2. Transmission and Re-Creation

1. Shen Zuxian, *Rong'an dizi ji*, 3.18a–18b. The date of the letter can be found in Zhang Jian, "Riji [Diary]," in *Zhang Jian quanji*, 6:529 (entry for GX30/5/13 [June 26, 1904]).
2. For instance, see the 1895 proposals contained in Zhang Jian, *Zhang Jizi jiu lu*, 1.12b–23b.
3. Wei Chunhui, *Zhang Jian pingzhuan*, 62–68.
4. Zhang Jian, "Bianfa pingyi [Reform Proposals]," in *Zhang Jian quanji*, 1:53.

5. Wei Chunhui, *Zhang Jian pingzhuan*, 75–76, and "Zhang Jizhi dianzhuan bianfa pingyi [Highest Ranked Examination Graduate Zhang Jian's Reform Proposals]," *Shenbao*, GX 27/3/22–GX 27/4/1 (May 10–May 18, 1901), 3.

6. Zhang Jian, "Ziding nianpu [Self-Written Chronology]," in *Zhang Jian quanji*, 6:865–66 (entries for GX 30/6 [ca. July–August 1904] and GX 30/8 [ca. September–October 1904]).

7. Luo Baoshan, "Qing mo xinzheng zhong de Yuan Shikai," 58–65.

8. The assessment is based on the Keio University Library's online database of Fukuzawa's published works at http://dcollections.lib.keio.ac.jp/en/fukuzawa/a15/48 (accessed March 31, 2015).

9. "Fukenkai kisoku [Prefectural Assembly Regulations]," in *Hōrei zensho*, 12–16. There is one exception in this law: elections held within the assemblies for leadership positions were described using a different phrase. Jichishō senkyobu, "Shūgiin giin senkyo hō [Lower House Election Law]," in *Senkyohō hyakunenshi*, 95–103.

10. See Liang's unambiguous use of *xuanju* for election in an 1899 essay on constitutions. Liang Qichao, "Ge guo xianfa yitong lun [On Similarities and Dissimilarities between the Constitutions of Various Countries]," in *Liang Qichao quanji*, 1:318–22.

11. Yang Tingdong, *Zhengzhixue jiaokeshu*.

12. Examples include Maruyama Toranosuke, *Putong xuanju lun*, and Kikuchi Gakuji, *Yihui zhengdang lun*.

13. Wang Rongbao and Ye Lan, *Xin Erya*, shi zheng 17.

14. *Commercial Press English and Chinese Pronouncing Dictionary*, 1st ed., 587. The definition includes a confusing sample phrase, "the election of members of the parliament." The Chinese gloss on this phrase (*xuan min wei guan*) included neither a clear term for elections nor a word for parliament. A better rendering would be "select people to appoint officials."

15. *Commercial Press English and Chinese Pronouncing Dictionary*, 2nd ed., 729.

16. Translation from Chung-li Chang, *Chinese Gentry*, 174; *Qinding Huangchao tongzhi*, 72:2b–3b.

17. Teng Ssu-yü, *Zhongguo kaoshi zhidu shi*, 337–55.

18. Chung-li Chang, *Chinese Gentry*, 164.

19. Elman, "Political, Social, and Cultural Reproduction," 8. See also Elman, *Cultural History of Civil Examinations*, 292–94.

20. Elman, *Cultural History of Civil Examinations*, 569–625.

21. Teng Ssu-yü, *Zhongguo kaoshi zhidu*, 268–76.

22. *Da Qing lichao shilu*, entries for GX 24/6/kuiwei (July 19, 1898), GX 24/7/jiayin (August 19, 1898), and GX 24/7/jimao (September 13, 1898).

23. Translation from Reynolds, *China, 1898–1912*, 201–4; *Da Qing lichao shilu*, entry for GX 26/12/dingwei (January 29, 1901).

24. Elman, *Cultural History of Civil Examinations*, 595–96.

25. *Da Qing lichao shilu*, entry for GX 29/2/jihai (March 12, 1903).

26. Gan Chunsong, "Kejuzhi de shuailuo," 116–17.

27. *Da Qing lichao shilu*, entry for GX 31/8/jiachen (September 2, 1905).

28. "Dianchuan shangyu [Imperial Edict Sent via Telegraph]," *Shenbao*, GX 32/8/8 (September 6, 1905), 2.

29. Untitled annotations following "Dianchuan shangyu [Imperial Edict Sent via Telegraph]," *Shenbao*, GX 31/8/8 (September 6, 1905), 2.

30. "Hui zou liting keju tuiguang xuetang zhe shu hou [In the Wake of the Memorial that Ended the Examinations and Promoted Schools]," *Shenbao*, GX 31/8/14 (September 12, 1905), 2.

31. Elman, *Cultural History of Civil Examinations*, 621–22.

32. "Tingzhi keju hou zhi shengyuan chulu [Post-examination System 'Paths Out' for Holders of the Licentiate Degree]," *Shenbao*, GX 31/8/9 (September 7, 1905), 2.

33. Strauss, "Creating 'Virtuous and Talented' Officials," and Guan Xiaohong, "Shutu nengfou tonggui."

34. Cao Yunyuan et al., *Minguo Wuxian zhi*, 9.1a.

35. Sun E-Tu Zen, "Chinese Constitutional Missions." For the published diaries, see Dai Hongci, *Chu shi jiu guo riji* and Zai-ze, *Kaocha zhengzhi riji*.

36. *Da Qing lichao shilu*, entry for GX 32/7/wushen (September 1, 1906).

37. Dai Hongci and Duan-fang, *Ou Mei zhengzhi yaoyi*, Sheli lixian junzhu zhengti zhi zongyi [The Basic Rationale for a Constitutional Monarchy], 1a.

38. Dai Hongci and Duan-fang, *Ou Mei zhengzhi yaoyi*, Guohui zhi sheli [Parliaments], 67b–68b.

39. Duan-fang, *Lieguo zhengyao*.

40. Duan-fang, *Duan Zhongmin gong zou gao*, 6.37a–37b.

41. Duan-fang, *Duan Zhongmin gong zou gao*, 6.36b–38b.

42. Duan-fang, *Duan Zhongmin gong zou gao*, 6.51b–52b.

43. Duan-fang, *Duan Zhongmin gong zou gao*, 6.56a–56b.

44. Xia Xiaohong, "Cong xin faxian shougao kan Liang Qichao."

45. Zhang Jian, "Riji," in *Zhang Jian quanji*, 6:526–28 (entries for GX 32/6/1 to GX 32/6/12 [July 21–August 1, 1906]), and Zai-ze, *Kaocha zhengzhi riji* (entries for GX 32/5/21 to GX 32/5/28 [July 12–19, 1906]).

46. Zhang Jian, "Riji," in *Zhang Jian quanji*, 6:575 (entry for GX 32/6/7 (July 27, 1906)).

47. Zheng Xiaoxu, the primary organizer of the group and a scrupulous diarist, recorded an early organizational meeting on September 10, 1906. Zheng Xiaoxu, *Zheng Xiaoxu riji*, 1056. Zheng records Zhang Jian in attendance at a meeting on September 23, 1906. Zheng Xiaoxu, *Zheng Xiaoxu riji*, 1058. Zhang's much briefer diary entries do not mention the Public Association until a month later.

48. Zheng Xiaoxu, *Zheng Xiaoxu riji*, 1060–61 and 1068.

49. "Yubei lixian gonghui kaihui jishi [The Public Association for Constitutional Preparation's Meeting]," *Shenbao*, GX 32/11/2 (December 17, 1906), 4.

50. "Yubei lixan gonghui dingqi kaihui [The Public Association for Constitutional Preparation Sets a Meeting Date]," *Shenbao*, GX 32/10/28 (December 13, 1906), 3.17.

51. Zheng Xiaoxu, *Zheng Xiaoxu riji*, 1079.

52. Chang Yu-fa, *Qing ji de lixian tuanti*, 365–70.

53. Thompson, *China's Local Councils*, 37–52.

54. "Shiban Tianjin xian difang zizhi gongjue cao'an [Proposal for Tianjin County Self-Government]," *Beiyang gongdu leizuan*, zizhi yi, 6b–13a.

55. "Beiyang dachen Yuan Shikai zou Tianjin shiban difang zizhi qingxing zhe [Beiyang Minister Yuan Shikai memorializes on Tianjin's Experiment in Local Self-Government]," in *Qingmo choubei lixian dang'an*, 719–21. The Tianjin population was reported at 420,000 in 1909. Cao Shuji, *Zhongguo renkou shi*, 790.

56. Zheng Xiaoxu, *Zheng Xiaoxu riji*, 1068.

57. "Zhili Tianjin xian difang zizhi gongjue cao'an [Draft Regulations for Tianjin County Local Self-Government]," *Dongfang zazhi*, GX 33/5/25 (July 5, 1907), neiwu 208–22.

58. "Shu li Guangxi tixueshi Li Hanfen tiao chen wu nian yubei lixian ji su li neige deng shi yi zhe [Guangxi Education Commissioner Li Hanfen Memorializes in Favor of a Five Year Constitutional Preparation Period and the Speedy Appointment of a Cabinet]," in *Qingmo chouban lixian dang'an*, 299–305.

59. Elvin, "Gentry Democracy in Chinese Shanghai," 53–54.

60. *Da Qing lichao shilu*, entry for GX 33/6/wuyin (July 28, 1907).

61. "Liangguang zongdu Cen Chunxuan zou qing su she Zizhengyuan dai shangyuan yi Duchayuan dai xiayuan bing she sheng ziyiju ji fu zhou xian yishihui zhe [Liangguang Governor-General Cen Chunxuan Memorializes on the Designation of the National Assembly as an Upper House of Parliament, the Designation of the Censorate as a Lower House of Parliament, and the Establishment of Provincial, Prefectural, and County Assemblies]," in *Qingmo choubei lixian dang'an*, 497–503.

62. "Zhuo ge sheng su she ziyiju yu [Imperial Edict for the Speedy Establishment of Provincial Assemblies]," in *Qingmo choubei lixian dang'an*, 667.

63. "Ji yi ziyiju cao'an [Gathering to Discuss a Provincial Assembly Proposal]," *Shenbao*, GX 33/9/15 (October 21, 1907), 4.

64. "Ziyiju zhangcheng cao'an ni gao [Draft Provincial Assembly Regulations]," *Shenbao*, GX 33/9/16 (October 22, 1907), 10, and *Shenbao*, GX 33/9/17 (October 23, 1907), 10–11.

65. "Jiangnan chouban ziyiju zhangcheng cao'an pingyi [Criticism of the Jiangnan Draft Provincial Assembly Regulations]," *Shenbao*, GX 33/12/17 [January 20, 1908], 2–3.

66. Zheng Xiaoxu received a copy of the Provincial Assembly Regulations at the Public Association's office on December 10, 1907; he did not explain which proposal this was or why the Public Association would have it. Zheng Xiaoxu, *Zheng Xiaoxu riji*, 1118.

67. "Difang zizhi huizhi [Collected Records on Local Government]," *Dongfang zazhi*, GX 34/4/25 (May 24, 1908), neiwu 266–68.

68. This theory is advocated in Thompson, *China's Local Councils*, 96–97.

69. "Xinzheng biancha guan ni xuanju ziyiju yiyuan zanxing zhangcheng [The Constitutional Drafting Office's Temporary Regulations for Provincial Legislature Elections]," *Shenbao*, GX 34/2/27 (March 29, 1908), 2.2.

70. "Qian Gongbu yuan wailang Liu Xun tiao chen yubei lixian zhi shi ying shili juban cheng [Former Board of Works Vice Director Liu Xun Memorializes Measures for Constitutional Preparation]," *Qingmo choubei lixian dang'an*, 340–43.

71. Many of these were published in the press. For two of many examples, see "Hunan quanti renmin minxuan yiyuan qingyuanshu [The Hunan People's Petition for a Popularly Elected Parliament]," *Shenbao*, GX 34/2/19 (March 21, 1908), 25–26, and "Jiangsu shenmin kai guohui gongcheng [Petition of the Jiangsu Gentry and People for the

Opening of Parliament]," *Shenbao*, GX 34/7/4 (July 31, 1908), 3–4, and GX 34/7/5 (August 1, 1908), 4.

72. Liu Jinzao, *Qing chao xu wenxian tongkao*, 11436–42. An English-language translation of the Provincial Assembly Regulations can be found in U.S. Department of State, *Papers Relating to the Foreign Relations of the United States*, 182–89.

73. Min Tu-ki, *National Polity and Local Power*, 21–49.

74. Zhang Jian, "Bianfa pingyi," in *Zhang Jian quanji*, 1:53.

75. Zheng, *Social Life of Opium*.

76. Madancy, *Troublesome Legacy of Commissioner Lin*.

77. The idea to represent these complicated election laws as a mathematical formula comes from historian Ye Lijun's *Minguo Beijing zhengfu shiqi xuanju zhidu*.

78. Hayashida Kazuhiro, "Development of Election Law in Japan."

79. Holt, *Introduction to the Study of Government*, 207; Suval, *Electoral Politics in Wilhelmine Germany*, 233–41.

80. Cited in A. J. P. Taylor, *Bismarck*, 97.

81. Dai Hongci, *Chu shi jiu guo riji*, 397 (entry for GX 32/2/23 [March 17, 1906]) and "Pulushiguo Xianfa [Prussian Constitution]," *Dongfang zazhi*, di 3 juan linshi zeng kan (1906 special issue), 12–19.

82. Municipal election laws can be found in "Xianzheng biancha guan zou heyi cheng zhen xiang difang zizhi zhangcheng bing ling ni xuanju zhangcheng zhe [The Constitutional Drafting Office Memorializes on the Local Governance Regulations and Election Regulations for Cities, Towns, and Villages]," in *Qingmo choubei lixian dang'an*, 724–41. County election laws can be found in "Xianzhengguan heding fu ting zhou xian difang zizhi zhangcheng qing dan [The Constitutional Drafting Office Ratifies Local Governance Regulations for Prefectures, Semi-Autonomous Prefectures, and Counties]," *Shenbao*, XT 2/1/14–XT 2/1/17 (February 23, 1910–February 26, 1910), 2.2.

83. "Xianzheng biancha guan deng zou niding ge sheng ziyiju bing yiyuan xuanju zhangcheng zhe [Constitutional Drafting Commission Memorial Proposing Regulations for Provincial Assemblies and the Regulations for Election to Provincial Assemblies]," in *Qingmo choubei lixian dang'an*, 667–83.

84. Meienberger, *Emergence of Constitutional Government*, 60–61.

85. Cao Rulin, *Cao Rulin yi sheng zhi huiyi*, 49–51.

86. *Qing shi gao*, 3247–61.

87. For one example, see Cao et al., *Minguo Wuxian zhi*, 9:16b–17a.

3. The First Elections and the Last Emperor

1. See, for example, "Xianzhengguan zizhengyuan hui zou ziyiju zhangcheng yu xuanju zhangcheng zhe [The Committee for Drawing Up Regulations for Constitutional Government and the National Assembly Joint Memorial on Provincial Assembly Regulations and Election Regulations]," *Shibao*, wushen/7/6 (August 2, 1908), 2 and 5; *Shibao*, wushen/7/7 (August 3, 1908), 5; *Shibao*, wushen/7/8 (August 4, 1908), 5; *Shibao*, wushen/7/9 (August 5, 1908), 5. See also "Xianzhengguan zizhengyuan zou ziyiju zhangcheng yu xuanju zhangcheng zhe [The Committee for Drawing Up Regulations

for Constitutional Government and the National Assembly Joint Memorial on Provincial Assembly Regulations and Election Regulations]," *Shenbao*, GX 34/7/4 (July 31, 1908), 1.4–1.5, and "Niding Ziyiju zhangcheng fujia anyu [Draft Provincial Assembly Regulations, with Annotations]," *Shenbao*, GX 34/7/4 (July 31, 1908), 4.2–4.8.

2. Bao Tianxiao, *Chuanyinglou huiyilu*, 328–33.
3. Judge, *Print and Politics*, 182–83.
4. Bao Tianxiao, *Chuanyinglou huiyilu*, 331–32.
5. "Xianzhengguan tongzi sheli ziyiju choubanchu [The Constitution Drafting Office Transmits an Order to Establish Provincial Assembly Preparatory Offices]," *Shenbao*, GX 34/7/15 (August 11, 1908), 1.5.
6. "Jiangsu shenshi jiyi ziyiju jishi [Jiangsu Gentry Gather to Discuss the Provincial Assembly]," *Shenbao*, GX 34/8/25 (September 20, 1908), 1.4.
7. *Jiangsu Su shu ziyiju*, 7a–8a.
8. Zhang Jian, "Riji," in *Zhang Jian quanji*, 6:607 (entries for GX 34/10/7 [October 31, 1908]–GX 34/10/13 [November 6, 1908]).
9. "Ge sheng chouban ziyiju [Provincial Assembly Preparations]," *Shenbao*, GX 34/9/25 (October 19, 1908), 3.2.
10. Yang Tingdong, *Zhengzhixue jiaokeshu*.
11. Xiao [Bao Tianxiao], "Piping er: Xianzhengguan zhi jieshi [Commentary Number Two: The Committee for Drawing Up Regulations for Constitutional Government's Explanation]," *Shibao*, wushen/11/20 (December 13, 1908), 3.
12. Yang Tingdong, *Ziyiju zhiwu xuzhi*, 2.
13. For one example, see untitled advertisement, *Shibao*, wushen/12/9 (December 31, 1908), 1.
14. "San zhi Changzhou huiyi ziyiju shi [Changzhou's Meeting on Preparations for the Provincial Assembly, Part Three]," *Shibao*, wushen/8/27 (September 22, 1908), 3. The Changzhou registration manual was reprinted as "Changzhou ziyiju diaocha xuzhi [Important Information for the Voter Census]," *Shibao*, wushen/9/8 (October 2, 1908), 1 and "Ziyiju diaocha shouxu [Procedures for the Voter Census]," *Shibao*, wushen/9/10 (October 4, 1908), 1; it also appears as "Wuyang chouban ziyiju shiwusuo diaocha shouxu [Wujin/Yanghu Provincial Assembly Preparation Office Procedures for the Voter Census]," *Shenbao*, GX 34/9/7 (October 1, 1908), 4.2, and "Wuyang chouban ziyiju shiwusuo diaocha xuzhi [Wujin/Yanghu Provincial Assembly Preparation Office Important Information for the Voter Census]," *Shenbao*, GX 34/9/8 (October 2, 1908), 4.2.
15. "Lai gao: ziyiju xuanju diaocha zhi shili [Letter: First Instances of Provincial Assembly Voter Censuses]," *Shibao*, wushen/9/16 [October 10, 1908], 1 and *Shibao*, wushen/9/18 [October 12, 1908], 1.
16. Xiao [Bao Tianxiao], "Piping er [Commentary Number Two]," *Shibao*, wushen/9/3 (September 27, 1908), 3.
17. "Changzhou fushu zhi xuanju diaocha [Changzhou Region Voter Census]," *Shibao*, wushen/10/6 (October 30, 1908), 3.
18. *Jiangsu Su shu ziyiju*, 7a–8a.
19. Yang Tingdong, *Ziyiju zhiwu xuzhi*, 5–6.
20. "Shelun: zouding Ziyiju zhangcheng boyi [Lead Editorial: Challenging the Provincial Assembly Regulations]," *Shibao*, wushen/7/8 (August 4, 1908), 1; *Shibao*,

wushen/7/9 (August 5, 1908), 1; *Shibao*, wushen/7/10 (August 6, 1908), 1; *Shibao*, wushen/7/11 (August 7, 1908), 1; *Shibao*, wushen/7/12 (August 8, 1908), 1; and *Shibao*, wushen/7/16 (August 12, 1908), 1.

21. Yang Tingdong, *Ziyiju zhiwu xuzhi*, 18–20.

22. Anhui ziyiju, *Xuanjuren zige shuomingshu*, 1a–3b.

23. Jiangxi ziyiju choubanchu, *Xuanju diaocha biyao*, "Xuanju zige zhangcheng jieshi [An Explantion of the Regulations for Voter Qualifications]," 1a–9b.

24. Jiangxi ziyiju choubanchu, *Xuanju diaocha biyao*, "Diaocha xuzhi [Necessary Knowledge for Registering Voters]," 1a–6a.

25. "Ge sheng chouban ziyiju: Jiading choubei ziyiju shiwusuo yanshuo yaoyi [Provincial Assembly Preparation Offices: A Summary of a Speech Given at the Jiading County Preparation Office]," *Shenbao*, GX 34/9/28 (October 22, 1908), 3.2–3.3, and *Shenbao*, GX 34/9/29 (October 23, 1908), 3.2–3.3.

26. Xiao [Bao Tianxiao], "Piping er: Jinggao ge sheng diaocha xuanju zhe [Commentary Number Two: A Message for All Voter Census Takers]," *Shibao*, wushen/10/9 (November 2, 1908), 3.

27. Historian Fu Huaifeng estimates that 60 percent of the population was age twenty or over and that half the population was male, thus the 0.48 percent of the Jiangsu provincial population (north and south) that registered to vote equaled approximately 1.7 percent of the adult male population. Fu Huaifeng, "Shi xi Qingmo minzhong de zhengzhi canyu." Here, the same assumptions have been applied to southern Jiangsu alone.

28. Chang Peng-yuan, *Zhongguo minzhu zhengzhi*, 55. The percentage of adult males was generated using Fu Huaifeng's assumptions.

29. C. Chang, *Chinese Gentry*, 164.

30. Xiao [Bao Tianxiao], "Piping er: Shen shang xue jie [Commentary Number Two: Gentry, Merchants, and Students]," *Shibao*, wushen/10/19 (November 12, 1908), 3.

31. These copies are held in the rare books rooms at the Nanjing Library, the Shanghai Municipal Library, and the National Library, respectively. Roger Thompson found an additional one, for Huichang County in Jiangxi Province, at the First Historical Archives in Beijing. Thompson, *China's Local Councils*, 139 and 226–27 (note 137).

32. *Changzhou xian xuanjuren mingce*.

33. *Hangzhou fu, Jiaxing fu xuanjuren mingce*.

34. *Chuxuanjuren mingce*.

35. *Shanghai xian xuanjuren xuanshi mingce*.

36. *Wu xian xuanjuren mingce*.

37. "Suzhoufu shu zhi xuanju diaocha [The Election Census in Suzhou Prefecture]," *Shibao*, wushen/10/3 (October 27, 1908), 3; *Jiangsu Su shu ziyiju*, 19a–21a.

38. Jiangxi ziyiju choubanchu, *Xuanju diaocha biyao*, "Diaochayuan zhuyi shixiang ba ze [Eight Points of Attention for Registrars of Voters]," n.p.

39. "Zai ji Changzhou chouyi ziyiju shi [A Further Record of Changzhou's Preparations for the Provincial Assembly]," *Shibao*, wushen/9/3 (September 27, 1908), 3.

40. "Xu zhi Changzhou huiyi ziyiju shi [Continued Record of Changzhou's Meeting Concerning the Provincial Assembly]," *Shibao*, wushen/8/26 (September 21, 1908), 3; "Changzhou chouban ziyiju shiwu zhi tebie da hui [Changzhou's Enormous Public Meeting on Preparations for the Provincial Assembly]," *Shibao*, wushen/9/2 (Septem-

ber 26, 1908), 3; and "Difang xinwen: Changzhou Wuyang liang yi xiangdong gongsuo he kai chouban ziyiju dahui [Local News: Joint Changzhou Wujin/Yanghu Counties Public Meeting on Preparations for the Provincial Assembly]," *Shibao*, wushen/9/11 (October 5, 1908), 3.

41. "San zhi Changzhou huiyi ziyiju shi [Third Record of Changzhou's Meeting Concerning the Provincial Assembly]," *Shibao*, wushen/8/27 (September 22, 1908), 3.

42. "Changzhouren zhi ziyiju re [Changzhou's Enthusiasm for the Provincial Assembly]," *Shibao*, wushen/9/3 (September 27, 1908), 3.

43. "Difang xinwen: Susheng ziyiju choubanchu jishi sanshiliu [Local News: Southern Jiangsu Provincial Assembly Preparation Office Records, Part Thirty-Six]," *Shibao*, wushen/12/3 (December 25, 1908), 3.

44. "Ge sheng chouban ziyiju: Jiading choubei ziyiju shiwusuo yanshuo.yaoyi [Provincial Assembly Preparation Offices: A Summary of a Speech Given at the Jiading County Preparation Office]," *Shenbao*, GX 34/9/28 (October 22, 1908), 3:2–3:3 and *Shenbao*, GX 34/9/29 (October 23, 1908), 3:2–3:3; "Changzhou xu ziyiju diaocha yi [Further Issues Concerning Changzhou's Provincial Assembly Voter Census]," *Shenbao*, GX 34/9/4 (September 28, 1908), 1:4.

45. "Difang xinwen: Wu Yang xuanju diaocha shiwusuo jin shi [Local News: Recent News from the Wu-Yang Voter Census Office]," *Shibao*, wushen/11/25 (December 18, 1908), 3.

46. For an extended discussion of the seminal importance of the Qing census, see Lam, *A Passion for Facts*, 50–90.

47. Yu [unidentified penname], "Shiping er: run er yue yi ri [Timely Commentary Number Two: The Day of March 22, 1909]," *Shibao*, jiyou/2/25 (March 16, 1909), 3.

48. Wei [ynidentified penname], "Lunshuo: Jinggao ziyiju zhi xuanjuren ji beixuanjuren [Editorial: A Message for Provincial Assembly Voters and Those Elected]," *Shenbao*, XT 1/2/29 (March 20, 1909), 1.2. For a similar editorial in *Shibao*, see Wang Hongfei, "Shelun: Jinggao you xuanju zige zhe [Editorial: A Message to Those Who Qualified for Suffrage]," *Shibao*, jiyou/2/29 (March 20, 1909), 1.

49. Translation from Mittler, *A Newspaper for China?*, 13–23; Liang Qichao, "Xuli [Preface]," *Guofengbao*, XT 2/1/11 [February 20, 1910], 7–8. See also Nathan, *Chinese Democracy*, 133–51.

50. Judge, *Print and Politics*, 40–41.

51. Judge, *Print and Politics*, 36–39; Janku, "The Uses of Genres in the Chinese Press," 137–53.

52. Bao Tianxiao, *Chuanyinglou huiyilu*, 236.

53. For a reconstruction of this data, see Fu Huaifeng, "Shi xi Qingmo minzhong de zhengzhi canyu," appendix 1.

54. "Xiangji Su yuan chuxuan toupiao qingxing [Detailed Account of Primary-Stage Voting in Suzhou]," *Shibao*, jiyou/run 2/3 (March 24, 1909), 3.

55. "Ge sheng chouban ziyiju juxing chuxuanju kaipiao [Provincial Assemblies: Ballot Counting Begins]," *Shenbao*, XT 1/run 2/5 (March 26, 1909), 3.2.

56. "Xi Jin chuxuan dangxuanren qingkuang [Primary-stage Election Winners in Wuxi and Jinshan]," *Shibao*, jiyou/run 2/10 (March 31, 1909), 3. Similar situations occurred in other counties. Xiao [Bao Tianxiao], "Shiping er: muyou wu xuanjuquan ji

bei xuanjuquan [Timely Commentary Number Two: Private Secretaries Employed by Government Officials Do Not Have the Right to Vote or Be Elected]," *Shibao*, jiyou/run 2/13 (April 3, 1909), 3.

57. Xiao [Bao Tianxiao], "Shiping er: fuxuan jiandu zhuyi [Timely Commentary Number Two: Things That the Secondary-Stage Election Supervisors Must Pay Attention To]," *Shibao*, jiyou/3/7 (April 26, 1909), 3.

58. "Suzhou zhi xuanju susong [Election Complaints in Suzhou]," *Shibao*, jiyou/run 2/25 (April 15, 1909), 3.

59. "Changzhou xuanju songsu huizhi [Compendium of Election Complaints in Changzhou]," *Shibao*, jiyou/3/16 (May 5, 1909), 3.

60. "Ge sheng chouban ziyiju juxing chuxuanju kaipiao [Provincial Assemblies: Ballot Counting Begins]," *Shenbao*, jiyou/run 2/5 (March 26, 1909), 18.

61. Xiao [Bao Tianxiao], "Shiping er: Ci you choubanchu suoji dang jijue zhe [Timely Commentary Number Two: These Are the Things Which the Preparatory Office Needs to Solve Quickly]," *Shibao*, jiyou/run 2/10 (March 31, 1909), 3.

62. This information can be culled from various March/April 1909 issues of *Shibao* and *Shenbao* and is helpfully collected in Fu Huaifeng, "Shi xi Qingmo minzhong de zhengzhi canyu," appendix 1.

63. Various communications collected in "Ziyiju choubanchu yu ge fu xian wanglai dianwen [Telegraphic Communication between the Provincial Assembly Preparatory Office and the Prefectures and Counties]," *Changsha ribao*, July 4, 1909–July 7, 1909.

64. Xiao [Bao Tianxiao], "Shiping er: yundong [Timely Comments Number Two: Campaigning]," *Shibao*, jiyou/2/7 (February 26, 1909), 3.

65. Mateer, *New Terms for New Ideas*, 122; see also Morgan, *Chinese New Terms*, 164.

66. By contrast, the late twentieth-century/early twenty-first-century standard term for "campaigning," *jingxuan* (lit. "competing for selection"), does not make an appearance in *Shenbao* before 1922 and only rarely for a decade thereafter. Mathews's 1931 Chinese–English dictionary lacks an entry for *jingxuan*, too.

67. "Lun zhengfu huiyi xuanjufa [On Election Laws for Government Meetings]," *Shenbao*, GX 32/7/11 (August 30, 1906), 2, and *Shenbao*, GX 32/7/12 (August 31, 1906), 2.

68. "Piping er: Xuanjuquan bei xuanjuquan [Commentary Number Two: The Right to Vote and the Right to Be Elected]," *Shibao*, wushen/10/3 (October 27, 1908), 3.

69. The promulgation of the law is recorded in *Da Qing lichao shilu*, entry for GX 34/2/yichou (March 11, 1908). The full text of the law can be found in *Dongfang zazhi*, GX 34/4/25 (May 24, 1908), neiwu 228–34.

70. For a useful comparison, see Shelley Rigger's analysis of how a single-vote, multiple-candidate election system produced "candidate-oriented voting and clientelistic campaigning" in post-1949 Taiwan. Rigger, *Politics in Taiwan*, 39–50.

71. "Xuanju yundong fa er [Election Campaigning Method #2]," *Shenbao*, XT 1/2/4 (February 23, 1909), 2.4.

72. Haishang xuanbaosheng [unidentified pseudonym], *Xuanju guai xianxiang* [Strange Tales from the Election] (N.p., ca. 1909), xuanju zazu 1–2 and 43.

73. Haishang xuanbaosheng, *Xuanju guai xianxiang*, 39.

74. "Xuanju yundong fa si [Election Campaigning Method #4]," *Shenbao*, XT 1/2/6 (February 25, 1909), 2:4.

75. For an alternative interpretation of these illustrations, see D. C. Chang, "Democracy Is in Its Details," 320–21.

76. "Xiangji Su yuan chuxuan toupiao qingxing [Detailed Account of Primary-Stage Voting in Suzhou]," *Shibao*, jiyou/run 2/3 (March 24, 1909), 3.

77. "Xuanju yundong san [Election Campaigning 3]," *Shibao*, jiyou/run 2/11 (April 1, 1909), 2, and "Xuanju yundong si [Election Campaigning 4]," *Shibao*, jiyou/run 2/12 (April 2, 1909), 2.

78. Xiao [Bao Tianxiao], "Shiping er: piru yi gua [Timely Commentary Two: Like a Melon]," *Shibao*, jiyou/run 2/11 (April 1, 1909), 3.

79. "Shiping san [Timely Commentary Three]," *Shibao*, jiyou/run 2/11 (April 1, 1909), 4.

80. "Lun Jiangsu chuxuanju zhi jieguo, shang pian [On the Results of the Primary-Stage Election in Jiangsu, Part One]," *Shibao*, jiyou/run 2/23 (April 13, 1909), 1.

81. "Difang xinwen: Jiangning chuxuanju kaipiao zhi fengbo [Local News: Primary Stage Election Dispute in Jiangning], *Shibao*, jiyou/run 2/20 (April 10, 1909), 3, and "Jiangning panding si kai piaogui zhi fajin [Ruling and Fine for Improperly Opening a Ballot Box in Jiangning]," *Shibao*, jiyou/run 2/27 (April 17, 1909), 3.

82. *Jiangsu Su shu ziyiju*, 64a–67a.

83. *Jiangsu Su shu ziyiju*, 82a–92a.

84. These numbers are compiled from the list of primary and secondary-stage winners printed in *Jiangsu Su shu ziyiju*, 82a–92a.

85. "Jiangsu sheng Sushu ziyiju choubanchu zhiyuan biao [Members of the Southern Jiangsu Provincial Assembly Preparatory Office]," *Shibao*, wushen/11/13 (December 6, 1908), 3.

86. "Ningshu ziyiju choubanchu zhiyuan mingdan [Members of the Northern Jiangsu Provincial Assembly Preparatory Office]," *Shibao*, wushen/11/3 [November 26, 1908], 3.

87. *Yubei lixian gonghui zhangcheng timing biao*.

88. "Lunshuo: Lun guomin yi you zizhi zhi jingshen [Editorial: Citizens Should Have the Spirit of Self-Government]," *Shenbao*, XT 1/run 2/7 (March 28, 1909), 1:2–3.

89. Leng [Chen Jinghan], "Shiping er: Zuo ri [Timely Commentary Two: Yesterday]," *Shibao*, jiyou/3/16 (May 5, 1909), 2.

90. G. E. Morrison, *Correspondence of G. E. Morrison*, 1:532–35.

91. "Zheng Guanying nianpu jianbian [Basic Chronology of Zheng Guanying's Life]," in *Zheng Guanying ji*, xia ce 1564.

92. Zheng Guanying, "Yu Li Jitang taishi shu [Letter to Li Jitang]," reprinted in *Zheng Guanying ji*, xia ce 315.

93. "Shiping san [Timely Commentary Three]," *Shibao*, jiyou/run 2/24 (April 14, 1909), 4.

94. "Yubei lixian gonghui fushe fazheng jiangxi suo xingkai jiangshi [The Public Association's Affiliated Law and Politics Lecturing Institute Opens], *Shenbao*, XT 1/2/2 (February 21, 1909), 3.3; "Fazheng jiangxi hui dingqi kaike [The Law and Politics Lecturing Institute Sets Time for Classes]," *Shenbao*, XT 1/2/6 (February 25, 1909), 2.4.

95. "Ge sheng chouban ziyiju juxing chuxuanju kaipiao [Provincial Assemblies: Ballot Counting]," *Shenbao*, XT 1/run 2/5 (March 26, 1909), 3.2; "Ge sheng chouban ziyiju juxing chong xuanju kaipiao [Provincial Assemblies: Ballot Counting for the Revote]," *Shenbao*, XT 1/run 2/13 (April 3, 1909), 3.2.

96. "Xiang zhi Su Song fuxuanju kaipiao qingxing [Detailed Account of Secondary-Stage Balloting in Suzhou and Songjiang Prefectures]," *Shenbao*, XT 1/3/17 (May 6, 1909), 1.6; "Juxing chong xuan houbu yiyuan [A Revote for Alternate Assemblymen]," *Shenbao*, XT 1/3/25 (May 14, 1909), 3.2

97. J. Wang, *Merry Laughter and Angry Curses*, 54–84.

4. Free Elections and the First Republic

1. Esherick, "Founding a Republic," 129–52.

2. Zheng Xiaoxu, *Zheng Xiaoxu riji*, 1382 (entry for XT 3/11/23 [January 11, 1912]).

3. Wei Chunhui, *Zhang Jian pingzhuan*, 103–5.

4. Zhang Jian, "Riji," in *Zhang Jian quanji*, 6:658–59 (entries for XT 3/8/19 [October 10, 1911] to XT 3/8/25 [October 16, 1911]).

5. Young-tsu Wong, "Popular Unrest and the 1911 Revolution."

6. *Jiangsu linshi shengyihui di yi jie huiqi baogao di san ce*, 3a–3b.

7. *Jiangsu linshi shengyihui yijue'an*, juan 3, 1a–5a; juan 4, 1a–30a; and juan 5,1a–50b. A locally designed law for provincial legislative elections was created in April 1912, but it was superceded by a national law in September and never used. *Jiangsu linshi yihui di er jie huiqi baogao di yi ce*, yijue huilu 1a–19a.

8. *Linshi gongbao*, March 20, 1912, mingling 1–2.

9. "Jiading xian fuxuan minzhengzhang [The Secondary-Stage Election for Jiading County Civil Commissioner]," *Shenbao*, July 12, 1912, 6.

10. "Shanghai xian yishihui dangxuan mingdan [List of People Elected to the Shanghai County Legislature]," *Shenbao*, July 17, 1912, 7; untitled, *Shenbao*, October 18, 1912, 6.

11. "Su dudu cuiban shi xiang xuanju zhi tongling [Jiangsu Military Governor's Order Promoting City and Countryside Elections]," *Shenbao*, September 21, 1912, 4.

12. Mo [Zhang Yunhe], "Shiping yi [Commentary on the Times, One]," *Shenbao*, August 31, 1912, 3.

13. "Zhuandian [Special Dispatches]," *Shenbao*, July 12, 1912, 2.

14. *Zhengfu gongbao*, July 13, 1912, fulu 9–15.

15. This representation is derived from Ye Lijun, *Minguo Beijing zhengfu shiqi xuanju*, 93.

16. *Zhengfu gongbao*, July 13, 1912, fulu 15–19.

17. *Zhengfu gongbao*, July 25, 1912, fulu 21–27.

18. *Zhengfu gongbao*, July 28, 1912, fulu 17–18.

19. *Zhengfu gongbao*, July 25, 1912, fulu 21–27.

20. *Zhengfu gongbao*, July 26, 1912, fulu 11–14.

21. *Zhengfu gongbao*, July 26, 1912, fulu 16.

22. "Mingling [Orders]," *Shenbao*, October 5, 1912, 2.

23. The national and provincial election laws can be found in, respectively, *Zhengfu gongbao*, August 11, 1912, falu 5–30, and *Zhengfu gongbao*, September 5, 1912, falu 7–12.

24. "Zhuandian [Special Dispatches]," *Shenbao*, July 12, 1912, 2.

25. Strand, *Unfinished Republic*, 38–51.

26. For one example, see Mo [Zhang Yunhe], "Shiping yi [Commentary One]," *Shenbao*, September 9, 1912, 3.

27. "Teyue lutou dian [Reuters Cable]," *Shenbao*, November 8, 1912, 2; "Nuzi canzhengquan you li yi jie [Women's Political Rights Are Struck Down Again]," *Shenbao*, November 13, 1912, 3.

28. Edwards, *Gender, Politics, and Democracy*, 68–102.

29. "Gongshangjie zhi yaoqiu xuanjuquan re [Enthusiasm in the Artisan and Merchant Communities for Demanding Suffrage]," *Shenbao*, November 4, 1912, 2.

30. "Teyue lutou dian [Reuters Cable]," *Shenbao*, October 30, 1912, 2.

31. "Luren shi fabian yu xuanju bing zhong [Shandong People See Elections and the Queue as Equally Important]," *Shenbao*, October 30, 1912, 6.

32. *Zhengfu gongbao*, October 30, 1912, mingling 1.

33. "Canyiyuan jishi [Proceedings of the Senate]," *Shenbao*, July 17, 1912, 2.

34. "Zhuandian [Special Dispatches]," *Shenbao*, November 23, 1912, 2.

35. "Canyiyuan zuijin huichang jishilu [Recent Proceedings of the Senate]," *Shenbao*, December 3, 1912, 3.

36. *Zhengfu gongbao*, August 31, 1912, gongdian 9. Also printed in "Gongdian [Public Telegrams]," *Shenbao*, September 3, 1912, 2.

37. "Susheng xuanju zhongyiyuan shuoming [An Explanation of the National Lower House Elections in Jiangsu]," *Shenbao*, September 9, 1912, 6.

38. "Xuanju zhongyiyuan yiyuan zhi yubei [Preparations for the Lower House Election]," *Shenbao*, September 23, 1912, 7.

39. "Shiping yi [Timely Commentary One]," *Shenbao*, October 3, 1912, 3. The reference to "mute orphans" is a complete mystery.

40. "Difang xinwen: Suzhou [Local News: Suzhou]," *Shenbao*, October 24, 1912, 6. For a county-by-county breakdown, see "Susheng xuanmin zongshu [Total Voter Numbers for Jiangsu]" and "Jiangsu zuijin renkou ce [The Most Recent Population Registers for Jiangsu]," *Shenbao*, October 26, 1912, 6.

41. "Zhuandian [Special Dispatches]," *Shenbao*, October 28, 1912, 3.

42. "Zhuandian [Special Dispatches]," *Shenbao*, November 2, 1912, 2.

43. "Zhuandian [Special Dispatches]," *Shenbao*, November 3, 1912, 2.

44. "Zhuandian [Special Dispatches]," *Shenbao*, November 14, 1912, 2.

45. "Suzhou bangshi xuanmin ce [Suzhou Posts Its Voter Rolls]," *Shenbao*, November 22, 1912, 6.

46. "Jiangning gongmin zhi buping ming [Nanjing-Area Citizens Claim Unfairness]," *Shenbao*, November 26, 1912, 6; "Zhuandian [Special Dispatches]," *Shenbao*, November 28, 1912, 2; and *Zhengfu gongbao*, November 25, 1912, gongdian 19.

47. *Zhengfu gongbao*, January 5, 1913, tonggao 72–74. This number was reprinted in contemporary newspapers. "Ge sheng zhongyiyuan, shengyihui xuanju [Parliamentary and Legislative Elections in Each Province]," *Shenbao*, January 5, 1913, 7; "Ge sheng zhongyiyuan shengyihui xuanjuren zongshu yi lan biao [Chart of Voter Totals for Parliament and Legislatures in Each Province]," *Shuntianbao*, January 18, 1913, 3.

48. Jiangsu neiwu si, *Jiangsu sheng neiwu xingzheng baogaoshu*, xia 83–87.

49. Registered voter totals are taken from *Zhengfu gongbao*, January 5, 1913, tonggao 72–74. National and provincial population estimates are taken from Chang Peng-yuan, *Zhongguo minzhu zhengzhi*, 80. (Note that several errors appear in Chang's data for reg-

istered voters.) An alternative set of population estimates is used in Ye Lijun, *Minguo Beijing zhengfu shiqi xuanju*, 123–24.

50. "Zaping yi: Cunluo sixiang wei xuanju shang zhi da zhang'ai [Miscellaneous Commentary, One: Village Mentality Is a Great Obstacle for the Election]," *Shenbao*, November 23, 1912, 3.

51. Liu Jianjun, *Ni suo bu shi de minguo mianxiang*, 130–32.

52. Untitled advertisement, *Shenbao*, October 19, 1912, 3.

53. *Shenbao* printed the full text of the election law for the lower house of parliament in daily segments, beginning on August 13 and concluding on August 19, 1912. The provincial legislature election law was likewise printed serially from September 2 to September 7, 1912.

54. *Zhengfu gongbao*, September 30, 1912, gongwen 10.

55. *Zhengfu gongbao*, November 3, 1912, gongdian 18.

56. Hunan sheng jiaoyu si, *Tongsu jiangyan ziliao*, "Guohui zhi zuzhi [The Structure of Parliament]."

57. Fu [unidentified pen name], "Shelun: jinggao xuanjuren (yi) [Lead Editorial: A Message for Voters, Part 1]," *Shenbao*, September 6, 1912, 1, and Fu [unidentified pen name], "Shelun: jinggao xuanjuren (er) [Lead Editorial: A Message for Voters, Part 2]," *Shenbao*, September 7, 1912, 1.

58. Xiao [Bao Tianxiao], "Shiping er: jinggao xuanjuren [Timely Commentary, Two: A Message for Voters]," *Shibao*, November 26, 1912, 4.

59. Chang Yu-fa, *Minguo chunian de zhengdang*, 35–36.

60. See, for example, advertisements for the "Minzhudang choubei zongshiwusuo [Democratic Party General Preparation Office]," *Shenbao*, October 13, 1912, 1, and "Guomindang zhengjian zhi yanjiu [Report on the Nationalist Party's Political Views]," *Shenbao*, October 13, 1912, 2.

61. Wang Shao'ao, "Xinhai geming shiqi zhengdang huodong," 405. The use of *jingxuan*, rather than *yundong*, for "campaigning," is an artifact of the period in which this account was written (sometime around 1961), not the time period it discussed (1912–13).

62. "Zhuandian [Special Dispatches]," *Shenbao*, November 8, 1912, 2.

63. "Zhuandian [Special Dispatches]," *Shenbao*, November 9, 1912, 2; "Zhuandian [Special Dispatches]," *Shenbao*, November 11, 1912, 2.

64. "Yang Zhen Minzhudang jinshiji [Recent Democratic Party Events in Yangzhou and Zhenjiang]," *Shenbao*, November 12, 1912, 6.

65. Hu Shi and Cai Dengshan, *"Nie hai hua,"* 30–31.

66. Zheng Xiaoxu, *Zheng Xiaoxu riji*, 1446–47 (entry for December 25, 1912).

67. Wang Shao'ao, "Xinhai geming shiqi zhengdang huodong," 404–5.

68. Wang Shao'ao, "Xinhai geming shiqi zhengdang huodong," 404–5.

69. "Songjiang shengyihui chuxuan zhi xianzhuang: wu wei xuanju qiantu ku [The Present Condition of the Songjiang County Elections for Provincial Legislature: I Cry for the Future of Elections]," *Shenbao*, December 8, 1912, 6.

70. *Zhengfu gongbao*, January 10, 1913, gongdian 9.

71. For one example from Dantu County, see "Dantu shenghui chuxuan shangwei jiexiao zhi yuanyin [The Reason Why Dantu County Has Not Announced the Results

for the Provincial Legislative Election]," *Shenbao*, December 13, 1912, 6; for another example from Shanghai County, see "Zhengming dangxuan ren zhi tonggao [Verifying the Election Results]," *Shenbao*, December 20, 1912, 7, and "Xuanbu Wang Zuocai bei xuan piao'e [Announcing Wang Zuocai's Vote Total]," *Shenbao*, December 22, 1912, 7.

72. Wang Shao'ao, "Xinhai geming shiqi zhengdang huodong," 405.

73. Xu Boxi, Ge Zhicheng, and Mei Dajun, "Fendou bu xi de zhongcheng zhanshi Wang Shao'ao tongzhi [Comrade Wang Shao'ao, A Tireless Loyal Fighter]," *Renmin ribao*, January 6, 1981, 5.

74. "Mingling [Orders]," *Shenbao*, May 19, 1914, 2.

75. "Chuxuanju toupiao zhi sheng kuang [The Excitement of Voting in the Primary Election]," *Shenbao*, December 7, 1912, 7; "Shanghairen xuanju zhi yongyue [Shanghainese Enthusiasm for the Election]," *Shibao*, December 7, 1912, 5; "Shiping san [Commentary 3]," *Shibao*, December 7, 1912, 6; and "Xuanju toupiao lengre guan [Seeing Enthusiasm and Indifference for Voting]," *Shishi xinbao*, December 7, 1912, 3.

76. Xiyi [unidentified pen name] "Laigao: shengyihui chuxuan zhi neimu [Received Article: The Behind-the-Scenes Story of the Provincial Legislative Election]," *Shenbao*, December 8, 1912, 1–2.

77. "Su Chang Zhen Yang shengyihui chuxuan xianzhuang [Primary Stage Provincial Legislature Voting in Suzhou, Changzhou, Zhenjiang, and Yangzhou]," *Shenbao*, December 9, 1912, 6.

78. "Zhuandian [Special Dispatches]," *Shenbao*, December 12, 1912, 2.

79. "Changzhou," *Shenbao*, December 22, 1912, 6; *Zhengfu gongbao*, January 15, 1913, gongwen 13.

80. "Suzhou shengyihui chuxuan toupiao ji [A Record of Primary-Stage Voting in Suzhou's Provincial Legislative Election]," *Shenbao*, December 8, 1912, 6; "Su Chang Zhen Yang shengyihui chuxuan xianzhuang [Primary Stage Voting in Suzhou, Changshu, Zhenjiang, and Yangzhou for the Provincial Legislature]," *Shenbao*, December 9, 1912, 6.

81. "Suzhou chuxuan zhi xianzhuang [The Primary-Stage Election in Suzhou]," *Shibao*, December 8, 1912, 4; "Suzhou shengyihui chuxuan toupiao jiwen [Report on Suzhou's Provincial Legislature Primary-Stage Election]," *Shibao*, December 10, 1912, 3.

82. Jiangsu neiwu si, *Jiangsu sheng neiwu xingzheng baogaoshu*, shang 114–17.

83. "Su Song shengyihui chuxuan jiexiao [Results from Suzhou and Songjiang's Provincial Legislative Primary-Stage Elections]," *Shenbao*, December 11, 1912, 6.

84. "Shiping san [Commentary Three]," *Shibao*, December 12, 1912, 6.

85. "Di er qu toupiaosuo jiwen [Report from the District Two Polling Station]," *Shenbao*, December 12, 1912, 7.

86. "Song Yang guohui chuxuan xianzhuang [The Primary-Stage Parliamentary Election in Songjiang and Yangzhou Regions]," *Shenbao*, December 13, 1912, 6.

87. "Wuxian guohui chuxuan jiexiao [Results of the Parliamentary Election in Wu County]," *Shenbao*, December 15, 1912, 6.

88. *Zhengfu gongbao*, December 25, 1912, gongdian 44.

89. Jiangsu neiwu si, *Jiangsu sheng neiwu xingzheng baogaoshu*, xia 91–99.

90. Haiyan Lee's analysis of Wang Dungen's 1913 magazine spin-off of "Free Talk" provides an introduction to this genre. Lee, "'A Dime Store of Words.'"

91. [Xu Tai], "Shoudie zhi shi xi [Skinny Butterfly's Ten Delights]," *Shenbao*, September 10, 1912, 9.

92. [Xu Tai], "Shoudie zhi shi bu [Skinny Butterfly's Ten No's]," *Shenbao*, September 10, 1912, 9.

93. Link, *Mandarin Ducks and Butterflies*.

94. Yehe [unidentified pen name], "Ziyoutan: Xi ni kaiban xuanju yundong yanjiuhui jianzhang [Free Talk: A Playful Proposed Charter for the Election Campaign Research Association]," *Shenbao*, December 4, 1912, 10.

95. Shuaigongxini [unidentified pen name], "Ziyoutan: sili yundongxue zhuanmen xuexiao yuanqi bingfu zhangcheng [Free Talk: Announcement for an Academy for Election Campaigners]," *Shenbao*, December 15, 1912, 10.

96. Shen Songxin, "Ziyoutan: xuanju baixiao lu [Free Talk: A Record of Many Laughable Things from the Election]," *Shenbao*, December 10, 1912, 10. Shen's identity is unknown; he never published another item in "Free Talk."

97. Shoudie [Xu Tai], "Ziyoutan: xuanju yundong ganyan [Free Talk: Words from the Heart about Election Campaigning]," *Shenbao*, December 16, 1912, 10.

98. Jiangong [unidentified pen name], "Shelun: xuanju zhi beiguan [Lead Editorial: A Pessimistic View of the Election]," *Changshu xunbao*, December 21, 1912, 1.

99. "Ying yingye hua (er) [Depictions of Sales, Two]," *Xibao*, March 22, 1913.

100. "Di er qu fuxuan zhanqi wu ri [District Two Secondary Stage Election Postponed Five Days]," *Shenbao*, January 7, 1913, 7.

101. Shuaini [unidentified pen name], "Ziyoutan: huaji guanggao [Free Talk: Humorous Advertisement]," *Shenbao*, December 23, 1912, 10.

102. "Zaping san: jinqian yiyuan [Miscellaneous Commentary Three: Money Legislators]," *Shenbao*, December 25, 1912, 7.

103. Dungen [Wang Dungen], "Ziyoutan: Paimai chuxuan dangxuanren [Free Talk: Auctioning Primary-Stage Election Winners]," *Shenbao*, January 7, 1913, 10.

104. "Zaping er: fuxuan ren xinli zhi shice [Miscellaneous Commentary, Two: An Examination of Voter Psychology]," *Shenbao*, January 11, 1913, 6. See also the very similar commentary provided in the same column several weeks earlier: "Zaping er: jin zhi suowei minxuan zhe [Miscellaneous Commentary, Two: Today's So-Called Popular Elections]," *Shenbao*, December 15, 1912, 6.

105. "Xin yiyuan kaiken qin hui jishi [Newly Elected Legislators Meet]," *Shenbao*, February 9, 1913, 6.

106. Jiangsu neiwu si, *Jiangsu sheng neiwu xingzheng baogaoshu*, shang 114–17.

107. "Zaping er: minguo zhi fuxuan zhi tong [Miscellaneous Commentary Two: The Pain of the Republic's Secondary-Stage Election]," *Shenbao*, February 27, 1913, 6.

108. "Jiangsu zhongyiyuan di san qu fuxuan jiexiao [Results of the House of Representatives Secondary-Stage Election in Jiangsu's Third District Announced]," *Shenbao*, January 13, 1913, 6.

109. *Zhengfu gongbao*, December 16, 1912, mingling 6–8.

110. Wu Xiangxiang, *Song Jiaoren zhuan*, 202.

111. Song Jiaoren, *Song Jiaoren ji*, 456–57.

112. Dungen [Wang Dungen], "Ziyoutan: ziyoutanhua hui [Free Talk: Free Talk Meeting]," *Shenbao*, January 7, 1913, 10.

5. Warlord Democracy

1. *Zhengfu gongbao*, November 5, 1913, mingling 4–12.
2. *Zhengfu gongbao*, November 10, 1913, tonggao 17.
3. *Zhengfu gongbao*, January 11, 1914, mingling 1–8.
4. *Zhengfu gongbao*, February 4, 1914, mingling 1–2; February 5, 1914, mingling 2–3; and March 1, 1914, mingling 3–4.
5. Leng [Chen Jinghan], "Shiping: Quanti tuifan zhi xianzai [Timely Commentary: Now Everything Is Overthrown]," *Shenbao*, February 6, 1914, 2.
6. *Zhongyiyuan yijue leibian*, 9:141–42; "Jiangsu yiyuan zhi huyu [Appeal from Jiangsu's Representatives], *Shenbao*, September 24, 1913, 3.
7. "Zuzhi xingzheng huiyi zhi xiangqing [Organizing the Political Conference]," *Shenbao*, November 11, 1913, 2; "Zhuandian [Special Dispatches]," *Shenbao*, November 17, 1913, 2; "Zhuandian [Special Dispatches]," *Shenbao*, July 21, 1914, 2.
8. Young, *The Presidency of Yuan Shih-k'ai*, 138–209.
9. *Zhengfu gongbao*, January 27, 1914, mingling 1–6.
10. *Yuefa huiyi jilu*, di 2 bian juan zhi 3, 46a–49b.
11. *Zhengfu gongbao*, October 28, 1914, mingling 1–25.
12. "Difang zizhi shi xing tiaoli [Experimental Local Self Government Regulations]," *Shenbao*, January 3, 1915, 11, and January 4, 1915, 10–11.
13. *Yuefa huiyi jilu*, di 2 bian juan zhi 3, 52a.
14. *Zhengfu gongbao*, March 13, 1915, mingling 4–9, and May 26, 1915, mingling 10–11.
15. "Jiangsu xuanju shixian ji [Preparations for Jiangsu's Elections]," *Shenbao*, October 7, 1915, 6.
16. Young, *The Presidency of Yuan Shih-k'ai*, 155 and 293, n. 55.
17. "Yangzhou: hege xuanmin liaoliao [Yangzhou: Few Qualified Voters]," *Shenbao*, October 3, 1915, 7.
18. Young, *The Presidency of Yuan Shih-k'ai*, 210–20.
19. "Shanghai chuxuan [The Primary-Stage Election in Shanghai]," *Shenbao*, October 21, 1915, 10.
20. "Jiangsu guomin daibiao toupiao ji [Jiangsu Citizen Representatives Vote]," *Shenbao*, November 2, 1915, 6.
21. Liu Dapeng, *Tuixiangzhai riji*, 220.
22. Hu Shi, "Manufacturing the Will of the People."
23. Liu Dapeng, *Tuixiangzhai riji*, 220–21; Harrison, "Experiencing the Modern State."
24. Guoqi Xu, *China and the Great War*, 203–33.
25. *Zhengfu gongbao*, September 29, 1917, mingling 1–2.
26. *Zhengfu gongbao*, December 1, 1917, gongdian 18; *Zhengfu gongbao*, March 3, 1918, gongdian 17.
27. *Zhengfu gongbao*, February 18, 1918, falu 5–28.
28. Chang Peng-yuan, *Zhongguo minzhu zhengzhi*, 112; Chang Peng-yuan, *Liang Qichao yu Minguo zhengzhi*, 80–83.
29. Chang Peng-yuan, *Zhongguo minzhu zhengzhi*, 128–37.

30. Xu Daolin, *Xu Shuzheng xiansheng wenji*, 212; Cao Rulin, *Cao Rulin yisheng zhi huiyi*, 140. Neither of these denials is creditable.

31. "Zhuandian [Special Dispatches]," *Shenbao*, May 7, 1918, 2.

32. "Nanjing kuaixin [News from Nanjing]," *Shenbao*, May 18, 1918, 7.

33. *Zhengfu gongbao*, March 22, 1918, gongdian 22; "Chouban guohui xuanju [Preparations for the Parliamentary Election]," *Xin Wuxi*, March 13, 1918, 2.

34. "Huainan liangyuan chuxuanju diaocha gaojun [Parliamentary Voter Registration Work Completed in Huainan]," *Wujin*, April 7, 1918, 3; "Kaihuaxiang choubei guohui chuxuanju zhiwen [News on Kaihua Township's Election Preparations]," *Xin Wuxi*, March 28, 1918, 2.

35. "Heding xuanju jingfei shumu [Confirmation of Election Appropriations]," *Wujin*, April 13, 1918, 2.

36. Nanhaiyinzi, *Anfu huoguo ji*, 31–32; "Funing [Funing County]," *Shenbao*, June 2, 1918, 7.

37. Jie had previously held elective office at the provincial and national levels. His role in organizing Anfu's election efforts in Jiangsu is alluded to (and briefly criticized) in a May 31, 1918 telegram from Xu Shuzheng to Wang Yitang. *Xu Shuzheng dian gao*, 193.

38. *Zhengfu gongbao*, April 25, 1918, gongdian 20.

39. *Zhengfu gongbao*, May 9, 1918, gongdian 19.

40. *Zhengfu gongbao*, May 14, 1918, gongdian 21; "Shenzhong xuanmin zige zhi shengling [Provincial Order on Being Careful about Voter Qualifications]," *Xin Wuxi*, May 14, 1918, 2.

41. *Zhengfu gongbao*, May 18, 1918, gongdian 18.

42. "Yundong xuanju zhi renao [The Hustle and Bustle of Election Campaigning]," *Xin Wuxi*, May 20, 1918, 2.

43. "Difang tongxin [Letters from Localities]," *Shenbao*, May 22, 1918, 7, and "Difang tongxin [Letters from Localities]," *Shenbao*, May 23, 1918, 7.

44. Nanhaiyinzi, *Anfu huoguo ji*, 20–21 and 29.

45. "Longmai," *Xin Wuxi*, May 24, 1918, 3; "Zhongyuan chuxuan ba zhi [Lower House Primary-Stage Election Report 8]," *Xibao*, May 28, 1918, 2.

46. "Xuanju jianchatuan zhi jinggao [A Warning from the Election Monitoring Team]," *Wujin*, June 5, 1918, 2. Similar groups may have been active even earlier; in late May, *Shenbao* noted the existence of a "citizens' monitoring group" involved in the election in northern Jiangsu's Huaiyin county. "Huaiyin," *Shenbao*, May 24, 1918, 7.

47. "Xuanju jianshituan zhi ge baoguan handie [Announcement from the Election Monitoring Team to All Newspapers]," *Wujin*, June 6, 1918, 3.

48. Naogong [unidentified pen name], "Qi huo ke ju [A Rare Commodity Worth Hoarding]," *Wujin*, June 9, 1918, 2.

49. "Maipiaotuan zhengqiu shan jia [The 'Vote-Buying Group' Vies for Good Prices]," *Wujin*, June 9, 1918, 2.

50. *Xu Shuzheng dian gao*, 205–6.

51. *Xu Shuzheng dian gao*, 220.

52. "Difang tongxin: Qingjiangpu [Local News: Qingjiangpu]," *Shenbao*, June 9, 1918, 7. For other examples, see "Zhongyiyuan fuxuan shi zhi zhongzhong [Various News

about the Secondary-Stage Election for the Lower House of the National Parliament]," *Xibao*, June 11, 1918, 2.

53. "Gonggong jueze [Public Choice]," *Xibao*, June 9, 1918, 3.

54. "Di er jie shengyiyuan xuanjuren shu [Voter Registration Totals for the Second Provincial Legislature]," *Wujin*, May 5, 1918.

55. *Zhengfu gongbao*, July 1, 1918, gongdian 7–8. The governor had expressed concern about inflated voter rolls as early as May. "Shenzhong xuanmin zige zhi shengling [Provincial Order on Being Careful about Voter Qualifications]," *Wujin*, May 15, 1918, 2.

56. *Zhengfu gongbao*, July 4, 1918, gongdian 13.

57. *Zhengfu gongbao*, July 10, 1918, gongdian 20.

58. "Nanjing kuaixin [Nanjing Fast News]," *Shenbao*, June 9, 1918, 7.

59. "Anshang gongmin zuzhi shenghui xuanju jianshi tuan [Citizens of Anshang Organize an Election Monitoring Team for the Provincial Elections]," *Wujin*, June 30, 1918, 2.

60. "Wang Qing qishi [Announcement from Wang Qing]," *Xibao*, July 8, 1918, 1. This advertisement ran on the four subsequent days.

61. "Jiang Zengyao lushi guanggao [Advertisement from Jiang Zengyao, Lawyer]," *Xibao*, July 7–12, 1918, 1.

62. "Jingzheng xuanju zhi guaizhuang [Strange Occurrences in Competing for Election]," *Lanyan ribao*, July 10, 1918, 2. See also "Zai zhi xuanju guaizhuang [More Strange Occurrences from the Election]," *Lanyan ribao*, July 12, 1918, 2.

63. "Shenghui chuxuan zhi bangshi [The Results of the Primary-Stage Election for Provincial Legislature]," *Lanyan ribao*, July 15, 1918, 2.

64. "Shengyihui chuxuan zhi zhongzhong [Various Reports on the Primary-Stage Elections for Provincial Legislature]," *Xibao*, July 12, 1918, 2.

65. "Chuxuan kaipiao hou zhi songsu liu [Post-Primary-Stage Election Complaints, Part 6]," *Xin Wuxi*, July 25, 1918, 2.

66. "Wuxi," *Shenbao*, July 13, 1918, 7; "Chuxuan kaipiao hou zhi songsu qi [Post-Primary-Stage Election Complaints, Part 7]," *Xin Wuxi*, July 27, 1918, 2.

67. Tianqi [unidentified pen name], "Yiping: Falu wuxiao [City Commentary: The Law Is Impotent]," *Xibao*, July 17, 1918, 3.

68. "Nanjing tongxin [Nanjing News]," *Shenbao*, July 18, 1918, 7.

69. For national election statistics, see Nathan, *Peking Politics*, 101.

70. Zhongzhang [unidentified pen name], "Pinglun: Xuanju ganyan er [Commentary: Thoughts on the Election, Part Two]," *Wujin*, July 31, 1918, 1.

71. *Zhengfu gongbao*, August 4, 1920, mingling 1.

72. *Zhengfu gongbao*, October 31, 1920, mingling 2.

73. *Zhengfu gongbao*, November 18, 1920, mingling 1.

74. *Zhengfu gongbao*, November 24, 1920, mingling 4–5.

75. "Tichang zuzhi gongmin xuanju jianshi tuan shixing xuanju wubi fa [Organize a Citizens' Election Monitoring Team in Order to Enforce the Laws against Election Fraud]," *Shenbao*, November 10, 1920, 17.

76. "Jiangsu gongmin jianshi xuanjutuan zhi choubei [Preparations for the Jiangsu Citizens Election Monitoring Team]," *Shenbao*, November 26, 1920, 10.

77. "Ge sheng gongmin zuzhi xuanju jianshituan chengbao bei an you guan wenxian [Documents Relevant to the Citizens' Formation of Election Monitoring Teams in the Various Provinces]." Second Historical Archives of China, 1001-2-1001.

78. "Jiangsu gongmin jianshi xuanju tuan huiyi ji [Meeting of the Jiangsu Citizens' Election Monitoring Team]," *Shenbao*, November 29, 1920, 10.

79. "Jiangsu gongmin jianshi xuanju tuan xiaoxi [Information on the Jiangsu Citizens' Election Monitoring Team]," *Shenbao*, December 7, 1920, 10.

80. "Jiangsu gongmin jianshi xuanju tuan Wuxi fenbu chengli bugao [Announcement of the Formation of the Jiangsu Citizen's Election Monitoring Team's Wuxi Chapter]," *Xin Wuxi*, January 2, 1921, 1. This advertisement ran for most of January.

81. Jiangsu sheng gongmin jianshi xuanju tuan, *Xuanju fagui*.

82. "Gongmin jianshi tuan kaihui yu zhi [Preparations for the Citizens' Election Monitoring Team's Meeting]," *Xin Wuxi*, January 21, 1921, 2.

83. "Liangxin xuanju [Voting in Good Conscience]," *Xin Wuxi*, February 28, 1921, 3.

84. Ne [unidentified pen name], "Zhongyuan chu xuanju [Lower House Primary-Stage Election]," *Shenbao*, March 1, 1921, 11.

85. 1921 numbers are reported in "Shenghui chuxuan xuanmin zongshu [Total Number of Registered Voters for the Provincial Primary-Stage Election]," *Xin Wuxi*, June 26, 1921, 2 and "Chengbao xuanmin zongshu [Reporting the Total Number of Registered Voters]," *Xibao*, June 28, 1921, 2–3; 1918 numbers in "Wuxi," *Shenbao*, April 13, 1918, 3; and 1912 numbers in Jiangsu neiwu si, *Jiangsu sheng neiwu xingzheng baogaoshu*, xia 83–87.

86. "Zhongyuan chuxuan kaipiao jishi [Primary-Stage Ballots Opened]," *Xin Wuxi*, March 5, 1921, 2.

87. "Suzhou," *Shenbao*, March 6, 1921, 7; Jiangsu neiwu si, *Jiangsu sheng neiwu xingzheng baogaoshu*, xia 83–87.

88. "Zhongyuan chuxuan zhi zhongzhong, er [Various Reports on the Primary-Stage Election, Two]," *Xin Wuxi*, March 2, 1921, 2; "Zhongyuan chuxuan zhi zhongzhong, san [Various Reports on the Primary-Stage Election, Three]," *Xin Wuxi*, March 3, 1921, 2; "Wuxi," *Shenbao*, March 3, 1921, 7.

89. "Jiangsu gongmin jianshi tuan jin dian [Recent Telegrams from the Citizens' Election Monitoring Team]," *Shenbao*, March 8, 1921, 10.

90. "Shanghai zhongyuan chuxuan dangxuanren zhi jieshi [Winners of the Shanghai Lower House Primary-Stage Election]," *Shenbao*, March 5, 1921, 10.

91. "Jianshi xuanju tuan zui jin liang dian [Two Recent Telegrams from the Election Monitoring Team]," *Shenbao*, April 26, 1921, 10.

92. Ne [unidentified pen name], "Zai lun xuanju [More on the Election]," *Shenbao*, March 2, 1921, 11.

93. Shen attended several dinners sponsored by an embryonic version of the Public Association in October 1906. Zheng Xiaoxu, *Zheng Xiaoxu riji*, 1060–61.

94. [Shen Enfu], "Shen Enfu diaocha zhongyiyuan yiyuan Shanghai chuxuan [Shen Enfu's Investigation of the Shanghai Primary Stage Election for the Lower House of Parliament]," *Shenbao*, March 5, 1921, 11.

95. "Xuanju susong kai ting ji [Opening of the Election Complaint Case]," *Shenbao*, March 15, 1921, 10. Yang later published a collection of documents related to the case. Yang Chunlü, *Minguo shi nian Shanghai*.

96. Elvin, "The Gentry Democracy in Chinese Shanghai," 41–65.

97. "Xuanju susong an panjue shu quanwen [Complete Text of the Election Complaint Ruling]," *Shenbao*, April 17, 1921, 10.

98. Laopu [Yang Yinhang], "Zhengzhi chouwei [The Stench of Politics]," *Shenbao*, April 2, 1921, 16.

99. "Xuanju panjue wuxiao hou zhi fandui sheng [Opposition to the Election's Invalidation]," *Shenbao*, April 21, 1921, 10; "Xuanju panjue wuxiao hou zhi fandui sheng, er [Opposition to the Election's Invalidation, 2]," *Shenbao*, April 22, 1921, 10; and Ne [unidentified pen name], "Xuanju wuxiao [Invalid Election]," *Shenbao*, April 16, 1921, 11.

100. "Resolution on Parliamentary Actions (July 1922) [Guanyu yihui xingdong jueyi'an]," translated in Saich, *Rise to Power*, 43–45.

101. Zhang Baicheng, "Gongmin changshi: Lun shengyihui zhi gaixuan—cui guomin zhuyi [Citizens' Knowledge: On the Provincial Legislature Election—Promoting Citizen Awareness]," *Shenbao*, May 30, 1921, 16.

102. Ne [unidentified pen name], "Zaping er: Shenghui chuxuan [Miscellaneous Commentary Two: Provincial Legislature Primary-Stage Election]," *Shenbao*, July 1, 1921, 15.

103. "Shenghui chuxuan toupiao xuzhi [A Continued Account of Primary-Stage Voting for the Provincial Legislature]," *Xibao*, July 3, 1921, 3.

104. "Shengyihui chuxuan kaipiao jishi [Ballot Counting for the Primary-Stage Election for the Provincial Legislature]," *Xibao*, July 4, 1921, 3.

105. "Su shenghui xuanju song'an bai ba shi yu qi [Over 180 Cases of Election Complaints from the Provincial Legislative Elections]," *Shenbao*, July 19, 1921, 17.

106. "Shenghui xuanju susong an zhi zuo xun [Yesterday's News about the Provincial Legislature Election Complaint]," *Shenbao*, July 15, 1921, 14; "Shanghai difang shenpanting [Shanghai Local Court]," *Shenbao*, September 15, 1921, 15.

107. Xiaowu [unidentified pen name], "Xiaoyan: Xuanju he toupiao [Brief Words: Elections and Casting Ballots]," *Xinbao*, July 8, 1921, 4.

108. Nanping [unidentified pen name], "Ni faxing shengyiyuan qianjuanpiao [A Proposal for Provincial Legislator Lottery Tickets]," *Wuyu*, July 9, 1921.

109. Nanping [unidentified pen name], "Huajiyu: shenghui fuxuan paimai gongsi guanggao [Humorous Essay: Advertisement for a Provincial Legislature Election Auction Company]," *Wuyu*, July 30, 1921.

110. "Pinglun: shengxuan zhi yuce [Opinion: Predictions for the Provincial Elections]," *Shangbao*, June 14, 1921, 2.

111. "Susheng xuanju tan [Talking about the Jiangsu Elections]," *Shenbao*, January 19, 1924, 11.

112. Zhen [unidentified pen name], "Changtan: Ai Jiangsu shengyihui [Common Discussions: Mourning the Jiangsu Provincial Legislature]," *Shenbao*, June 11, 1924, 17.

113. "Susheng xuanju tan, er [Talking about the Jiangsu Elections, Part Two]," *Shenbao*, January 21, 1924, 11.

114. This order is reprinted in "Su yihui linshi hui kaimu [The Provisional Session of the Jiangsu Legislature Opens]," *Shenbao*, April 2, 1925, 10. See also *Jiangsu sheng zhi: yihui renmin daibiao dahui zhi*, 64–65.
115. *Zhengfu gongbao*, January 6, 1924, mingling 3–5.
116. Nathan, *Peking Politics*, 201–20.

6. Elections as Education

1. Luo Zhitian, *Zai zao wenming zhi meng*, 248–50 and 279–88; Grieder, *Hu Shih and the Chinese Renaissance*, 173–216.
2. Grieder, *Hu Shih and the Chinese Renaissance*, 191.
3. Hu Shi, "Women de zhengzhi zhuzhang [Our Political Proposals]," in *Hu Shi wenji*, 3:328–31. See also Fung, *Intellectual Foundations of Chinese Modernity*, 172–82.
4. Lou Mingyuan, "Jianjie xuanju zhi quedian [Defects of Indirect Elections]," *Shenbao*, October 18, 1920, 16. Little is known about Lou, a semi-frequent *Shenbao* writer (focusing mainly on legal issues) in 1920–23 and again in 1926. After 1927, he served as a Nationalist-appointed county magistrate in Zhejiang Province.
5. Hu Shi, "'Zhengzhi gailun' xu [Preface to 'An Overview of Politics']," in *Hu Shi wenji*, 3:322–26. A portion of this document, including the first sentence quoted here, is translated in Grieder, *Hu Shih and the Chinese Renaissance*, 197–98.
6. Hu Shi, "Zhei yi zhou 28: Wu Peifu yu lianzheng zizhi [This Week #28: Wu Peifu and Provincial Autonomy]," in *Hu Shi wenji*, 3:425–26; emphasis added.
7. Hu Shi, "Zai lun jianguo yu zhuanzhi [On National Construction and Autocracy, Part II]," in *Hu Shi wenji*, 11:373–78; Hu Shi, "Da Ding Zaijun xianzheng lun minzhu yu duzai [A Response Ding Wenjiang's 'On Democracy and Dictatorship']," in *Hu Shi wenji*, 11:529–31. See also Fung, *In Search of Chinese Democracy*, 115–19.
8. Wang Shijie, "Xinjin xianfa de qushi—daiyizhi zhi gaizao [Recent Trends in Constitutionalism—The Reform of Representative Systems]," *Dongfang zazhi*, November 15, 1922.
9. Lou Mingyuan, "Jiming toupiao yu wu jiming toupiao zhi deshi [A Comparison of Open Ballots and Secret Ballots]," *Shenbao*, November 23, 1920, 16.
10. Bergère, *Golden Age of the Chinese Bourgeoisie*, 217–27, and Chesneaux, "The Federalist Movement in China," 122–23.
11. Huang Baoyi [Huang Yanpei], "Sheng zizhi [Provincial Autonomy]," *Shenbao*, October 10, 1920, 46.
12. Tang Zhijun, *Zhang Taiyan nianpu changbian*, 605–6.
13. Copies of these constitutions can be found in Xia Xinhua, *Jindai Zhongguo xianzheng licheng*, 741–47 (Jiangsu), 685–97 (Zhejiang), 657–70 (Hunan), 711–21 (Guangdong), 721–38 (Henan); Zhou Yezhong and Jiang Guohua, *Zi xia er shang de lixian changshi*, 381–94 (Sichuan) and 424–45 (Fujian).
14. See Edwards, *Gender, Politics, and Democracy*, 103–38, for an extended discussion of this era.
15. "Jiangsu shengzhi cao'an [Proposed Provincial Structure for Jiangsu]," *Shenbao*, November 27, 1920, 11; November 28, 1920, 11; and November 29, 1920, 11. A draft may have been completed as early as June. See *Sushe tekan* [Special Periodical of the Jiangsu

Society], March 1922, reprinted in *Minguo Beijing zhengfu zhixian shiliao erbian*, 17:187–99.

16. Leslie H. Chen, *Chen Jiongming and the Federalist Movement*.

17. For the county legislative election law, see "Guangdong sheng zanxing xianyihui yiyuan xuanju tiaoli [Guangdong Provisional Election Law for County Legislatures]," reprinted in Chen Dingyan, *Chen Jingcun (Jiongming) xiansheng nianpu*, 1031–43; for the county magistrate election law, see "Guangdong zanxing xianzhang xuanju tiaoli [Guangdong Provisional Election Regulations for County Magistrates]," reprinted in Chen, *Chen Jingcun (Jiongming) xiansheng nianpu*, 1027–30.

18. "Guangdong zhi nüquan chao [The Women's Rights Movement in Guangdong]," *Shenbao*, March 31, 1921, 3; for a more extensive report, see "Guangdong nüzi canzheng zhi da yundong [The Great Campaign for Guangdong Women's Political Rights]," *Shenbao*, April 4, 1921, 7.

19. "Guangzhou tongxin: Nüzi canzheng an yi foujue [News from Guangzhou: Proposal for Women's Political Rights is Rejected]," *Shenbao*, April 7, 1921, 6.

20. Edwards, *Gender, Politics, and Democracy*, 121, and Fu Jinzhu, "Chen Jiongming yu jindai Guangdong nüquan yundong."

21. See, for example, the reference to Guangzhou women voting in "Xuanju shicanshi zhi toupiao qingxing [Voting for City Council Members]," *Huazi ribao*, June 2, 1921.

22. Chen Dingyan, *Chen Jingcun (Jiongming) xiansheng nianpu*, 410.

23. Xia Xinhua, *Jindai Zhongguo xianzheng licheng*, 711–21; "Guangdong laodong funü puxuan taolunhui [Laboring Women in Guangdong Discuss Mass-Suffrage Elections]," *Shenbao*, April 9, 1922, 7.

24. Chen Jiongming, "Zhongguo tongyi chuyi [Modest Proposal for China's Unification]," in *Chen Jiongming ji*, 1045.

25. Chang Peng-yuan, "Jindai difang zhengzhi canyu de mengya."

26. "Shengxianfa gao cheng de tongdian [Announcement of the Passage of the Provincial Constitution]," *Hunan tongsu ribao*, December 13, 1921; "Changsha xian shengxian zongtoupiao zhi jinkuang [Current Situation of the Constitutional Plebiscite in Changsha County]," *Dagongbao* (Changsha), November 6, 1921, 7.

27. Hunan zhiding xianfa choubei chu, *Hunan zhixian baogaoshu*, zalu 7–16.

28. "Hunan sheng sheng yihui yiyuan xuanjufa," reprinted in Liu Jianqiang, *Hunan zizhi yundong shilun*, 285–319.

29. Edwards, *Gender, Politics, and Democracy*, 121–29.

30. "Nü yuan canyu xuanzheng zhi dianling [Telegrams on Women's Electoral Participation]," *Dagongbao* (Changsha), March 14, 1922, 6; "Liling xuanju zhi da fengchao [Electoral Unrest in Liling]," *Dagongbao* (Changsha), March 21, 1922, 6; and "Zuo ri xuanju xunshi ji [Observations of Yesterday's Election]," *Dagongbao* (Changsha), March 26, 1922, 6.

31. "Hengyang teyue tongxin [Hengyang Report]," *Dagongbao* (Changsha), February 8, 1922, 6.

32. "Yundong xuanju zhi jiahua [Talking Points about Election Campaigning]," *Dagongbao* (Changsha), February 11, 1922, 6.

33. "Hengyang teyue tongxin [Hengyang Report]," *Dagongbao* (Changsha), February 21, 1922, 6.

34. "Changsha xuanju de yu wen pianpian [Miscellaneous News on the Election in Changsha]," *Hunan tongsu ribao*, March 31, 1922; "Changsha xian xuanju de ji jian yu wen [News about the Election in Changsha County]," *Hunan tongsu ribao*, April 1, 1922; "Changsha sheng yiyuan jiexiao [Changsha Provincial Legislators Announced]" and "Changsha xuanju zhi da chaban an [Investigation of the Changsha Election]," *Hunan tongsu ribao*, April 11, 1922.

35. Tang Dechang, "Liansheng zizhi yu xianzai zhi Zhongguo [Provincial Autonomy and Present-Day China]," *Taipingyang yuekan*, September 1922, 3.

36. Li Jiannong, *Zuijin sanshi nian Zhongguo zhengzhi shi*, 519.

37. Sun Yat-sen, "Jiuren da zongtong zhi dui wai xuanyan [Presidential Inaugural Statement to Foreign Countries]," in *Sun Zhongshan quanji*, 5:532–33.

38. For evidence of his enduring anger, see Sun's lengthy tirade against provincial federalism in Sun Yat-sen, "Minzhuquan di si jiang [Democracy—Fourth Lecture]," in *Sun Zhongshan quanji*, 9:299–314.

39. "Zhongguo Guomindang xuanyan [Proclamation of the Chinese Nationalist Party]," in *Zhongguo Guomindang xuanyan ji*, 67–71.

40. "Zhongguo Guomindang di yi ci quanguo daibiao dahui xuanyan [Proclamation of the Chinese Nationalist Party's First National Conference]," in *Zhongguo Guomindang xuanyan ji*, 84–94.

41. "Jian guo dagang [Fundamentals of National Reconstruction]," in Xia Xinhua, *Jindai Zhongguo xianzheng licheng*, 598–600.

42. Sun Yat-sen, "Zhonghua geming dang zongzhang [China Revolutionary Party Charter]," in *Sun Zhongshan quanji*, 3:97–102.

43. Sun Yat-sen, "Zai Shanghai Zhongguo Guomindang benbu huiyi de yanshuo [Speech to the Nationalist Party Headquarters in Shanghai]," in *Sun Zhongshan quanji*, 5:400–401.

44. "Zhonghua minguo zhengfu zuzhifa [Organic Law of the Republic of China]," in Xia Xinhua, *Jindai Zhongguo xianzheng licheng*, 786–89.

45. Ch'ien, *Government and Politics of China*, 133–49, and Fung, *In Search of Chinese Democracy*, 30–31.

46. "Guomin huiyi daibiao xuanju fa [Election Law for Citizen's Conference Representatives]" and "Guomin huiyi daibiao xuanju fa shixingfa [Method of Implementing the [Election Law for Citizen's Conference Representatives]," in Xia Xinhua, *Jindai Zhongguo xianzheng licheng*, 837–45.

47. An exception is the Guangzhou city election law designed by Sun Yat-sen's son, Sun Ke, in the early months of Chen Jiongming's administration. It reserved ten seats on the city council for representative from business, labor, and professional associations. Chen Dingyan, *Chen Jingcun (Jiongming) xiansheng nianpu*, 287–88. A similar system was implemented in the nearby city of Shantou, too. Chen Dingyan, *Chen Jingcun (Jiongming) xiansheng nianpu*, 449.

48. John A. Fairlie, "Constitutional Developments in China."

49. "Zhonghua minguo xunzheng shiqi yuefa [Tutelary Era Constitutional Compact for the Republic of China]," in Xia Xinhua, *Jindai Zhongguo xianzheng licheng*, 830–35.

50. Eastman, "Nationalist China during the Nanking Decade," 160–63.

51. "Zhonghua minguo xianfa cao'an ('Wu-wu xian cao') [Draft Constitution of the Republic of China (May 5, 1936 Draft)]," in Xia Xinhua, *Jindai Zhongguo xianzheng licheng*, 982–92.

52. "Guomin dahui daibiao xuanjufa [National Assembly Election Law]" and "Guomin dahui daibiao xuanjufa shixing xizi [Detailed Regulations for the National Assembly Election Law]," in Xia Xinhua, *Jindai Zhongguo xianzheng licheng*, 1001–15.

53. "Guomin dahui daibiao xuanjufa [National Assembly Election Law]" and "Guomin dahui daibiao xuanjufa shixing xizi [Detailed Regulations for the National Assembly Election Law]," in Xia Xinhua, *Jindai Zhongguo xianzheng licheng*, 1001–15.

54. Details about the oath can be found in *Guomin zhengfu gongbao*, May 21, 1930, 1–6, and *Guomin zhengfu gongbao*, May 30, 1930, 8–9.

55. "Gongmin xuanshi dengji gongwuyuan mingri kaishi [Citizen's Oath and Registration for Civil Servants Begins Tomorrow]," *Shenbao*, August 13, 1936, 10, and "Gongmin xuanshi jiu yue shisan ri quantian jinxing [The Citizen's Oath Will Be Given All Day on September 13]," *Shenbao*, September 13, 1936, 12.

56. "Guoxuan shiwusuo juxing sheng da xuanchuan [The National Assembly Election Office Embarks on a Major Propaganda Effort]," *Shenbao*, July 1, 1937, 19; "Zuo ri kaipiao, Guoda xuanju daibiao quyu nong, gong, shang jiexiao [Ballot Boxes Opened Yesterday; National Assembly Results for Geographical, Farmer, Worker, and Merchant Constituencies Announced]," *Shenbao*, July 20, 1937, 13.

57. "Guomin dahui daibiao xuanju zong shiwusuo gongzuo baogao [Work Report of the National Assembly Election Office]," Hoover Archives KMT Records microfilm 5.2 reel 27.

58. "Zhonghua minguo xianfa [Constitution of the Republic of China]," reprinted in Xia Xinhua, *Jindai Zhongguo xianzheng licheng*, 1104–18; "Guomin dahui daibiao xuanju bamian fa [National Assembly Election and Recall Law]" and "Guomin dahui daibiao xuanju bamian fa shixing tiaoli [Operational Regulations for the National Assembly Election and Recall Law]," in Xia Xinhua, *Jindai Zhongguo xianzheng licheng*, 1130–42. The only significant differences were the addition of "women's organizations" to the list of special constituencies allowed to elect their own National Assembly members and the reconfiguration of the Legislative Yuan and Control Yuan into bodies elected directly by the people.

59. "Fei Jiangsusheng guomin daibiao dahui xuanmin renshu juan [Voter Registration Numbers for Jiangsu's National Assembly Elections]," Jiangsu Provincial Archives 1002-yi-109. Less than half of Jiangsu's counties are represented in this file.

60. "Shishi xianzheng kuoda xuanchuan gangyao [Framework for Spreading Propaganda for Constitutional Government]," *Jiangsu sheng zhengfu gongbao*, October 31, 1947, 22–23.

61. "Fei Jiangsu sheng xuanju xuanchuan dagang [Outline of Jiangsu Province's Propaganda for the Election]," Jiangsu Provincial Archives 1026-yi-257.

62. "Jiaofei kanluan tuixing daxuan Hu gejie juxing xuanchuan dahui [All Sectors of Shanghai Society Hold a Publicity Meeting to Promote the Election and the Campaign against the Bandit Insurrection]," *Shenbao*, November 20, 1947, 2; "Ziyou toupiao, gongkai jingsai: Nanhui xuanjiao yundong yi pie [Vote Freely, Compete Openly: A Brief Overview of Nanhui's Voter Education Movement]," *Shenbao*, January 29, 1948, 5.

63. "Ge di jingxuan jian bairehua [Election Competition Heats Up across the Nation]," *Shenbao*, November 18, 1947, 2.

64. "Shelun: Zhenzhong ziji de zhei yi piao [Commentary: Cherish Your Ballot]," *Shenbao*, November 19, 1947, 2.

65. Henry Lieberman, "Chinese Election Stirs No Fervor," *New York Times*, October 23, 1947, 22, and Henry Lieberman, "Assembly Election Set in China Today," *New York Times*, November 21, 1947, 22.

66. "General Apathy Reported," *New York Times*, November 22, 1947, 3; "Pan yizhang xiwang shizhengfu chu bugao [Speaker Pan Hopes for an Announcement from the City Government]," *Shenbao*, November 22, 1947, 4. Additional examples can be found in Chang Peng-yuan, *Zhongguo minzhu zhengzhi*, 178–82.

67. "Guodai xuanju di yi ri toupiao yue wu liu wan [500,000 to 600,000 Ballots Cast on the Election's First Day]," *Shenbao*, November 22, 1947, 4.

68. "Shanghai shi xuanju shiwusuo guanyu guoda daibiao, lifa weiyuan xuanju dian suo dian cui Shanghai shi toupiao diaocha biao ji liwei xuanren ming ce [Shanghai Municipal Election Office's Telegram on the National Assembly and Legislative Yuan Voting Stations, with a Ballot Chart and Electoral Rolls]," Shanghai Municipal Archives Q105-1-156.

69. "China's First General Election," *China Magazine*, December 1947, 4. For a range of other voter estimates, see Chang Peng-yuan, *Zhongguo minzhu zhengzhi*, 172.

70. "China's First General Election," *China Magazine*, December 1947, 5.

71. "Fei guoda daibiao Jiangsu sheng zhi fu tuanti huimin xuanju jieguo tongjibiao [Results of Jiangsu Elections for National Assembly from Occupational, Women's Groups, and Hui Muslim Constituencies]," Jiangsu Provincial Archives 1026-yi-95.

72. Chang Peng-yuan relates several examples of this. Chang Peng-yuan, *Zhongguo minzhu zhengzhi*, 182–83.

73. "Fei Jiangsu sheng ge xian shi guoda daibiao xuanju kaipiao jieguo baogaoshu [National Assembly Election Results Reports from Various Jiangsu Counties]," Jiangsu Provincial Archives 1026-yi-109.

74. Wang Shijie, *Wang Shijie riji*, 1:893.

75. "Fei Jiangsu sheng Wuxian Guofa gaibiao xuanju jiufen [Wu County National Assembly Election Controversies]," Jiangsu Provincial Archives 1026-yi-174.

76. "Fei Jiangsu sheng gexian Guoda daibiao xuanju jiufen [National Assembly Election Disputes from Various Jiangsu Counties]," Jiangsu Provincial Archives 1026-yi-177. For additional examples, see Pepper, *Civil War in China*, 137–43, and Chang Peng-yuan, *Zhongguo minzhu zhengzhi*, 183–89.

77. Ch'ien, *Government and Politics of China*, 331–36.

78. "Fei Jiangsu sheng Suqian xian Guoda houxuanren Lu Xuanzhi jingxuan wenti [The Issue of Suqian County, Jiangsu Resident Lu Xuanzhi's Competition for Office]," Jiangsu Provincial Archives 1026-yi-35. Lu had been active in the Nationalist government for over a decade before the 1947 election and had served as a county magistrate in northern Jiangsu during the war with Japan; he was not an outsider by any means.

79. Lu's candidacy for the Legislative Yuan is reported in "Su sheng quyu liwei houxuanren zong'e sa wu ming funü san ming [35 Candidates and 3 Female Candidates for Jiangsu's Legislative Yuan Geographical Constituencies]," *Shenbao*, December 23, 1947, 5.

His withdrawal from the National Assembly seat must have occurred at approximately the same time—it was reported to the provincial government in a telegram dated December 26. "Fei Jiangsu sheng Suqian xian Guoda houxuanren Lu Xuanzhi jingxuan wenti," Jiangsu Provincial Archives 1026-yi-35. Nationalist Party–nominated candidates for the Legislative Yuan are listed in "Zhengdang liwei houxuanren xuanzong zuo gongbu mingdan [The Party's Candidates for Legislative Yuan Announced Yesterday by the Election Commission]," *Shenbao*, December 28, 1947, 1.

80. Chang Peng-yuan, *Zhongguo minzhu zhengzhi*, 189–97.

81. "Hu Shi dui puxuan yuan zuo yi xuanmin [Hu Shi Is Willing to Be an Ordinary Voter during the Mass Suffrage Election]," *Shenbao*, August 27, 1947, 6. See, too, Grieder, *Hu Shih and the Chinese Renaissance*, 293–313.

82. "On China's First General Election," *China Magazine*, December 1947, 6–7.

83. "Shelun: Puxuan jieshu yu zhengzhi jiaoyu [Lead Editorial: The Mass Suffrage Election and Political Education]," *Shenbao*, November 24, 1947, 2.

84. Rigger, *Politics in Taiwan*, 34–54.

85. "Taiwan sheng xiang (zhen) min daibiao xuanju guize [Taiwan Province Regulations for Village (Township) Resident Assemblies]," *Taiwan sheng xingzhengzhang guangongshu gongbao*, February 8, 1946, 3–4 (Chinese text) and 11–13 (Japanese text). Village, township, and urban district assemblies were established in some places in the mainland, but no accounts of voting for these positions survive. In all likelihood, members were simply appointed by local governments. For regulations permitting this in Shanghai, see "Qu gongsuo zuzhi guize [District Office Organizational Regulations]," *Shenbao*, January 19, 1946, 5.

86. "Tainan xian dudao xuanju bing jiangxi xiang zhen daibiao xuanju [Tainan County Supervises the Election and Assembly Member Training Classes]," *Minbao* (Taiwan), March 5, 1946, 2.

87. "Shelun: Mo qing qi yi piao [Editorial: Don't Abandon Your Ballot Lightly]," *Minbao* (Taiwan), March 14, 1946, 1; "Shelun: Xuanju hou de huixiang [Editorial: Reflecting on the Election]," *Minbao* (Taiwan), March 18, 1946, 1.

88. Kerr, *Formosa Betrayed*, 120.

89. "Xuanju jingshen yao you er shi peiyang qie kan mandian xuanchuan chengji [Election Spirit Must Be Cultivated from Childhood, with Great Results for the Propaganda Effort]," *Minbao* (Taiwan), March 6, 1946, 2. See also Kerr, *Formosa Betrayed*, 116–20 (for an account of the overall propaganda campaign) and 194–96 (for a brief account of the election).

90. "Taiwan sheng ge xian shi zhengfu juban xiang zhen mindaibiao zizhi jiangxi hui banfa [Plan for Cities and Counties of Taiwan Province to Hold Self-Government Training Classes for Township Representatives]," *Taiwan sheng xingzhengzhang guangongshu gongbao*, February 22, 1946, 91–92.

91. Rigger, *Politics in Taiwan*, 22.

92. For a series of examples from the 1950s and 1960s, see Chao and Myers, "How Elections Promoted Democracy," 394–97; for vote buying, see Rigger, *Politics in Taiwan*, 94–99.

93. A substantial number of districts for county/municipal legislatures, district/township representative assemblies, and the provisional provincial legislature were as-

signed multiple members, although voters were limited to a single vote. "Taiwan sheng ge xian shi yihui yiyuan xuanju ba mian guicheng [Election and Recall Regulations for County/Municipal Legislatures in Taiwan Province]," *Taiwan sheng zhengfu gongbao*, April 26, 1950, 338–43; "Taiwan sheng xiang zhen min daibiao xuanju ba mian guicheng [Election and Recall Regulations for District/Township Representative Assemblies in Taiwan Province]," *Taiwan sheng zhengfu gongbao*, July 15, 1950, 147–49; "Taiwan sheng linshi sheng yihui yiyuan xuanju bamian guicheng [Election and Recall Regulations for the Provisional Provincial Legislature of Taiwan Province]," *Taiwan sheng zhengfu gongbao*, August 22, 1953, 611–17. Legislative elections in Taiwan continued to use a single-vote, multiple-member model until the 2008 elections. Shelley Rigger traces the origins of these laws to the Japanese colonial era, rather than the mainland Republic. Rigger, *Politics in Taiwan*, 36–37 and 39.

94. Rigger, *From Opposition to Power*, 41–45.

95. See, for example, Arthur Lerman's rich ethnographic study of the Taiwanese provincial legislature, conducted in 1971–72. Lerman, *Taiwan's Politics*.

96. Hu Fu, "Electoral Mechanism and Political Change," 140–41.

97. Rigger, *From Opposition to Power*, 6–7 and 16–35; Chao and Myers, *The First Chinese Democracy*, esp. 59–65 and 82–88; Chao and Myers, "How Elections Promoted Democracy in Taiwan."

98. Rigger, *Politics in Taiwan*, 82. For a similar claim, see Tien, "Elections and Taiwan's Democratic Development," 8.

99. Specific examples are recounted in Ts'ai and Myers, "Winds of Democracy," 367–70. Ts'ai and Myers offer a positive evaluation of this election overall, despite the excesses of campaigning. For a response to this anxiety, see Sullivan and Sapir, "Nasty or Nice?"

100. Chao and Myers, *First Chinese Democracy*, 109–15; Taylor, *The Generalissimo's Son*.

101. For one way to measure this change: occurrences of the phrase "political tutelage [*xunzheng*]" in official government gazettes basically disappear after December 1947, whereas sixty-eight examples can be found in issues published between 1928 and 1944. This is based on a keyword search of historical government gazettes digitized by the National Central Library (http://gaz.ncl.edu.tw/).

7. Voting without a Choice

1. Dai Xiuzan, Wu Chuanyi, and Li Haopei, "Jiu Zhongguo xuanju zhidu de shizhi [The True Character of Old China's Election Systems]," *Renmin ribao*, June 8, 1953, 3.

2. Zhonghua Suwei'ai gongheguo zhongyang zhixing weiyuanhui, *Zhonghua Suwei'ai gongheguo de xuanju xize*.

3. Niu and Mi, *Dou xuan*, 80–131 and 192–202.

4. For a list of bean voting elections culled from a variety of sources, see Niu and Mi, *Dou xuan*, 215–41. A detailed discussion of wartime elections can be found in Chen Yung-Fa, "Rural Elections."

5. Hinton, *Fanshen*, 319–31 and 535–47.

6. "Shelun: Renzhen zhaokai ge di renmin daibiao hui [Editorial: Diligently Hold People's Assemblies in Every Area]," *Renmin ribao*, October 27, 1949, 1.

7. Liu Shaoqi, *Jianguo yilai Liu Shaoqi wengao*, 4:525–35; *Zhou Enlai nianpu 1949–1976*, 1:274–79.

8. "Guanyu zhaokai quanguo renmin daibiao dahui de jidian shuoming [Several Thoughts about the Opening of a People's Congress] (January 13, 1953)," in Mao Zedong, *Mao Zedong wenji*, 6:257–62.

9. "Yingjie puxuan, shixing renmin daibiao dahui zhidu [Welcome the Mass Suffrage Election and Implement the People's Congress System]," *Renmin ribao*, January 15, 1953, 1.

10. Deng Xiaoping, "Guanyu 'Zhonghua renmin gongheguo quanguo renmin daibiao dahui xuanjufa' cao'an de shuoming [Explanation of the Draft Resolution of the 'Election Law of the National People's Congress of the People's Republic of China']," *Renmin ribao*, March 3, 1953, 1–2.

11. The full text of the law can be found at "Zhonghua renmin gongheguo quanguo renmin daibiao dahui ji difang geji renmin daibiao dahui xuanju fa [Election Law for the National and Local People's Congresses]," *Renmin ribao*, March 2, 1953, 1.

12. Jiangsu sheng xuanju weiyuanhui bangongshi, *Jiangsu sheng puxuan ziliao huibian* [Collected Materials from the Election in Jiangsu Province] (N.p., 1954), 469. Jiangsu Provincial Archives.

13. "Quan shi shiqu jiaoqu puxuan ganbu qingkuang tongji biao [Statistics on Cadre Activity during the Election in (Shanghai's) Urban and Suburban Districts]," Shanghai Municipal Archives B52-2-61.

14. "Shanghai shi renkou diaocha yu xuanmin dengji shibanfa [Shanghai Population Census and Voter Registration Methods]," Shanghai Municipal Archives B52-1-10.

15. Ledong xian xuanju weiyuanhui, *You guan shaoshu minzu xuanju*, 14–15.

16. Mullaney, *Coming to Terms with the Nation*, 18–19.

17. A sample registration log can be found in "Guanyu xuanmin dengji biao de shuoming [Instructions for Voter Registration Logs]," *Renmin ribao*, April 6, 1953, 3.

18. Wang Li, "Yige putong nongfu de xuanpiao."

19. *Jiangsu sheng puxuan ziliao huibian*, 461–65. Jiangsu Provincial Archives (no reference number).

20. "Guanyu renkou diaocha yu xuanmin zige shencha wenti [Issues Concerning the Population Census and Investigation of Voting Rights]," Shanghai Municipal Archives B52-2-36.

21. "Jiangsu sheng xuanju weiyuanhui baogao [Jiangsu Provincial Election Committee Report]," July 3, 1953, Jiangsu Provincial Archives 3087-chang-0002.

22. "Jiji canjia xuanju, gong renmin minzhuquan, tuijin guojia de jianshe shiye [Enthusiastically Participate in the Election, Strengthen the People's Democratic Rights, and Promote National Construction]," Shanghai Municipal Archives A22-1-90.

23. "Jiangsu sheng jiceng xuanju dianxing shiban gongzuo qingkuang [Work Reports on Jiangsu Provincial Grassroots Election Model Districts]," *Jiangsu sheng xuanju gongzuo qingkuang* [Jiangsu Provincial Election Work Report], issue 1 (July 20, 1953). Jiangsu Provincial Archives 3087-duanqi-21.

24. "Guanyu ben shi mouxie xianxingqu xuanchuan gongzuo zhong fasheng ruogan quedian he cuowu de jiancha tongbao [Investigatory Report Concerning Several De-

fects and Errors in the Propaganda Work in Several Shanghai Election Test Districts]," Shanghai Municipal Archives A22-1-90.

25. "Shanghai shi xuanju weiyuanhui puxuan qiangkuang huibao [Shanghai City Election Committee Collected Reports on the General Election]," report 3, Shanghai Municipal Archives B52-1-41.

26. "Jiangsu sheng jiceng xuanju gongzuo zongjie [Jiangsu Provincial Grassroots Election Final Work Report]," Jiangsu Provincial Archives 3087-yong-0003; "Hebei sheng jiceng puxuan zhong cunzai de wenti [Existing Problems in the Hebei Local Elections]," *Neibu cankao*, March 22, 1954; "Zhongnan qu puxuan gongzuo cunzai de wenti [Existing Election Problems in the Southwest]," *Neibu cankao*, March 23, 1954; "Liaoxi di er pi jiceng puxuan fasheng zisha shijian shisi qi [At Least 14 Cases of Suicide in the Second Round of Liaoxi Local Elections]," *Neibu cankao*, April 3, 1954; "Anhui sheng jiceng xuanju gongzuo zhong cunzai de wenti [Existing Problems in Local Election Work in Anhui]," *Neibu cankao*, April 6, 1954.

27. "Puxuan shiban gongzuo zhong yi fasheng zisha shijian gedi ying yinqi yanzhong jingti [Incidents of Suicide during Test Elections Should Result in Vigilance Everywhere]," *Jiangsu sheng xuanju gongzuo qingkuang* [Jiangsu Provincial Election Work Report], July 30, 1953. Jiangsu Provincial Archives 3087-duanqi-21.

28. "Puxuan shiban gongzuo zhong yi fasheng zisha shijian gedi ying yinqi yanzhong jingti [Incidents of Suicide during Test Elections Should Result in Vigilance Everywhere," *Jiangsu sheng xuanju gongzuo qingkuang* [Jiangsu Provincial Election Work Report]," July 30, 1953. Jiangsu Provincial Archives 3087-duanqi-21.

29. "Gan, qun sixiang qingkuang diandi cailiao huiji [Collected Bits of Material about the Mindset of the Masses and the Cadres]," *Jiangsu sheng xuanju gongzuo qingkuang* [Jiangsu Provincial Election Work Report]," September 5, 1953. Jiangsu Provincial Archives 3087-duanqi-21.

30. "Jiangsu Danyang deng xian shencha xuanmin zige shi ba bufen zhong fu nong cuo huawei dizhu [In Danyang and Other Jiangsu Counties, Some Middle and Wealthy Peasants Were Incorrectly Categorized as Landlords during Voter Registration]," *Neibu cankao*, July 2, 1953.

31. "Jiangsu sheng xuanju weiyuanhui baogao [Report of the Jiangsu Provincial Election Committee]," December 2, 1953, Jiangsu Provincial Archives 3087-chang-002.

32. Nanjing shi renmin zhengfu gong'an ju, "Boduo xuanjuquan he bei xuanjuquan liju [Examples of People Deprived of Voting and Election Rights]," Jiangsu Provincial Archives 3087-13.

33. "Jiangsu sheng xuanju weiyuanhui baogao [Report of the Jiangsu Provincial Election Committee]," Jiangsu Provincial Archives 3087-chang-002.

34. "Wuxi shi puxuanju shiban diqu puxuan xuanchuan gongzuo zongjie [Final Work Report on Election Propaganda Work in Wuxi Test Districts]," *Jiangsu sheng xuanju gongzuo qingkuang* [Jiangsu Provincial Election Work Report]," issue 12 (September 24, 1953). Jiangsu Provincial Archives 3087-duanqi-21.

35. Puyi, *From Emperor to Citizen*, 479.

36. *Jiangsu sheng puxuan ziliao huibian* [Collected Materials from the Election in Jiangsu Province] (N.p., 1954), 271–76. Jiangsu Provincial Archives (no reference number).

37. Jiangsu sheng xuanju weiyuanhui bangongshi, *Jiangsu sheng puxuan ziliao huibian*, 320–23. Jiangsu Provincial Archives (no reference number).

38. Yuexi banshichu, *Lianjiang xian di yi qu jiceng siban gongzuo zuofa*, 1–4.

39. Guangdong sheng renmin zhengfu, *Puxuan wenyi xuanchuan cailiao*, 2.

40. "Shanghai shi xuanju weiyuanhui xuanchuanchu puxuan xuanchuan gongzuo qingkuang huibao [The Shanghai Election Committee Propaganda Office's Collected Reports on Election Propaganda Work]," December 19, 1953. Shanghai Municipal Archives B52-1-47.

41. For these examples, see Zhang Jishun, "Creating 'Masters of the Country.'"

42. "Tianjin zichan jieji wei zhengqu dangxuan huodong pinfan [The Tianjin Capitalist Class Frequently Engages in Activities to Win Election]," *Neibu cankao*, June 12, 1953.

43. "Nanjing Muxuyuan xiang Muxuyuan xuanqu xuanju dahui shibai de jiaoxun [Lessons of the Failed Election Meeting in Nangjing's Muxuyuan Village Electoral District]," *Jiangsu sheng xuanju gongzuo qingkuang* [Jiangsu Provincial Election Work Report]," September 12, 1953. Jiangsu Provincial Archives 3087-duanqi-21.

44. "Shanghai shi xuanju weiyuanhui xuanchuanchu puxuan xuanchuan gongzuo qingkuang huibao [The Shanghai Election Committee Propaganda Office's Collected Reports on Election Propaganda Work]," issue 13, January 16, 1954. Shanghai Municipal Archives B52-1-47.

45. "Jiangsu sheng jiceng xuanju gongzuo zongjie [Jiangsu Provincial Grassroots Election Final Work Report]," Jiangsu Provincial Archives 3087-yong-0003.

46. Li Youyi, "Lun wo guo de xuanju zhidu [Our Country's Election System]," *Renmin ribao*, November 29, 1957, 7.

47. "Shanghai shi xuanju weiyuanhui xuanchuanchu puxuan xuanchuan gongzuo qingkuang huibao [The Shanghai Election Committee Propaganda Office's Collected Reports on Election Propaganda Work]," January 20, 1954. Shanghai Municipal Archives B52-1-47. For more on the notion of "masters of the country," see Zhang Jishun, "Creating 'Masters of the Country.'"

48. "Jiangsu sheng jiceng xuanju gongzuo zongjie [Jiangsu Provincial Grassroots Election Final Work Report]," Jiangsu Provincial Archives record group 3087-yong-0003.

49. Jiangsu sheng xuanju weiyuanhui bangongshi, *Jiangsu sheng puxuan ziliao huibian*, qianyan. Jiangsu Provincial Archives (no reference number).

50. "Shanghai shi xuanju weiyuanhui xuanchuanchu puxuan xuanchuan gongzuo qingkuang huibao [The Shanghai Election Committee Propaganda Office's Collected Reports on Election Propaganda Work]," issue 13, January 16, 1954. Shanghai Municipal Archives B52-1-47.

51. "Puxuan qingkuang fanying di er hao [Reactions to the Election, Number Two]," Shanghai Municipal Archives B52-1-37.

52. "Wenjiang xian Hesheng xiang puxuan shidian xuanchuan lliangzhou hou duoshu qunzhong de xuanju reng mo bu guanxin [Even After Two Weeks of Propaganda Effort, the Majority in the Hesheng Township, Wenjiang County Election Test District Do Not Care about the Election]," *Neibu cankao*, March 22, 1953; "Xi'an shi you xie jiguan gongzuo renyuan dui xuanjufa you cuowu renshi [Some Employees in Xi'an Gov-

ernment Agencies Have Mistaken Understandings of the Election Law]," *Neibu cankao*, May 22, 1953; and "Hunan nongmin dui puxuan de renshi qingkuang [The Status of Hunan Peasant Knowledge of the Election]," *Neibu cankao*, May 27, 1953.

53. "Beijing Zhongnanhai xuanqu jinxing jiceng xuanju, Mao Zedong tongzhi canjia toupiao [Grassroots Elections Held in Beijing's Zhongnanhai Precinct, Comrade Mao Zedong Votes]," *Renmin ribao*, December 11, 1953, 1. Mao's brief remarks at the opening session of the first National People's Congress in September 1954 also say nothing about the election that produced the body. Mao Zedong, "Wei jianshe yige weida de shehui zhuyi guojia er fendou [Strive to Build a Great Socialist Nation]," in *Mao Zedong xuanji*, 5:132–33.

54. "Canjia xuanju de renshu gaoyu shangji xuanju shi de bili [Voter Participation Greater in This Election Than in the Previous Election]," *Renmin ribao*, December 28, 1956, 4.

55. "Quanguo gedi kaishi xuanju [Voting Begins across the Nation]," *Renmin ribao*, March 18, 1958, 4; "Quanguo jiceng xuanju jiben wancheng [The Nation's Local Elections Are Basically Finished]," *Renmin ribao*, May 19, 1958, 1; "Rang da yuejin zhong xianjin renwu lai yindao da yuejin [Let the Advanced Individuals of the Great Leap Forward Lead the Great Leap Forward]," *Renmin ribao*, May 19, 1958, 1; and "Renzhen relie xingshi minzhu quanli [Conscientiously and Enthusiastically Exercise Democratic Rights]," *Renmin ribao*, May 19, 1958, 1.

56. "Beijing Shanghai jiceng xuanju zhong guangda xuanmin relie toupiao [The Broad Masses of Voters in Beijing and Shanghai's Grassroots Elections Enthusiastically Cast Ballots]," *Renmin ribao*, December 5, 1960, 1.

57. I was not able to examine post-1957 archival material at the Jiangsu Provincial Archives, so I cannot draw case studies from that province.

58. "Xuan hao dang jia ren, geng hao de jianshe shehuizhuyi [Select Good Leaders to Better Build Socialism]," *Renmin ribao*, April 9, 1963, 1, and "Renzhen tiaoxuan jianshe shehuizhuyi de hao dang jia ren [Diligently Select Good Leaders to Build Socialism]," *Renmin ribao*, April 13, 1963, 2.

59. For example, "Renzhen zuo hao xuanju gongzuo [Diligently Carry Out Election Work]," *Renmin ribao*, April 13, 1963, 1, and "Tiaoxuan hao dang jia ren [Select Good Leaders]," *Renmin ribao*, April 15, 1963, 2.

60. Ji Xianlin, *The Cowshed*, 27. No description of this election appears in the *People's Daily*, however.

61. This observation is based on a keyword search in the "*Renmin ribao* tuwen shuku [*People's Daily* Text and Picture Database]," http://data.people.com.cn/rmrb.

62. "Zhongguo gongchandang zhongyang weiyuanhui guanyu wuchan jieji wenhua da geming de jueding [Central Committee Decision Concerning the Great Proletarian Cultural Revolution]," *Hongqi* 1968.10 (August 10, 1966), 1–9.

63. "Xuexi shi liu tiao, shuxi shi liu tiao, yunyong shi liu tiao [Study the Sixteen Points, Understand the Sixteen Points, Utilize the Sixteen Points]," *Renmin ribao*, August 13, 1966, 1.

64. For an example from the state-sanctioned media, see "Bali gongshe shixing de quanmian xuanju zhi [The Comprehensive Election System Practiced in the Paris

Commune]," *Renmin ribao*, August 15, 1966, 2, and the much longer (but similar) Liu Huiming, "Bali gongshe de quanmian xuanju zhi [The Paris Commune's Comprehensive Election System]," *Hongqi* 1966.11 (August 21, 1966), 36–37. Even oppositional Red Guard figures, such as the Beijing University students who suggested that "comprehensive elections" be used to allow the population to select party leadership, never defined the term. Qiao Jianwu and Du Wenge, "Three Big Rebellions." The Chinese-language original of Qiao and Du's essay can be found online at https://ccradb.appspot.com/post/4074 (accessed March 11, 2018).

65. Chang Ying, "Xin Beida zai gaoge mengjin [The New Beijing University Advances Triumphantly]," *Hongqi* 1966.13 (October 1, 1966), 18–19.

66. Macciocchi, *Daily Life in Revolutionary China*, 153–56.

67. Thornton, "The Cultural Revolution as a Crisis of Representation."

68. "He Kabo, Baluku tongzhi de tanhua [Conversation with Comrades Hysni Kapo and Beqir Balluku]," in *Mao Zedong sixiang wansui*, 5:288–89. For the Albanian version of this conversation, see "Memorandum of Conversation between Chairman Mao Zedong and Comrades Hysni Kapo and Beqir Balluku," February 3, 1967, History and Public Policy Program Digital Archive, AQSH, F. 14/AP, M- PKK, V. 1967, Dos. 6, Fl. 12-32. Obtained and translated by Elidor Mëhilli. http://digitalarchive.wilsoncenter.org/document/117302. The Chinese version, which is translated here, differs in a number of respects from the Albanian.

69. Potter, *From Leninist Discipline to Socialist Legalism*.

70. "Zhonghua renmin gongheguo quanguo renmindaibiao dahui he difang geji renmin daibiao dahui xuanju fa [Election Law for the National and Local People's Congresses]," *Renmin ribao*, July 5, 1979, 1.

71. For a discussion of competitive races in 1980, see Nathan, *Chinese Democracy*, 193–223. Yao Lifa's story is told in Zhu Ling, *Wo fandui*. Other recent examples of independent candidates for local People's Congresses can be found in Javier C. Hernandez, "'We Have a Fake Election': China Disrupts Local Campaigns," *New York Times*, November 16, 2016, A6.

72. An Chen, *Restructuring Political Power in China*, 63–95.

73. Methods of election control are discussed in Zhongyuan Wang, "Playing by the Rules."

74. Truex, *Making Autocracy Work*; Manion, "Authoritarian Parochialism."

75. Zhang Mingshu, *Zhongguoren xiangyao shenmeyang minzhu*, 225, 231, and 235.

76. These additional voting rights can be found, respectively, in articles 17 and 111 of the 1982 Constitution of the People's Republic of China. The 1975 constitution, written during the final phase of the Cultural Revolution, is the exception: it did not specify that local People's Congresses would be elected.

77. One of the few descriptions of such elections can be found in An Chen, *Restructuring Political Power in China*, 31–35.

78. Read, *Roots of the State*, 73–78.

79. For a history of the village election law and the public discourse that surrounded it, see Kelliher, "Chinese Debate over Village Self-Government" and O'Brien and Li, "Accommodating 'Democracy' in a One-Party State."

80. Peng Zhen zhuan bianxie zu, *Peng Zhen zhuan*, 4:1522.

81. Zhan Chengfu et al., *Quanguo cunmin weiyuanhui xuanju*, 18–19 and 22–23.
82. Zhonghua renmin gongheguo minzheng bu [Ministry of Civil Affairs of the People's Republic of China], "2016 nian shehui fuwu fazhan tongji gongbao [2016 Statistical Report on the Development of Social Services]," available at http://www.mca.gov.cn/article/sj/tjgb/201708/20170800005382.shtml (accessed March 12, 2018).
83. O'Brien and Han, "Path to Democracy?," 363–67.
84. O'Brien and Han, "Path to Democracy?," 367–76. There are exceptions to this, such as Kerry Brown's cautiously hopeful assessment of village elections during the middle of the Hu Jintao era. Brown, *Ballot Box China*.
85. Tsai, *Accountability without Democracy*.
86. Zhihu.com has a number of examples of this, including "Nongcun xuanju zhende hen hei'an ma? [Are Village Elections Really So Sleazy?]," https://www.zhihu.com/question/41981251, and "Canjia huo guancha guo nongcun xuanju de pengyou, ni suo liaojie de cun xuanju she shenme qingkuang [Friends Who Have Participated In or Observed Village Elections: What Are They Like?]," https://www.zhihu.com/question/20531282.
87. For information on turnout in People's Congress elections based on employment status, see Wang and Sun, "Social Class and Voter Turnout in China."

Conclusion

1. "Xi Jinping zai Buluri Ouzhou xueyuan de yanjiang [Xi Jinping's Speech at the College of Europe in Bruges]," *Renmin ribao*, April 2, 2014, 2. Translation from "Xi Jinping Says Multi-Party System Didn't Work for China," Reuters, April 2, 2014, http://in.reuters.com/article/2014/04/02/china-politics-xi-jinping-idINDEEA3I01U20140402 (accessed January 13, 2017).
2. Xi Jinping, *Governance of China*, 117–18.
3. Yu, *Democracy Is a Good Thing*, 3–5; Yu Keping, "Minzhu shi ge hao dongxi."
4. Compare this, for instance, to the history of the expansion of suffrage in the United States, which Alex Keyssar ascribes to three "powerful forces": the efforts of mass social movements, the influence of changing concepts of democracy, and the impact of war. Keyssar, *Right to Vote*, 296.
5. A few examples of this genre include Zhang Weiwei, *The China Wave*, 111–38, and Bell, *The China Model*.
6. The literature on Chinese democratization is vast, but a handy summary of obstacles to democratization in twentieth-century China can be found in Nathan, "Chinese Democracy: The Lessons of Failure."
7. Feng Xiaocai, "Counterfeiting Legitimacy."
8. Harrison, *The Making of the Republican Citizen*, 240.
9. Strand, *An Unfinished Republic*, 1–12 and 289–90.
10. For a handful of examples, see Chang Peng-yuan, *Zhongguo minzhu zhengzhi de kunjing*, 90, 179, 182, 221. In English, see Chang Peng-yuan, "Provincial Assemblies."
11. Chang Peng-yuan, *Zhongguo minzhu zhengzhi de kunjing*, 207–21.
12. Chang Peng-yuan, "Guomindang kongzhi xia de guohui xuanju," 187. This article is reprinted as a chapter in *Zhongguo minzhu zhengzhi de kunjing*, although the final paragraph quoted here is omitted from that publication.

13. *Please Vote for Me*, directed by Weijun Chen, produced by Steps International and ITVS International, 2007.

14. Davies, *Worrying about China*.

15. Shi, *Cultural Logic of Politics*, 192.

16. For a detail assessment of mainland policy toward elections as of 2016, see Cao, "For over 36 Years, Grassroots Elections in China Have Made No Progress."

17. Chao and Myers, *The First Chinese Democracy*; Chao and Myers, "How Elections Promoted Democracy"; Rigger, *Politics in Taiwan*.

18. Jacobs, *Democratizing Taiwan*, 5–16. See also Christian Schafferer, who lists a history of elections as one of seven "forces behind the transition" to democracy. Schafferer, *Power of the Ballot Box*, 11–26.

Bibliography

Archival Collections

Jiangsu Provincial Archives (Nanjing, Jiangsu).

KMT Records, Hoover Archives (Stanford, CA).

Second Historical Archives of China (Nanjing, Jiangsu).
Shanghai Municipal Archives (Shanghai).

Periodicals

Changsha ribao 長沙日報 (Changsha, Hunan).
Changshu xunbao 常熟旬報 (Changshu, Jiangsu).
China Magazine (Nanjing).

Dagongbao 大公報 (Changsha, Hunan).
Dagongbao 大公報 (Tianjin).
Dongfang zazhi 東方雜誌 (Shanghai).

Guofengbao 國風報 (Shanghai).
Guomin xinbao 國民新報 (Hankou, Hubei).
Guomin zhengfu gongbao 國民政府公報 (Nanjing).

Hongqi 紅旗 (Beijing).
Huazi ribao 華字日報 (Hong Kong).
Hunan gongbao 湖南公報 (Changsha, Hunan).
Hunan tongsu ribao 湖南通俗日報 (Changsha, Hunan).

Jiangsu sheng zhengfu gongbao 江蘇省政府公報 (Zhenjiang, Jiangsu).

Lanyan ribao 蘭言日報 (Wujin, Jiangsu).
Linshi gongbao 臨時公報 (Beijing).
Linshi zhengfu gongbao 臨時政府公報 (Nanjing).

Minbao 民報 (Taipei).

Neibu cankao 內部參考 (Beijing).
Nuli zhoubao 努力週報 (Beijing).

Renmin ribao 人民日報 (Beijing).
Rugao xian gongshu tongsu bao 如皋縣公署通俗報 (Rugao, Jiangsu).

Shangbao 商報 (Wujin, Jiangsu).
Shenbao 申報 (Shanghai).
Shibao 時報 (Shanghai).
Shishi xinbao 時事新報 (Shanghai).
Shuntianbao 順天報 (Beijing).

Taipingyang 太平洋 (Shanghai).
Taiwan sheng xingzhengzhang guangongshu gongbao 臺灣省行政長官公署公報 (Taipei).
Taiwan sheng zhengfu gongbao 台灣省政府公報 (Taipei/Nantou).

Wujin 武進 (Wujin, Jiangsu).
Wuyu 吳語 (Suzhou, Jiangsu).

Xiaoshuo xinbao 小說新報 (Shanghai).
Xibao 錫報 (Wuxi, Jiangsu).
Xin Wuxi 新無錫 (Wuxi, Jiangsu).

Yuyangbao 虞陽報 (Changshu, Jiangsu).

Zhengfu gongbao 政府公報 (Beijing).

Books and Articles

Achen, Christopher, and Larry Bartels. *Democracy for Realists: Why Elections Do Not Produce Responsive Government.* Princeton, NJ: Princeton University Press, 2016.
Anhui ziyiju [Anhui Provincial Assembly] 安徽諮議局. *Xuanjuren zige shuomingshu* 選舉人資格說明書 [Explanation of Voter Qualifications]. N.p., 1910.

Bailey, Paul. *Strengthen the Country and Enrich the People: The Reform Writings of Ma Jianzhong.* Richmond, Surrey: Curzon Press, 1998.
Bao Tianxiao 包天笑. *Chuanyinglou huiyilu* 釧影樓回憶錄 [Reminiscences]. Hong Kong: Dahua chubanshe, 1971.

Beiyang gongdu leizuan 北洋公牘類纂 [Northern China Public Documents, Organized by Classification]. Gan Houci 甘厚慈, ed. 1907. Reprint, Taipei: Wenhai chubanshe, 1966.

Bell, Daniel. *The China Model: Political Meritocracy and the Limits of Democracy*. Princeton, NJ: Princeton University Press, 2015.

Bergère, Marie-Claire. *The Golden Age of the Chinese Bourgeoisie, 1911–1937*. Janet Lloyd, trans. Cambridge: Cambridge University Press, 1989.

Brennan, Jason. *Against Democracy*. Princeton, NJ: Princeton University Press, 2016.

Brown, Kerry. *Ballot Box China: Grassroots Democracy in the Final Major One Party State*. London: Zed Books, 2011.

Cao Rulin 曹汝霖. *Cao Rulin yi sheng zhi huiyi* 曹汝霖一生之回憶 [Cao Rulin's Memoirs]. Taipei: Zhuanji wenxue chubanshe, 1980.

Cao Shuji 曹樹基. *Zhongguo renkou shi, di 5 juan: Qing shiqi* 中国人口史，第五卷：清时期 [China's Population History, Volume 5: The Qing Period]. Shanghai: Fudan daxue chubanshe, 2001.

Cao, Yaxue. "For over 36 Years, Grassroots Elections in China Have Made No Progress—An Interview with Hu Ping." *China Change*, November 1, 2016. https://chinachange.org/2016/11/01/for-over-36-years-grassroots-elections-in-china-have-made-no-progress/.

Cao Yunyuan 曹允源 et al. *Minguo Wuxian zhi* 民國吳縣志 [Wu County Gazetteer]. 1933. Reprint, Nanjing: Jiangsu guji chubanshe, 1991.

Caplan, Bryan. *The Myth of the Rational Voter: Why Democracies Choose Bad Policies*. Princeton, NJ: Princeton University Press, 2007.

Chang, Chung-li. *The Chinese Gentry: Studies on Their Role in Nineteenth-Century Chinese Society*. Seattle: University of Washington Press, 1955.

Chang, David Cheng. "Democracy Is in Its Details: The 1909 Provincial Assembly Elections and the Print Media." In Sherman Cochran and Paul Pickowicz, eds., *China on the Margins*. Ithaca, NY: Cornell University Press, 2010, 195–220.

Chang Peng-yuan 張朋園. "Guomindang kongzhi xia de guohui xuanju (1947–1948) 國民黨控制下的國會選舉 (1947–1948) [Legislative Elections under Nationalist Control (1947–1948)]." *Zhongyang yanjiuyuan jindaishi yanjiusuo jikan* 中央研究院近代史研究所集刊 [Bulletin of the Institute of Modern History, Academia Sinica] 35 (June 2001), 145–95.

Chang Peng-yuan 張朋園. "Jindai difang zhengzhi canyu de mengya—Hunan sheng juli 近代地方政治參與的萌芽——湖南省舉例 [The Early Stage of China's Political Participation—A Case Study of Hunan]." *Lishi xuebao* 歷史學報 [Bulletin of Historical Research] 4 (1976), 381–405.

Chang Peng-yuan 張朋園. *Liang Qichao yu Minguo zhengzhi* 梁啓超與民國政治 [Liang Qichao and Republican Politics]. Taipei: Zhongyang yanjiuyuan jindaishi yanjiusuo, 2006.

Chang Peng-yuan 張朋園. *Zhongguo minzhu zhengzhi de kunjing (1909–1949): wan Qing yilai lijie yihui xuanju shulun* 中國民主政治的困境 (1909–1949)：晚清以來歷屆議會選舉述論 [The Dilemma of Chinese Democracy, 1909–1949: Legislatures and Elections since the Late Qing]. Taipei: Lianjing chuban, 2007.

Chang Peng-yuan. "Provincial Assemblies: The Emergence of Political Participation, 1909–1914." *Zhongyang yanjiuyuan jindaishi yanjiusuo jikan* 中央研究院近代史研究所集刊 [Bulletin of the Institute of Modern History, Academia Sinica] 12 (June 1983), 273–99.

Chang Yu-fa 張玉法. *Minguo chunian de zhengdang* 民國初年的政黨 [Political Parties in the Early Republic of China]. Taipei: Zhongyang yanjiuyuan jindaishi yanjiusuo, 1985.

Chang Yu-fa 張玉法. *Qing ji de lixian tuanti* 清季的立憲團體 [Constitutionalists of the Ch'ing Period]. Taipei: Zhongyang yanjiuyuan jindaishi yanjiusuo, 1985.

Changzhou xian xuanjuren mingce 長洲縣選舉人名冊 [Changzhou County Voter Rolls]. N.p., ca. 1909.

Chao, Linda, and Ramon H. Myers. *The First Chinese Democracy: Political Life in the Republic of China on Taiwan*. Baltimore: Johns Hopkins University Press, 1998.

Chao, Linda, and Ramon H. Myers. "How Elections Promoted Democracy in Taiwan under Martial Law." *China Quarterly* 162 (June 2000), 387–409.

Chen, An. *Restructuring Political Power in China: Alliances and Opposition, 1978–1998*. Boulder, CO: Lynne Rienner, 1999.

Chen Dingyan 陳定炎. *Chen Jingcun (Jiongming) xiansheng nianpu* 陳競存(炯明)先生年譜 [Chronological Biography of Chen Jiongming]. Taipei: Li Ao chubanshe, 1995.

Chen Jiongming 陈炯明. *Chen Jiongming ji* 陈炯明集 [Collected Writings of Chen Jiongming]. Duan Yuanzhang 段雲章 and Ni Junming 倪俊明, eds. Guangzhou: Zhongshan daxue chubanshe, 1998.

Chen, Leslie H. Dingyan. *Chen Jiongming and the Federalist Movement: Regional Leadership and Nation Building in Early Republican China*. Ann Arbor: Center for Chinese Studies, the University of Michigan, 1999.

Chen Qitai 陈其泰 and Liu Lanxiao 刘兰肖. *Wei Yuan pingzhuan* 魏源评传 [Critical Biography of Wei Yuan]. Nanjing: Nanjing daxue chubanshe, 2004.

Chen Yung-Fa. "Rural Elections in Wartime Central China: Democratization of the Subbureaucracy." *Modern China* 6.3 (1980), 267–310.

Chesneaux, Jean. "The Federalist Movement in China, 1920–3." In Jack Gray, ed., *Modern China's Search for a Political Form*. Oxford: Oxford University Press, 1969, 96–137.

Ch'ien, Tuan-sheng. *The Government and Politics of China*. Cambridge, MA: Harvard University Press, 1950.

Chouban yiwu shimo (Daoguang chao) 籌辦夷務始末(道光朝) [Complete Account of the Management of Barbarian Affairs (Daoguang Era)]. Reprint, Taipei: Guofeng chubanshe, 1963.

Chuxuanjuren mingce 初選舉人名冊 [Primary Election Voter Rolls]. N.p., ca. 1909.

Commercial Press English and Chinese Pronouncing Dictionary, 1st ed. Shanghai: Commercial Press, 1902.

Commercial Press English and Chinese Pronouncing Dictionary, 2nd ed. Shanghai: Commercial Press, 1908.

Da Qing lichao shilu 大清歷朝實錄 [Veritable Records of the Qing Dynasty]. Reprint, Beijing: Zhonghua shuju, 1985–1987.

Dai Hongci 戴鴻慈. *Chu shi jiu guo riji* 出使九國日記 [Diary of a Diplomatic Mission to Nine Countries]. 1907. In Zhong Shuhe 钟叔河, comp., *Zou xiang shijie congshu* 走向世界丛书 [From East to West: Chinese Travelers before 1911]. Reprint, Changsha: Yuelu shushe, 2008.

Dai Hongci 戴鴻慈 and Duan-fang 端方. *Ou Mei zhengzhi yaoyi* 歐美政治要義 [Essentials of European and American Politics]. N.p., 1907.

Davies, Gloria. *Worrying about China: The Language of Chinese Critical Inquiry*. Cambridge, MA: Harvard University Press, 2007.

Duan-fang 端方. *Duan Zhongmin gong zou gao* 端忠敏公奏稿 [Duan-fang's Draft Memorials]. N.p., ca. 1918. Reprint, Taipei: Wenhai chubanshe, 1967.

Duan-fang 端方. *Lieguo zhengyao* 列國政要 [Survey of the Policies of the Various States]. N.p., 1907.

Eastman, Lloyd. "Nationalist China during the Nanking Decade, 1927–1937." In John King Fairbank and Denis Twitchett, eds., *The Cambridge History of China, Volume 13: Republican China 1912–1949, Part 2*. Cambridge: Cambridge University Press, 1986, 116–67.

Edwards, Louise P. *Gender, Politics, and Democracy: Women's Suffrage in China*. Stanford, CA: Stanford University Press, 2008.

Elman, Benjamin A. *A Cultural History of Civil Examinations in Late Imperial China*. Berkeley: University of California Press, 2000.

Elman, Benjamin. "Political, Social, and Cultural Reproduction via Civil Service Examinations in Late Imperial China." *Journal of Asian Studies* 50.1 (1991), 7–28.

Elvin, Mark. "The Gentry Democracy in Chinese Shanghai, 1905–1914." In Jack Gray, ed., *Modern China's Search for a Political Form*. Oxford: Oxford University Press, 1969, 41–65.

Esherick, Joseph W. "Founding a Republic, Electing a President: How Sun Yat-sen Became *Guofu*." In Eto Shinkichi and Harold Z. Schiffrin, eds., *China's Republican Revolution*. Tokyo: University of Tokyo Press, 1994, 129–52.

Fairlie, John A. "Constitutional Developments in China." *American Political Science Review* 25.4 (1931), 1016–22.

Feng Guifen 馮桂芬. *Jiaobinlu kangyi* 校邠廬抗議 [Essays of Protest]. Nanchang: N.p., 1884.

Feng Xiaocai. "Counterfeiting Legitimacy: Reflections on the Usurpation of Popular Politics and the 'Political Culture' of Urban China, 1912–49." Joshua Hill, trans. *Frontiers of History in China* 8.2 (June 2013), 202–22.

Fincher, John H. *Chinese Democracy, the Self-Government Movement in Local, Provincial, and National Politics, 1905–1914*. New York: St. Martin's Press, 1981.

Fu Huaifeng 傅懷鋒. "Shi xi Qingmo minzhong de zhengzhi canyu–jiyu Qingmo Jiang Zhe ziyiju yiyuan xuanju de ge'an yanjiu 試析清末民眾的政治參與——基於清末江浙諮議局議員選舉的個案研究 [A Preliminary Analysis of Late Qing Popular Political Participation—A Case Study of the Jiangsu and Zhejiang Provincial Assembly Elections]." *Ershiyi shiji* 二十一世紀 [Twenty-First Century] 81.2 (2004), 28–38.

Fu Jinzhu 付金柱. "Chen Jiongming yu jindai Guangdong nüquan yundong 陈炯明与近代广东女权运动 [Chen Jiongming and the Modern Feminist Movement of Guangdong]." *Zhonghua nüzi xueyuan xuebao* 中华女子学院学报 [Journal of China Women's University] 29.1 (2009), 101–5.

Fung, Edmund S. K. *In Search of Chinese Democracy: Civil Opposition in Nationalist China, 1929–1949*. Cambridge: Cambridge University Press, 2000.

Fung, Edmund S. K. *The Intellectual Foundations of Chinese Modernity: Cultural and Political Thought in the Republican Era*. Cambridge: Cambridge University Press, 2010.

Gan Chunsong 干春松. "Kejuzhi de shuailuo he zhiduhua Rujia de jietie 科举制的衰落和制度化儒家的解体 [The Decline of Imperial China's Examination System and the Disintegration of Institutionalized Confucianism]." *Zhongguo shehui kexue* 中国社会科学 [Social Sciences in China] 2002.2, 107–17.

Giles, Herbert Allen. *A Chinese-English Dictionary*, 1st ed. London: B. Quaritch; Shanghai: Kelly and Walsh, 1892.

Giles, Herbert Allen. *A Chinese-English Dictionary*, 2nd ed. 1912. Reprint, Taipei: Ch'eng Wen, 1972.

Grieder, Jerome. *Hu Shih and the Chinese Renaissance: Liberalism in the Chinese Revolution, 1917–1937*. Cambridge, MA: Harvard University Press, 1970.

Guan Xiaohong 關曉紅. "Shutu nengfou tonggui—liting keju hou de kaoshi yu xuancai 殊途能否同歸—立停科舉後的考試與選材 [Can All Roads Lead to Rome? Examinations and Candidate Selection after the End of the Imperial Civil Service Examination System]." *Zhongyang yanjiuyuan jindaishi yanjiusuo jikan* 中央研究院近代史研究所集刊 [Bulletin of the Institute of Modern History, Academia Sinica] 59 (2008), 1–28.

Guangdong sheng renmin zhengfu 廣東省人民政府 [People's Government of Guangdong Province]. *Puxuan wenyi xuanchuan cailiao* 普選文藝宣傳材料 [Literary and Artistic Propaganda Materials for the Mass Suffrage Election]. N.p., 1953.

Guo Songtao 郭嵩燾. *Lundun yu Bali riji* 伦敦与巴黎日记 [A Diary of London and Paris]. In Zhong Shuhe 钟叔河, comp., *Zou xiang shijie congshu* 走向世界丛书 [From East to West: Chinese Travelers before 1911]. Reprint, Changsha: Yuelu shushe, 2008.

[Gutzlaff, Karl.] *Gujin wanguo gangjian lu* 古今萬國綱鑑錄 [An Outline of Countries of the World, Ancient and Modern]. Singapore: Jianxia shuyuan, 1838.

Hangzhou fu, Jiaxing fu xuanjuren mingce 杭州府嘉興府選舉人名冊 [Hangzhou Prefecture and Jiaxing Prefecture Voter Rolls], ca. 1909.

Harrison, Henrietta. "Experiencing the Modern State in Rural Shanxi: Money and Democracy in the 1916 Elections for National Assembly." Conference paper presented at "Zhongguo jindai guojia de suzao 中國近代國家的塑造 [Constructing the Modern Chinese Nation-State]." Taipei, Taiwan, December 13–14, 2002.

Harrison, Henrietta. *The Making of the Republican Citizen: Political Ceremonies and Symbols in China, 1911–1929*. Oxford: Oxford University Press, 2000.

Hauf, Kandice. "The Community Covenant in Sixteenth Century Ji'an Prefecture, Jiangxi." *Late Imperial China* 17.2 (1996), 1–50.

Hayashida Kazuhiro. "Development of Election Law in Japan." *Hōsei kenkyū* 法政研究 [Studies in Law and Politics] 34.1 (1967), 51–104.

Hernandez, Javier C. "'We Have a Fake Election': China Disrupts Local Campaigns." *New York Times*, November 16, 2016, A6.
Hinton, William. *Fanshen: A Documentary of Revolution in a Chinese Village.* New York: Vintage Books, 1966.
Holt, Lucius Hudson. *An Introduction to the Study of Government.* New York: Macmillan, 1915.
Hōrei zensho 法令全書 [Complete Laws and Orders]. [Japan]: Naikaku kanpōkyoku, 1878.
Hsiao, Kung-chuan. *Rural China: Imperial Control in the Nineteenth Century.* Seattle: University of Washington Press, 1967.
Hu Fu. "The Electoral Mechanism and Political Change in Taiwan." In Steve Tsang, ed., *In the Shadow of China: Political Developments in Taiwan since 1949.* London: Hurst, 1993, 134–68.
Hu Shi 胡适. *Hu Shi wen ji* 胡适文集 [Collected Writings of Hu Shi]. Ouyang Zhesheng 欧阳哲生, ed. Beijing: Beijing daxue chubanshe, 1998.
Hu Shi. "Manufacturing the Will of the People." *Journal of Race Development* 7.3 (1917), 319–28.
Hu Shi 胡適 and Cai Dengshan 蔡登山. "*Nie hai hua*" *yu Sai Jinhua*《孽海花》與賽金花 ["Nie hai hua" and Sai Jinhua]. Taipei: Xiuwei, 2013.
Huang Liuhong 黃六鴻. *Juguan fuhui quanshu* 居官福惠全書 [A Complete Book of Prosperity and Benevolence for Appointed Officials]. 1699. In *Guanzhenshu jicheng* 官箴書集成 [Collection of Magistrate's Manuals]. Reprint, Hefei: Huangshan shushe, 1997.
Huang Zunxian 黃遵憲. *Huang Zunxian quanji* 黃遵憲全集 [Complete Works of Huang Zunxian]. Chen Zheng 陈铮, ed. Beijing: Zhonghua shuju, 2005.
Huang Zunxian 黃遵憲. *Renjinglu shi cao* 人境廬詩草 [Draft Poetry from the Hut within the Human Realm]. 1911. Reprint, n.p., 1930.
Huang Zunxian 黃遵憲. *Renjinglu shi cao jianzhu* 人境廬詩草箋注 [Annotated Edition of Draft Poetry from the Hut within the Human Realm]. Qian Zhonglian 錢仲聯, ed. Shanghai: Shanghai guji chubanshe, 1981.
Huangfu, Zhengzheng. "Internalizing the West: Qing Envoys and Ministers in Europe, 1866–1893." PhD diss., University of California, San Diego, 2012.
Hunan sheng jiaoyu si 湖南省教育司 [Hunan Provincial Bureau of Education]. *Tongsu jiangyan ziliao* 通俗講演資料 [Materials for Public Lecturing]. N.p., 1912.
Hunan zhiding xianfa choubei chu 湖南製定憲法籌備處 [Hunan Provincial Constitution Drafting Office]. *Hunan zhixian baogaoshu* 湖南製憲報告書 [Report on the Hunan Constitution]. N.p., 1922.

Jacobs, J. Bruce. *Democratizing Taiwan.* Leiden: Brill, 2012.
Janku, Andrea. "The Uses of Genres in the Chinese Press from the Late Qing to the Early Republican Period." In Cynthia Brokaw and Christopher A. Reed, eds., *From Woodblocks to the Internet: Chinese Publishing and Print Culture in Transition, circa 1800 to 2008.* Leiden: Brill, 2010, 111–57.
Ji Xianlin. *The Cowshed: Memories of the Chinese Cultural Revolution.* Chenxin Jiang, trans. New York: New York Review of Books, 2016.

Jiangsu linshi shengyihui di yi jie huiqi baogao di san ce 江蘇臨時省議會第一屆會期報告第三冊 [Report on the First Meeting of the Jiangsu Provisional Provincial Legislature, Volume 3]. N.p., ca. 1911.

Jiangsu linshi shengyihui yijue'an 江蘇臨時省議會議決案 [Proceedings of the Jiangsu Provisional Provincial Legislature]. N.p., ca. 1912.

Jiangsu linshi yihui di er jie huiqi baogao di yi ce 江蘇臨時議會第二屆會期報告第一冊 [Report on the Second Meeting of the Jiangsu Provisional Provincial Legislature, Volume 1]. N.p., ca. 1912.

Jiangsu neiwu si 江蘇內務司 [Jiangsu Bureau of Internal Affairs]. *Jiangsu sheng neiwu xingzheng baogaoshu, Zhonghua Mingguo er nian* 江蘇省內務行政報告書, 中華民國二年 [Jiangsu Province Report on Internal Affairs Administration, 1913]. N.p., 1914.

Jiangsu sheng gongmin jianshi xuanju tuan 江蘇省公民監視選舉團 [Jiangsu Citizens' Election Monitoring Team]. *Xuanju fagui* 選舉法規 [Election Laws and Regulations]. Shanghai: Zhonghua shuju, 1921.

Jiangsu sheng zhi: yihui renmin daibiao dahui zhi 江苏省志: 议会人民代表大会志 [Jiangsu Provincial Gazetteer: Legislatures and People's Congresses]. Jiangsu sheng difangzhi bianzuan weiyuanhui 江苏省地方志编纂委员会 [Jiangsu Provincial Gazetteer Compilation Committee], comp. Nanjing: Jiangsu renmin chubanshe, 1999.

Jiangsu Su shu ziyiju choubanchu baogaoshu 江蘇蘇屬諮議局籌辦處報告書 [Southern Jiangsu Provincial Assembly Preparatory Office Report]. Suzhou: ca. 1909.

Jiangxi ziyiju choubanchu 江西諮議局籌辦處 [Jiangxi Provincial Assembly Preparatory Office]. *Xuanju diaocha biyao si zhong* 選舉調查必要四種 [Four Chapters of Necessary Knowledge for Election Registrars]. N.p., 1909.

Jichishō senkyobu 自治省選挙部 [Elections Division of the Ministry of Home Affairs]. *Senkyohō hyakunenshi* 選挙法百年史 [A Centennial History of Election Law]. Tokyo: Daiichi hōki, 1990.

Judge, Joan. *Print and Politics: "Shibao" and the Culture of Reform in Late Qing China*. Stanford, CA: Stanford University Press, 1996.

Kelliher, Daniel. "The Chinese Debate over Village Self-Government." *China Journal* 37 (January 1997), 63–86.

Kerr, George H. *Formosa Betrayed*, 2nd ed. Upland, CA: Taiwan Publishing, 1992.

Keyssar, Alexander. *The Right to Vote: The Contested History of Democracy in the United States*, rev. ed. New York: Basic Books, 2009.

Kikuchi Gakuji 菊池學而. *Yihui zhengdang lun* 議會政黨論 [On Deliberative Assemblies and Political Parties]. Shanghai: Shangwu yinshuguan, 1903.

Kishlansky, Mark A. *Parliamentary Selection: Social and Political Choice in Early Modern England*. Cambridge: Cambridge University Press, 1986.

Kuhn, Philip A. *Origins of the Modern Chinese State*. Stanford, CA: Stanford University Press, 2002.

Kwang Ki-Chaou. *An English and Chinese Dictionary*. Shanghai: Wah Cheung, 1887.

Lam, Tong. *A Passion for Facts: Social Surveys and the Construction of the Chinese Nation State, 1900–1949*. Berkeley: University of California Press, 2011.

Ledong xian xuanju weiyuanhui 樂東縣選舉委員會 [Ledong County Election Committee]. *You guan shaoshu minzu xuanju cankao wenjian, di yi ji* 有關少數民族選舉參考文件, 第一集 [Documents on Elections in Minority Areas, Volume I]. N.p., 1953.

Lee, Haiyan. "'A Dime Store of Words': *Liberty* Magazine and the Cultural Logic of the Popular Press." *Twentieth-Century China* 33.1 (2007), 53–80.

Lerman, Arthur J. *Taiwan's Politics: The Provincial Assemblyman's World*. Washington, DC: University Press of America, 1978.

Li Jiannong 李劍農. *Zuijin sanshi nian Zhongguo zhengzhi shi* 最近三十年中國政治史 [The Political History of the Last Thirty Years]. Shanghai: Taipingyang shudian, 1930.

Liang Chi-Chao [Liang Qichao]. *History of Chinese Political Thought during the Early Tsin Period*. L.T. Chen, trans. New York: Harcourt, Brace, 1930.

Liang Qichao 梁启超. *Liang Qichao quanji* 梁启超全集 [Complete Works of Liang Qichao]. Yang Gang 杨钢 and Wang Xiangyi 王相宜, eds. Beijing: Beijing chubanshe, 1999.

Liang Tingnan 梁廷枏. *Haiguo si shuo* 海國四說 [Four Accounts of the Maritime Countries]. 1846. Reprint, Beijing: Zhonghua shuju, 1993.

Lin Qingyuan 林庆元. *Lin Zexu pingzhuan* 林则徐评传 [A Critical Biography of Lin Zexu]. Nanjing: Nanjing daxue chubanshe, 2000.

Lin Yongyu 林永俣. "Lun Lin Zexu zuzhi de yiyi gongzuo 论林则徐组织的移译工作 [Lin Zexu's Organization of Translation Work]." In *Lin Zexu yu yapian zhanzheng yanjiu lunwen ji* 林则徐与鸦片战争研究论文集 [Collected Essays on Lin Zexu and the Opium War]. Fuzhou: Fujian renmin chubanshe, 1985, 118–37.

Lin Zexu 林則徐. *Lin Wenzhonggong zhengshu* 林文忠公政書 [Political Writings of Lin Zexu]. 1885. Reprint, Taipei: Wenhai chubanshe, 1966.

Lin Zexu 林则徐. *Lin Zexu quanji* 林则徐全集 [Collected Writings of Lin Zexu]. Fuzhou: Haixia wenyi chubanshe, 2002.

Lin Zexu 林則徐. *Si zhou zhi* 四洲志 [Gazetteer of the Four Continents]. 1840. In Wang Xiqi 王錫祺, comp., *Xiaofanghuzhai yudi congchao zaibubian* 小方壺齋輿地叢鈔再補編 [Collections of Historical Writings from the Xiaofanghu Studio, Second Addendum]. Reprint, Shanghai: Zhuyitang, 1897.

Link, E. Perry, Jr. *Mandarin Ducks and Butterflies: Popular Fiction in Early Twentieth-Century Chinese Cities*. Berkeley: University of California Press, 1981.

Liu Dapeng 刘大鹏. *Tuixiangzhai riji* 退想斋日记. Qiao Zhiqiang 乔志强, ed. Taiyuan: Shanxi renmin chubanshe, 1990.

Liu Jianjun 刘建军. *Ni suo bu shi de minguo mianxiang: Zhili difang yihui zhengzhi, 1912–1928* 你所不识的民国面相：直隶地方议会政治, 1912–1928 [The Unrecognized Face of the Republic: Local Legislative Politics in Zhili, 1912–1928]. Guilin: Guangxi shifan daxue chubanshe, 2009.

Liu Jianqiang 刘建强. *Hunan zizhi yundong shilun* 湖南自治运动史论 [The Hunan Provincial Self-Government Movement]. Xiangtan, Hunan: Xiangtan daxue chubanshe, 2008.

Liu Jinzao 劉錦藻. *Qing chao xu wenxian tongkao* 清朝續文獻通考 [General Documentary History of Qing Institutions, Continued]. Shanghai: Shangwu yinshuguan, 1935.

Liu Shaoqi 刘少奇. *Jianguo yilai Liu Shaoqi wengao* 建国以来刘少奇文稿 [Post-1949 Liu Shaoqi Documents]. Beijing: Zhongyang wenxian chubanshe, 2005.

Liu, Lydia He. *Translingual Practice: Literature, National Culture, and Translated Modernity—China, 1900–1937.* Stanford, CA: Stanford University Press, 1995.

Lobscheid, William. *English and Chinese Dictionary.* Hong Kong: Daily Press Office, 1866.

Luo Baoshan 骆寶善. "Qing mo xinzheng zhong de Yuan Shikai yu Zhang Jian lianmeng 清末新政中的袁世凱與張謇聯盟 [The Alliance between Yuan Shikai and Zhang Jian during the Late Qing New Policies]." *Ershiyi shiji shuangyuekan 二十一世紀雙月刊* [Twenty-First Century] 99 (December 2006), 58–65.

Luo Zhitian 罗志田. *Zai zao wenming zhi meng—Hu Shi zhuan 再造文明之梦—胡适传* [The Dream of Civilizational Reconstruction: A Biography of Hu Shi]. Chengdu: Sichuan renmin chubanshe, 1995.

Ma Jianzhong 馬建忠. *Shikezhai jiyan 適可齋紀言* [Recorded Sayings of the Shike Studio]. 1896. Reprint, Taipei: Wenhai chubanshe, 1968.

Macciocchi, Maria Antonietta. *Daily Life in Revolutionary China.* New York: Monthly Review Press, 1972.

Mackenzie, Robert. *The Nineteenth Century: A History—The Times of Queen Victoria.* London: T. Nelson, 1889.

Madancy, Joyce A. *The Troublesome Legacy of Commissioner Lin: The Opium Trade and Opium Suppression in Fujian Province, 1820s to 1920s.* Cambridge, MA: Harvard University Asia Center, 2003.

Mair, Victor. "Language and Ideology in the Written Popularizations of the Sacred Edict." In David Johnson and Andrew Nathan, eds., *Popular Culture in Late Imperial China.* Berkeley: University of California Press, 1985, 325–59.

Manion, Melanie. "Authoritarian Parochialism: Local Congressional Representation in China." *China Quarterly* 218 (June 2014), 311–38.

Mao Zedong 毛泽东. *Mao Zedong wenji 毛泽东文集* [Collected Works of Mao Zedong]. Beijing: Renmin chubanshe, 1993–1999.

Mao Zedong 毛泽东. *Mao Zedong xuanji 毛泽东选集* [Selected Works of Mao Zedong]. Beijing: Renmin chubanshe, 1977.

Mao Zedong sixiang wansui 毛泽东思想万岁. N.p., n.d.

Maruyama Toranosuke 丸山虎之助. *Putong xuanju lun 溥通選舉論* [Discussion of Mass Sufferage Elections]. Li Mingyou 李銘又, trans. Shanghai: Kaiming shudian, 1902.

Mateer, A. H. *New Terms for New Ideas: A Study of the Chinese Newspaper.* Shanghai: Presbyterian Mission Press, 1913.

Mathews, Robert H. *A Chinese-English Dictionary.* Shanghai: China Inland Mission and Presbyterian Mission Press, 1931. Reprint, Cambridge, MA: Harvard University Press, 1972.

Medhurst, Walter Henry. *English and Chinese Dictionary.* Shanghai: Printed at the Mission Press, 1847–48.

Meienberger, Norbert. *The Emergence of Constitutional Government in China (1905–1908): The Concept Sanctioned by the Empress Dowager Tz'u-Hsi.* Bern: P. Lang, 1980.

Min Tu-ki. *National Polity and Local Power: The Transformation of Late Imperial China.* Cambridge, MA: Council on East Asian Studies Harvard University, 1989.

Minguo Beijing zhengfu zhixian shiliao erbian 民國北京政府制憲史料二編 [Constitutional Materials from the Republic of China's Beijing Government, Series 2]. Beijing: Xianzhuang shuju, 2008.

Mittler, Barbara. *A Newspaper for China?: Power, Identity, and Change in Shanghai's News Media, 1872–1912*. Cambridge, MA: Harvard University Asia Center, 2004.

Morgan, Evan. *Chinese New Terms and Expressions with English Translations*. Shanghai: Kelly and Walsh, 1913.

Morrison, G. E. *The Correspondence of G. E. Morrison*. Lo Hui-min, ed. Cambridge: Cambridge University Press, 1976.

Morrison, Robert. *A Dictionary of the Chinese Language*. Macao: East India Company's Press, 1815–23.

Mosca, Matthew W. *From Frontier Policy to Foreign Policy: The Question of India and the Transformation of Geopolitics in Qing China*. Stanford, CA: Stanford University Press, 2013.

Mullaney, Thomas. *Coming to Terms with the Nation: Ethnic Classification in Modern China*. Berkeley: University of California Press, 2010.

Murray, Hugh. *An Encyclopædia of Geography*. London: Longman, 1834.

Nanhaiyinzi 南海胤子. *Anfu huoguo ji* 安福禍國記 [A Record of Anfu's Harm to Our Country]. 1920. Reprint, Beijing: Zhonghua shuju, 2007.

Nathan, Andrew J. *Chinese Democracy*. Berkeley: University of California Press, 1986.

Nathan, Andrew J. "Chinese Democracy: The Lessons of Failure." In Suisheng Zhao, ed., *China and Democracy: The Prospect for a Democratic China*. New York: Routledge, 2000, 21–32.

Nathan, Andrew J. *Peking Politics, 1918–1923: Factionalism and the Failure of Constitutionalism*. Berkeley: University of California Press, 1976.

Niu Mingshi 牛銘實 and Mi Youlu 米有录. *Dou xuan* 豆選 [Bean Voting]. Beijing: Zhongguo renmin daxue chubanshe, 2014.

O'Brien, Kevin J., and Lianjiang Li. "Accommodating 'Democracy' in a One-Party State: Introducing Village Elections in China." *China Quarterly* 162 (June 2000), 465–89.

O'Brien, Kevin J., and Rongbin Han. "Path to Democracy? Assessing Village Elections in China." *Journal of Contemporary China* 18.60 (June 2009), 359–78.

Ogden, Suzanne. *Inklings of Democracy in China*. Cambridge, MA: Harvard University Asia Center, 2002.

Peng Zhen zhuan bianxie zu 彭镇传编写组 [Peng Zhen Biography Compilation Group]. *Peng Zhen zhuan* 彭镇传 [Biography of Peng Zhen]. Beijing: Zhongyang wenxian chubanshe, 2012.

Pepper, Suzanne. *Civil War in China: The Political Struggle, 1945–1949*, 2nd ed. Lanham, MD: Rowman and Littlefield, 1999.

Platt, Stephen R. *Provincial Patriots: The Hunanese and Modern China*. Cambridge, MA: Harvard University Press, 2007.

Polachek, James M. *The Inner Opium War*. Cambridge, MA: Harvard University Council on East Asian Studies, 1992.

Potter, Pittman B. *From Leninist Discipline to Socialist Legalism: Peng Zhen on Law and Political Authority in the PRC*. Stanford, CA: Stanford University Press, 2003.

Puyi. *From Emperor to Citizen—The Autobiography of Aisin-Gioro Pu Yi*, 2nd ed. W. J. F. Jenner, trans. Beijing: Foreign Languages Press, 1979.

Qiao Jianwu and Du Wenge, "Three Big Rebellions: Reform the Old World and Build a New World with Mao Zedong Thought." *Contemporary Chinese Thought* 32.4 (Summer 2001), 37–44.

Qinding huangchao tongzhi 欽定皇朝通志 [Comprehensive Treatise on the Institutions of the Qing Dynasty]. 1767. Reprint, Taipei: Taiwan shangwu yinshuguan, 1983.

Qing huidian shili 清會典事例 [Collected Statutes and Substatutes of the Qing Dynasty]. 1899. Reprint, Beijing: Zhonghua shuju, 1991.

Qing shi gao 清史稿 [Draft History of the Qing Dynasty]. Zhao Erxun 趙爾巽 et al., eds. 1927. Reprint, Beijing: Zhonghua shuju, 1976.

Qing ting qianyi "Jiaobinlu kangyi" dang'an huibian 清廷签议《校邠庐抗议》档案汇编 [Documentary Collection of Comments Appended to *Essays of Protest* by Qing Court Officials]. Zhongguo di yi lishi dang'anguan [First Historical Archives of China], ed. Beijing: Xianzhuang shuju, 2008.

Qingmo choubei lixian dang'an shiliao 清末籌備立憲檔案史料 [Archival Materials on Late Qing Constitutional Preparations]. Gugong bowuyuan Ming-Qing dang'an bu 故宮博物院明清檔案部 [Palace Museum, Division of Ming-Qing Archives], ed. Beijing: Zhonghua shuju, 1979.

Qingmo-Minchu xianzheng shiliao jikan 清末民初憲政史料輯刊 [Historical Materials Related to Late Qing and Early Republican Constitutional Government]. Beijing: Beijing tushuguan chubanshe, 2006.

Read, Benjamin J. *Roots of the State: Neighborhood Organization and Social Networks in Beijing and Taipei*. Stanford, CA: Stanford University Press, 2012.

Reynolds, Douglas R. *China, 1898–1912: The Xinzheng Revolution and Japan*. Cambridge, MA: Harvard University Council on East Asian Studies, 1993.

Richard, Timothy. *Forty-Five Years in China*. New York: Frederick A. Stokes, 1916.

Richard, Timothy, and Cai Erkang 蔡爾康. *Taixi xinshi lanyao* 泰西新史攬要 [A New Historical Overview of the West]. Shanghai: N.p., 1895.

Rigger, Shelley. *From Opposition to Power: Taiwan's Democratic Progressive Party*. Boulder, CO: Lynne Rienner, 2001.

Rigger, Shelley. *Politics in Taiwan: Voting for Democracy*. London: Routledge, 1999.

Saich, Tony, ed. *The Rise to Power of the Chinese Communist Party: Documents and Analysis*. Armonk, NY: M. E. Sharpe, 1996.

Schafferer, Christian. *The Power of the Ballot Box: Political Development and Election Campaigning in Taiwan*. Lanham, MD: Lexington Books, 2003.

Schmidt, J. D. *Within the Human Realm: The Poetry of Huang Zunxian, 1848–1905*. Cambridge: Cambridge University Press, 1994.

Schram, Stuart, ed. *Mao's Road to Power: Revolutionary Writings, 1912–1949*, vol. 1, Armonk, NY: M. E. Sharpe, 1992.

Shanghai tushuguan 上海图书馆. *Zhongguo jindai qikan bianmu huilu* 中国近代期刊编目汇录 [Collected Table of Contents for Modern Chinese Periodicals]. Shanghai: Shanghai renmin chubanshe, 1979.

Shanghai xian xuanjuren xuanshi mingce 上海縣選舉人宣示名冊 [Shanghai County Sworn Voter Rolls]. N.p., ca. 1909.

Shen Xiaomin 沈晓敏. *Chuchang yu qiubian: Qingmo Minchu de Zhejiang ziyiju he shengyihui* 处常与求变：清末民初的浙江咨议局和省议会 [Continuity and Change: Zhejiang's Provincial Assemblies in the Late Qing and Early Republic]. Beijing: Shenghuo Dushu Xinzhi sanlian shudian, 2005.

Shen Zuxian 沈祖憲. *Rong'an dizi ji* 容菴弟子記 [A Record of Yuan Shikai and His Followers]. 1913. Reprint, Taipei: Wenxing shudian, 1962.

Shi, Tianjian. *The Cultural Logic of Politics in Mainland China and Taiwan*. New York: Cambridge University Press, 2015.

Snow, Edgar. *Red Star over China*. 1937. Reprint, New York: Grove Press, 1994.

Somin, Ilya. *Democracy and Political Ignorance: Why Smaller Government Is Smarter*. Stanford, CA: Stanford University Press, 2016.

Song Jiaoren 宋教仁. *Song Jiaoren ji* 宋教仁集 [Collected Works of Song Jiaoren]. Chen Xulu 陈旭麓, ed. Beijing: Zhonghua shuju, 2011.

Strand, David. *An Unfinished Republic: Leading by Word and Deed in Modern China*. Berkeley: University of California Press, 2011.

Strauss, Julia C. "Creating 'Virtuous and Talented' Officials for the Twentieth Century: Discourse and Practice in Xinzheng China." *Modern Asian Studies* 37.4 (2003), 831–50.

Sullivan, Jonathan, and Eliyahu Sapir, "Nasty or Nice? Explaining Positive and Negative Campaign Behavior in Taiwan." *China Journal* 67 (January 2012), 149–70.

Sun Yat-sen. *San min chu i: The Three Principles of the People*. Frank W. Price, trans. Shanghai: Commercial Press, 1928.

Sun Yat-sen 孫中山. *Sun Zhongshan quanji* 孙中山全集 [Complete Works of Sun Yat-sen]. Beijing: Zhonghua shuju, 1981.

Sun, E-Tu Zen. "The Chinese Constitutional Missions of 1905–1906." *Journal of Modern History* 24.3 (1952), 251–68.

Suval, Stanley. *Electoral Politics in Wilhelmine Germany*. Chapel Hill: University of North Carolina Press, 1985.

Tang Shouqian 湯壽潛. *Wei yan* 危言 [Words of Warning]. 1890. Reprint, n.p., 1895.

Tang Zhijun 汤志钧. *Zhang Taiyan nianpu changbian* 章太炎年谱长编 [Chronological Biography of Zhang Taiyan]. Beijing: Zhonghua shuju, 1979.

Taylor, A. J. P. *Bismarck: The Man and the Statesman*. New York: Knopf, 1955.

Taylor, Jay. *The Gerneralissimo's Son: Chiang Ching-kuo and the Revolutions in China and Taiwan*. Cambridge, MA: Harvard University Press, 2000.

Teng Ssu-yü 鄧嗣禹. *Zhongguo kaoshi zhidu shi* 中國考試制度史 [A History of the Chinese Examination System]. Taipei: Taiwan xuesheng shuju, 1967.

Teng Ssu-yü and John King Fairbank. *China's Response to the West: A Documentary Survey, 1839–1923*. Cambridge, MA: Harvard University Press, 1954.

Thompson, Roger R. *China's Local Councils in the Age of Constitutional Reform, 1898–1911*. Cambridge, MA: Harvard University Council on East Asian Studies, 1995.

Thomson, John. *Illustrations of China and Its People*. London: S. Low, Marston, Low, and Searle, 1873.

Thornton, Patricia M. "The Cultural Revolution as a Crisis of Representation." *China Quarterly* 227 (September 2016), 697–717.

Tien, Hung-mao. "Elections and Taiwan's Democratic Development." In Hung-mao Tien, ed., *Taiwan's Electoral Politics and Democratic Transition*. Armonk, NY: M. E. Sharpe, 1996, 3–26.

Truex, Rory. *Making Autocracy Work: Representation and Responsiveness in Modern China*. New York: Cambridge University Press, 2016.

Ts'ai Ling and Ramon H. Myers. "Winds of Democracy: The 1989 Taiwan Elections." *Asian Survey* 30.2 (April 1990), 360–79.

Tsai, Lily L. *Accountability without Democracy: Solidary Groups and Public Goods Provision in Rural China*. Cambridge: Cambridge University Press, 2007.

U.S. Department of State. *Papers Relating to the Foreign Relations of the United States with the Annual Message of the President Transmitted to Congress December 8, 1908*. Washington, DC: U.S. Government Printing Office, 1908.

Wang Li 王力. "Yige putong nongfu de xuanpiao 一個普通農婦的選票 [A Common Peasant Woman's Ballot]." *Shanghai jiefang shi nian* [The Tenth Anniversary of Shanghai's Liberation]. Shanghai: Shanghai wenyi chubanshe, 1960, 146–53.

Wang Rongbao 汪榮寶 and Ye Lan 葉瀾. *Xin Erya* 新爾雅 [New Erya Dictionary]. Shanghai: Mingquanshe, 1903.

Wang Shao'ao 王紹鰲. "Xinhai geming shiqi zhengdang huodong de diandi huiyi 辛亥革命時期政黨活動的點滴回憶 [Brief Recollections of Political Party Activities in the Period of the 1911 Revolution]." In *Xinhai geming huiyilu* 辛亥革命回憶錄 [Recollections of the 1911 Revolution]. Zhongguo renmin zhengzhi xieshanghuiyi quanguo weiyuanhui wenshi ziliao yanjiu weiyuanhui 中國人民政治協商會議全國委員會文史資料研究委員會 [The Chinese People's Political Consultative Conference's Committee for Research on Historical and Literary Materials], ed. Beijing: Zhonghua shuju, 1961, 398–409.

Wang Shijie 王世杰. *Wang Shijie riji* 王世杰日記 [Wang Shijie Diary]. Taipei: Zhongyang yanjiuyuan jindaishi yanjiusuo, 2012.

Wang Shu-hwai 王樹槐. "Qingmo Minchu Jiangsu sheng de ziyiju yu sheng yihui 清末民初江蘇省的諮議局與省議會 [The Late Qing Provincial Assembly and Early Republican Provincial Legislature in Jiangsu]." *Lishi xuebao* 歷史學報 [Bulletin of Historical Research] 6 (1978), 313–33.

Wang Wuwei 王無為. *Hunan zizhi yundong shi shangpian* 湖南自治運動史上篇 [History of the Hunan Self-Government Movement, Part I]. Shanghai: Taidong tushuju, 1920.

Wang, Juan. *Merry Laughter and Angry Curses: The Shanghai Tabloid Press, 1897–1911*. Vancouver: University of British Columbia Press, 2012.

Wang, Zhengxu, and Long Sun. "Social Class and Voter Turnout in China: Local Congress Elections and Citizen-Regime Relations." *Political Research Quarterly* 70.2 (2017), 243–56.

Wang, Zhongyuan. "Playing by the Rules: How Local Authorities Engineer Victory in Direct Congressional Elections in China." *Journal of Contemporary China* 26.108 (2017), 870–85.

Wei Chunhui 卫春回. *Zhang Jian pingzhuan* 张謇评传 [A Critical Biography of Zhang Jian]. Nanjing: Nanjing daxue chubanshe, 2001.

Wei Yuan 魏源. *Haiguo tuzhi* 海国图志 [Illustrated Gazetteer of the Maritime Countries]. 1852. Chen Hua 陈华 et al., ann. Reprint, Changsha: Yuelu shushe, 1998.

Wei, Yang. "Popular Opinion and Public Reasoning: Intellectual Changes and Institutional Innovations in Late Ming China (1580s–1640s)." PhD diss., Harvard University, 2014.

Wong, Lawrence Wang-chi. "Translators and Interpreters during the Opium War between Britain and China (1839–1842)." In Myriam Salama-Carr, ed., *Translating and Interpreting Conflict*. Amsterdam: Rodopi, 2007, 41–57.

Wong, Young-tsu. "Popular Unrest and the 1911 Revolution in Jiangsu." *Modern China* 3.3 (1977), 321–44.

Wu xian xuanjuren mingce 吳縣選舉人名冊 [Wu County Voter Rolls]. N.p., ca. 1909.

Wu Xiangxiang 吳相湘. *Song Jiaoren zhuan* 宋教仁傳 [Biography of Song Jiaoren]. Taipei: Wenxing shudian, 1965.

Wuxu bianfa 戊戌變法 [The 1898 Reform Movement]. Jian Bozan 翦伯贊 et al., eds. Shanghai: Shenzhou guoguangshe, 1953.

Xi Jinping. *The Governance of China*. Beijing: Foreign Languages Press, 2014.

Xia Dongyuan 夏东元. *Zheng Guanying zhuan* 郑观应传 [Biography of Zheng Guanying]. Shanghai: Huadong shifan daxue chubanshe, 1981.

Xia Xiaohong 夏晓红. "Cong xin faxian shougao kan Liang Qichao wei chuyang wu dachen zuo qiangshou zhenxiang 从新发现手稿看梁启超为出洋五大臣做枪手真相 [Finding the Truth of Liang Qichao's Ghostwriting for the Late Qing Constitutional Overseas Missions in Newly Discovered Manuscripts]." *Nanfang zhoumo* 南方周末 [Southern Weekend], November 13, 2008, 23.

Xia Xinhua 夏新华. *Jindai Zhongguo xianzheng licheng: shiliao huicui* 近代中国宪政历程: 史料荟萃 [The Course of Modern China's Constitutional Government: A Collection of Historical Materials]. Beijing: Zhongguo zhengfa daxue chubanshe, 2004.

Xiong Yuezhi 熊月之. *Feng Guifen pingzhuan* 冯桂芬评传 [A Critical Biography of Feng Guifen]. Nanjing: Nanjing daxue chubanshe, 2004.

Xiong Yuezhi 熊月之. *Zhongguo jindai minzhu sixiang shi* 中国近代民主思想史 [A History of Modern Democratic Thought in China]. Shanghai: Shanghai renmin chubanshe, 1986.

Xiong, Yuezhi. "Difficulties in Comprehension and Differences in Expression: Interpreting American Democracy in the Late Qing." William Rowe, trans. *Late Imperial China* 23.1 (2002), 1–27.

Xu Daolin 徐道鄰. *Xu Shuzheng xiansheng wenji nianpu hekan* 徐樹錚先生文集年譜合刊 [Writings and Chronological Biography of Xu Shuzheng]. Taipei: Taiwan shangwu yinshuguan, 1962.

Xu Jiyu 徐繼畬. *Yinghuan zhilue jiaozhu* 瀛寰志略校注 [A Brief Description of the Ocean Circuit, Annotated Edition]. 1848. Song Dachuan 宋大川, ann. Reprint, Beijing: Wenwu chubanshe, 2007.

Xu Shuzheng dian gao 徐树铮电稿 [Xu Shuzheng's Telegrams]. Zhongguo kexueyuan jindaishi ziliao bianjizu 中国科学院近代史资料编辑组 [Chinese Academy of Sciences Modern Historical Materials Editorial Group], ed. Beijing: Zhonghua shuju, 1962.

Xu, Guoqi. *China and the Great War: China's Pursuit of a New National Identity and Internationalization*. Cambridge: Cambridge University Press, 2005.

Xuanju guai xianxiang 選舉怪現象 [Strange Tales from the Election]. N.p., ca. 1909.

Xue Fucheng 薛福成. *Chushi siguo riji* 出使四國日記 [Record of a Diplomatic Mission to Four Countries]. 1894–98. In Zhong Shuhe 钟叔河, comp., *Zou xiang shijie congshu* 走向世界丛书 [From East to West: Chinese Travelers before 1911]. Reprint, Changsha: Yuelu shushe, 2008.

Yang Chunlü 楊春綠. *Minguo shi nian Shanghai zhongyiyuan yiyuan xuanju susong lu* 民國十年上海眾議院議員選舉訟訴錄 [Record of the Legal Challenge to the 1921 Parliamentary Election in Shanghai]. N.p., 1921.

Yang Tingdong 楊廷棟. *Zhengzhixue jiaokeshu* 政治學教科書 [Political Science Textbook]. Shanghai: Zuoxinshe, 1902.

Yang Tingdong 楊廷棟. *Ziyiju zhiwu xuzhi, di yi bian: bianzao xuanjuren mingce* 諮議局職務須知, 第一編: 編造選舉人名冊 [Manual for Provincial Assembly Work, Volume 1: Creating Voter Rolls]. Shanghai: Commercial Press, 1908.

Yapian zhanzheng dang'an shiliao 鸦片战争档案史料 [Archival Materials Relating to the Opium War]. Zhongguo di yi lishi dang'anguan 中国第一历史档案馆 [First Historical Archives of China], ed. Shanghai: Shanghai renmin chubanshe, 1987.

Ye Lijun 叶利军. *Minguo Beijing zhengfu shiqi xuanju zhidu yanjiu* 民国北京政府时期选举制度研究 [The Republic of China's Election System in the Beijing Era]. Changsha: Hunan renmin chubanshe, 2007.

Young, Ernest P. *The Presidency of Yuan Shih-k'ai: Liberalism and Dictatorship in Early Republican China*. Ann Arbor: University of Michigan Press, 1977.

Yu Keping 俞可平. "Minzhu shi ge hao dongxi 民主是个好东西 [Democracy Is a Good Thing]." *Renmin wang* 人民网 (December 28, 2006). http://theory.people.com.cn/GB/49150/49152/5224247.html (accessed on January 3, 2017).

Yu, Keping. *Democracy Is a Good Things: Essays on Politics, Society, and Culture in Contemporary China*. Washington, DC: Brookings Institution Press, 2009.

Yubei lixian gonghui zhangcheng timing biao 預備立憲公會章程提名表 [Public Association for Constitutional Preparation Charter and Membership List]. N.p., ca. 1910.

Yuefa huiyi jilu 約法會議記錄 [Proceedings of the Constitutional Conference]. Yuefa huiyi mishuting 約法會議秘書廳 [Constitutional Conference Secretariat], ed. 1914. Reprint, Taipei: Wenhai chubanshe, 1968.

Yuexi banshichu 粤西辦事處 [Western Guangdong Administrative Office]. *Lianjiang xian di yi qu jiceng siban gongzuo zuofa* 廉江縣第一區基層選舉試辦工作做法 [Work Methods Used for the Trial-Run Local Election in Lianjiang County's First District]. N.p.: n.p., 1954.

Zai-ze 載泽. *Kaocha zhengzhi riji* 考察政治日記 [A Record of the Investigation of Politics and Government]. 1909. In Zhong Shuhe 钟叔河, comp., *Zou xiang shijie congshu* 走

向世界丛书 [From East to West: Chinese Travelers before 1911]. Reprint, Changsha: Yuelu shushe, 2008.

Zhan Chengfu 詹成付 et al. *Quanguo cunmin weiyuanhui xuanju gongzuo jinzhan baogao (2005–2007 nian)* 全国村民委员会选举工作进展报告 (2005–2007 年) [Progress Report on Nationwide Election Work for Villagers' Committees (2005–2007)]. Beijing: Zhongguo shehui chubanshe, 2008.

Zhang Deyi 张德彝. *Ou-Mei huanyou ji (Zai shu qi)* 欧美环游记 (再述奇) [Record of a Journey to Europe and the United States (A Second Record of Wonders)]. 1872. In Zhong Shuhe 钟叔河, comp., *Zou xiang shijie congshu* 走向世界丛书 [From East to West: Chinese Travelers before 1911]. Reprint, Changsha: Yuelu shushe, 2008.

Zhang Deyi 张德彝. *Sui shi Ying E ji* 随使英俄记 [Record of Accompanying the Ambassadors to Great Britain and Russia]. 1883. In Zhong Shuhe 钟叔河, comp., *Zou xiang shijie congshu* 走向世界丛书 [From East to West: Chinese Travelers before 1911]. Reprint, Changsha: Yuelu shushe, 2008.

Zhang Jian 张謇. *Zhang Jian quanji* 张謇全集 [Complete Works of Zhang Jian]. Hu Duojia 胡多佳, ed. Nanjing: Jiangsu guji chubanshe, 1994.

Zhang Jian 张謇. *Zhang Jizi jiu lu* 张季子九錄 [Nine Records of Zhang Jian]. Zhang Yizu 张怡祖, ed. Shanghai: n.p., 1931.

Zhang Jishun. "Creating 'Masters of the Country' in Shanghai and Beijing: Discourse and the 1953–54 Local People's Congress Election." Trans. Joshua Hill. *China Quarterly* 220 (December 2014), 1071–91.

Zhang Mingshu 张明澍. *Zhongguoren xiangyao shenmeyang minzhu: Zhongguo "zhengzhi ren" 2012* 中国人想要什么样民主：中国 "政治人" 2012 [What Democracy Does Chinese Want—Chinese "Political Man" 2012]. Beijing: Shehui kexue wenxian chubanshe, 2013.

Zhang Weiwei. *The China Wave: Rise of a Civilizational State*. Hackensack, NJ: World Century Publishing, 2012.

Zheng Guanying 郑观应. *Zheng Guanying ji* 郑观应集 [Collected Works of Zheng Guanying]. Xia Dongyuan 夏东元, ed. Shanghai: Shanghai renmin chubanshe, 1982.

Zheng Xiaoxu 郑孝胥. *Zheng Xiaoxu riji* 郑孝胥日记 [Zheng Xiaoxu's Diary]. Lao Zude 劳祖德, comp. Beijing: Zhonghua shuju, 1993.

Zheng, Yangwen. *The Social Life of Opium in China*. Cambridge: Cambridge University Press, 2005.

Zhi-gang 志刚. *Chushi Taixi ji* 出使泰西记 [Record of the First Embassy to the West]. 1877. In Zhong Shuhe 钟叔河, comp., *Zou xiang shijie congshu* 走向世界丛书 [From East to West: Chinese Travelers before 1911]. Reprint, Changsha: Yuelu shushe, 2008.

Zhongguo di er lishi dang'anguan 中國第二歷史檔案館 [Second Historical Archives of China]. *Zhonghua Minguo shi dang'an ziliao huibian, di 2 ji Nanjing linshi zhengfu* 中華民國史檔案資料滙編，第 2 輯：南京臨時政府 [Collected Documentary Materials on the History of the Republic of China, Series 2: The Nanjing Provisional Government]. Nanjing: Jiangsu guji chubanshe, 1991.

Zhongguo di er lishi dang'anguan 中國第二歷史檔案館 [Second Historical Archives of China]. *Zhonghua Minguo shi dang'an ziliao huibian, di 3 ji Nanjing linshi zhengfu* 中華民國史檔案資料滙編，第 3 輯：政治(一) [Collected Documentary Materials on the

History of the Republic of China, Series 2: Politics (Part 1)]. Nanjing: Jiangsu guji chubanshe, 1991.

Zhongguo Guomindang xuanyan ji 中國國民黨宣言集 [Collection of Nationalist Party Proclamations]. In Xiao Jizong 蕭繼宗, ed., *Geming wenxian* 革命文獻 [Documents of the Revolution]. Taipei: Zhongyang wenwu gongyingshe, 1976.

Zhonghua renmin gongheguo minzheng bu 中华人民共和国民政部 [Ministry of Civil Affairs of the People's Republic of China]. "2016 nian shehui fuwu fazhan tongji gongbao 2016 年社会服务发展统计公报] [2016 Statistical Report on the Development of Social Services]." Available at http://www.mca.gov.cn/article/sj/tjgb/201708/20170800005382.shtml (accessed March 12, 2018).

Zhonghua Suwei'ai gongheguo zhongyang zhixing weiyuanhui 中華蘇維埃共和國中央執行委員會 [Central Executive Committee of the Chinese Soviet Republic]. *Zhonghua Suwei'ai gongheguo de xuanju xize* 中華蘇維埃共和國的選舉細則 [Election Regulations for the Chinese Soviet Republic]. N.p., 1931.

Zhongyiyuan yijue leibian 眾議院議決類編 [Lower House of Parliament Collected Decisions]. N.p. In Zhou Guangpei 周光培, comp., *Zhonghua minguo shi shiliao san bian* 中華民國史史料三編 [Historical Materials on the Republic of China, Third Series]. Reprint, Shenyang: Liaohai chubanshe, 2007.

Zhou Enlai nianpu 1949–1976 周恩来年谱 1949–1976 [Chronological Biography of Zhou Enlai 1949–1976]. Beijing: Zhongyang wenxian chubanshe, 1997.

Zhou Yezhong 周叶中 and Jiang Guohua 江国华. *Zi xia er shang de lixian changshi: shengxian pinglun* 自下而上的立宪尝试：省宪评论 [An Attempt at Constitutionalism from the Bottom Up: A Critique of the Provincial Constitutions]. Wuchang: Wuhan daxue chubanshe, 2010.

Zhu Ling 朱凌. *Wo fandu: Yige renda daibiao de canzheng chuanqi* 我反对：一个人大代表的参政传奇 [I Object: The Legend of a Local People's Congress Representative]. Haikou: Hainan chubanshe, 2006.

Zhu Xi 朱熹. *Zhu Xi ji* 朱熹集 [Zhu Xi's Collected Works]. Chengdu: Sichuan jiaoyu chubanshe, 1996.

Index

Page numbers for figures and tables are in italics.

Achen, Christopher, 6
age, of voting, 63–64, 108
Albania, 196, 212
Anfu Club [*Anfu julebu*], 145–48, 151
Anhui Province, 15–16, 80, 202
apportionment, 146
Australia, 140

ballot, *124*; beans as, 194–95; Hu Shi on, 165; in "open ballot voting [*jiming toupiao*]," 140, 167; secret, 140, 167; selling of, 147
Bao Tianxiao, 78, 81–82; on campaigning, 97–98; campaigning and, 93–94; as editorialist, 87–89, 97–98; on Mansion of Repose, 75; on opium use, 81, 90; on voter choices, 120
Bartels, Larry, 6
bean voting, 194–95
Bland, J. O. P., 102
"Blunt Root," 129, 132, 135
Boxer Rebellion, 38, 50, 61
bribery, 27, 38, 121, 151, 161
business community, 78, 83

Cai Erkang, 30–32
campaigning, 7–8, 93–100, *94*, *97–99*, 135, 153–54, 167
"Campaigning for Beginners" (anonymous), 95–96
Cao Kun, 161
Cao Rulin, 70–71, 145, 151
cards, identification, 203–4
cartoons, 96–100, *97–99*
"cash campaigning," 159
Catholics, 205
Cen Chunxuan, 61–62
Chang Peng-yuan, 4, 224–25
Changsha, 1–2, 5, 169, 172, 209, *215*, *220*
Changzhou (Jiangsu), 78–79, 82, 84–85, 126
Chao, Linda, 227
Charter Oath, 55–56
Chen Jiongming, 170–71, 175–76
Chen Weijun, 225
Chen Yi, 200
Cheng Dequan, 107–8, 117, 121
Chiang Ching-kuo, 190
Chiang Kai-shek, 176–77, 179, 186–87, 189–90
China Magazine, 182

China Vocational School, 153
Chinese Revolutionary Party, 176
Citizens' Conference, 140–41, 177
civil service examination system, 48–52
civil war, 161–62, 179–81
Cixi, Empress Dowager, 38, 42, 50, 54–56, 61, 70–72
classification, of voters, 198–200
Common Program, 195
Communist Party, 1–2, 125, 163, 179–80, 195–98, 222. *See also* political parties
Communist Revolution, 1, 193, 199
community compacts [*xiangyue*], 9, 15
Confucian ethics, 8
Confucianism, civil service examinations and, 48–49
Congress of Citizens' Representatives, 141
constitutional activism, 56–57
Constitutional Drafting Commission, 70
Constitutional Reform Office, 62, 78
coordination, political, 120–28, 142–51
corruption, 13–14, 27, 151. *See also* bribery; election fraud
Cultural Revolution, 9, 125, 210–13, 270n76

Dai Hongci, 53–54, 57–58, 68–69
Daoguang emperor, 18–19
Davies, Gloria, 225
decentralization, 17, 42
deliberative assemblies [*yiyuan*], 33–35, 38, 52–53, 57–59, 72
democracy, 213–17, *215*; folk theory of, 6; "gentry," 157; Hu Shi on, 166; Mao and, 1–2; Song Jiaoren and, 135
"Democracy Is a Good Thing" (Yu), 221
Democratic Party, 122
Deng Xiaoping, 196–97
Di Baoxian, 57, 74–75
Di Fuding, 153
dictatorship, 139–42
dictionaries, 14, 18, 29, 236n5, 240n14
disenfranchisement, 64
Dongtai County (Jiangsu), 204
Draft History of the Qing Dynasty, 71

Duan-fang, 52–56, 58, 67, 76
Duan Qirui, 143–45
dynastic histories, 44

editorials, 87–89, 101–2, 128–34
education: Chen Jiongming and, 170–71; Chiang Kai-shek and, 176–77; Hu Shi and, 163–67; Lou Mingyuan and, 167–68; in Nanjing Decade, 175–85, *183*; Nationalist Party and, 176–77, 180–81; propaganda and, 180–81, 185; provincial autonomy and, 167–74; Sun Yat-sen and, 193; Taiwan and, 186–90; as voter qualification, 112; Wang Shijie and, 166–67
education system; 50–52, 66–67
Edwards, Louise, 4
election fraud, 100–101, 148–50, 159, 173, 223
election law(s): campaigning and, 94; early, 7–8; education of populace on, 119–20; in Japan, 44–45; legal scholars on, 192; Tianjin system and, 60–61; transformation of, 221–22. *See also* 1908 Regulations
election monitoring teams, 152–55, 173, 255n46
elections: after 1982, 214–15; communism and, 195–96; European political ideas and, 12; examinations and, 72; in Feng, 22–24; functions of, 7–8; "grassroots," 207, 210; observation of, 25–29; pessimistic view of, 13–14; as political ritual, 193–94; in Qing dynasty, 3; resources dedicated to, 3–4; "single-candidate," 197; Stalin on, 196; talking freely about, 128–34; terminology for, 204–5; village, 216–17
electoral colleges, 139
electoral formulas, 67, 90, 95, 110–11
electoral manipulation: as coordination, 142–51; idealism and, 151–60
elites, local, formal participation of, 16–17
Encyclopedia of Geography (Murray), 19

ethics, Confucian, 8
ethnic categories, 198
European political ideas, 12
examinations: elections and, 72; end of civil service, 48–52; as "selection and appointment" [*xuanju*], 44–48, *46–47*

famine, 210
Fang Shu, 140
Feng Guifen, 21–25, 34–43, 54, 60, 63, 69–70
Feng Xiaocai, 222–23
Fincher, John, 4
"folk theory," 6
formulas, electoral, 67, 90, 95, 110–11
France, 27
fraud: election, 100–101, 148–50, 159, 173, 223; voter registration, 145–46
"Free Talk," 129–35
Fu Huaifeng, 245n27
Fukuzawa Yukichi, 44–45
Funing County (Jiangsu), 146, 149

gender equality, 113–14
gentry class, 49, 112
Germany, 68–69
Giles, Herbert, 14, 236n5
Gong, Prince, 31
gongju (public appointment), 13–17, 24, 29–31, 44, *46*, 46–47
"grassroots elections [*jiceng xuanju*]," 207, 210
Great Britain, 27, 31, 165
Great Leap Forward, 210
Guangdong Province, 170–73
Guangxi Province, 82
Guangxu emperor, 31, 36, 38, 41–43, 49, 61, 85
Guo Songtao, 37
Guomin ribao (newspaper), 157
Gutzlaff, Karl, 20

Haiguo tuzhi [Illustrated Gazetteer of the Maritime Countries] (Wei), 21–22
Hainan Island, 198

Harrison, Henrietta, 223–24
Hengyang County (Hunan), 173
Hinton, William, 195
HMS Nemesis, 12
Hong Kong, 172, 219–20
House of Commons, 19
Hu Fu, 189
Huaixia township (Wuxi), 159
Huaiyin County (Jiangsu), 182
Huang Bihun, 171
Huang Junlong, 38
Huang Yanpei, 75, 169
Huang Zongxi, 108
Huang Zunxian, 27–28, 93
Huating County (Jiangsu), 126
Hunan: provincial autonomy in, 172–74
Hunan provincial legislature, 1–2
"Hundred Days of Reform," 41, 49, 53
Hu Shi, 163–67, 184–85, 193

idealism, 151–60
identification cards, 203–4
illiteracy, 207

Jacobs, J. Bruce, 227
Japan: early election law in, 44–45; as model, 55–56, 70–71; in Russo-Japanese War, 40, 42; Taiwan and, 186; Zhang and, 41–43
Jiading County (Jiangsu), 109
Jiang Zengyao, 149
Jiang Zengyu, 149
Jiangsu Education Association, 88, 155
Jiangsu Province, 76–77, 81–82, 89, 119, 127–28, 132–33, 152, 158–59; census and, 117–18; Communist elections in, 197; electoral formulas and, 111; fraud in, 149–50; provincial autonomy and, 170; revote in, 92; women's suffrage in, 200
Jiangxi Province, 80, 83–84, 194
Jiangyin County (Jiangsu), 180
Jiaobinlu kangyi [Essays of Protest] (Feng), 22, 34, 36, 41
Jiaqing emperor, 16
Jie Shuqiang, 146

Kang Youwei, 31, 37–38, 41, 45
Kangxi Emperor's Sacred Edict, 9
Kerr, George, 187
Kishlansky, Mark, 7
Kong Zhaojin, 90, 101
Kwang Ki-Chaou, 29

Land Reform Campaign, 202–3
landlords, 198–200, 203
law. *See* election law(s)
lectures, public, 119–20
Ledong County (Guangdong Province), 198
Li Dazhao, 163
Li Hongzhang, 28, 31, 35, 37–38, 93
Li Jiannong, 175
Li Timotai, 30
Liang Qichao, 3, 6–7, 31, 45, 56, 74, 86–87, 138
Liang Shuming, 164
Lin Zexu, 17–22, 24–25, 66
literacy, 81, 207
literati, 17, 33–34
Liu Chongyou, 122
Liu Dapeng, 141–42
Liu Guangdi, 38
Liu, Lydia, 12
Liu Shaoqi, 196
Lobscheid, William, 29
London, 27
Lou Mingyuan, 164, 167–68, 259n4
Lower House Election Law, 113
Lu Wenlu, 156–57
Lu Xuanzhi, 184, 263nn78–79

Ma Jianzhong, 28
Mackenzie, Robert, 30–32
Manchu conquest, 15
manipulation, electoral: as coordination, 142–51; idealism as, 151–60
"Mansion of Repose," 74–76, 153, 155
Mao Zedong, 1–3, 5, 169, 194–97, 208–12
Medhurst, Walter Henry, 29
Mei Lien-hua, 182, *183*
Meiji emperor, 42, 55–56

membership, in political community, 193–94
merchants, 83, 86, 115
Ming dynasty, 48
monitoring teams, 152–55, 173, 255n46
Morrison, G. E., 102
Morrison, Robert, 18
Murray, Hugh, 19
Myers, Ramon, 227

names, with characters from personal name of emperor, 85
Nanhui County (Jiangsu), 181
Nanjing, 77, 138
Nanjing Decade, 175–85, *183*
National Assembly, 63
National Election Preparation Office, 179
Nationalist Party, 121, 123, 134, 136, 138; democratization and, 179–80; exclusion of members of, 137, 194; propaganda and, 180–81, 185; protests against, 114; provincial autonomy and, 175; purge of, 125; regularization and, 179–80; Song and, 135; Taiwan and, 186, 188–89; tutelage and, 176–77; voter qualifications and, 115
National People's Congress, 208
"New New Parliament," 158
New York Times (newspaper), 181
newspapers, 4–5, 30, 86–87, 120. *See also Shenbao* (newspaper); *Shibao* (newspaper)
1908 Regulations, 63–70, 74–79; Hu Shi and, 164; in new Republic, 104–5; pushing boundaries of, 110–16; restoration of, 139–40; Taiwan and, 188. *See also* election law(s)
Nineteenth Century, The: A History—The Times of Queen Victoria (Mackenzie), 30–31
nominations, 23–24, 178, 183, 205–6
Nuli zhoubao [Endeavor Weekly], 163–64

oath-taking, 178, 185
observation, of elections, 25–29

"On the New Democracy" (Mao), 195
"open ballot voting [*jiming toupiao*]," 140
opera, 204–5
opium, 18, 67, 90, 113, 140
Opium War, 18
Oumei zhengzhi yaoyi [Essentials of European and American Politics], 54–55
"Our Political Proposals" (Hu), 163–64

Pan Gongzhan, 181
Paris, 27
Paris Commune, 211–12
parties, political, 120–28
partisanship, 13–14
pedagogy. *See* education
Peng Zhen, 213–16
People's Congresses, 192–93, 196, 198, 203, 206, 208–10, 213–14
People's Daily (newspaper), 125, 196, 210, 212
Please Vote for Me (documentary), 225
political coordination, 120–28, 142–51
political parties, 120–28. *See also* Communist Party, Nationalist Party
political tutelage. *See* education
Progressive Party, 125
propaganda, 180–81, 185, 199, *201*, 204
property ownership, 59, 64–66, 80–82
Provincial Assembly Election Regulations, 63. *See also* 1908 Regulations
Provincial Assembly Preparatory Offices, 76–80, 83–84
Provincial Assembly Regulations, 63. *See also* 1908 Regulations
provincial autonomy, 167–74
Provincial Legislature Election Law, 113
Provisional Senate, 144
Prussian system, 68–69
public appointment [*gongju*], 13–17, 24, 29–31, 44, *46*, 46–47, *47*
public lectures, 119–20
public voting, 206–7
Puyi (emperor), 204, 210

Qi Yaolin, 146
Qing dynasty, 3, 7, 11–16, 20, 26, 29–30, 48

Qiying, 20
qualifications, voter, 59, 64–65, 79–83, 108, 111–13, 144

real estate ownership, 59, 64–66, 80–82
Red Flag (newspaper), 212
Red Guards, 211
Reform Bill (1832, Britain), 31
registration fraud, 145–46
registration, voter, 78–86, 94–95, 116–19, 145, 152–57, 198–99, 245n27
Republic of China Parliamentary Organizational Law, 113
Republican Party, 121, 123
revolts, 106–9
Revolutionary Alliance, 114, 153
revote, 91–92
Richard, Timothy, 30–32
Rigger, Shelley, 4, 189, 227
ritual, elections as, 193–94
Rousseau, Jean-Jacques, 77, 108
Russo-Japanese War, 40, 42

school system, 50–52, 66–67. *See also* education
secret ballots, 140
selection, 7–8; in Feng, 23; foreign methods of, importation of, 52–58; in newspapers, 120
"selection and appointment" [*xuanju*], 44–48, *46–47*
Shanghai, 74–75, 127, 132, 141, 158; Communist elections in, 197; provincial autonomy and, 168; voter classification in, 199–200; voter registration in, 116–17
Shanghai-Nanjing Railway, 80–81
Shanxi Province, 58
Shen Baochang, 156
Shen Enfu, 74–75, 155
Shen Tongfang, 77
Shenbao (newspaper), 41, 87, 101–2; on choices in voting, 86, 120; critique of census work in, 117; education in, 51; "Free Talk" in, 129–34; on Jiangsu

Shenbao (newspaper) (*continued*)
  provincial elections, 158; on 1912 elections, 109–10; public appointment in, 30, 46, *46*; as source, 4
Shengshi weiyan [Words of Warning to a Prosperous Age] (Zheng), 32–35, 39, 57
Shi Liangcai, 75
Shi, Tianjian, 225–26
Shibao (newspaper), 57, 74–75, 80, 86–88, 96–100, *97–99*
"show of hands" voting, 206–7
"single-candidate elections [*deng'e xuanju*]," 197
Sino-Japanese War, 30, 36, 40–41, 45, 87
"Sixteen Points," 211
Sizhou zhi [Gazetteer of the Four Continents] (Lin), 19
"Skinny Butterfly," 129–30
Snow, Edgar, 1–2
Social Contract (Rousseau), 77
Society for the Diffusion of Useful Knowledge, 30
Song Jiaoren, 114, 134–35
source materials, 4–5
Soviet Union, 194, 199, 206, 218
Spencer, Herbert, 98
Stalin, Joseph, 195–96
Strand, David, 224
student suffrage, 115–16
suffrage. *See* student suffrage; voter qualifications; women's suffrage
suicides, 202–3
Sun Jia'nai, 31
Sun Ke, 261n47
Sun Yat-sen, 106–7, 143–44, 153, 171–72, 176–77, 187, 193
Suqian County (Jiangsu), 184
Sushe [The Jiangsu Society], 170
Suzhou, 77, 107–8

Taiping, 21
Taiping Rebellion, 22
Taiwan, 9, 186–90, 219–20, 226–27

Taixi xinshi lanyao [A New Historical Overview of the West] (Richard and Cai), 31
Taixing County (Jiangsu), 155
Tang Hualong, 122
Tang Qunying, 114
Tang Shouqian, 33, 36, 57
taxation: voter qualification and, 66, 68, 111–12; voter registration and, 85–86
Thompson, Roger, 4
Three Principles of the People, 178, 187
Tiananmen Square, 153
Tianjin system, 59–61, 65–67
Tongshan County (Jiangsu), 182
translation, 19–20
tutelage. *See* education

United States: early Chinese conceptions of elections in, 14–15, 237n24; observation of elections, 27–28, 165
unrest, 106–9, 187

village elections, 216–17
voice voting, 206–7
von Bismarck, Otto, 68
voter classification, 198–200
voter identification cards, 203–4
voter qualifications, 59, 63–65, 79–83, 108, 111–13, 144, 171
voter registration, 78–86, 90, 94–95, 113, 116–19, 145, 152–57, 178, 198–99, 245n27
voter registration fraud, 145–46
voting age, 63–64, 108

Wang Chonghui, 164
Wang Hui, 129, 132, 135
Wang Qing, 149–50
Wang Rongbao, 46
Wang Shao'ao, 121–25, 127, 143
Wang Shijie, 166–67, 179, 183–84
Wang Xinrun, 111
Wanguo gongbao [Chinese Globe] (newspaper), 30